Anthropocentrism and Its Discontents

Anthropocentrism

AND ITS DISCONTENTS

 The Moral Status of Animals in
the History of Western Philosophy

GARY STEINER

University of Pittsburgh Press

Published by the University of Pittsburgh Press, Pittsburgh, Pa., 15260

Copyright © 2005, University of Pittsburgh Press

Manufactured in the United States of America

Printed on acid-free paper

First paperback edition, 2010

10 9 8 7 6 5 4 3 2

ISBN 10: 0-8229-6119-9

ISBN 13: 978-0-8229-6119-2

In loving memory of Ajax Steiner (1985–2003) and Cleopatra Steiner (1985–2004), who taught me more about the human–animal bond than all the philosophers combined

CONTENTS

ACKNOWLEDGMENTS

The single greatest inspiration to me in writing this book was Urs Dierauer's incomparable *Tier und Mensch im Denken der Antike*. Meticulous and insightful, Dierauer's book sets the standard for investigations of conceptions of animals and their moral status in the history of Western philosophy.

My work on this book benefited from a painstaking critique of the systematic chapters provided by Richard Watson, the support of Richard Wolin and Paul Waldau, and an ongoing series of discussions with Marc Lucht concerning environmental philosophy, ethics, and cognitive ethology. Special thanks are also due to Jeff Turner for his continued efforts to secure support for my research at Bucknell. Additional support was provided by Esther Bauer, Cindy Benton, Douglas Candland, Angela Cozea, Kevin Daly, Otis Daly-Larson, Daniel Dombrowski, Peter Groff, Sheridan Hough, Michael James, Janet Jones, Larry Kay, Stephanie Larson, Janice Mann, Peter Markie, George Matthews, Scott McElreath, Jeff Scheckter, Elaine Steiner, James Steiner, Cornelia Tsakiridou, and the students in my "Western Perspectives on Animals" course from 2001 to 2004 at Bucknell University. Capable research assistance was provided by Joseph Trullinger in 2002 and Nate Bridge in 2004.

My editor at the University of Pittsburgh Press, Kendra Boileau Stokes, took unusual initiative in soliciting this project for publication, and she invested a great deal of energy in ensuring that my vision for the book would be realized.

Chapter 6 is adapted from my article "Descartes on the Moral Status of Animals," *Archiv für Geschichte der Philosophie* 80 (1998): 268–91.

Anthropocentrism and Its Discontents

INTRODUCTION

But the life of a man is of no greater importance to the universe than that of an oyster.

—David Hume, "Of Suicide"

The pre-Socratic philosopher Xenophanes said that "if cattle and horses or lions had hands, or were able to draw with their hands and do the works that men can do, horses would draw the forms of the gods like horses, and cattle like cattle, and they would make their bodies such as they each had themselves."[1] The fact that the Greeks drew their gods as likenesses of human beings reveals their anthropocentrism, the view that human beings are primary and central in the order of things. Philosophers in the West conceptualize the human condition as a middle station between animality and divinity and maintain that of all earthly beings, human beings are closest to the gods. This prejudice persists even in Kant's cosmopolitanism, in which human beings stand alone among earthly beings as capable of perfecting their natures and achieving the status of "lord[s] of nature."[2] Standing in close proximity to the gods gives human beings license to exercise lordship over animals and other created beings. To call our representations of the gods into question is to challenge our privileged status as lords of nature. This challenge forces us to reevaluate our sense of ourselves and, in turn, our sense of animals. The example of Xenophanes illustrates the tendency throughout the history of Western philosophy to recognize the limits of old conceptions of ourselves and animals and to seek new conceptions that adequately reflect our experience of humanity and animality.

Thinkers such as Xenophanes pose a challenge to advocates of anthropocentrism. Even when the world is conceived as theocentric, that is, as centered on a god or gods rather than on human beings, the fact that we picture the gods in human form shows the influence of anthro-

1

pocentric thinking. A theocentric worldview is compatible with an anthropocentric view, according to which animals are inferior to humans in the cosmic order. In fact, many anthropocentric thinkers assert that the gods created animals expressly for the sake of human beings. Anthropocentric arguments have long exercised their influence on thinking about animals in the history of Western philosophy. These arguments have their roots in Aristotle, and particularly in the thought of the Stoics, Saint Augustine, Saint Thomas Aquinas, Descartes, and Kant. These philosophers' views about animals are linked by an underlying logic: that all and only human beings are worthy of moral consideration, because all and only human beings are rational and endowed with language. Only such beings are capable of genuine self-determination and moral responsibility, and are moral beings in the most complete and authentic sense. As nonrational beings, animals are due less moral consideration than human beings, and on some accounts animals are due no moral consideration whatsoever.

Alongside this dominant view in the history of Western philosophy, there are a number of heterodox thinkers who seek to vindicate the moral status of animals. But in most cases, philosophers will acknowledge the fundamental continuity or kinship between human beings and animals, only to conclude that human beings nonetheless enjoy priority over animals in considerations of moral worth. Anthropocentric conceptions of animals and their moral status begin to play a significant role early in the history of Western philosophy. The influence of these considerations undercuts the force of arguments advanced on behalf of animals. At the same time, heterodox philosophers have continued to express themselves in the midst of a predominantly anthropocentric tradition.

The expression "anthropocentrism and its discontents" is intended to capture this ambivalence in our cultural history. Freud's title *Das Unbehagen in der Kultur*, known in English as *Civilization and Its Discontents*, literally means "the [element of] discontent in culture," and it refers to the fact that culture itself includes an irreducible sense of dissatisfaction—that satisfaction and dissatisfaction in civilization are inseparable from one another. Similarly, the sense of self-satisfaction we have derived from representing ourselves as superior to animals has been inseparable from an underlying discontent about the fundamental limits of this sense of superiority and the consequent injustices that have been done to animals.

The increasing interest in animals and their moral status in recent decades has been accompanied by a greater willingness to challenge the conventional wisdom that only human beings possess mental capacities such as self-awareness, intentional states (such as beliefs), deliberation, and conceptual abstraction. Moved by the desire to establish a more edified view of the moral status of animals than the sense that has prevailed in the Western philosophical tradition, an increasing number of ethologists and philosophers have marshaled insights concerning the evolutionary continuity and physiological similarity between animals and human beings to argue that many animals are conscious, sentient beings that deserve substantial moral consideration.

These contemporary efforts are beset with many questions and disagreements. Are capacities such as rationality relevant to considerations of moral worth? Is sentience, the capacity to experience pleasure and pain, morally significant, and if so, how are we to compare the value of animal pleasures and pains with those of human beings? If we agree that mammals are sentient, do we avoid moral problems by killing them painlessly? Can a being possess moral worth if it lacks rationality or sentience? Are animals to be treated differently in this regard than, say, an infant or a persistently comatose human being? Are there grounds other than experiential capacities that are of fundamental relevance to the moral status of animals? Should we take Hume seriously when he places the cosmic value of a human being on a par with that of an oyster?

These are important and troubling questions for which there are no settled answers. Philosophers have struggled with these questions since antiquity, and the terms of the contemporary debates about animals take their bearings from a complex lineage of thinking that extends back to Homeric Greece. The more we learn about that lineage, the more insight we can gain for the task of rethinking the nature and moral status of animals.

CONTEMPORARY DEBATES ON
THE STATUS OF ANIMALS

Martha Nussbaum concludes her review discussion of Steven Wise's *Rattling the Cage* with the observation that the moral status of animals "is an area in which we will ultimately need good theories to winnow our judgments because our judgments are so flawed and shot through with self-serving inconsistency."[1] The clearest sign that such theories are needed is that, often against their proponents' best intentions, the leading contemporary theories of the moral status of animals ultimately privilege the interests of human beings over nonhuman animals. Academic philosophers use such terms as "robust" to characterize theories that are well grounded, persuasive, and effective in shaping insights about the subject matter of theories. For a theory of the moral status of animals to deserve such a characterization, it must counter the self-serving inconsistencies of contemporary theories.

A different approach is proposed by Richard Sorabji, who states that "from a philosophical point of view, I do not think that we have to adopt any moral theory at all, and certainly not any moral theory . . . which seeks, as far as possible, to boil down all considerations to one."[2] In particular, Sorabji criticizes the limitations and problematic conclusions of Peter Singer's utilitarian theory and Tom Regan's inherent value theory. Singer bases judgments about moral worth on sentience (the ability to experience pleasure and pain) and the capacity to satisfy preferences, whereas Regan appeals to capacities such as cognition, self-awareness, and self-determination. Advocates of virtue ethics also rely on the notion of capacities and, like advocates of utilitarianism and inherentism, they tend to conceptualize the capacities of human beings as superior to those of animals in ways that are morally significant. The central limitation of these approaches is that they lead to the sort of self-serving prejudice that motivates Nussbaum's cautionary remark. By focusing on capacities such as preference satisfaction, selfhood, virtue, or a self-reflective awareness of the future, these philosophers base judgments of moral worth on the degree of sophistication or complexity of a being's subjective inner life. In doing so, they implicitly support the notion of the autonomous human individual that has become the linchpin of liberal political theory. At the same time, the moral upshot of these theories is that animals ultimately compare unfavorably to human beings on the relevant measures and are inevitably branded with an inferior moral status vis-à-vis human beings. The resulting dilemma is that we cannot dispense with the liberal ideal of the individual in the political realm, but this ideal is ill-suited to protect the moral status of animals.

Sorabji's response to the limitations of inherentism and utilitarianism is to call into question the very endeavor to marshal a moral "theory" to vindicate the moral status of animals, and to recommend instead that we appeal to our "own values, rather than offering theoretical support for any values."[3] This is intriguing, but it is not the approach that I pursue in this book. Appeals to "our own values" are like appeals to our intuitions: these values are often prejudices that stand in need of evaluation and revision. It is here that theories can assist us in reevaluating our moral relationship to animals. What is needed is a view of animals that includes considerations of capacities such as cognition and sentience, while not making these considerations exclusive or paramount. Sorabji's approach to animals can accommodate such a view. He says that "multiple considerations are needed" in the study of animals, because "elaborations of the one-dimensional theories do not seem to get at the reasons that move us, even if they help those theories to reach more acceptable verdicts."[4] My working hypothesis is that cognition and sentience are each sufficient conditions for establishing the moral status of animals, but that neither is a necessary condition. This leaves open the possibility that other considerations are fundamental to the moral status of animals. It poses no challenge to the importance of sophisticated capacities such as reflection and self-determination in the sphere of human relations, but it remains open to the limitations of such capacities in considerations of the moral worth of animals.

Hume suggested that "the life of a man is of no greater importance to the universe than that of an oyster."[5] From the standpoint of contemporary prejudices about the relative value of human beings and animals, Hume's statement is ridiculous. Oysters possess no central nervous system and thus are not even capable of sensations of pain; they are so lacking in sentience that it seems absurd to accord them any moral status, let alone a status on a par with human beings. Nevertheless, my working hypothesis leaves open this possibility. If we proceed on the a priori assumption that creatures such as oysters cannot possibly have anything like the moral status of human beings, our arguments will be undermined by anthropocentric prejudice. Even if we ultimately conclude that oysters do not enjoy the same moral status as human beings, I argue that we must start with openness to the possibility that they do.

Such an openness is expressed in Homeric and pre-Socratic thought, but Aristotle presents a serious challenge to it that remains dominant throughout the history of Western philosophy. Nonetheless, some aspects of that early openness persist in Western thought and conflict with the dominant line of thought. This is evident in contemporary debates about animals and their moral status.

Current Philosophical Discussions of the Moral Status of Animals

The two most influential contemporary philosophers working in animal ethics are Peter Singer and Tom Regan. Although their philosophical positions are opposed in fundamental ways, they share a common goal: to inspire a wholesale rethinking of the moral status of animals, and to move people to change their received values and prejudices about the treatment of animals. Singer advocates a utilitarian approach, while Regan advocates a deontological or "inherentist" approach. As different as these two approaches are, their implications for the valuation of animals are strikingly similar.

Singer proposes "a broadly utilitarian position" in which utility is not to be understood simply in terms of pleasure and pain, but in terms of "the interests of those affected."[6] Singer focuses on the ability to have interests because he believes that some sense of "subjectivity" or selfhood is necessary if a being is to be considered to possess moral status. For Singer, all sentient beings are subjects or selves. Sentience can be understood in a number of ways. Often it is understood as a capacity for thought or cognition; but Singer conceives of it as the capacity to experience pleasure or pain, and he makes this capacity requisite for moral status.

To have interests, "a being must be capable of suffering or experiencing pleasure."[7] Singer emphasizes interests because on his view, pleasure and pain are part of a larger complex of ways of relating to the world. They are not merely discrete experiences that some beings have. Mountain ecosystems, the Grand Canyon, coral reefs, and giant sequoias lack moral status because they are incapable of experiencing pleasure or pain, and hence are incapable of having interests. Because they have no interests, it makes no sense to consider whether their interests are being promoted or frustrated. Beings such as sequoia redwoods and oysters cannot be benefited or harmed, hence they have no claim to inclusion in any utilitarian calculus. The interests of people or certain animals may be affected by the things we do to forests or ecosystems, and to this extent our actions affecting these sorts of beings often do figure in our utilitarian calculations. But in such cases, the harms or benefits are not to the forests or ecosystems but to the people or animals in question.

If we grant that many animals experience pleasure and pain, then on Singer's view we must also grant that these animals have inner lives that involve them in a web of interests and at least quasi-intentional behaviors. For example, Singer considers it obvious that apes that use language must necessarily employ concepts, and he likewise considers it obvious that animals that engage in deceptive behavior must possess "self-consciousness and the consciousness of another."[8] But such sophisticated behavior is not needed for an animal to have intentional states. Just in virtue of the capacity to experience pleasure and pain, an animal can be said to have "wants and desires."[9] Although Singer does not focus on beliefs, he could argue that if an animal has desires, it also has beliefs and hence possesses intentionality, selfhood, interests, awareness of self in contrast with others, and similar capacities for sentience. As noted, however, Singer restricts his focus and his argumentation to sentience conceived as the capacity to experience pleasure and pain.

On the basis of this conception of sentience, Singer argues that utilitarian considerations demand not equal treatment but rather equal *consideration* of interests.[10] This means that the interests of all sentient beings must be considered equally, but that utilitarian considerations may justify unequal treatment. Several years ago, when Singer was given a chair in ethics at Princeton University, many people were outraged because Singer argues that it is more justifiable to experiment on low-functioning ("marginal") humans than on high-functioning nonhumans such as apes. Singer's rationale is that an irretrievably comatose human's interests count less because the comatose condition apparently makes it impossible for that human to experience any pleasure or pain at all, whereas a conscious bonobo has a rich sentient life. Thus the comatose human's interests are outweighed by the interests of a healthy bonobo or chimpanzee (which on some accounts have mental functioning equivalent to a three-year-old human), and we should give priority to the interests of the ape. An important part of Singer's argument is that our inclination to give preference to any human over any animal is simply a vestige of dogmatic speciesism—dogmatic, because our preference is based on nothing but the sheer fact of membership in our own species, without regard to that being's capacity for sentience.[11]

Thus Singer argues for the abolition of factory farming and adoption of a vegetarian diet for human beings. This would alleviate the suffering of animals and enhance their prospects for pursuing their interests. Singer acknowledges the costs to humanity of abolishing factory farming, but he notes that these costs will occur only once. Regarding changes in our diet, Singer stresses that his call for vegetarianism is not categorical: "Whether we ought to be vegetarians depends on a lot of facts about the situation in which we find ourselves."[12] It is incumbent on us to be vegetarians only to the extent that doing so contributes to optimal utilitarian results. Thus, as Cora Diamond observes, "your Peter Singer vegetarian should be perfectly happy to eat the unfortunate lamb that has just been hit by a car," because eating the lamb inflicts no harm on the decedent, and it (ex hypothesi) benefits the diner.[13] Only a moral absolutist would argue that a person should not eat the lamb; Singer explicitly disavows "all . . . forms of moral absolutism." "Vegetarianism is, for [Singer], a means to an end rather than an end in itself."[14] Singer no more places an absolute value on the lives of animals than he does on the lives of human beings. Depending on the circumstances, we should be prepared to sacrifice one or the other if doing so will result in a better utilitarian outcome.

Except in highly unusual circumstances, such as that involving a trade-off between the interests of an irretrievably comatose human being and a high-functioning primate, the principle of "equal consideration" of interests constitutes the basis for preferential treatment of human beings. Notwithstanding Singer's intention to improve the lives of animals, the principle of equal consideration functions much as Marx says the liberal principle of legal equality does: by treating unequal beings as if they were equal, the principle of equal consideration of interests preserves underlying de facto inequalities. The root inequality in Singer's position follows from his orientation on interests. Outwardly, his analysis of interests in terms of the capacity to experience pleasure and pain seems to put human beings and animals on an equal plane. But the concept of interests in utilitarianism is more complex than this suggests. John Stuart Mill articulates the unexpressed presupposition of Singer's utilitarianism: that human beings have a fundamentally more sophisticated capacity for happiness than animals, because human beings possess rationality. Even though all sentient creatures' interests must be taken into account in the utilitarian calculus, "a beast's pleasures do not satisfy a human being's conceptions of happiness. Human beings have faculties more elevated than the animal appetites, and when once made conscious of them, do not regard anything as happiness which does not include their gratification."[15] Thus intellectual pleasures are fundamentally superior to brute pleasures, just as Aristotle argues in the *Nicomachean Ethics*. Regan notes that Singer views humans and animals alike as "receptacles" that can accommodate quanta of pleasure or pain.[16] To the extent that human beings are fundamentally capable of being "filled" to a greater degree than animals, in all or most utilitarian comparisons between human beings and animals, the interests of human beings take precedence.

Singer emphasizes eliminating practices, such as factory farming, in which the most egregious offenses against animals are committed. The potential of utilitarianism to counter practices such as animal experimentation is less clear, particularly in cases in which the gain to human beings promises to be great. Thus Stuart Hampshire states that utilitarianism "places men at the very center of the universe, with their states of feeling as the source of all value in the world."[17] Utilitarianism does not imply this inherently, to the extent that all the interests of all sentient beings are considered; but utilitarians do so as a matter of practice, because human beings ultimately make the calculations. A basic tenet of utilitarianism is that only the individual in question can say definitively what his or her interests are and how much enjoyment or suffering he or she will experience from the promotion or frustration of those interests. When humans make utilitarian calculations on behalf of animals, the likelihood of anthropocentrism is high. It is easy to provide rationalizations—that we can minimize animal suffering, that it is "natural" for people to eat meat, that we will eat only free-range cattle, that we will provide the animals with a comfortable life right up to the moment when we kill them painlessly, that the true value of our uses of animals can be properly grasped only when viewed in the larger context of a web of interests and projects whose range and sophistication are possible only for human beings. None of this is to say that utilitarianism is of no use in considerations of moral worth, but only that utilitarianism is insufficient *on its own* for evaluating the moral status of animals.

Tom Regan attempts to avoid this limitation of Singer's utilitarianism by taking a deontological approach to the moral status of animals. Instead of focusing on sentience and the capacity to satisfy preferences or pursue interests, Regan focuses on the complex cognitive apparatus of "perception, memory, desire, belief, self-consciousness, intention, [and] a sense of the future."[18] Any being that possesses these capacities possesses inherent worth and merits moral consideration; for Regan, this includes at least "mentally normal mammals of a year or more," and may include other animals as well, although Regan makes his case only for mature mammals.[19] These animals are "autonomous" in the sense that "they have preferences and the ability to initiate action with a view to satisfying them"; they are "individuals who act intentionally."[20] Autonomy in animals is thus not as sophisticated as it is in human beings; it is not the full-blown autonomy of a Kantian moral subject. But it is nonetheless sufficient for the initiation of projects and the cultivation of an individual life, and for Regan this is sufficient to qualify animals as moral patients if not as moral agents. For thinkers such as Kant to deny inherent value to animals when they clearly possess intentional agency (the ability to form and act on the basis of beliefs and desires, and to engage in acts of abstraction) is "arbitrary in the extreme."[21] According to Regan, Kant's mistake is to draw a sharp distinction between "persons" and "things," and to classify all and only rational, language-using beings as "persons" while relegating all subhuman beings to the class of mere "things." Kant thus maintains—incorrectly, in Regan's view—that only those beings capable of moral responsibility can have inherent value and thus be proper objects of direct moral consideration. Regan notes that animals are fundamentally "innocent," that is, they are incapable of committing redressable wrongs, but they nonetheless possess inherent value just as we consider severely mentally impaired human beings to possess inherent value.[22]

Even if animals are not "persons" in the Kantian sense, on Regan's view they merit inclusion in deontological moral considerations because they are "subjects-of-a-life" with "beliefs and desires; perception, memory, and a sense of the future, including their own future; an emotional life together with feelings of pleasure and pain; preference- and welfare-interests; the ability to initiate action in pursuit of their desires and goals; a psychophysical identity over time; and an individual welfare in the sense that their experiential life fares well or ill for them, logically independently of their utility for others and logically independently of their being the object of anyone else's interests."[23] All subjects-of-a-life possess inherent value, and all such beings possess inherent value equally. This means that animals possess inherent value and deserve respect, just as human beings do. Regan rounds out this picture of the basis for animal rights by noting that the subject-of-a-life criterion is a sufficient but not a necessary condition for attributing inherent worth to a being.[24] He makes this qualification because he believes that natural objects can have inherent value even though they are not subjects-of-a-life.[25] Regan thus seeks to avoid the problem of anthropocentrism by acknowledging the possibility of making a case for the moral status of natural beings that does not depend on mental capacities.

Regan's position in *The Case for Animal Rights* has the same limitation as Singer's utilitarianism. This is evident in Regan's lifeboat example. "Imagine five survivors are on a lifeboat. Because of limits of size, the boat can only support four. All weigh approximately the same and would take up approximately the same amount of space. Four of the five are normal adult human beings. The fifth is a dog. One must be thrown overboard or all will perish. Who should it be?" Regan's answer is that "no reasonable person would suppose that the dog has a 'right to life' that is equal to the humans'."[26] The dog should unquestionably be thrown overboard, because "the harm that death is, is a function of the opportunities for satisfaction that it forecloses, and no reasonable person would deny that the death of any of the four humans would be a greater prima facie loss, and thus a greater prima facie harm, than would be true in the case of the dog."[27] Moreover, "numbers make no difference in this case. A million dogs ought to be cast overboard if that is necessary to save the four normal humans."[28]

Thus on Regan's view, two beings that have inherent moral worth are not necessarily to be treated equally. On Regan's view, the human being's "prima facie loss" is so incomparably greater than that of *any* number of dogs that a human's life, under "normal" circumstances, is *never* to be sacrificed for the sake of even a million dogs. On this reasoning, it would appear to be morally acceptable to sacrifice the life of every animal on earth for the sake of one human being, at least in the hypothetical situation in which we could ignore the environmental devastation that would ensue. As Dale Jamieson has observed, Regan's view entails that

> animals in lifeboats, like animals on farms, are all equal; but some are more equal than others. Recall the governing metaphor: inherent value is the value of the receptacle rather than the value of the contents. If inherent value is to play any well-motivated role in Regan's theory, it would seem that it must block inferences from the content of a creature's life to conclusions about the creature's moral entitlements. Yet despite his denials it appears that Regan makes exactly this sort of inference in his discussion of the lifeboat case.[29]

At its core, then, Regan's rights-based approach to the moral status of animals is subject to the same anthropocentric prejudice as Singer's utilitarian approach. It is important to consider the question how awareness of the long-term future, the ability to envision and cultivate a more complex and self-aware life, and the ability to reflect on the meaning of enjoyment and suffering entail a superior *moral* status for human beings vis-à-vis animals. Is it not possible that a being can suffer harm whether or not it is aware of the harm it suffers, and regardless of how similar its modes of awareness are to those of a human being? This is the possibility Regan proposes when he says cognition is sufficient but not necessary for moral status. I now examine this possibility as a supplemental basis for assessing the harm that a being such as a dog might suffer if it were thrown overboard.

In his poem "The Lizard," Theodore Roethke expresses an appreciation of this possibility, by depicting a person's reflection on the experience of a lizard with whom he is sharing a terrace. Both have just eaten, and both are sitting calmly on the terrace, eyeing each other. The person wonders whether lighting a cigarette would disturb the lizard, proceeds to light the cigarette, and calmly observes the lizard while being calmly observed. Roethke clothes this encounter in a mood of repose and ancient memory, in which the person comes to wonder whose standpoint really has primacy in this encounter.

> To whom does this terrace belong?—
> With its limestone crumbling into fine grayish dust,
> Its bevy of bees, and its wind-beaten rickety sun-chairs.
> Not to me, but to this lizard,
> older than I, or the cockroach.[30]

Roethke's reflection on the life of the lizard draws attention to the fact that the lizard has a life of its own that is unknown to us, and whose significance may not be captured adequately by the language of intentionality and "psychophysical identity over time." For Regan as for Singer, the basis for giving priority to the life of a human being over that of a lizard is that "in the vast majority of cases, a human's death wipes out greater opportunities for satisfaction than does the life of a trout, lizard, or alligator. The mental lives of these animals are presumably pretty dim. Of course, that means they suffer less, a point with which we need to come to terms."[31] We must also come to terms with the possibility that the moral worth of such animals may be due in part to considerations that have nothing to do with how "dim" those animals are. The mental lives of severely mentally impaired human beings "are presumably pretty dim," but it is not clear that this gives us license to treat such human beings as many people treat trout, lizards, and alligators. If we believe that "marginal" human beings (infants, the severely mentally impaired, and so on) have moral worth despite their limited capacities for cognition and sentience, then the same should hold for a wide variety of animals.[32]

Although no systematic attempt has yet been made to marshal virtue ethics on behalf of animals, the central concepts of virtue ethics have been appealed to with increasing frequency in recent years, together with their underpinnings in Aristotelian ethical naturalism. The terms of Aristotle's naturalism attribute to each creature a good that is its proper end in life, and the pursuit of which characterizes that creature's activity. The virtue of each being is to be evaluated by its capacities, which determine its proper end. A basic distinction between humans and animals is that we possess the freedom to determine ourselves (and thus to succeed or fail in pursuing our ends), whereas animals lack this freedom; their natures are fixed, and they live in accordance with their nature because they are not free to do otherwise. The only factor that can prevent an animal from living in accordance with its nature is a birth defect. Thus, for example, "a good elephant is one which has good tusks, follows the leader, does not attack other elephants, looks after its young, is not frightened of water, etc."[33] It is "virtuous" in the sense that these capacities are its excellences; they enable it to flourish. Moral virtue is the exclusive end of human beings on this view, because only human beings are rational. Animals, by comparison, can act so as to continue their species and they live in accordance with the life expectancy proper to their kind and circumstances. They have no higher ends than the optimization of these material considerations that lead to their thriving.

According to virtue ethics, morality is defined not in terms of duties or utility, but in terms of the moral life. Such a life is understood primarily in terms of Aristotle's notion of character and the ideal of cultivating particular moral virtues such as courage, temperance, and compassion. Aristotle envisions a whole human life or the life of a human community as the proper unit of measure for morality. Particular actions are not moral unless they are chosen for their own sake, are in accordance with right reason, and proceed from a stable character state that the agent has developed over a long period of time.[34] On Aristotle's view, animals are incapable of moral virtue because they lack the rationality requisite for satisfying these conditions. "Animals and plants can flourish, but *eudaimonia* [Aristotle's term for the moral life] is only possible for human beings."[35]

Aristotle never classifies concern for animals among the virtues. For virtue ethics to support the endeavor to vindicate the moral status of animals, a case would have to be made that some virtue or combination of virtues grounds the respectful treatment of animals. "The concept of a virtue is the concept of something that makes its possessor good; a virtuous person is a morally good, excellent, or admirable person who acts and reacts well, rightly, as she should—she gets things right."[36] I now consider whether we simply do not "get things right" when we exhibit indifference to the suffering that we inflict on animals. Rosalind Hursthouse's remarks on vegetarianism are instructive in this connection. Noting that vegetarianism is a practice rather than a virtue, Hursthouse says it is right for "people in the circumstances that make it possible for them to write or read this sort of book" to practice vegetarianism—not because we "get things right" when we recoil at the thought of killing an animal for our gastronomic pleasure, but rather "on the grounds that (i) temperance (with respect to the pleasures of food) is a virtue, and (ii) that for most of 'us', eating meat is intemperate (greedy, self-indulgent)."[37] These appear to be the grounds on which Socrates proposes a vegetarian *kallipolis* (ideal or "good" city) in the *Republic*.[38] Hursthouse adds that virtue ethics implies that all "ethical evaluations are made from within an ethical outlook, an outlook which already has its own conceptions of the virtues, and related conceptions of what is good, beneficial, advantageous, worthwhile, important, enjoyable (and their opposites), and of what we have reason to do."[39] Thus virtue ethics might be pursued from an ethical outlook in which considerations other than temperance recommend vegetarianism. We simply do not "get things right" if we take animals as sources of food.

Rather than exploring such an outlook, Hursthouse states that she and readers like her should embrace vegetarianism because it is temperate to do so. She conceives of temperance not with respect to meat eating, but rather "with respect to the pleasures of food." This is in accordance with Aristotle's definition of temperance as moderation or a mean "with regard to pleasures and pains."[40] More specifically, temperance is moderation with regard to bodily pleasures such as eating and drinking; the corresponding excess is self-indulgence, and for the corresponding deficiency there is no name.[41] Given this account of temperance, to advocate vegetarianism on grounds of temperance is to evaluate meat eating as self-indulgent in principle, which is to say that we derive too much pleasure from the practice. Because meat eating is not a virtue, but rather a practice, it makes no sense to speak of moderation in meat eating, but only of moderation in the amount of bodily pleasure we permit ourselves. So Hursthouse's analysis does not permit us to "get things right" simply by refraining from overindulgence in meat; she construes meat eating per se as self-indulgent—there just is no such thing as eating meat moderately, because eating *any* meat at all provides intemperate (excessive) pleasure.

Hursthouse's analysis of meat eating exposes two key features of the virtue ethics approach to animals. First, according to virtue ethics, meat eating, and by extension a variety of other uses of animals such as experimentation for the benefit of human beings, is not inherently pernicious. Instead, the moral status of such uses of animals is determined in each case by the underlying moral outlook and the specific virtues that it accommodates. Second, virtue ethics makes moral evaluations from the standpoint of the good life for human beings. It promotes the cultivation of character states that enable human agents to live in moderation with regard to those virtues acknowledged by the prevailing moral outlook. According to the terms of the moral outlook that prevails in our society, specifically *human* welfare is of such central concern in virtue ethics that Hursthouse challenges the proposition that concern for animals should be placed on a par with concern for our own species:

> With respect to the continuance of the species and the good functioning of the social group, our natural tendency to bond to other human

beings and our children seems to be serving us rather well. The onus is on those who recommend impersonal benevolence as a virtue to provide at least a speculation about how a species of rational animals who had brought themselves to care naught for their own children or each other's company might still be a species of *social* animals who, moreover, nurtured their young—and, indeed, went to the trouble of giving them a moral education and bringing them up to be impersonally benevolent in their turn.[42]

Thus, deep concern for nonhuman species is incompatible with virtue ethics, at least according to the terms of our inherited moral outlook.

This shows the limits of virtue ethics as it has been conceived in our culture. As DeGrazia notes, an animal is "a being who [can be] wrongfully harmed, not simply a practicing ground for virtue." Virtue ethics "leaves entirely unexplained why cruelty to animals is a vice and compassion to them a virtue—if, as the position assumes, animals lack moral status and therefore cannot be directly wronged."[43] Whether this limitation of virtue ethics can be overcome depends on the extent to which virtue ethics can be incorporated in an ethical naturalism in which the significance of animals in the cosmos is a basic commitment. Martha Nussbaum, for example, argues that the same considerations requiring us to permit the development of human capabilities also require us to permit the development of animal capabilities. With regard to human beings, Nussbaum maintains that "the presence of certain powers, deemed valuable in themselves, gives rise to justified claims on the part of the person who has the powers, that they not be stunted or wasted, but given a chance to develop."[44] With regard to animals, she notes that "the language of capabilities equips us to move beyond the species barrier. Just as it prepares us to see dignity in our own animal faculties . . . so, too, the capabilities approach, already seeing in animality something valuable and dignified, prepares us to turn to the difficult issue of animal entitlements." Nussbaum considers an extension of the capabilities approach to animals to be "essential to the theory's integrity and its completeness."[45]

Even though Nussbaum's intent is not to vindicate virtue ethics but rather to present her own "capabilities" approach, her remarks nonetheless provide grounds for envisioning a virtue ethics that can contribute to a robust animal ethic. Against the background of a holistic view of the inner kinship or commonality between human beings and animals, such a virtue ethics would make virtues such as piety and compassion the basis of moral regard for animals. It would be a virtue to recognize and promote the capacity of an animal to flourish.

Whether such a revised conception of virtue ethics is possible is unclear. It does not meet DeGrazia's challenge that because virtue ethics by its very nature is concerned with *human* excellence, it reduces animals to "a practicing ground for virtue." Thus the underlying outlook guiding virtue ethics would have to be radically revised to make a place for animals as participants in a sphere of moral relations. Along these lines, S. F. Sapontzis argues that animals can be virtuous even though they are incapable of being moral agents. "Only rational beings can be fully moral agents," because only rational beings are capable of being "moral$_{ad}$." "Moral$_{ad}$" refers to "the agent-dependent dimensions of moral value. . . . These are the dimensions of moral value that depend on the agent's understanding of the situation and of his own action, including their moral significance, and on his motive for acting." "Animals cannot be fully moral$_{ad}$ beings . . . because their actions are not part of an attempt to fulfill an ideal way of life."[46] Sapontzis acknowledges Hursthouse's distinction between beings that are free to determine themselves and those that are not. Even though animals are not capable of self-determination and hence are not moral agents, Sapontzis maintains that "many animals are virtuous."[47] They exhibit loyalty, affection, courage, and a variety of other qualities that we call virtues.

Sapontzis does not address the question how a being that acts entirely in accordance with its nature can be considered virtuous; he simply follows commentators such as Mary Midgley in observing that many animals behave in ways that we associate with virtues such as loyalty. "Although [animals] may be unable to recognize how virtuous action contributes to the attainment of an ideal world, they do recognize the needs of others and respond to those needs compassionately, courageously, responsibly, loyally, and so forth. To that degree, they do recognize and respond to moral values. That is enough to earn them a place in the moral$_{ad}$ arena and to discredit the claim that only rational beings can occupy that place of honor."[48] Sapontzis's approach has the advantage of presenting animals as beings with lives, endeavors, and a moral status that corresponds to capacities to act that are much more sophisticated than most people are inclined to suppose. Here a conception of cosmic holism, the notion of an essential commonality between human beings and animals, might provide the necessary background for the emergence of a revised virtue ethics that would incorporate a sense of concern for animals as well as for human beings. The roots of such a sense of cosmic holism lie in early Greek antiquity, and I examine this in the next chapter.

A central argument underlying the present study is that none of the approaches examined above—utilitarianism, deontology, and virtue ethics—is capable on its own of adequately addressing the problem of the moral status of animals. Capacities approaches work well for animals that exhibit relatively sophisticated cognitive skills and conduct that strikes us as loyal, courageous, and so on. But these approaches are ill-suited to the moral evaluation of other sorts of animals—Hume's oyster, say, or Roethke's lizard. What is needed is an ethical naturalism or cosmic holism according to which human beings are part of a larger cosmic whole and have a fundamental kinship relation to animals. On this basis, utilitarianism, deontology, and virtue ethics can be united and their limitations overcome.

Contemporary Ethology and the Question of Animal Capacities

Two responses are possible to the argument that animals lack certain capacities required for moral status: one can argue that the possession of such capacities is not really relevant to the question of moral status, or that animals do in fact possess the capacities in question and thus do possess moral status. Most of the animal advocates I discuss above take the latter approach. As a result, they often attribute too much to animals, whereas the major exponents of the tradition attribute too little. The crucial question about animal awareness is what sorts of capacities must be attributed to animals to account for the complex discriminatory and problem-solving behavior many of them exhibit. In short, what must their awareness must be like for them to act teleologically? Recent ethologists have done a great deal to confirm that many animals possess some sort of sophisticated cognitive apparatus. What remains at issue is how animal cognition is best to be understood, and whether and to what extent cognitive capacities are relevant to considerations of moral worth. Philosophers such as Regan attribute to animals complex abilities modeled on human cognition, such as self-awareness, a sense of the future, and a "psycho-physical identity over time." Martha Nussbaum asserts that animals (she is not clear exactly which ones) possess the full apparatus of intentionality, and that emotion in animals is predicative and eudaimonistic.[49] And some contemporary cognitive ethologists believe that animals such as pigeons and bees possess at least quasi-linguistic communication skills.

The main historical prejudice to which such defenders of animal consciousness are responding is one inherited from the Stoics. That prejudice is that only human beings possess rationality and language, and that these interrelated capacities are absolutely necessary conditions for the possession of moral status. In the first half of this book, I show that this assumption was challenged in the ancient world, but that the prejudice of Stoic anthropocentrism became the dominant voice in the West with regard to animals and their moral status. Defenders of animals have always reacted with indignation to the suggestion that animal behavior is determined by instinct or mechanistic-biological principles. In their zeal to overturn the conventional wisdom about animals, these defenders have attributed to animals qualities and quantities of consciousness that are both indemonstrable and implausible—indemonstrable because of a fundamental problem identified by the philosopher Thomas Nagel, and implausible for reasons developed by the Soviet psychologist Lev Vygotsky.

Some of the earliest philosophers and naturalists recognize a fundamental kinship between humans and animals, without assuming that the experience of animals is necessarily like that of human beings. They are aware that the inner experiences of animals are in principle inaccessible to us, and that the nature of these experiences must remain a matter of speculation. Other ancient philosophers established the terms of much contemporary thinking about animal experience by assuming that the experience and capacities of animals must be the same or similar to those of human beings. In the past century, philosophers have appealed increasingly to research in ethology to support their claims about the nature of animal awareness. This appeal to science has brought with it an implicit sense of the legitimacy of the philosophers' claims. But these claims can be only as legitimate as the conclusions of the underlying ethological research. Ethology, for its part, has undergone a revolution in the past generation, and its basic concepts have not become settled to the point that the results of ethological research can be relied upon with full confidence. The basic problem lies in the axiomatic assumptions made by ethologists.

Contemporary ethology has been shaped by a strong reaction against behavioral ethology, which is based on a rejection of any appeal to "inner" states in accounting for animal behavior. Spearheaded by revolutionaries such as Donald Griffin, the study of animal behavior has been transformed in the past generation into cognitive ethology, based on the axiom that the behavior of animals must be understood by using an anthropomorphic vocabulary of consciousness and cognition. On Griffin's view, to attribute consciousness to animals is to recognize that animals are capable of "thinking about objects and events" and that some animals may be capable of "memories of past perceptions, or anticipations of future events."[50] Griffin argues on the basis of analogy to human experience that animals in all likelihood possess self-consciousness and intentional agency. Behavioristic appeals to genetic programming are not categorically incorrect, but "it does seem more parsimonious" to suppose that animals employ conscious thought in adapting to their environments.[51] Such thought includes the capacity for "if-then" inferences and the use of concepts, even in invertebrates such as bees.[52]

Philosophers following Griffin's logic have appealed to evolutionary continuity and neurophysiological similarities between animals and human beings to strengthen the case for cognition in animals. DeGrazia, for example, takes these considerations, together with the explanatory power of the intentional stance, as persuasive grounds for concluding that many animals possess the full apparatus of intentionality, which includes self-consciousness, conceptual understanding, and the capacity for intentional states such as beliefs and desires.[53] Much research in cognitive ethology has been done to test and defend the hypothesis that animals employ intentional cognition. The basis most often appealed to in claims about animal cognition is that the behavior and versatility of animals seem incomprehensible in the absence of intentionality. How are chimpanzees able to cooperate in problem-solving tasks, pigeons able to engage in highly complex discrimination, and bees able to convey so much information with the bee dance, if these animals have no intentional agency or capacity to form and use concepts?

The problem with this sort of reasoning is, as Thomas Nagel points out, that it relies too heavily on analogy to human experience, and thereby anthropomorphizes the experience of animals. The differences between our perceptual encounter with the world and that of nonhuman animals are sufficiently great that we cannot ultimately know what it is like to be, say, a bat. Our reflections on animal consciousness are irretrievably speculative.[54] Implicit in Nagel's observation is the acknowledgment that evolutionary continuity gets us only so far in the endeavor to understand the nature of consciousness and subjective experience in animals, as well as a recognition that some differences of degree between human beings and animals are so great as to constitute differences of kind. In the remainder of this chapter, I focus primarily on the interrelated capacities for intentionality and conceptual abstraction: Does it make sense to attribute these capacities to animals, particularly those with extremely high levels of cognitive ability such as dolphins and great apes? Is there any reason to suppose that the possession of these capacities is relevant to considerations of the moral worth of animals?

In the three decades since Nagel advanced his thesis about animal consciousness, philosophers and ethologists have sought in a variety of ways to overturn his claim. Some have flatly denied it, proceeding from the putatively "obvious" kinship between humans and animals to the conclusion that our capacity for empathy can disclose some fundamental truths about animal experience. Others have appealed to evolution by arguing that similarities between human physiology and that of many animals, and the similar adaptive demands faced by humans and animals, are a plausible basis for concluding that many animals possess cognitive and emotional capacities similar to those of human beings. But Nagel's challenge is not easily dismissed. Most people who have spent much time studying or interacting with animals conclude that the linguistic and reflective abilities of human beings make our experience different in fundamental respects from the experience of most if not all animals. Even if we consider it plausible to attribute to animals complex emotional lives and the ability to provide for themselves and their offspring in ways that seem to require capacities such as intentionality and a sense of the future, few if any animals exhibit the capacities for language and abstraction that have long been almost universally considered to be the exclusive possession of human beings. But if intentionality and a fully developed sense of the future depend on the ability to conceptualize things, as most philosophers believe they do, then it seems impossible that animals could be capable of intentionality unless they also possess something like human language.

More specifically, to be capable of intentionality, a sense of the future, and so on, animals would have to be able to employ concepts. They would have to be capable not only of making complex discriminations between different objects, but also of doing so by means of abstractions from concrete particulars that enable animals to associate the particulars with one another. The cognitive ethologists Colin Allen and Marc Hauser distinguish "between recognizing an *X*, and recognizing something *as* an *X* or recognizing it to be an *X*." The first ability simply reflects "a discriminatory ability," whereas the second "says something about the organism's system of internal representation. To have a concept of X where the specification of X is not exhausted by a perceptual characterization, it is not enough just to have the ability to discriminate X's from non-X's. One must be able to have a representation of X that abstracts away from the perceptual features that enable one to identify X's."[55]

On the basis of this definition, Allen and Hauser argue that it makes sense to attribute conceptual abilities to at least some animals, and that it might be possible to design experiments to support such attributions. Allen develops this suggestion cautiously by noting that the attribution of concepts to animals is hypothetical. As an example of animal behavior that can be explained by an appeal to conceptual ability, he offers vervet monkeys' alarm calls, which vary according to predator.[56] Vervet alarm calls differ depending on whether the predator is a martial eagle, a python, or a large mammal such as a leopard. And the responses exhibited by vervets hearing the call differ according to the specific threat; vervets alerted to the presence of a python run away, those threatened by a martial eagle climb into a tree, and those protecting themselves from a leopard climb onto the small outermost branches of a tree. Vervets also appear to be able to distinguish the calls of individual members of their group. Behaviors and abilities of this sort are difficult to explain unless we assume that vervets are capable of conscious thought and conceptual ability. Another example cited by Allen and Hauser is the apparent ability of vervets to understand the concept of death: vervet mothers seem to grasp the difference between dead and missing offspring. Mothers that take their young to be dead soon "turn off" their concerned response when they hear distress calls of their young that were recorded before the young died.[57]

Other key examples of animal capacities and behaviors that seem to depend on predication and conceptual abstraction include the sophisticated linguistic abilities of some apes, deceptive behavior in a variety of animals, and the ability of pigeons to make highly complex discriminations between different types of object.[58] Each of these examples is fraught with interpretive difficulties. The apes that learn language, such as Kanzi and Washoe, have limited vocabularies, and although they do comprehend some syntax, they seem unable to reproduce it on their own. In the cases of deception and complex discrimination tasks, if Nagel's observation about the irreducible particularity of the consciousness of different animals is correct, then we can only speculate about the mechanisms at work. For example, de Waal has confirmed that a non-alpha male seeking to have sex with a prized female while the alpha male is away will, if the alpha male returns unexpectedly, cover his erection with his hands to conceal his endeavor.[59] But it remains unclear how such an action is to be interpreted: Is it inexplicable without recourse to concepts and intentional states such as beliefs and desires? Are mental states such as beliefs and desires not predicatively structured in the consciousness of the animal in question, even though from our standpoint as observers such states are incomprehensible in nonpredicative terms? Is it reasonable to suppose that a being that seems largely or completely incapable of language is nonetheless capable of acts of predication?

There are questions of comparable difficulty concerning the interpretation of pigeon discriminatory abilities and the abilities of animals such as the Clark's nutcracker, which is able to bury and later retrieve large numbers of seeds that it has stored for food. Herrnstein's experiments on discrimination in pigeons show that pigeons possess remarkable abilities to discriminate objects such as human beings, water, and trees. The pigeons were able not only to select each sort of object, but to do so even when they were shown only parts of the objects and even when they were shown new items that were not exact matches for the original objects of each kind that they had been shown.[60] Allen and Hauser note that Herrnstein's conclusions were widely taken to show that pigeons employ concepts, but that Herrnstein et al. never actually argued that pigeons employ concepts, only that they employ "categories," which, unlike concepts, do not involve mental content separate from the particulars classified.[61]

Ethologists such as Allen and Hauser want to account for the complex discriminations and adaptive choices made by animals. They reason that conceptual ability is a plausible basis, given its adaptive value. The examples they focus on involve vervet monkeys, which are extremely high-functioning primates. The relative similarity between the brain physiology of higher mammals such as vervets and that of human beings leads John Searle to conclude that intentional states are a more or less obvious feature of the mental capacities of higher mammals, and that the explanation of animal behavior becomes "unintelligible" if we do not have recourse to beliefs and desires.[62] Searle's claim is most plausible with regard to those animals closest to human beings, the higher primates. But what about other animals, such as dogs and cats? Is it reasonable to suppose, as some do, that any animals exhibiting purposive behavior must possess intentionality and conceptual ability?[63] A number of influential discussions of the question of concepts in animals center on examples involving dogs. Norman Malcolm set off a chain reaction when he proposed in the early 1970s that a dog is presumably thinking when it chases a cat, loses track of it, and sits barking excitedly up the wrong tree.[64] Donald Davidson argues in "Rational Animals" that Malcolm cannot possibly be right about this, because the capacity for thought presupposes the capacity for beliefs, and having a belief presupposes both an abstract conception of what a belief is and a whole network of beliefs in terms of which any given belief derives its meaning. To the extent that beliefs are propositional attitudes, only beings capable of language can have beliefs. Animals such as dogs, therefore, cannot have any beliefs. Davidson does not appear to conceive of animals as simple machines. He acknowledges their ability to respond to the world in intricate ways, but he maintains that none of this requires the attribution of beliefs to animals. "A creature may react to the world in complex ways without entertaining any propositions. It may discriminate among colors, tastes, sounds and shapes. It may 'learn', that is, change its behavior in ways that preserve its life or increase its food intake. It may 'generalize', in the sense of reacting to new stimuli as it has come to react to similar stimuli. Yet none of this, no matter how successful by my standards, shows that the creature commands the subjective-objective contrast, as required by belief."[65]

Other philosophers offer related reasons why it does not make sense to attribute concepts to animals. Wittgenstein asks, "A dog believes his master is at the door. But can he also believe his master will come the day after tomorrow?—And *what* can he not do here?"[66] The context of Wittgenstein's remark suggests that the dog cannot have expectations beyond the immediate moment, because to do so requires having a language, which means being engaged in a social network of meaningful exchanges. "Rationality," as Davidson puts the point, "is a social trait."[67] Steven Stich argues that it makes no sense to attribute beliefs and concepts to a dog in an example such as Malcolm's, because doing so would entail that the dog understood all sorts of abstract notions that the dog just does not seem to understand.

> To explain Fido's behavior it would be perfectly natural to say he believes that the squirrel is up in the oak tree. But suppose now that some skeptic challenges our claim by focusing attention on the differences separating Fido's belief from ours. "Does Fido really believe it is a squirrel up

in the oak tree? Are there not indefinitely many logically possible creatures which are not squirrels but which Fido would treat indistinguish-
ably from the way he treats real squirrels? Indeed does he believe, or even
care, that the thing up the tree is an animal? Would it not be quite the
same to Fido if he had been chasing some bit of squirrel-shaped and
squirrel-smelling machinery, like the mechanical rabbits used at dog-
racing tracks? The concept of animal is tied to the distinction between
animals and plants. But Fido has little grasp of these distinctions. How
can you say that he believes it is a squirrel if he doesn't know that squirrels
are animals?" Confronted with the challenge, which focuses attention
on the ideological gap that separates us from Fido, intuition begins to
waver. It no longer sounds quite right to say that Fido believes there is
a *squirrel* up in the oak tree.[68]

Stich's challenge is like Allen and Hauser's distinction between recognizing an X and recognizing something *as* an X or recognizing that something
is an X: To recognize that something *is* an X presupposes that we understand what an X is, how it differs from Ys, Zs, As, Bs, and Cs, and what it
means to be a Y, a Z, and so forth. The extreme consequence of Stich's
argument is that we cannot attribute to dogs anything like our concept
of, say, a bone, because our concept of bone involves the concept of a
physical object, which the dog patently seems to lack.[69] Daniel Dennett
argues, along similar lines, that the attribution of concepts to the dog can
be no more than a heuristic device, because it is ultimately impossible to
specify the content of the dog's concept of a given thing, for example, a
piece of steak. "What the dog recognizes this object as is something for
which there is no English word."[70]

There are different ways to respond to the difficulty raised by Stich
and Dennett. One is to observe, as Allen does, that the difficulty involved
in specifying the content of the dog's concept of something (of a piece
of steak, for example) is no bar to the possibility of arriving at some sort
of description of the dog's concept. "If we think of the list of concepts,
such as nourishment or edibility, that are related to the concept of food,
then it might be possible to specify the deletion or addition of links to
specific concepts from this list and thereby end up with a concept which
does match the dog's." Dennett's argument does not exclude the possibility
"that there is some suitably complicated sentence which we lack enough
ingenuity (or are too lazy) to discover" that can capture the dog's sense
of steak, or food, or a bone, or a squirrel.[71] The fact that the dog has no

concept of physical objects, the law of gravity, osteology, or nutrition in general, does not preclude the possibility that the dog has some kind of concept of steak or bones, even if the dog's concepts are quite unlike human concepts of these same things. Regan employs a comparable strategy in arguing for a "more or less" notion of concepts rather than an "all or nothing" one: It is not necessary for a being, whether it be a human or a nonhuman animal, to possess all of the possible associations relevant to a given concept in order to have that concept. Human beings prior to the chemical revolution had a less adequate conception of bones than we have today, and yet they nonetheless had some concept of bone.[72] Similarly, young children know little if anything about abstract notions such as "physical object," and yet they are able to distinguish very effectively between cookies and spinach. For Allen and Regan, the same reasoning holds, mutatis mutandis, for animals. Even if it turned out to be impossible for us to specify the content of animals' concepts or beliefs, and even if those concepts or beliefs are fundamentally less rich than human concepts and beliefs, it still makes sense to attribute to animals mental states with *content* that the animals can apply to new, unfamiliar cases that are relevantly similar to familiar ones.

This sort of response to Stich and Dennett is intended to preserve the idea that animals are capable of propositional attitudes (intentional states) such as beliefs and desires. The act-object structure of intentional states, for example, "(I believe that) there is one sun in our solar system," is a propositional structure in which the subject and the object are explicitly conceptualized. For the dog to believe that the cat ran up this tree, the dog must be able to conceptualize the objects that we understand under the terms "cat" and "(this) tree." For the dog to desire a particular bone or a steak, the dog must have the concept of bones and steak. How, otherwise, could the dog seek out the objects that command its attention? How could a bull succeed in using its horns rather than its tail to defend itself, unless it had a conceptual awareness of the different parts of its body and proper functions of each?

But do such abilities as self-defense and discrimination between potential sources of food necessarily presuppose conceptualization and intentionality? Allen and Hauser's distinction between recognizing an *X* and recognizing something to *be* an *X* is illuminating here, for it makes it possible to imagine an animal recognizing the different parts of its body and different sorts of potential food without having a concept of any of these. This distinction helps explain Davidson's claim that animals can be capable of complex discriminations without employing concepts or beliefs at all, and Wittgenstein's claim that the dog cannot believe that someone will come home the day after tomorrow. The consciousness of the dog, as thinkers from the Stoics to Aquinas to Schopenhauer argue, is confined to the present (and perhaps the very near future) in a way that human beings are not, because human beings are capable of conceptual abstraction and a sense of the future as such; human agents are, in turn, able to contemplate different possible objects of desire in relation to one another and in relation to the agent's overall aims, which makes free choice possible for human beings. Animals, in contrast, are moved by objects of desire in a comparatively (if not entirely) mechanical way. Animals, from the Thomistic viewpoint, are *non agunt sed magis aguntur*—they do not act, but are instead acted upon.

Although I do not believe that animals are incapable of choice, I do believe that there is something essentially correct in the traditional view, according to which the consciousness of animals is confined to the present and perhaps the very near term, and according to which animals do not contemplate various objects of desire conceptually. I also think that Davidson is right to propose that the capacity for belief presupposes linguistic ability. Where I disagree with traditional thinkers such as the Stoics and Descartes is in their wholesale denial of consciousness in animals. The Stoics argue that the perceptual states of animals are fundamentally different than those of human beings because animals lack linguistic ability; and Descartes argues that animals "perceive" in nothing more than the way in which we might speak offhandedly of a thermometer "perceiving" a change in temperature. For both the Stoics and Descartes, whose ideas about animal experience are the most influential in the history of Western philosophy, animals are fundamentally incapable of beliefs and desires.[73] The Stoics and Descartes arrive at this conclusion because they are sensitive to the limitations imposed on animal experience by the lack of linguistic ability, which includes the capacity for conceptual abstraction. But they err by going to the extreme of denying most (the Stoics) or all (Descartes) aspects of inner experience to animals, thereby leaving us with an impoverished view of animal mentality.

Fundamental to the task of understanding animal experience is the problem of conceptualizing animal consciousness in terms that do not require recourse to concepts and propositional attitudes. The real puzzle of animal behavior is how animals can engage in acts of discrimination that are sometimes enormously complex, without employing concepts or intentional states. What is needed is a way of accounting for the complex discriminatory and communicative abilities of a wide variety of animals, without unduly anthropomorphizing them. In addition to the examples of animal resourcefulness already mentioned, the remarkable capacities of bees merit brief mention in this connection. Gould and Gould have shown that bees use the "bee dance" to communicate detailed information about location, distance, and the kind of object available (nectar, water, or the site for starting a new colony).[74] To account for such communication, Donald Griffin enthusiastically embraces the intentional stance. He argues that the "versatile behavior patterns and apparently intentional communication" exhibited by creatures all the way down to some invertebrates support "tentatively considering animals as conscious, mindful creatures with their own points of view." For example, "directional orientation" and the use of a "symbolic communication system" may constitute evidence that honeybees employ concepts. Regarding Herrnstein's pigeons, which exhibit highly complex discriminatory ability in an experimental setting, "it seems reasonable to suppose that when the pigeons are working hard in Skinner boxes to solve these challenging problems, they are thinking something like: 'Pecking that thing gets me food.'"[75]

Griffin bases his assimilation of human and animal consciousness on the "clearly demonstrated evolutionary continuity between human and nonhuman communication and thinking."[76] Davidson, on the other hand, says that "the intrinsically holistic character of the propositional attitudes makes the distinction between having any and having none dramatic."[77] There is strong support for Davidson's argument. He does not deny any of the apparent facts about evolutionary continuity. But he argues that certain differences in degree are so significant as to constitute differences in kind and that linguistic capacity is one such "dramatic" difference. He acknowledges the sophisticated capacities of animals to negotiate their environments; but he recognizes that their teleological behavior does not entail that they conceptualize their experience nor that they *think* teleologically. Regarding the endeavor to characterize emotion in animals, Konrad Lorenz argues that "terminology derived from human language is insufficient from the outset for the description of the internal processes of animals, i.e., *the number of terms is too small*."[78] What Lorenz notes about emotion appears to hold for the mental lives of animals generally: dependence on human language, concepts, and experiential perspective distorts, perhaps unavoidably, our appreciation of animal mentality. What is needed is a radicalization of our understanding of animals to overcome the tendency to attribute overly sophisticated cognitive abilities to them.

Addressing a related concern, Nagel concludes his essay "What is it like to be a bat?" with the suggestion that the solution to the mind-body problem may depend on the devising of new concepts that are themselves neither mental nor physical. This has important implications for the endeavor to conceptualize animal experience. We need to devise a vocabulary that both dispenses with the anthropocentric language of linguistic intentionality and avoids the traditional tendency to reduce animals to unconscious machines. In the twentieth century, one thinker did more than any other to contribute to the possibility of developing such a vocabulary. The great Soviet psychologist Lev Vygotsky's experimental and theoretical explorations of the relationship between thought and language help explain both why it is unreasonable to attribute conceptual ability to most if not all animals and how we might develop a notion of associations or "complexes" that is central to our conceptualization of animal consciousness

Vygotsky published *Thought and Language* (literally "thought and speech") in 1934. His central concern is the relationship between the development of linguistic competence and the development of thought in human beings. Drawing on the research of Piaget, Stern, and Claparède as well as on his own extensive experimental work, Vygotsky argues that the capacities for language and thought are not inherently interrelated.[79] At first, each pursues a course of development independent of the other. Thus the development of thought has a prelinguistic phase and the development of speech a preintellectual phase.[80] But at certain crucial junctures, their paths of development cross and mutually inform one another. At one of these crucial junctures, around the age of two, speech is first marshaled to express thoughts; at another, which occurs at the onset of puberty, human beings develop the capacity to form abstract concepts. Conceptual capacity is the product of a long developmental process, and it depends fundamentally on the use of words.[81] One consequence of Vygotsky's analysis is that only beings capable of linguistic signification are capable of truly abstract thought; another is that even healthy, intelligent human beings are incapable of such thought until puberty.[82]

The latter conclusion is particularly counterintiutive. How can children and adults effectively communicate with one another, and how can children engage in acts of apparent generalization, if preadolescent humans are incapable of conceptual abstraction? Vygotsky's answers to these questions are outdated in certain respects as regards language development in humans, but they nonetheless shed light on the differences between human beings and animals. According to Vygotsky, the basis for child-adult communication as well as for the limitations of such communication lies in the fact that "the child's and the adult's words coincide in their referents but not in their meanings."[83] "In the dialogue between child and adult . . . both of them may refer to the same object, but each will think of it in a fundamentally different framework. The child's framework is purely situational, with the word tied to something concrete, whereas the adult's framework is conceptual. . . . Mental acts based on the child's speech do not coincide with the mental acts of the adult, even if they are uttering one and the same word."[84] Prior to the acquisition of abstract concepts, the mental processes of the child are characterized by "complex" thinking. Thinking in complexes enables children to group or associate different particular objects in virtue of perceived similarities, commonalities, or relationships. Vygotsky identifies five types of complex: associations, collections, diffuse complexes, chain complexes, and pseudoconcepts. Each is "first and foremost a concrete grouping of objects connected by factual bonds. . . . The bonds that create it, as well as the bonds that it helps to create, lack logical unity; they may be of many different kinds." This distinguishes complexes from concepts: "While a concept groups objects according to one attribute, the bonds relating the elements of a complex to the whole and to one another may be as diverse as the contacts and relations of the elements are in reality."[85] In a complex there is no "hierarchical organization of the relations between different traits of the object. All attributes are functionally equal."[86] A child is able to form complex associations between objects without being able to order them in a logically coherent manner, because "he masters syntax of speech before syntax of thought. Piaget argues that grammar develops before logic and that the child learns relatively late the mental operations corresponding to the verbal forms he has been using for a long time."[87]

Of the different forms of complex, the pseudocomplex comes the closest to true conceptual generalization. But even the pseudoconcept falls short of genuine abstraction, because it is "only an associative complex limited to a certain kind of perceptual bond" based on a "concrete, visible likeness."[88] For example, when an individual is presented with a yellow triangle and is asked to pick out all the triangles in an array, the selection process can be based on a concept or on a concrete image. That an adult and a child may make the same selection simply obscures the fact that a fundamentally different thought process is going on in each. "The functional equivalence between complex and concept" has "led to the false assumption that all forms of adult intellectual activity are already present in embryo in the child's thinking and that no drastic change occurs at the age of puberty."[89]

Even though the pseudoconcept is fundamentally different than a concept, it "serves as a connecting link between thinking in complexes and thinking in concepts. It is dual in nature: a complex already carrying the germinating seed of a concept."[90] But for a child to develop the capacity for conceptual abstraction, two conditions must be met. First, as in the development of consciousness generally, practical needs must be encountered whose satisfaction demands the formation of abstractions.[91] Second, symbolic communication must be involved for "the germinating seed" to mature into a genuine abstraction. "It is a functional use of the word, or any other sign, as means of focusing one's attention, selecting distinctive features and analyzing and synthesizing them, that plays a central role in concept formation. . . . Real concepts are impossible without words, and thinking in concepts does not exist beyond verbal thinking. That is why the central moment in concept formation, and its generative cause, is a specific use of words as functional 'tools.'"[92]

Because the child's pseudoconcepts "already coincide in content with adult concepts," the transition to conceptual thought occurs without being noticed; "the child begins to operate with concepts, to practice conceptual thinking, before he is clearly aware of the nature of these operations."[93] The functional equivalence of the child's pseudoconcepts and the adult's concepts, together with the fact that child and adult communicate with a shared vocabulary, conceals the fact that the thinking processes of the child and the adult are quite different from one another. The underlying difference between the thought processes of children and adults does a great deal to help account for the reasons why children are incapable of the same levels of comprehension and responsibility as adults: The thought processes of children involve some capacity for generalization, but they fall short of genuine abstraction. A key consequence of this limitation is that the judgments that children make are fundamentally more primitive than those possible for adults. The mental lives of children are tied to concrete particulars in experience, whereas adults are capable of transcending these particulars in acts of cognitive-linguistic abstraction.

The child's capacity to make judgments depends on forms of complex thinking, such as pseudoconcepts, that have been ramified through language. Given that the child "masters syntax of speech before syntax of thought," the functional equivalence between the "judgments" of children and those of adults should not mislead us into supposing that children possess the full intentional agency of adults. The thought processes at work in each are of a fundamentally different nature.

Vygotsky's claim about a fundamental difference between intellect in children and adults has important implications for understanding the mental lives of animals. Drawing on the research of Köhler, Bühler, and Yerkes, Vygotsky notes that language establishes the key difference between the thinking of human beings and animals. Intellect in animals "is in no way related to language," and the "language" of the chimpanzee "functions apart from its intellect."[94] The crucial points of intersection between thought and language that give rise to conceptualization in human beings are absent, on Vygotsky's view, even in higher primates. As a result, the "language" of chimpanzees is fundamentally different than mature human language, in that its "phonetics is entirely 'subjective', and can only express emotions, never designate or describe objects. . . . The gestures and mimicries of apes do not bear any objective reference; i.e., they do not carry out a function of signification."[95] An excellent occasion for testing these claims is provided by the current state of knowledge about vervet alarm calls, discussed above. If vervets have distinct alarm calls that enable their companions to identify the type of predator (martial eagle, predatory mammal, or python), does this not confirm that the calls are more than mere subjective expressions of emotions, that the calls do designate objects?

When Vygotsky wrote *Thought and Language*, some key facts about animal communication, such as the versatility of vervet alarm calls and the ability of some apes to master some symbolic communication, were unknown. Thus it is not surprising to encounter Vygotsky's blunt assertion that "not a hint of [chimpanzees'] using signs has ever been heard of."[96] Nor is his claim that, in problem-solving tasks with tools, "even the best tool for a given problem is lost on the chimpanzee if it cannot see it simultaneously or quasi-simultaneously with the goal," a claim that is disproved by Sue Savage-Rumbaugh's work with the chimpanzees Sherman and Austin, who cooperatively solve problems that require the use of tools that are not immediately present to the chimpanzees.[97] Vygotsky is on more solid ground when he observes that the linguistic utterances of animals are overwhelmingly if not exclusively "affective vocal reactions, more or less differentiated and to some degree connected, in a conditional-reflex fashion, with stimuli related to feeding or other vital situations: a strictly emotional language."[98] While the linguistic abilities of apes and the alarm calls of vervets are more sophisticated than this account allows, these instances are the exception rather than the rule in the animal world. There is no evidence that the linguistic abilities of these apes are indicative of the linguistic abilities of most other animals; at best these cases show how difficult it is to draw a sharp line of demarcation between the "human" and the "nonhuman." Moreover, little in the annals of contemporary cognitive ethology lends support to the hypothesis that any but the most sophisticated primates employ concepts in their cognitive encounters with the world. Nor is there any clear reason to suppose that the question whether animals can employ concepts or master linguistic phenomena such as syntax has any *moral* significance whatsoever.[99]

These limitations in the linguistic abilities of animals suggest that intellect in animals—at least that of the vast majority of animals—is fundamentally different than the intellect of adult humans. Vygotsky's contention that animals never "reach the stage of objective representation in any of their activities" seems plausible for most animals except the higher primates.[100] Animals engage in complex thinking, the principal function of which "is to establish bonds and relations." At its most sophisticated level, the complex thinking of animals even includes the formation of "potential concepts," which are formed by "grouping [different perceived objects] on the basis of a single attribute—e.g., only round objects or only flat ones." Potential concepts, however, are not genuine abstractions; "being a precursor of intellectual judgment, the potential concept by itself bears no sign of intelligence." In this connection, Vygotsky notes that "even hens can be trained to respond to one distinct attribute in different objects, such as color or shape. . . . There is no necessity to assume any involvement of logical processes in order to account for the use of potential concepts."[101] Even in human children, the relation between a word and its meaning is at first simply an associative one, that is, the child's "first words are potential concepts indeed—they have a potential to become concepts, but this potential is still idle in them."[102]

Here the crucial difference between verbal and nonverbal beings becomes apparent. For complex thinking to make the transition from associative relations to genuine conceptual abstraction, words or comparable linguistic symbols must be employed. "The decisive role in this process [of concept formation] . . . is played by the word, deliberately used to direct all the subprocesses of advanced concept formation."[103] Only in conjunction with symbolic language is it possible to transcend the concrete particulars of experience and to enter the world of specifically verbal thinking, which differs in kind from complex thinking. Only in the realm of verbal thinking are such uniquely human phenomena as inner speech possible.[104] In nonverbal beings, by contrast, the transcendence of concrete particulars, and hence capacities such as intellectual judgment, are impossible. Examples such as vervet alarm calls or the dog barking up the wrong tree require no appeal to judgment or intentional states such as beliefs; they are fully explicable through appeal to complex thinking alone, without any verbal component.

Moreover, the fact that complex thinking in human beings is augmented by the play of language suggests that complex thought in nonverbal beings is functionally equivalent to that in humans, but that it is nonetheless qualitatively different. Vygotsky says that "from our point of view, there is an essential difference between naturally biologically grounded intelligence and historically developed human intelligence."[105] A main focal point for Vygotsky in the exploration of this thesis is the role of formal education in the development of human concepts and mental life. One of his key conclusions is that "verbal thought is not an innate, natural form of behavior, but is determined by a historico-cultural process and has specific properties and laws that cannot be found in the natural forms of thought and speech."[106] The lack of such a historico-cultural process in animals (leaving aside those few apes who have been partially indoctrinated into the cultural processes of symbolic language in experimental conditions) makes capacities such as intellectual judgment and intentionality impossible. The fact that animals exhibit some capacities that are functionally equivalent to human intelligence tends to conceal the basic differences between animal and human consciousness. The decisive point is that the consciousness of animals lacks the historico-cultural sense that serves as the foundation for the formation of specifically verbal intelligence. Thus to assume, as Nussbaum and others have done, that purposiveness in animals is a clear sign of their capacities for predication, intentionality, and self-awareness is hasty. Vygotsky's analysis gives us a way of conceiving of animal experience as driven by a sophisticated ability to make associations between experiences that is independent of conceptual abstraction. This makes it possible to account for the purpo-

sive conduct of animals without attributing to them the formal apparatus of language and intentionality.

One of Vygotsky's most controversial claims is that language capacity
in human beings is not innate. Another is that language ability is initially
the ability to form associations between particulars. Both of these ideas
have been refuted by Noam Chomsky, whose ideas on language provide
a way to correct Vygotsky's views. According to Chomsky, language is a
"biologically isolated" capacity that is more than the capacity to make
associations.[107] Human beings possess "an innate representation of universal grammar" that serves as the basis for initiation into particular
natural languages such as English or French.[108] Moreover, language in this
sense is unique to human beings. Chomsky argues that "it is conceivable,
but not very likely" that "other organisms [possess] faculties closely analogous to the human language capacity"; the discovery of language capacity
in nonhuman animals "would constitute a kind of biological miracle,
rather similar to the discovery, on some unexplored island of a species
of bird that had never thought to fly until instructed to do so through
human intervention."[109] The symbolic communication systems taught to
apes "have only the most superficial resemblance to human language";
higher apes "apparently lack the capacity to develop even the rudiments
of the computational structure of human language," though they "nevertheless may command parts of the conceptual structure" of human
language.[110] In short, "there is no serious reason today to challenge the
Cartesian view that the ability to use linguistic signs to express freely
formed thoughts marks 'the true distinction between man and animal.'"[111]

In the light of Chomsky's views, Vygotsky's picture of human language
acquisition needs to be revised so as to admit the possibility of conceptual ability in human children. In other respects, however, Chomsky's
views serve to clarify Vygotsky's conception of the fundamental differences
between human beings and animals. The full possession of concept-based
linguistic ability is unique to human beings. Animals, with the possible
exception of extremely high-functioning species, are capable of making
associations of differing levels of complexity between particulars. On this
view, animals possess "linguistic" abilities much like those attributed by
Vygotsky to young children, whereas human beings are capable of the
conceptual abstraction that forms the basis of self-understanding, comprehension of the distant future, and comparably complex objects of
understanding. Thus the Cartesian view that the capacities for language
and abstract reason fundamentally distinguish human beings from ani-

mals would be correct, but the Cartesian conclusion that the lack of linguistic and rational abilities in animals deprives them of all moral worth would not follow.

Prospects for Overcoming Anthropocentrism

Vygotsky's reflections on human and animal intelligence make a tremendous if heretofore unrecognized contribution to the endeavor to conceptualize the mental lives and capacities of animals. His research helps us to understand why contemporary attempts to attribute intentionality and conceptual ability to animals are misguided, and how we might begin to rethink the nature of animal experience in terms of complex associations that are devoid of intellectual logical judgment. In the light of Vygotsky's work and the reflections of contemporary philosophers such as Davidson, the central problems that beset current debates about animals become clear: The leading advocates of the moral status of animals focus on the wrong capacities, or—to state the point more precisely—they mischaracterize animal capacities by unduly anthropomorphizing them. The anthropocentrism of these contemporary approaches is evident in the fact that their exponents describe the experience of animals from a markedly human standpoint, as when Griffin describes the pigeon as thinking "pecking this thing gets me food" or bees as employing concepts in executing or interpreting the bee dance. By opening the prospect that animals relate to their environments in complex ways that are ultimately unlike human ways of relating (because uninformed by verbal language), Vygotsky enables us to acknowledge a richness to animal awareness that we will never fully grasp, and to which we will completely fail to do justice as long as we adhere to anthropomorphic categories such as intentionality. Once we acknowledge a richness to animal experience that defies categorization in terms of anthropomorphic categories, and once we abandon the effort to attribute to animals the most sophisticated sorts of cognitive functioning that we find in ourselves, we can seriously raise the question whether these sorts of functioning are morally relevant in the first place.

It is in this connection that a careful examination of conceptions of animals and their moral status in the history of Western philosophy is needed. Too often, contemporary philosophers discuss animals without any apparent awareness of the long tradition of thinking about animals, their capacities, and the question of the relevance of capacities to moral status. Some of the most insightful and sophisticated discussions of animals are those of Greco-Roman antiquity. The earliest texts bearing on animals exhibit sensitivity to the fundamental kinship between humans and animals, and the most influential philosophers in antiquity show a remarkable knowledge of the capacities of animals. But in Greco-Roman times there was also a fundamental shift in thinking about animals, away from a sense of kinship and toward a capacities-based approach according to which animals were denigrated in relation to human beings. Starting in late antiquity, defenses of animals became based on capacities as well. Subsequent thinkers about animals, through the Middle Ages and into modernity, adhered to and progressively modified the capacities approach, first under the influence of Christianity and later under the influence of Cartesian dualism. This entire trajectory of thinking culminates in the confusions and misconceptions that characterize contemporary debates about animals.

I examine the history of Western thinking about animals to help clarify the contemporary debates, both by showing how the great philosophers conceptualize the experience and the moral status of animals, and by showing that the basis for an edified view of animals and their moral status is contained in this tradition. By focusing on the historical development of thinking about animals, one can understand the sources of our own anthropocentric prejudices and use that history as the basis for a radical rethinking of the moral status of animals. The historical study that follows extends from Hesiod to Heidegger and shows both the dominant views and the recurrence of heterodox voices in the tradition. My goal is not to be exhaustive, but to exhibit the essential thread that connects all Western philosophers with the epic and pre-Socratic thinkers.

EPIC AND PRE-SOCRATIC
THOUGHT

Carol J. Adams wrote *The Sexual Politics of Meat* "in memory of six billion each year, 16 million each day, 700,000 each hour, 11,500 each minute."[1] What is most shocking about these numbers is not that they open our eyes to the extent of factory farming of animals for human consumption, but that they are an underestimation. In 1994, in North America alone seven *billion* broiler chickens were slaughtered for human consumption.[2] In the United States, one hundred thousand cattle are slaughtered daily.[3] The use of animals to satisfy human needs is firmly entrenched in our culture's value system. The insights of cognitive ethology into the experiential capacities of the animals we consume have done little if anything to alter our behavior toward these animals.

The dominant view in the history of Western philosophy is that human beings are fundamentally superior to nonhuman animals, typically on the grounds that only human beings possess reason, language, and self-awareness. In one way or another, such thinkers as Aristotle, the Stoics, Saint Augustine, Saint Thomas Aquinas, Descartes, and Kant all appeal to this dividing line between humans and animals. But alongside this dominant voice there has been a set of dissenting voices that challenge the view that human beings are superior to nonhuman animals, some of these voices going so far as to insist on strict vegetarianism as part of a life well led. This much is fairly well known. What is less well known is that some of these "dissenting" voices were once the dominant voices in the West. Specifically, Homer and Hesiod characterize the human-animal relation as a continuum rather than as a strict opposition. Even though they ultimately attribute superiority to human beings over ani-

mals, they do so against the background of a sense of the underlying likeness of the two; this sense of likeness or kinship leads Homer to appeal
to animals in some cases as exemplars or standards of human excellence,
and it inspires Hesiod to give a characterization of a long-past golden age
in which human beings and animals coexisted peacefully.

We are accustomed to taking our cultural bearings on the human-animal question from philosophers such as Aristotle and the Stoics, who
make their appearance relatively late in the history of thinking about this
question in antiquity. By this time, our culture had incorporated concepts and values that place a clear priority on the abilities and the moral
status of human beings over those of animals. "Somewhere between the
time of Homer and the time of Aeschylus a shift occurred in the manner in which the human person was conceived—a gradual shift towards
moral responsibility and towards the notion of soul as the dominant
partner in the soul-body complex."[4] This shift affects not only the
conceptualization of humanity, but inevitably the conceptualization of
animals and the boundary between the two. In the next two chapters, I
examine the shift that occurred beginning around the fifth century BCE.
In this chapter, I explore the way in which the human-animal boundary
was conceived by the epic thinkers Homer and Hesiod, and by two pre-
Socratic thinkers, Pythagoras and Empedocles. All four acknowledge
important differences between human beings and animals but do so
against the background of a commitment to the fundamental continuity
between humans and animals as natural kinds subject to fate and the
ravages of time.

Homer

It is as difficult to ascribe dates to Homer as it is to determine the time
when the early books of the Bible were written. There is evidence that
Homer had composed the *Iliad* and the *Odyssey* by around 700 BCE, about
five centuries after the events described in these texts were to have taken
place, but scholars have been unable to make more precise determinations.[5]

In the *Iliad*, particularly in battle scenes, Homer draws parallels between the temperaments of human individuals and types of animals. In
these parallels, emotional reactions and dispositions to act are of fundamental significance. Beasts of prey such as the lion figure prominently.
Book 3 opens with Paris bursting "from the Trojan forward ranks, / a

challenger, lithe, magnificent as a god," ready to take on any foe, until Menelaus meets his challenge "like a lion lighting on some handsome carcass," whereupon Paris turns tail, recedes into the Trojan ranks, and is duly taunted by Hector for his cowardice.[6] In book 5, Aeneas has just killed Tydides and stands over his dead body, "proud in his fighting power like some lion / . . . burning to kill off any man who met him face-to-face / and he loosed a bloodcurdling cry."[7] Diomedes is "claw-mad as a lion" and proceeds to "maul" Trojans.[8] The tenacity and courage of warriors are several times described as leonine, Achilles being described as "that lionheart who mauls battalions wholesale."[9] Just as great warriors are described as beasts of prey, the cowardly or vanquished are likened to herd animals. In book 11, the Trojans flee Agamemnon and his troops "like cattle driven wild by a lion lunging / in pitch darkness down on the whole herd."[10]

The first of the analogies cited above shows the underlying meaning of the image of the lion in these battle scenes. Paris at first comes forward "magnificent as a god," and Menelaus counters him "like a lion" setting upon its prey. The juxtaposition is not accidental. It establishes an association, now long familiar to us, between the lion and the ideal of sovereignty.[11] The other qualities associated with the lion in the analogies cited serve to fill out this ideal for human aspiration: courage, tenacity, singularity of purpose, dominance over one's enemy. This image of the lion as a symbol of supremacy has long held a place in our cultural imagination, serving to fix a dignified sense of identity in such far-flung connections as the establishment of the Lands of the United Netherlands subsequent to the Union of Utrecht in 1579 to the twentieth-century hawking of beer in the United States.[12] Our cultural memory is so saturated with the image of the lion that it is easy to overlook its deep significance in Homer. To draw an analogy between a magnificent warrior and a lion is to say that both are driven by the imperative to survive and conquer. Each faces the threat and uncertainty posed by natural adversaries and is ultimately dependent upon his own resources—strength, persistence, ingenuity, rage, ardent desire—and the grace of the gods for the prospect of victory. The triumphant warrior is preeminent among men, just as the lion is the most magnificent of beasts. Both are analogous to gods in reigning supreme in their respective domains.

Other comparisons between human warriors and animals reinforce the sense of shared life conditions and emotional responses to adversity.

Consider three vivid examples from the *Iliad*. As the enraged Aeneas charges him, Idomeneus "stood his ground like a wild mountain boar, / trusting his strength, standing up to a rout of men / that scream and swoop against him off in a lonely copse, / the ridge of his back bristling, his eyes flashing fire, / he grinds his teeth, champing to beat back dogs and men."[13] Hector, resolved to face Achilles, lies in wait "as a snake in the hills, guarding his hole, awaits a man— / bloated with poison, deadly hatred seething inside him, glances flashing fire as he coils round his lair."[14] Just before Achilles kills Polydorus, Hippodamus leaps from his chariot and runs in terror from Achilles, who drives his spear through Hippodamus's back. Hippodamus "gasped his life away, bellowing like some bull / that chokes and grunts when the young boys drag him round / the lord of Helice's shrine and the earthquake god delights to see them dragging—so he bellowed now / and the man's proud spirit left his bones behind."[15] The unyielding tenacity of the boar, the coiled repose of the snake, and the shrill despair of the vanquished bull all converge on the finality of death and the ineluctable logic of kill-or-be-killed. In this, human beings and animals are exactly like one another.[16]

Homer also acknowledges an important respect in which humans are unlike animals. The juxtaposition of two scenes in the *Odyssey* brings this difference into relief. The first is Odysseus's encounter with the Cyclopes in book 9. The Cyclopes are "giants, louts, without a law [θέμις] to bless them. / . . . Cyclopes have no muster and no meeting, / no consultation or old tribal ways, / but each one dwells in his own mountain cave / dealing out rough justice to wife and child, / indifferent to what the others do."[17] The barbarism and cannibalism of the Cyclopes are presented in the light of beastliness rather than humanity. When Polyphemus devours some of Odysseus's men, he "dismembered them and made his meal, / gaping and crunching like a mountain lion—/everything: innards, flesh, and marrow bones."[18] Here Odysseus and his comrades lift their hands to Zeus, reinforcing the connection between humanity, the gods, and the law (θέμις) that serves to bind the two. Custom, law, right, divine decree (θέμις) is what separates human beings from savage beasts like mountain lions and the Cyclopes. This word (θέμις) returns in book 18, when Odysseus confronts the suitors: "No man should flout the law [ἀθεμίστιος, be lawless], but keep in peace what gifts the gods may give."[19] One basis that Odysseus gives for obeying the law is the fact that "of mortal creatures, all that breathe and move, / earth bears none frailer than mankind."[20] In contrast with the violent pathos of the *Iliad*, the weary Odysseus at the end of the *Odyssey* characterizes violence as a necessary last resort in the face of human beings who conduct themselves like savages. The suitors are less than fully human in their disregard of the law (θέμις) handed down by the gods. Their barbarism justifies the same trickery and blood vengeance that Odysseus employed against Polyphemus. But when Odysseus deploys his tricks and his violence in the closing books of the *Odyssey*, he does so in a controlled way, subjecting his passions to calculation and the voice of reason. Thus when he sees the women servants in his household going off to the suitors' beds, he checks his anger and bides his time.[21]

Homer's view of the relationship between human beings and animals is not, for all that, a conception of the fundamental superiority of humans over animals. Like the *Iliad*, the *Odyssey* gives prominence to a sense of continuity. The most poignant testimonial to this continuity is the moment when Odysseus is recognized by his dog Argus. Disguised as a beggar, Odysseus approaches his home unrecognized by his adversaries. Argus has not seen Odysseus since he was a puppy, and "had grown old in his master's absence. / . . . But when he knew he heard Odysseus' voice nearby, he did his best / to wag his tail, nose down, with flattened ears, / having no strength to move nearer his master."[22]

Argus is aged, neglected, and barely alive when he encounters Odysseus. He musters what little strength he has left to wag his tail in a gesture that speaks volumes. Odysseus, needing to conceal his identity, must constrain himself to exhibit no more emotion than Argus has been able to show. "And the man looked away, / wiping a salt tear from his cheek."[23] The inward exchange of feeling and regard between these two old companions is as intense as its outward expression is muted. The exchange is so intense that "death and darkness in that instant closed / the eyes of Argus, who had seen his master, / Odysseus, after twenty years."[24] Sextus Empiricus takes this scene as a sign that dogs are "valiant and smart in [their] defending," and that their powers of discrimination are in some respects superior to those of human beings.[25] Particularly when contrasted with the depravity of the suitors and the utter disarray of Odysseus's home upon his return, the encounter between Odysseus and Argus bespeaks an intimate sense of kinship and community that puts to shame Odysseus's relationships with many other human beings. The intimacy of this kinship is reinforced by the fact that Homer considers death to entail the loss of soul not only in human beings but in animals as well.[26]

Hesiod

Hesiod, also writing around the eighth century BCE, establishes the first fundamental distinction in the West between human beings and animals. In *Works and Days*, Hesiod says that Zeus gave justice to human beings but not to animals: "Here is the law [νομός] as Zeus established it for human beings; / as for fish, and wild animals, and the flying birds, / they feed on each other, since there is no idea of justice among them; / but to men he gave justice [δίκη], and she in the end is proved the best thing / they have."[27] Where Homer places emphasis on the distinction between divine and mortal beings, Hesiod shifts the focus to a basic distinction between human and nonhuman. This distinction is not, as it is later for thinkers such as the Stoics, based on the claim that human beings are rational and animals nonrational. The capacity for justice is not based on abilities that human beings possess and animals lack. Instead, justice is a gift of the gods pure and simple, as is the flourishing that ensues when we act justly: "If a man sees what is right and is willing to argue it, / Zeus of the wide brow grants him prosperity."[28] Hesiod's is a view according to which human beings enjoy a status that elevates them above animals, but they are entirely dependent upon the gods for that status and for the fruits that come with it.

In *Works and Days*, Hesiod tells two stories about Zeus's reasons for bestowing justice on human beings. The first is the myth of Prometheus. In Hesiod's version of the myth, "the gods have hidden and keep hidden what could be men's livelihood. / . . . Zeus in the anger of his heart hid it away / because the devious-minded Prometheus had cheated him; / and therefore Zeus thought up dismal sorrows for mankind."[29] Prometheus steals fire and gives it to mortals. When Zeus discovers this, he says that "as the price of fire I will give them an evil, and all men shall fondle / this, their evil, close to their hearts, and take delight in it."[30] He has the gods fashion a woman, and he instructs Hermes "to put in her the mind of a hussy, and a treacherous nature." This woman is called Pandora, "because all the gods who have their homes on Olympus / had given her each a gift." Zeus has Hermes give Pandora to Epimetheus as a gift. Epimetheus, forgetting that his brother Prometheus has warned him "never to accept a gift from Olympian Zeus, but always to send it back, for fear it might prove to be an evil for mankind," accepts Pandora, who opens the jar of sicknesses and troubles and unleashes them on the world.

Hesiod does not spell out the relevance of this story of the origin of evil in the world to Zeus's bestowal of justice on human beings, but the implicit connection becomes clear in Plato's retelling of the Prometheus myth in the *Protagoras*. In Plato's account, Prometheus steals fire and skill in the arts and gives these to mortals. "In this way man acquired sufficient resources to keep himself alive, but had no political wisdom. This was in the keeping of Zeus." The bestowal of the arts led to "articulate speech and names, and [the invention of] houses and clothes and shoes and bedding and . . . food from the earth." These in turn led to human communities, "but when they gathered in communities they injured one another for want of political skill." To prevent the destruction of these communities, Zeus "sent Hermes to impart to men the qualities of respect for others and a sense of justice, so as to bring order into our cities and create a bond of friendship and union."[31]

The second story that Hesiod tells about Zeus's reasons for bestowing justice on humanity clarifies Hesiod's conviction that the qualities of respect and justice pertain to human beings and not to animals. This is the story of the five ages of man, according to which humanity originated in an idyllic golden age and progressively degenerated into the contemporary age of iron.[32] In the golden age, human beings "lived as if they were gods, their hearts free from all sorrow, / by themselves, and without hard work or pain; no miserable / old age came their way; their hands, their feet, did not alter." They lived a carefree existence, and "when they died, it was as if they fell asleep." Humanity enjoyed plenty, and "the fruitful grainland yielded its harvest to them / of its own accord." Implied here is the bucolic vegetarian repose that Milton later attributes to the prelapsarian Adam and Eve.[33] Only in the course of subsequent ages do human beings begin to age, perpetrate "reckless crime against each other," and involve themselves in "evil war and . . . terrible carnage." Some people left these circumstances and settled "at the end of the world," living, like those in the golden age, off the bounty of the "fruitful grainland." These people live their peaceful existence even today, but most people live in the age of iron, beset with toil and weariness. This age will persist until people lose their sense of decency and respect and turn back to the life of violence and evil that Zeus's law of justice was designed to prevent.

In reverting to violence and evil, human beings devolve from their full humanity to a bestial state. Hesiod concludes his telling of the myth of the five ages with the story of the hawk and the nightingale. A hawk has caught a nightingale, and is flying along with her in his claws. To the nightingale's mournful wails, the hawk replies:

> What is the matter with you? Why scream? Your master has you.
> You shall go wherever I take you, for all your singing.
> If I like, I can let you go. If I like, I can eat you for dinner.
> He is a fool who tries to match his strength with the stronger.
> He will lose his battle, and with the shame will be hurt also.[34]

The hawk obeys the law that might makes right, but human beings are meant to follow Zeus's law of justice. Hesiod tells the story of the hawk and the nightingale, and implores human beings to "listen to justice; do not try to practice / violence." When Hesiod later says that Zeus gave justice to men but not to animals, he uses the same expression that he uses here— "listen to justice."[35] To do so is to obey the law promulgated by Zeus for fallen human beings.

To listen to justice is also to emulate the peaceful conditions of life enjoyed in the golden age, which symbolizes a long lost moment of perfect harmony from which human beings have progressively fallen away in the course of time. This conception of time has captured the imagination of philosophers from Hesiod to Spengler and Heidegger, who characterize history as a *Verfallsgeschichte*, as a history of decline from an original moment of perfect integration or complete satisfaction. In the case of ancient thinkers such as Hesiod and Ovid, the complete satisfaction enjoyed in our golden beginnings had as its gastronomic component a diet of fruits and grains that corresponded to the peaceful coexistence of human beings and animals in a gardenlike paradise.[36] Neither Hesiod nor Ovid explicitly recommends vegetarianism. But one clear implication of their conception of the course of time as a *Verfallsgeschichte* is that the suffering, corruption, and overall dissatisfaction of later generations such as our own are products of the turn to violence against both human beings and animals. Some later advocates of vegetarianism such as Porphyry appeal to Hesiod's story of the ages of man in arguing that the killing and eating of animals is fundamentally impious.[37]

Pythagoras

In the sixth century BCE, Pythagoras espoused an ethic of kinship with animals based on the doctrine of metempsychosis or transmigration of souls. Diogenes Laertius reports that Pythagoras "was the first . . . to declare that the soul, bound now in this creature, now in that, thus goes on a round ordained of necessity."[38] Ovid writes that Pythagoras "was the first to decry the placing of animal food upon our tables."[39] But there is disagreement on whether Pythagoras based his advocacy of vegetarianism on the doctrine of metempsychosis or simply on an interest in promoting the health of the human body and mind.[40] This question has important implications for Pythagoras's position on the moral status of animals.

Views of metempsychosis take one of two basic forms. On one view, the soul has the capacity to ascend through various embodiments toward ultimate liberation from embodiment. This is the view of metempsychosis that Socrates presents in the *Phaedrus,* where the lowest form of human embodiment is that of a tyrant and the highest "a seeker after wisdom or beauty."[41] On the other view, souls move endlessly from one embodiment to another. The moral status of animals on either view depends upon whether souls are considered to be able to move between human and animal bodies or whether souls simply move from one human embodiment to another. If metempsychosis involves only human bodies, the ethical focus of the doctrine is how to live one's life properly so as to secure the prospect of ascending to a higher form of existence. This endeavor to ascend may or may not have implications for meat eating and the treatment of animals, depending on the particular view. On one account, attributed by some interpreters to Pythagoras, even if transmigration involves only human bodies, it is still important to maintain a vegetarian diet and to be kind to animals because these activities are conducive to the purification of the soul.

But if transmigration is considered to involve animal bodies as well as human bodies, then the ethical stake on the treatment of animals becomes much higher—one could be eating or otherwise mistreating a kindred spirit. This is the view of metempsychosis attributed to Pythagoras by Iamblichus, Ovid, and Sextus Empiricus. Iamblichus writes that Pythagoras abstained from animal food and sacrifice on the grounds that we "should not destroy the creatures which share our nature. . . . Animals are akin to us, sharing our life and basic constituents and composition, linked in a kind of brotherhood."[42] Animals are our "friends and kinsfolk," and thus we should not "harm or kill or eat any."[43] Pythagoras claimed to have lived through a number of human incarnations, and Xenophanes says that Pythagoras implored a man to stop whipping a dog because "'Tis a friend, a human soul; / I knew him straight whenas I heard him yelp!"[44] Ovid traces Pythagoras's prohibitions on eating and sacrificing animals to the view that metempsychosis involves animal as well as human bodies. "The spirit wanders, comes now here, now there, and occupies whatever frame it pleases. From beasts it passes into human bodies, and from our bodies into beasts, but never perishes."[45] Those who sacrifice animals make "the gods themselves partners of their crime," by making it look as if "the heavenly ones took pleasure in the blood of the toiling bullock!"[46] To eat animals is to indulge in a hideous "Thyestean banquet."[47] "For," as Sextus Empiricus reports, Pythagoras and Empedocles believe that "there is one spirit [πνεῦμα] which pervades, like a soul [ψυχῆς], the whole Universe, and also makes us one with" irrational animals (ἄλογα τῶν ξώων).[48]

According to Plutarch, this sense of kinship with animals led Pythagoras "to try to accustom us to act justly toward other creatures." One specific duty of justice toward animals is to avoid "slicing off portions from a dead father or mother."[49] Plutarch's account accords with the statements of Mnesimachus and Heraclides that Pythagoras observed and recommended a strictly vegetarian diet.[50] But the accounts of Diogenes Laertius, Iamblichus, and Porphyry all include statements that make it unclear whether Pythagoras really advocated strict vegetarianism, and whether Pythagoras's dietary restrictions were motivated by a sense of justice toward animals or simply by an interest in the purification of the human soul. An additional question is whether Pythagoras believes it is ever permissible to kill animals. At one point Pythagoras's position is said to be that we should never "kill or injure trees that are not wild, nor even any animal that does not injure man."[51] This suggests that we may kill animals in self-defense, but not otherwise. But Pythagoras may have made other exceptions to the rule against killing animals, in connection with animal sacrifice as well as with diet.

Regarding animal sacrifice, Diogenes Laertius provides conflicting accounts. At one point he reports that Pythagoras's position was "not to let victims be brought for sacrifice to the gods, and to worship only at the altar unstained with blood."[52] But at another point he says that, according to Apollodorus, Pythagoras "offered a sacrifice of oxen on finding that in a right-angled triangle the square of the hypotenuse is equal to the squares on the sides containing the right angle."[53] The possibility that Pythagoras countenanced some animal sacrifice has support in Iamblichus, who attributes to Pythagoras the view that "the souls of humans may enter any living creature except those it is lawful to sacrifice. So we must eat only sacrificial animals, those that are fit to eat, not any other living creature."[54] Porphyry reports that "the Pythagoreans . . . abstained from animal-eating all their lives, and when they did assign some animal to the gods as an offering in place of themselves, they ate only that, but continued to live for truth, not touching the others."[55] This account is at odds with Ovid's suggestion in *Metamorphoses* 15, noted above, that Pythagoras considered one of the impieties of animal sacrifice to be that it makes "the gods themselves partners of [our] crime."

This account is also at odds with the view that Pythagoras advocated strict vegetarianism. In addition to the statements of Iamblichus and Porphyry that Pythagoras approved of the consumption of sacrificial animals, Diogenes Laertius equivocates on Pythagoras's views about diet. Together with the reports of Mnesimachus and Heraclides that Pythagoras advocated strict vegetarianism, Diogenes states that Pythagoras is "said to have been the first to diet athletes on meat"; that "above all, he forbade as food red mullet and blacktail, and he enjoined abstinence from the hearts of animals and from beans, and sometimes, according to Aristotle, even from paunch and gurnard"; and that he recommended simply that we "avoid excess of flesh."[56] On the interrelated questions of animal sacrifice and consumption, we are told that "he used to practice divination by sounds or voices and by auguries, never by burnt-offerings, beyond frankincense. The offerings he made were always inanimate; though some say that he would offer cocks, sucking goats and porkers, as they are called, but lambs never. However, Aristoxenus has it that he consented to the eating of all other animals, and only abstained from ploughing oxen and rams."[57] This conflict of interpretations about Pythagoras again raises the question whether his views about duties toward animals were motivated primarily by a sense of justice toward animals or by an interest in purifying the human soul. Several commentators cited by Diogenes maintain that the appeal to an animal soul [ψυχή] as the basis for abstaining from meat was simply "the excuse put forward," but that Pythagoras's "real reason for forbidding animal diet was to practice people and accustom them to simplicity of life, so that they could live on things easily procurable, spreading their tables with uncooked foods and drinking pure water only, for this was the way to a healthy body and a keen mind."[58] This account is consistent with Pythagoras's emphasis on moderation and the need for purification in preparation to worship the gods. "Purification is by cleansing baptism and lustration, and by keeping clean from all deaths and births and all pollution, and abstaining from meat and flesh of animals that have died, mullets, gurnards, eggs and egg-sprung animals, beans, and the other abstinences prescribed by those who perform mystic rites in the temples."[59]

If Pythagoras is advocating duties toward animals not for the sake of the animals but instead to promote the spiritual purity of human beings, then he is advocating "indirect duties" toward animals. This means that we should treat animals in certain ways, for example, we should refrain from killing them or being cruel to them, not because we value animals in their own right but because it is better for the well-being of humans. Aquinas is best known for advocating kindness toward animals on these grounds: if we are cruel toward animals, this will make us more likely to be cruel toward our fellow human beings. The ultimate duty is not toward animals but toward humanity. Sorabji notes that Clement of Alexandria, Plutarch, and Iamblichus trace the origin of the indirect duties view in ethics to Pythagoras.[60] The available evidence does not make it possible to conclude with confidence whether Pythagoras advocated direct duties to animals or simply indirect duties. In either case, however, as Long observes, the doctrine of metempsychosis had clear moral implications for the Pythagoreans; we have a fundamental continuity with at least some nonhuman living beings, and the way we treat those beings has implications at least for the purification of the soul if not for the sake of nonhuman beings themselves.[61]

One last consideration sheds some additional light on the question of Pythagoras's views concerning the moral status of nonhuman beings and the kinship between human and nonhuman creatures. I note in passing above that Diogenes Laertius lists beans as one of the foods from which Pythagoras abstained. It appears that even though Pythagoras did not generally consider plants to have soul, he did consider beans to have it.[62] Pythagoras had two reasons for abstaining from beans, namely, "because they are flatulent and partake most of the breath of life; and besides, it is better for the stomach if they are not taken, and this again will make our dreams in sleep smooth and untroubled."[63] Several stories told about Pythagoras suggest that his abstinence from beans was motivated primarily by the belief that beans share in soul or "the breath of life." Diogenes Laertius tells the story of Pythagoras's willingness to die rather than tread upon a bean field as he was being pursued by tyrannical adversaries.[64] Iamblichus reports that Pythagoras whispered into the ear of a bull that saw eating beans, and made such a persuasive case that "the bull promptly stopped eating the bean-plant, of his own accord, and they say he never ate beans again. He lived to a very great age at Taras, growing old in the temple of Hera. Everyone called him 'Pythagoras' holy bull' and he ate a human diet, offered him by people who met him."[65] Iamblichus also tells of Pythagoras's taming of a she-bear through stroking, feeding, and the administration of an oath; Iamblichus stresses the kinship between human beings and animals such as the she-bear as the basis for Pythagoras's confidence that he would be able to tame the she-bear, who afterward "was never again seen to attack even a non-rational animal."[66] Taken together, these stories suggest that Pythagoras considered a variety of living beings, not simply human beings, to possess soul, and that such beings should be not be killed, sacrificed, eaten, or otherwise defiled.

Empedocles

Empedocles, probably active in the mid-fifth century BCE, refined Pythagoras's sometimes conflicting views on the human-animal relationship and their implications for diet. Aristotle states in the *Rhetoric* that Empedocles "bids us kill no living creature" on the grounds that "an all-embracing law" demands justice for all living beings.[67] According to Aetius, Empedocles, along with Parmenides and Democritus, equates reason [νοῦς] and soul [ψυχή].[68] Hippolytus takes this to mean that, for Empedocles, "all things . . . have wisdom [φρόνησιν] and take part in thinking."[69] This leads Empedocles to appeal to the notion of a golden age that recalls Hesiod's myth. But in addition to the absence of war, Empedocles' golden age is characterized by matriarchy and nonviolent sacrifices to the gods: "They had no god Ares nor Kudiomos, nor king Zeus nor Poseidon, but Kupris as queen. Her did they propitiate with holy images, with paintings of living creatures, with perfumes of varied fragrance and with sacrifice of pure myrrh and sweet-scented frankincense, casting to the ground libations of golden honey. Their altar was not steeped in the pure blood of bulls, but rather was this the greatest abomination among men, to tear out the life from the goodly limbs and eat them."[70] Where Pythagoras can be seen to be equivocating between direct and indirect duties toward animals in his ethic of abstinence, Empedocles is much clearer about the direct violation involved in practices such as blood sacrifice. Thus he recommends supplication of the gods through the sacrifice of aromatics, honey, and pictures of animals.

Closely related to his prohibition of animal sacrifice is Empedocles' prohibition on meat eating. He attributes humanity's fall from the golden age to the advent of blood sacrifice and meat eating: "Father lifts up his own dear son, his form changed, and, praying, slays him—witless fool;

and the people are distracted as they sacrifice the imploring victim; and he, deaf to its cries, slays it and makes ready in his halls an evil feast. And likewise son seizes father, and children their mother, and, tearing out the life, eat the flesh of their dear ones."[71] The reference to the son's "changed form" indicates that Empedocles bases his view on the doctrine of metempsychosis. The animal that we sacrifice or kill for food could house the soul of our own child or a parent. Seen in this light, killing, sacrificing, and eating animals are barbaric transgressions against nature. Reports by Porphyry and Diogenes Laertius suggest that Empedocles lived his life in strict observance of the principle of justice toward animals. He laments that "the pitiless day of death did not first destroy me before I contrived the wretched deed of eating flesh with my lips."[72] Diogenes Laertius reports that he "found in the *Memorabilia* of Favorinus a statement that Empedocles feasted the sacred envoys on a sacrificial ox made of honey and barley meal."[73]

On Empedocles' view of metempsychosis, human souls can enter animal bodies as well as vice versa. This is clear from the passage cited above in which Empedocles warns of the danger of killing one's child or parent, and from Empedocles' statement that he himself has previously been not only other people, but also various sorts of animals and even a plant: "Before now I was born a boy and a maid, a bush and a bird, and a dumb fish leaping out of the sea." The soul "assumes all the various forms of animals and plants."[74] But it seems that the soul was not always in a condition of transmigration. The golden age, as noted above, had no need for a "king Zeus," and hence it implicitly had no need for the imposition of law that Zeus represents for the Greeks. In contrast, the advent of such practices as blood sacrifice and meat eating led to a fallen condition in which "the soul is a fugitive and a wanderer, banished by the decrees and laws of the gods."[75] This condition of perpetual wandering is Empedocles' basis for abstaining from meat.[76]

None of the extant fragments explain why, on Empedocles' account, we should not abstain from plants as well. This may be one of several indications of anthropocentrism in the thought of Empedocles. Diels states in a footnote that transmigration on Empedocles' view follows a trajectory from plant to animal to human being to god.[77] This is a highly speculative thesis, but there may be some support at least for the idea that human beings are closest to the gods.[78] And Diogenes Laertius reports a story out of Timaeus implying that Empedocles' views about the human–animal relationship were less than egalitarian. According to Timaeus, "when the etesian winds once began to blow violently and to damage the crops, [Empedocles] ordered asses to be flayed and bags to be made of their skin. These he stretched out here and there on the hills and head-lands to catch the wind and, because this checked the wind, he was called the 'wind stayer.'"[79] One need only imagine this story involving the flaying of human beings rather than asses, to draw out its implications.

These passages are difficult to reconcile with the majority of extant fragments describing Empedocles' views and with the received picture of Empedocles as an advocate of abstinence based on a sense of kinship with animals. The received view is expressed well by Plutarch, who considers it "certain" that Empedocles believed that "man is not altogether inno-cent of injustice when he treats animals as he does," and according to whom both Pythagoras and Empedocles "try to accustom us to act justly toward other creatures also."[80] Whether or not Empedocles' views are beset with anthropocentric prejudices, his core beliefs about the continuity of human souls with other living things in the cosmos show a fundamen-tal connection between Empedocles and Homer, Hesiod, and Pythagoras. Each of these early thinkers subscribes to a conception of living things as sharing a common basic nature. These thinkers recognize the distinc-tiveness of humans among living beings, but they do not assert a meta-physical distinction between human beings and animals in the manner of many later thinkers. The fundamental distinction for these thinkers is not between human and nonhuman beings, but rather between mortal and immortal beings. This is the crucial background for the emergence of the predominant theories of human and animal natures. The emer-gence of those theories signals the beginning of a long and complex his-torical turn against the notion of natural continuity that I examine in the remainder of this book. What is remarkable, and crucial, about the pre-Socratic background is that it anticipates all the appeals made by later Western thinkers to the need to rethink our relationship to animals in a way that does better justice to animals. Even more remarkable is the fact that later critics of anthropocentrism sometimes mistakenly assume that they themselves were the first to conceive of animals as our kin.

ARISTOTLE AND THE STOICS
The Evolution of a Cosmic Principle

Richard Sorabji opens his study of ancient views of animals with the powerful claim that "a crisis was provoked when Aristotle denied reason to animals."[1] None of the pre-Socratic thinkers make any rigorous distinction between faculties of the soul such as understanding and perception. They all acknowledge differences between human beings and animals, but they do not see human reason as the sign of an essential distinction between the two. Instead they either emphasize the commonality of humans and animals (this was particularly the case for exponents of metempsychosis), or they base their arguments for differential treatment of human beings and animals on the idea of divine bequest. The terms of the controversy over the moral status of animals shifted fundamentally once it became a philosophical commonplace to assert that reason or understanding distinguishes human beings from "the beasts." This shift signals the beginnings of a distinctively anthropocentric approach to an understanding of the boundary separating us from animals. And, as Sorabji observes, it provokes a crisis.

Prior to Aristotle's time, a distinction between the soul's functions of understanding and perception had been asserted by at least one thinker. Alcmaeon of Croton grants sense perception (αἰσθάνεται) to animals but, explicitly departing from Empedocles, he considers understanding (ξυνεῖναι) to be the exclusive prerogative of human beings.[2] Urs Dierauer notes the fundamental significance of this assertion: "If the overcoming of an original animal condition and the advent of human civilization is explained on the basis of human beings having been endowed with the ability to interpret sense perception, then this suggests at the same time that the lack of culture in animals derives from their lack of understanding." This in turn means that human civilization is no longer understood as a gift of the gods, but instead is seen as the product of "an independent capacity for invention on the part of human beings."[3] For Alcmaeon, human understanding is different in kind than divine understanding. Human understanding is capable only of "inference from evidence," whereas "only the gods have certain knowledge."[4] Thus Alcmaeon sees a gulf between divine and human understanding that makes it necessary for us to invent or manufacture means for our survival. This sense of a gulf signifies a loss of faith in divine inspiration to guide human beings. The assertion of a fundamental distinction between human beings and animals in terms of the faculty of understanding brings with it "the emergence of a new scale of values that assigns to the intellectual moment an unequivocal priority over pure physical force."[5]

The emergence of this new scale of values suggests that the crisis of which Sorabji speaks has roots that predate Aristotle. Alcmaeon's distinction between understanding and sense perception brings with it a new understanding of perception. Now perception is understood to accomplish less than it had previously been thought to accomplish. With the rise of the idea of an intellectual faculty that stands above sensation, sensation is conceived less as an interpretive faculty and more as a data-collecting faculty. This raises the question how animals are able to negotiate their environment and take care of themselves. How do they make discriminations between healthful food and dangerous poisons, between family members and outsiders, and between dangerous enemies and nonthreatening beings? If animals lack understanding, how are they able to defend themselves? How does a bull, for example, "know" to fight with its horns rather than with its tail? And if the word "know" does not properly apply to a bull, then what vocabulary are we to use in describing the bull's ability to negotiate its environment?

Ancient thinkers were well aware that animals exhibit a wide variety of abilities conducive to their well-being. The denial of understanding to animals made it impossible (or at least very difficult) to appeal to explanations that attributed to animals capacities such as insight and reflection. Thinkers such as Xenophon and Hippocrates appeal to what later is called instinct to account for the seemingly spontaneous abilities of animals to care for themselves, relate to their kin, and so on. But in antiquity, as today, notions such as instinct appear to have struck many in the philosophical community as question begging. More precise answers to the sorts of questions posed above were demanded, and answers were sought through reflections on the experiential faculties possessed by human beings and animals respectively.

These reflections are taken to an unheralded level of sophistication in the work of Aristotle. But before I examine his complex views on animals and their place in the cosmos, I note the impetus to Aristotle's thinking on these matters provided by Plato.[6] The crisis of which Sorabji speaks cannot occur in the thought of Plato. There are two interrelated reasons for this. First, Plato is not at pains to study the boundary between human beings and animals, but focuses instead on human beings proper. Plato does hold up the notion of animality as a symbol of what human beings should not aspire toward—he equates irrational human beings with the irrationality of animals, and urges us to cultivate our rationality so as to elevate ourselves above our animal tendencies—but he never makes an essential distinction between human beings and animals. Human beings can try to live a life of pure pleasure, but to do so is to aspire to the life conditions of a very low animal.[7] Plato's central concern is the cultivation of reason (νοῦς, nous) in human beings and the subjugation or regulation of our desire for pleasure. He sees, though, that all people are not equally liable to employ their reason to regulate their desires. Thus he equates the statesman to the shepherd who keeps watch over his flock and guides them away from danger.[8]

Plato starts, then, from the proposition that human beings are a type of animal, although he places primary emphasis on our capacity to subjugate our desires for pleasure to the demands of wisdom. This brings me to the second reason why the crisis does not come to fruition in Plato. Plato subscribes to a conception of soul as an immortal entity that transcends the body. In a number of places he also subscribes to the doctrine of metempsychosis. Because it is possible for souls to move back and forth between animal and human bodies, animals cannot be viewed as essentially inferior to human beings; at best the difference is one of degree. Nonetheless, Plato places a clear priority on human over animal form in his conception of metempsychosis. The *Phaedrus* contains a discussion of the movement of souls back and forth between animal and human bodies, with the qualification that "only the soul that has beheld truth may enter into this our human form."[9] The ideal of transmigration in the *Phaedrus* is one according to which the soul moves from animal to human form, progresses through a hierarchy of human embodiments starting with the form of a tyrant and ending with the form of "a seeker after wisdom or beauty," and ultimately escapes embodiment altogether.[10] In the *Phaedo* and the *Timaeus*, the movement from animal to human form is given a clear premium, with movement from human to animal form being viewed as a punishment for evil.[11] The cultivation of reason and reflection on the forms are the means of the soul's ascent through incarnations.

This makes it impossible to view animals as fundamentally different or inferior to human beings, because animals at least potentially (and in some cases actually) contain the souls of beings who can be liberated to human form and perhaps eventually to pure communion with the gods. Animals are explicitly included in the community of beings capable of realizing the superiority of the life of soul over the life of body.[12] This commitment leads Plato to attribute to animals at least some of the capacities that we associate with rationality, although he is not entirely consistent on the matter. At one point in the *Laws*, Plato says that the souls of all living organisms possess intelligence (νούς, *nous*) as "the fitting protector" in all their life activities.[13] In the *Philebus*, Socrates implies that "thought, intelligence, memory, and things akin to these, right opinion and true reasoning" can be found in "all animate beings," though the context is not clear.[14] In the *Republic*, dogs are described as having the capacity to judge, to be lovers of learning, and hence to be philosophical.[15] In the *Republic*, Socrates says that both children and animals are spirited from birth and can develop rational calculation later in life.[16] In the *Phaedo*, in a discussion of metempsychosis, animals such as bees, wasps, and ants are classified as political beings (πολιτικόν γένος).[17] But the greater emphasis in the Platonic corpus is on denying rational capacities to animals. In the *Symposium*, Diotima attributes care for one's young to reason in human beings but to instinct or nature (φύσει) in animals.[18] Animals are explicitly denied reason in the *Cratylus* and the *Laches*.[19] In book 9 of the *Republic*, Socrates appeals to animals as exemplars a life led by unreason: "Those who have no experience of wisdom and virtue . . . have never transcended all this and turned their eyes to the true upper region . . . but with eyes ever bent upon the earth and heads bowed down over their tables they feast like cattle, grazing and copulating, ever greedy for more of these delights . . . vainly striving to satisfy with things that are not real the unreal and incontinent part of their souls."[20]

Despite these equivocations on the question whether and to what extent animals possess rational abilities, Plato is clear that animals have beliefs.[21] This view is a corollary of Plato's view that the lower, nonrational parts of the soul can have beliefs. Part of the process of maturation involves supplanting irrational beliefs acquired early in life with rationally substantiated beliefs.[22] In this way, irrational appetites and the distorted opinions that they produce are brought under the yoke of rational reflection. Likewise, spirited desire can be brought into willing accord with reason, the ruling part of the soul.[23] Beasts and slaves are capable of rudimentary beliefs.[24] In the case of animals, these beliefs seem to correspond to the beliefs held by the appetitive and spirited parts of the soul. Animals can form beliefs that certain objects are desirable, threatening, and so on. But because animals act "from nature" (φύσει) rather than from reason, they are incapable of stepping back from these beliefs and scrutinizing them with an eye toward assessing their suitability to the higher concerns of the soul. Animals are imprisoned in a life of sheer physicality, and their beliefs are restricted to considerations of material welfare.[25]

Aristotle

The "crisis" of which Sorabji speaks occurs when Aristotle denies that animals possess reason and the capacity to form beliefs. Where Plato and other pre-Aristotelian thinkers are able to account for animal awareness by attributing such states as belief to animals, Aristotle, by conceiving of belief as a function of reason, must develop an elaborate conception of capacities such as perception and desire to account for the ways in which animals negotiate their environments. Aristotle remarks about animal capacities in two sets of texts. In the zoological texts, such as *History of Animals* and *Parts of Animals*, Aristotle attributes to animals a wide array of capabilities and in many instances appears to attribute to them abilities that presumably require belief. In the psychological, metaphysical, and ethical texts, particularly *On the Soul* and the *Nicomachean Ethics*, Aristotle offers his explicit denial that animals are capable of rationality and belief, and he attributes to animals what appears to be a much more limited array of capacities. In one of these latter texts Aristotle baldly asserts that animals exist entirely for the sake of human beings. This assertion has done much to cement Aristotle's reputation as a hard-line speciesist. But is this reputation deserved?

The answer to this question depends on the force accorded to Aristotle's statements in the two sets of texts bearing on animals. The remarks attributing capacities such as intelligence and wisdom to animals occur in texts with a naturalist bent, while the remarks denying political status and subordinating animals to the interests of human beings occur in texts whose primary focus is the human condition. Aristotle's aims in the two sets of texts are quite different. In the one he characterizes the variety and richness of animal behavior, while in the other he explores the place of human beings in the cosmos. Aristotle has a tendency to speak more loosely about animal capacities in the zoological treatises than he does in the psychological and ethical texts, that is, he is much more willing in the zoological texts to attribute capacities such as intelligence and technical capacity to animals by way of analogy to human capacities, whereas he speaks more strictly and precisely about the respective capacities of human beings and animals in the psychological and ethical texts.[26]

There is a further complication in interpreting Aristotle that bears directly on his statement in the *Politics* that animals exist for the sake of human beings. Often in texts such as *On the Soul* and the *Politics*, Aristotle makes statements in such a way as to make it unclear whether he is presenting his own view or simply a view held by popular common sense. In these cases, the passage must be interpreted with a special sensitivity to its context. The passage about human supremacy over animals is a case in point: "After the birth of animals, plants exist for their sake, and . . . the other animals exist for the sake of man, the tame for use and food, the wild, if not all, at least the greater part of them, for food, and for the provision of clothing and various instruments. Now if nature makes nothing in vain, the inference must be that she has made all animals for the sake of man."[27] If, as I argue, Aristotle denies reason and belief to animals, then this statement about a natural hierarchy in which animals stand below human beings might appear to follow quite directly: In virtue of our rational capacity we humans stand above all nonrational beings in the hierarchy of nature, and these nonrational beings exist simply to satisfy our needs and desires.

This conventional wisdom about Aristotle correctly identifies his conviction that human beings are superior to animals in the order of nature, but it misrepresents Aristotle's reasoning. It attributes to Aristotle a conception of nature as a teleologically ordered whole that he never asserts in his writings. It does so by taking a preliminary statement of human common sense as if it were an assertion of Aristotle's considered position. Martha Nussbaum points out that "this passage is from an introductory section of the work, a section concerned with stating the appearances; it assumes an anthropocentric vantage point and asks what use various parts of the natural world are to man in his efforts to establish himself in the world. It is a preliminary *phainomenon*, from the human-practical viewpoint, not a serious theoretical statement."[28] Urs Dierauer notes that this is the only place in all of Aristotle's writings where he commits himself to such a view, which invites the conclusion that Aristotle never treats this idea as a cosmic principle.[29]

The conventional wisdom about the passage in the *Politics* is that Aristotle has a conception of universal teleology that he never actually proposes. In the *Physics*, Aristotle appeals to four "causes" (αἰτίαι) as principles underlying the explanation of changes in nature. Causes in Aristotle's sense are ways of being responsible for something. Plants, animals, and simple elements each possess within themselves "a principle of motion and of stationariness (in respect of place, or of growth and decrease, or by way of alteration)."[30] Aristotle's view is at odds with the mode of explanation employed in Newtonian physics, according to which changes in the state of an object or a system are explained through appeal to universal forces exterior to the objects that act upon them. On Aristotle's view, natural beings possess principles of growth internally rather than having them imposed externally. Aristotle sometimes refers to the internal principle of development as a thing's "nature," by which he means "the shape or form which is specified in the definition of the thing" and which is attained through a process of growth or development.[31] A thing's "nature" in this sense is the shape that it takes in the course of its development, a process that is accounted for by the four causes specific to that thing. The four causes are the matter out of which the being is composed; its form; "the primary source of the change or rest, e.g. the man who deliberated" or the artisan who created a particular artifact; and, most important for our purposes, the "end or that for the sake of which a thing is done."[32] This last cause, the "final" cause, is the "end" in the sense that it is the highest point of a being's development. "That for the sake of which tends to be what is best and the end of the things that lead up to it."[33] The "end" (τέλος, *telos*) of exercise, proper diet, and medical care is good health. The developmental process exhibited by a pig embryo takes place "for the sake of" a mature pig.

The conventional wisdom sketched out above suggests that, for Aristotle, the "end" of the pig is to be used by human beings. As I show below, the Stoics express this sort of commitment in their doctrine of providence; according to Porphyry, Chrysippus even maintains that pigs exist simply to be sacrificed and eaten by human beings.[34] But Aristotle does not go this far. His doctrine of causes includes a teleological component in the idea of ends or final causes for particular beings, but he never asserts that the cosmos as a whole has an overarching teleology.[35] What he does say is that if "artificial products are for the sake of an end, so clearly also are natural products. . . . This is most obvious in the animals other than man," though it holds for plants as well.[36] In accordance with this conception of teleology in nature, Aristotle says that plants and animals "come to be and are by nature." To say that these creatures are "by nature" (φύσει) is to say that their functioning is regulated "neither by art nor after inquiry or deliberation" but rather by natural causes that human beings are able to observe only through the mediation of their outward effects.[37]

Thus human beings may never be able to ascertain the true ends of creatures such as pigs or trees. But Aristotle is unequivocal in his commitment to the proposition that the end of human beings is "happiness" (εὐδαιμονία, eudaimonia), by which he means not pleasure or material prosperity but rather a complex ideal of moral virtue achieved in community by dint of long practice and reflection. Happiness in this sense depends crucially on the capacity for rational contemplation (θεωρία), which makes human beings most like the gods. Animals, on Aristotle's view, lack this capacity and hence do not have any share in happiness.[38] This makes animals "inferior in their nature to men," but it does not entail that animals exist for the sake of human beings.[39]

Even if the passage from the Politics should not be taken at face value, then, it contains an important clue to Aristotle's evaluation of animals. There is a cosmic scheme of things, and human beings are superior to animals in that scheme because only humans possess the contemplative ability that likens us to the gods. In the zoological treatises, Aristotle treats human beings and animals as existing on a natural continuum and differing primarily in degree rather than in kind with respect to capacities such as intelligence. Even if Aristotle is presenting a popular opinion in the Politics when he says that animals exist for human beings, he is doing something more. He is reflecting a set of values that he has woven into the very fabric of his view of human social life. I argue that, in interpreting statements such as this one from the Politics, it is very important to maintain sensitivity to the larger context. I now examine this context.

Aristotle conceives of human political associations as necessary for the pursuit of happiness. Lone individuals cannot pursue happiness, but must pursue the higher satisfactions of life in concert with their fellow human beings. In this sense, "the state is by nature clearly prior to the family and to the individual."[40] The state is prior to the individual not chronologically, but rather in being the necessary precondition for the pursuit of virtue. "The individual, when isolated, is not self-sufficing; and therefore he is like a part in relation to the whole."[41] The state is an exclusively human association, not because animals are entirely apolitical, but rather because they are not sufficiently capable of political existence. "Man is more of a political animal than bees or any other gregarious animals."[42] Aristotle is well aware of the social nature of animals such as bees and ants. What makes human beings peculiarly suited to the form of political association in which happiness is the end, is the fact that human beings have been endowed by nature "with the gift of speech" (λόγος, *logos*), whereas other animals merely possess "voice" (φωνὴ), which "is but an indication of pleasure and pain."[43] Speech is the exclusive possession of rational beings. Even slaves possess reason and speech, but animals "cannot even apprehend reason [λόγου]; they obey their passions [παθήμασιν]."[44] Tame animals and slaves "both with their bodies minister to the needs of life," the key difference in this regard being that the slave "participates in reason enough to apprehend, but not to have" reason.[45] Animals and slaves minister to the needs of life in the sense that they perform tasks, notably but not exclusively physical labor, that help to secure the material prosperity of the state. In doing so, they free the citizens for the more lofty work of political participation, which consists chiefly in service in the legislature and the law courts.[46]

Because the end of the state is the shared pursuit of virtue, Aristotle treats the *Politics* and the *Nicomachean Ethics* as companion pieces.[47] This means that the context for interpreting the statement from the *Politics* includes the theory of virtue developed in the *Nicomachean Ethics*. There Aristotle characterizes virtue in a way that unequivocally excludes animals. One cannot be virtuous if one is not a rational being. Aristotle characterizes virtue in a number of ways in the *Ethics*, but several key constants emerge in his discussion. In particular, virtue or excellence (ἀρετὴ) is "a state concerned with choice [προαιρετική], lying in a mean relative to us, this being determined by reason and in the way in which the man of practical wisdom [φρόνιμος] would determine it."[48] On Aristotle's view, virtue is to be measured not against particular actions, but against the long-term trajectory of a person's life. A person's mature and virtuous character state is an index of long practice and struggle that has been guided by the acquisition of knowledge and the ongoing endeavor to bring one's actions into conformity with what rational principles demand. The shaping of one's character into that of a virtuous person thus depends in part on rational capacity. Adult human beings are capable of rational deliberation (βούλευσις) and rationally grounded choice (προαίρεσις) and thus are moral agents in the full sense of the term.[49] Children and animals, in contrast, are guided not by reason but by spirited desire (θυμός) and appetite (ἐπιθυμία).[50] Their actions are "voluntary" (ἑκούσιον) but do not count as "choice" in the morally weighty sense.[51] Aristotle conceives of choice as a subset of volition. Aristotle confines his discussion of virtue and vice within the more narrowly circumscribed boundaries of choice.

Because animals lack rational capacity, Aristotle excludes them from the ethico-political realm altogether. We cannot have friendships with animals, because "there is nothing common [κοινωνῆσαι] to the two parties."[52] What is lacking is rationality. For the same reason, there is no justice relation between human beings and animals: Justice is a virtue; participation in virtue requires articulate speech, deliberative capacity, and the capacity for reciprocal dealings with human beings, all of which animals categorically lack.[53] The inability to reflect on proper ends for conduct, and to deliberate about possible courses of action in the service of chosen ends, excludes animals from the realm of moral virtue and political associations. Thus when we say, for example, that a particular animal is "temperate," "self-indulgent," and so on, we must acknowledge that we are speaking only "by a metaphor," because capacities such as temperance presuppose the ability to think about one's conduct and to understand the relationship between an action in the present instant and the larger trajectory of one's life.[54] We also cannot, strictly speaking, consider animals to be incontinent, that is, animals are incapable of experiencing a conflict between passion and reason in which passion is victorious.[55]

Aristotle's understanding of animals gives rise to a crisis because, in addition to denying that animals possess rationality and the capacities that depend on reason, he is denying animals the very ability to form a belief. In the passage in the *Ethics* in which he denies that animals can be incontinent, Aristotle says that animals "have no universal beliefs [καθόλου ὑπόληψιν] but only imagination and memory of particulars [ἕκαστα φαντασίαν καὶ μνήμην]."[56] This statement should be read together with Aristotle's statement in *On the Soul* that "in the brutes though we often find imagination we never find belief [πίστις]."[57] This denial of belief in animals follows from Aristotle's broad conception of *logos* (λόγος), which includes a variety of meanings such as articulate speech and logic. One of Aristotle's terms for reasoning or calculation is *logismos* (λογισμός, reckoning), which reflects the close proximity of language and rationality in Aristotle's thought. Animals are incapable of articulate speech, because speech symbolizes mental experiences.[58] At most, as I note above, animals have "voice," and, as I show below, some animals, on Aristotle's view, are merely capable of emitting noises or sounds. In denying animals capacities for reason, language, and belief, Aristotle denies them the richness and complexity of mental experience that is evident in human beings and makes it possible to explain human activities such as planning, forming strategies, and dealing with unanticipated contingencies. But Aristotle is well aware that animals exhibit a wide variety of abilities to provide for themselves and their offspring. So he must reconceive the faculties of experience in animals so as to account for these abilities.

The faculties that Aristotle acknowledges in animals are sense perception (αἴσθησις) and, in most but not all animals, imagination (φαντασία).[59] Animals also exhibit two modes of desire: appetite (ἐπιθυμία) and spirited desire (θυμός).[60] Human beings possess these capacities and modes of desire as well, but the possession of rationality affects their functioning in ways that give rise to a much higher ideal of full human flourishing than is possible for animals. The possession of rationality enables human beings to form universal concepts, which makes contemplation and practical deliberation possible. This in turn makes it possible for human beings to regulate their desires by subjecting them to rational insight. Whereas animals are moved simply by the prospect of pleasure or pain, human beings can be moved by three different sorts of object of desire.[61] Appetites seek pleasure and avoid pain, and thus are fundamentally irrational but can be persuaded to obey reason. Spirited desire, a competitive drive concerned with noble objects, can be regulated through habituation, so as to be brought into conformity with reason. The third type of human desire, rational wish (βούλησις), relies on deliberative capacity and is directed at objects that are advantageous for the individual agent.

In human beings, the regulation of these three sorts of desires converges on the ideal of rationally informed deliberate choice (προαίρεσις). As I note above, the lack of rationality in animals makes such choice impossible for them.[62] This by itself, however, does not constitute the crisis brought about by Aristotle. The deeper problem is how, if animals are not even capable of forming beliefs, they are able so effectively to perform actions that in a human being we would describe as planning for the future, discriminating between alternatives, and the like. In human beings, these capacities can be attributed to rational abilities such as deliberation. By denying rational abilities in animals, Aristotle must attribute animal ingenuity to the remaining capacities that he acknowledges animals to possess, namely, sense perception and imagination.

In sensation we perceive particular qualities such as colors, sounds, or tastes. On Aristotle's account there are also "common sensibles" perceivable by multiple senses simultaneously, namely, "movement, rest, number, figure, magnitude," and unity.[63] Sensation also perceives differences between qualities, as when we distinguish white and black or white and sweet.[64] Sorabji proposes that, in conceiving sensation in these terms, Aristotle is attributing to animals a *predicative* ability, that is, an ability to perceive "*that* something is the case." Perceiving, in other words, is "propositional perceiving," such that "one can perceive that the thing is this or something else, whether the white thing is a man or not, that the approaching thing is a man and is white, what the coloured or sounding thing is, or where," and so on.[65] If this interpretation is correct, it would do much to solve the problem of how animals come to recognize a threat as a threat as opposed to a family member, a piece of food as opposed to something inedible, and so forth. There is textual support for this interpretation. Aristotle says that the sheer hearing of a sound cannot err, but that perception can err regarding the location of the sound. Aristotle does not make it clear whether we are to conceive of such an error as predicative or not. Moreover, the term "predicative" seems suspiciously linguistic. How are we to envision a dog hearing a sound and erring as to where the sound is coming from? For example, we can say that a dog hears a gunshot and makes the immediate (nonlinguistic) association "gunshot—over there!" but is mistaken about the direction because of an echo effect. (The same kind of association would be made in a case in which the dog is *not* mistaken about the direction.) On Sorabji's view, any such immediate association must be conceived as propositional or predicative—*that* the gunshot came from over there. On this interpretation, sensation has the character of intentionality, that is, it does not simply receive pixels of color, discrete bits of sound, and the like, but is directed toward objects of attention, and is directed toward them *as such*. This seems to accord with Aristotle's suggestion that "it is through sense that we are aware that we are seeing or hearing" and with his suggestion that "whether this is bread or has been baked as it should

. . . are matters of perception."[66] It also seems to accord with Aristotle's way of treating perception as "speaking." Aristotle attributes to perception the ability to "say" that an object is pleasant, to "say" "here's drink" in response to an appetite that "says" it has to drink, and the like.[67] It also calls to mind Aristotle's example of a lion's perception of a potential meal: "Nor does the lion delight in the lowing of the ox, but in eating it; but he perceived by the lowing that it was near, and therefore appears to delight in the lowing; and similarly he does not delight because he sees 'a stag or a wild goat', but because he is going to make a meal of it."[68] If perception is propositional, then we must conceive of the lion perceiving that an ox is nearby, that the ox is tonight's dinner, and that this is occasion for delight.

This account places a great burden on sensation. It appears to attribute to sense perception concepts, predication, the act-object structure of intentionality, and a very clear and determinate sense of what things are and how they differ from one another. In short, this interpretation appears to read back into sense perception most everything we associate with linguistic ability other than words. Nussbaum offers a somewhat different interpretation that avoids the imposition of this burden on sensation. She states that sensation on Aristotle's view is passive, and that active, selective focusing occurs in imagination. On this interpretation, it is not in sensation but in imagination that the agent, be it human or animal, selectively seizes upon specific aspects of its environment. It is here that a particular thing can be seen "as a thing belonging to a certain class of objects and not just as a particular materially distinct item."[69] Thus "when we perceive a rose by sight, it is not the rose qua rose, but the rose qua white that acts upon our sight. But to be moved to action an animal has to become aware of something qua what-it-is-called; he has to see the man as a man, not just as pale," that is, "as a unitary object under some description, not just as an assortment of various perceptible characteristics."[70] Like Sorabji's account, this account appears to attribute to animals highly sophisticated capacities to recognize and classify that are difficult to attribute to a being that lacks linguistic ability. It may simply push back the problem of recognition and discrimination between objects from sensation to imagination. But Aristotle's account of imagination or *phantasia* is complex, and I examine it to shed light both on his conception of animal capacities and on the question of the plausibility of Nussbaum's account of Aristotelian *phantasia* in animals. What is ultimately at stake in this examination of *phantasia* is the question whether it can account for capacities in animals that correspond to or resemble practical, deliberative wisdom (φρόνησις) in human beings.

So far I have translated *phantasia* as "imagination" but Aristotle's remarks in book 3 of *On the Soul* make it necessary to speak more precisely about this capacity. Aristotle notes that *phantasia* (φαντασία) is etymologically derived from *phaos* (φάος), which means light.[71] The connection with terms such as *phaino* (φαίνω, to bring to light, to make appear) indicates the sense that something appears or shows up in *phantasia*. In this respect the translation "imagination" is potentially misleading, for example, if it is taken to mean that *phantasia* always involves the production of a visual image. A *phantasma* may, but need not, be a visual image. *Phantasia* is a capacity that presupposes sensation and makes discriminations about what has been perceived in sensation. This would appear to introduce the possibility that *phantasia* can be inaccurate if not downright false. Although Aristotle sometimes says that sensation can be false, he seems to be conflating sensation and imagination in those instances. His more precise view seems to be that "sensations are always true" while "imagination may be false."[72] Aristotle gives as an example of false *phantasia* the case in which "we imagine the sun to be a foot in diameter though we are convinced that it is larger than the inhabited part of the earth."[73] The perception of the sun is simply our perception of the sun, and in itself it cannot be false; the mistake or falsity enters into the experience when we associate the perception with an inaccurate sense of actual size. Aristotle says that most if not all animals exhibit *phantasia*, and he says that in animals *phantasia* plays the role in action that thinking plays in human beings.[74] Both human beings and animals need more than sensation and appetite to be moved to action; certain objects must be viewed *as* desirable or undesirable to initiate movement toward or away from the objects. In *On the Soul* 3.10, Aristotle says that this movement can be completed in human beings either by imagination (which in humans can function as a kind of quasi-thinking) or by reflection on a principle of reason, while in animals it is imagination alone that can complete the movement.

Aristotle explains the role of *phantasia* in action by distinguishing between two forms of *phantasia*. "All imagination is either calculative [λογιστικὴ] or sensitive [αἰσθητική]. In the latter all animals partake."[75] In both cases, *phantasia* draws out of sensation something that the perceiver associates with other aspects of experience, whether rightly or wrongly— as when I wrongly take the sun to be a foot wide, or when my cat rightly takes me to be the same person with whom she has been living for the past eighteen years. In this sense, *phantasia* "is some interpretation of what has been seen," although interpretation in this connection is not (in the case of animals, cannot be) linguistic.[76] Calculative imagination differs from sensitive imagination in having recourse to "a single standard to measure by," which facilitates deliberation about what is to be done. In both cases, however, *phantasia* involves the ability "to make a unity out of several images."[77] When my cat recognizes me, she is making a unity out of her present perception of me and her previous perceptions of me. Whether she is making an immediate, nonpredicative association (you—Gary!) or whether she is predicating of me *that* I am the person with whom she is already familiar is not made clear by Aristotle's remarks. But I incline toward the nonpredicative interpretation. Predication, as a form of synthesis, is subject to truth and falsity. And even though Aristotle says that *phantasia* can be false, I believe that Nussbaum is right when she observes that Aristotle must mean in the "loose" sense that *phantasia* can be "inaccurate."[78] Aristotle reserves the possibility of falsity for composites such as predicative assertions.[79] *Phantasia*, in contrast, appears to be an immediate, noncomposite sense of something *as* something.

Aristotle says that *phantasia* consists in the ability to form a unity out of a number of particulars. Does this imply that animals are capable of forming concepts of the things that they perceive? This question arises because Aristotle has to be able to account for acts of discrimination in animals without appealing to belief, which Aristotle associates with cognition and language. If my cat is to recognize me as me, how can she do this if she does not have a concept of me? Sorabji's solution to this problem is to attribute to Aristotle a conception of sensation as predicative. If recognition and seeing-as occur not in sensation but instead in *phantasia*, then *phantasia* must be predicative.[80] But predicative determinations such as "the being I am looking at now is Gary" are not possible without recourse to concepts. Determinations of the form "*X* is the case" or "*X* is a *Y*" presuppose a stabilized sense of what *X*s and *Y*s are. In the "*X* is a *Y*" sort of experience, the agent of experience must have had sufficient prior encounters with *Y*s to be able to invoke the notion of a *Y* in the present determination. On the assumption that *phantasia* is predicative, the example of my cat recognizing me has the form "*X* is a *Y*." Hence the question whether Aristotle is saying that an animal such as my cat is employing a concept in *phantasia*, and, if so, whether Aristotle's account of *phantasia* can account for concept formation in a noncognitive being.

In the *Metaphysics*, Aristotle links intelligence and learning to memory.

Animals possessing memory are "more intelligent and apt at learning than those which cannot remember," because memory facilitates "knowledge of individuals."[81] Without this kind of memory, there is no way my cat could recognize me as her longtime companion. The essence of memory is the recognition that a present image or idea is the same as what I experienced in the past.[82] Memory is a capacity that requires "the faculty of perceiving time" and "essentially . . . belongs to the primary faculty of sense-perception."[83] But there are limits to memory in animals. Although animals with memory can recall past experiences of an object experienced in the present, only human beings are capable of calling up a memory of a past experience when there is no present impression to inspire the memory; Aristotle employs the Platonic term "recollection" (ἀνάμνησις) to characterize this specifically human mnemonic ability, and he characterizes it as "a mode of inference" possible only for beings "endowed with the faculty of deliberation."[84] The overall picture of animal memory that Arisotle presents in *On Memory* is this: At best, animals can make immediate associations between present experiences and past experiences of the same objects, but they cannot call memories to mind at will, that is, in the absence of a present impression of the relevant object. Moreover, Aristotle states in *On Memory* that the future "is an object of opinion or expectation."[85] This suggests that animals, which lack the capacity for opinion, have no relation to the future. The scope of their dealings is confined to the present and a limited capacity to retrieve the past—and, in accordance with Aristotle's example of the lion and the ox in *Nichomachean Ethics* 3.10, some limited capacity to be related to the near (perhaps the immediate) future.

In the *Posterior Analytics*, Aristotle may locate within the scope of animal dealings a place for what he calls "primitive universals." Animals possess "a connate discriminatory capacity, which is called perception." Memory occurs when "retention of the percept comes about"; animals possessing this capacity are able "to have an account [λόγον] from the retention of such things." For beings with such cognitive abilities, "from perception comes what we call memory, and from memory (when it occurs often in connection with the same thing), experience; for memories that are many in number form a single experience."[86] Whether this amounts to attributing to animals the power to form universals depends on the meaning of the following passage: "When one of the undifferentiated things makes a stand, there is a primitive universal in the mind [πρῶτον μὲν ἐν τῇ ψυχῇ καθόλου] (for though one perceives the particu-

lar, perception is of the universal—e.g. of man but not Callias the man):
again a stand is made in these, until what has no parts and is universal
stands—e.g. *such and such* an animal stands, until animal does, and in this
a stand is made in the same way."[87] This passage has been widely interpreted to attribute the capacity for concept formation to animals, or at
least the capacity to form the "primitive universals" of which Aristotle
speaks. Dierauer says that Aristotle is attributing to animals the capacity
to "feel, somehow, the commonality" between members of a class of
perceived objects.[88] Sorabji takes Aristotle to be saying that "for the lion
to have a rudimentary concept of an ox is no more than for it to have many
memories of individual oxen."[89] Labarrière interprets the *Posterior Analytics*
passage to mean that animals possess "pre-predicative sub-universals" and
a sort of "proto-recollection" that falls short of rational wish but suffices
for the purposes of making prudent discriminations.[90]

The attribution of rudimentary concepts to animals has the tremendous advantage of facilitating a clear explanation of prudent behavior.
Sorabji does the best job of attributing rudimentary concepts to animals
with a minimum of cognitive baggage—the lion's rudimentary concept of
an ox *just is* its several memories of an ox. Whether this account is sufficient
to explain the lion's recognition *as* an ox, an ox that the lion has never seen
before, is unclear. A more fundamental problem is whether it makes sense
to call a collection of memories a "concept." Aristotle does say that "a
number of memories constitute a single experience," but he does not
explain what he means by this. And even if it is plausible to suppose that
such an experience can amount to, or perhaps become, a concept in the
thought processes of a rational being, Aristotle goes on in the *Posterior
Analytics* to say that "it is necessary for us to become familiar with the primi-
tives by induction; for perception too instils the universal in this way."[91]
This means that even the most "primitive universals" are produced by
means of induction. Induction is a mode of inference, and we typically
think of inference as an activity reserved for rational beings. To this extent, it would seem implausible to suppose that Aristotle is attributing
the capacity for inductive inference to animals, especially given his statement in the *Metaphysics* that it is specifically in *human beings* that memories
produce "a single experience."[92]

But Aristotle's views on this question are troublingly ambiguous. This
ambiguity is also evident in his views on the question whether animals are
capable of practical wisdom. The connection between the two questions
is relatively straightforward. Aristotle conceives of practical wisdom as a

process of syllogistic inference-making that terminates in an action oriented on the well-being of the agent. Aristotle defines practical wisdom (φρόνησις, phronesis) as "a true and reasoned state of capacity to act with regard to the things that are good or bad for man." The rational component of practical wisdom, and the fact that Aristotle classifies practical wisdom as a virtue, suggest that animals are incapable of phronesis.[93] Phronesis "is concerned with things human and things about which it is possible to deliberate."[94] Deliberation, in turn, "involves reasoning . . . The man who is deliberating, whether he does so well or ill, is searching for something and calculating."[95] When calculating well, the individual will achieve "true apprehension" with regard to the end in question.[96] But Aristotle conceives of truth and falsity as properties of cognitive-linguistic predication.[97] Thus a nonrational being would appear to be incapable of phronesis. For the same reasons, it is doubtful that Aristotle would deem animals capable of any kind of inferential capacity.

But Aristotle does sometimes speak as if animals are capable of inference and phronesis. In his discussion of memory at the beginning of the Metaphysics, when Aristotle says that animals with memory are "more intelligent" than those lacking it, he uses the term phronimotera [φρονιμώ-τερα].[98] In On the Soul, Aristotle says that "understanding [φρονεῖν, phronein] . . . is found in only a small division of" the animal world, though he does not clarify whether he means human beings only or some nonhuman animals as well.[99] One interpretation of the passage in Nicomachean Ethics 3.10, in which the lion perceives an ox nearby, is that the lion has an expectation of dinner in the near future—though this interpretation is beset with the problem of explaining how the lion can have a sense of the future, given Aristotle's statement that only beings capable of opinion can have a relation to the future. Another textual passage that might appear to support the contention that Aristotle grants phronesis to some animals is one in which he states that "we say that some even of the lower animals have practical wisdom, viz. those which are found to have a power of foresight with regard to their own life."[100] Like the passage about the lion and the ox, this statement conflicts directly with Aristotle's claim that anticipation of the future depends on opinion and thus depends on cognitive ability. But Aristotle is not really contradicting himself here. As Fortenbaugh points out, Aristotle is not presenting his considered view in this passage, but is simply presenting a popular view about animal ingenuity, namely, that animals outwardly appear to employ foresight and calculation.[101]

There is one other key passage in which Aristotle seems to attribute *phronesis* to animals. In *Movement of Animals* 6, Aristotle takes up the question "how the soul moves the body, and what is the origin of an animal's motion."[102] Aristotle's aim here is to argue that the bodily movements of animals are not simply mechanical but are caused by *phantasia* and appetite. Aristotle gives the following example, which has the outward form of a practical syllogism. "'I have to drink', says appetite. 'Here's drink', says sense-perception or *phantasia* or thought. At once he drinks."[103] It is tempting to interpret Aristotle to mean that a thirsty animal engages in a process of practical deliberation, however quick, whose conclusion is the act of drinking. But this is incompatible with Aristotle's characterization of deliberation as a rational capacity. Moreover, the context of this example seems to exclude such an interpretation. Aristotle presents this example as an illustration of the principle that "whatever we do without calculating, we do quickly."[104] This suggests that Aristotle is speaking metaphorically when he characterizes the movement to drink as a practical syllogism. There is no reason to believe that the process *could not* occur as a practical syllogism, but Aristotle makes clear with his prefatory remark that he is describing a situation in which *there is no* calculation. Thus he seems to mean that the movement to drink in such a situation takes place *as if* it were arrived at through a practical syllogism, even though in such a situation there is no deliberation any more than appetite utters the words "I have to drink."

I take Sorabji's remark about a "crisis" in thinking about animal capacities to be focused in Aristotle's struggle to reconcile his staunch denial of belief and other rational capacities in animals with the obvious fact that animals exhibit capacities for survival and flourishing whose precise nature is a mystery to us. Particularly in the zoological writings, Aristotle attributes to animals capacities that he treats in the psychological and ethical writings as applying only to human beings—capacities such as character, intelligence, ingenuity, and emotion. Aristotle provides a hint to the interpretation of such attributions when he says that "we call the lower animals neither temperate nor self-indulgent except by a metaphor" because "these have no power of choice or calculation."[105] The same metaphorical usage is at work, on Aristotle's view, when we attribute emotions such as fear to animals. If emotions such as fear or pity involve belief, then it is impossible for animals to have them "except by a metaphor."[106] Similarly, animals cannot properly be said to possess the virtue of courage, because they do not possess the relation to the future that courage presupposes; but we may call animals courageous in a figurative sense.[107]

Aristotle is well aware of the appeal of anthropomorphic language in characterizing animal behavior, but he is equally sensitive to the limitations of such language. The limitations, as Aristotle understands them, are clearly sketched out in the ethical and psychological writings. In the zoological writings, Aristotle allows himself to slip into metaphor as a means for exploring the capacities of animals. My working hypothesis is that Aristotle's metaphorical usage is born of a sensitivity to the richness of animal capacities, but that this sensitivity is later attenuated by Aristotle's intensive focus on the human condition in the ethical and psychological writings. Aristotle is clearly fascinated by the animal kingdom and devotes numerous texts to the discussion of animals and their capacities. At the same time, he recognizes the sui generis character of human reason and attempts to do justice to capacities that are uniquely human. Ultimately he is unable to do justice to both sides of the dichotomy between the human and the animal realms. But he may come closer to doing so than any other Western advocate of the superiority of human beings over animals.

Aristotle devotes much of his *History of Animals* to an examination of abilities in animals that bring to mind the human capacities for foresight, ingenuity, sociability, and various forms of intelligence. The anthropomorphic language of this text stands in stark contrast to the typical characterizations of animals found in texts such as *On the Soul* and the *Nicomachean Ethics*. In attributing to animals capacities such as intelligence or emotion, Aristotle sometimes qualifies his remarks by saying that animals behave "as if" they possess such capacities. But in many cases he omits the qualification and simply attributes capacities such as *phronesis* to animals. Aristotle tends to deny in the ethical and psychological texts that animals possess such capacities, so I now examine his remarks in the zoological texts against the background of an important distinction that he makes at the beginning of book 7 of *History of Animals*. There Aristotle says that many animals exhibit "resemblances of intelligent understanding. . . . [S]ome characters differ by the more-and-less compared with man . . . while others differ by analogy: for corresponding to art, wisdom and intelligence in man, certain animals possess another natural capability of a similar sort."[108] In some respects, the differences between human beings and animals are matters of degree ("more-and-less"), while in other respects the differences are differences in kind ("by analogy"). Aristotle says that characteristics such as "tameness and wildness, gentleness and roughness, courage and cowardice" differ by "more-and-less" in human beings and in animals. This suggests that human beings and animals differ only in degree with respect to qualities such as courage, and it leaves open the possibility that some animals surpass human beings in such qualities. With regard to intelligence in animals, Aristotle moves back and forth between treating it as different in degree from human intelligence and as merely analogous to human intelligence.[109] To say that animals exhibit qualities analogous to human intelligence is to acknowledge that animals do not really possess capacities such as *dianoia* (thought, understanding) or *phronesis*. It is to recognize, as Dierauer puts the point, that animals act for their own well-being in ways that are mysterious to us and that we can do no better than characterize as operating "by nature" (φύσει) in animals, which is to say that they operate by means of learning and what a modern biologist such as Lorenz would call instinct.[110]

In the zoological texts Aristotle freely grants that animals can exhibit capacities such as courage, while in the *Ethics* he denies this possibility. What he does not do in the zoological texts is provide an account of the precise nature of capacities such as courage in animals. Instead he simply observes that many animals exhibit behavior that could be described as "courage," for example, and he rests satisfied to employ such descriptive terms with their commonsense meanings rather than seeking to give a rigorous account of what such terms can mean in the case of animals. For example, given Aristotle's characterization of courage in the *Ethics* as involving a sense of the future, he should reconcile the attribution of courage to animals with his conviction, expressed even in the zoological treatises, that "man is the only animal that has hope and expectation of the future."[111] His omission to provide the needed reconciliation in the zoological treatises underscores the loose, commonsense character of his attribution of emotional states to animals in those treatises. It also highlights the fact that, notwithstanding Aristotle's fascination with the animal kingdom and the great value that he places on the study of animals, he ultimately seems more interested in human beings and shared pursuit of virtue in the human community.[112]

Aristotle remarks in a number of places in the zoological texts that animals exhibit intelligence. In these passages, Aristotle variously employs terms such as reasoning (νοῦς, *nous*), thought or understanding

(διάνοια), sagacity (σύνεσις), and practical wisdom (φρόνησις, phronesis).
Thus different animals exhibit "mind" (νοῦς, nous) in different degrees,
though Balme notes that Aristotle "does not intend nous in the technical sense of de An. [On the Soul], which is applicable only to humans, but
the context suggests that he is distinguishing between animals that learn
from experience or teaching and those that remain 'ignorant.'"[113] Goats,
hounds, panthers, deer, and other animals exhibit different sorts of
phronesis; for example, wild goats on Crete struck by arrows seek out a
particular herb to help expel the arrows, and deer give birth near roads
because the proximity to human beings scares away predators.[114] Different
birds exhibit various sorts of intelligence (διάνοια) in providing for their
well-being.[115] Some animals demonstrate skill or ingenuity (τεχνικά,
technika), which is implicitly denied to animals in the Metaphysics on the
grounds that art or skill requires knowledge of universals.[116] One specific
form of ingenuity of interest to Aristotle is the deceptive behavior of
animals such as the octopus and the cuttlefish, which conceal themselves
in ink when posed with a threat.[117] He also speaks of foresight in bees, and
he speaks of the "actions" (πράξεις) of animals in terms that, in the ethical
and psychological texts, he strictly reserves for human beings.[118] And, in
a remarkable anticipation of the contemporary experiments demonstrat-
ing different forms of alarm calls in vervet monkeys, Aristotle notes that
pigeons learn to discriminate between hawks that attack in the air and
those that attack on the ground.[119] Aristotle even tells stories, without any
apparent irony, of a camel and a horse, each of which reacted violently
to the discovery that it had been deceived into having sex with its mother.[120]

Aristotle's clearest departure from the ethical and psychological texts
may be his attribution of linguistic ability to some animals in the zoological texts. I note above that Aristotle makes a distinction in the Politics between voice and articulate speech and that he grants voice to some
animals but categorically denies speech to animals on the grounds that
they lack the requisite rational capacity. In the zoological treatises, on the
other hand, Aristotle distinguishes between animals "that hear sounds"
and "those that distinguish the differences between the signs."[121] He also
distinguishes between animals capable of producing sounds (ψόφος), those
capable of voice (φωνή), and those capable of speech (διάλεκτος).[122] Only
animals with a pharynx are capable of producing voice. Hence bees, for
example, can emit buzzing sounds but cannot produce voice. A lowing
cow, on the other hand, has voice. But the cow is incapable of speech

because its tongue is incapable of the fine articulation that transforms voice into speech. The human tongue "is the freest, the broadest, and the softest of all," which enables it "to articulate the various sounds and to produce speech."[123] But whereas Aristotle strictly reserves this capacity to human beings in the *Politics*, in the zoological writings he says in a number of places that birds share the capacity for speech with human beings. "All birds use their tongues as a means of communication with other birds, and some to a very considerable extent, so much so that it is probable that in some cases information is actually conveyed from one bird to another."[124]

Aristotle also comments extensively on the emotional capacities (πάθη) of animals in the zoological writings. Regarding some emotional states, Aristotle hedges and says only that certain animals behave "as though" out of pity, for example, in a case in which two dolphins tended a dead baby dolphin.[125] On the other hand, he attributes emotional states such as jealousy, fear, and courage to various animals without any such qualification, even though he notes in the *Politics* that courage requires a capacity for foresight that animals lack.[126] In *Parts of Animals* Aristotle reaffirms his conviction that "man is the only animal that has hope and expectation of the future."[127] What he does not do there is explain how we are to conceive of courage in creatures that cannot anticipate future events. The implicit answer is that, as in the case of "foresight" in bees, such a capacity must be understood by way of analogy rather than in terms of "more-and-less." Seen in this light, Aristotle's attributions of ingenuity, courage, and the like to beings that he consistently treats as nonrational reflect his sensitivity to the complexity of animal behavior, the difficulties involved in thinking the boundary between human and animal, and perhaps even the potential inadequacy of seizing upon rationality as the dividing line between human beings and animals. Aristotle's fascinating acknowledgement that some birds may be able to exchange information through articulate speech is not far removed from the contemporary cognitive ethologist Donald Griffin's efforts to argue for conceptual ability and self-consciousness in a wide variety of animals. Taken seriously, this acknowledgment threatens to undermine, or at least erode, the very basis to which Aristotle appeals in the *Politics* for excluding animals from community with human beings. For all his attempts to adhere to a position according to which human beings differ in kind from animals, Aristotle ultimately admits that animals exhibit "traces" of human "character" (ἦθος, *ethos*) and that human beings differ from animals only in degree—that "man's nature is the most complete, so that these dispositions [viz. characters such as spirit and cunning] too are more evident in humans" rather than being exclusive to humans.[128]

Aristotle's conflicting comments about animals do not constitute a simple inconsistency but rather reflect Aristotle's recognition of a continuum between human beings and animals while seeking to distinguish human beings on the basis of their rational capacities. In the zoological writings, Aristotle notes that there is no sharp dividing line between plants and animals.[129] He implicitly recognizes that the possession of rational soul in human beings does not distinguish them in a cosmically absolute sense from animals, but distinguishes them only by degree. This recognition is a corollary of one of Aristotle's key criticisms of Plato, namely, that soul is not a substance independent of body, but instead is "a substance [οὐσία] in the sense of the form of a natural body having life potentially within it. . . . Soul [ψυχή] is the actuality [ἐντελέξεια] of a body."[130] Soul "is substance in the sense which corresponds to the account [λόγον] of a thing."[131] Soul in this sense is the capacity or potentiality of a given kind of body, understood teleologically. Aristotle discusses five kinds of soul: nutritive, sensory, appetitive, locomotive, and rational.[132] In each case, the type of soul characterizes the highest end or potentiality that the being can attain. Plants, for example, seek nutrition. Some animals possess in addition to nutritive soul sensory and appetitive soul as well, which means that they are moved by sensation and desire as well as by the need for nutrition. Other animals exhibit, in addition to these, the power of locomotion, and human beings possess all of these as well as the power of thought. Understood in this sense, reason or rational soul (nous) is inseparable from the body that it animates. Aristotle does not subscribe to the idea of an immortal soul, except in the strictly limited sense that reason itself (nous) is immortal.[133] All this brings into clearer relief Aristotle's sense of continuity between human beings and animals: the possession of rational soul does not set us radically apart from animals, but simply reflects a difference in the ways in which our bodies function in the world.

The full force of Aristotle's position regarding animals, then, can be grasped only when we acknowledge the uneasy tension between his commitment to the natural continuity between animals and human beings on the one hand, and his categorical exclusion of animals from the polis on the other.

The Stoics

Where Aristotle is willing to acknowledge the fundamental tension between the idea of humans as a special kind of animal and the idea that ethical life is the exclusive prerogative of humans among earthly beings, the Stoics resolve this tension by elevating the dividing line between human beings and animals to the status of a cosmic principle. The Stoics thereby neutralize any sense of ambivalence on the question whether animals are capable of powers such as conceptual abstraction. They drastically restrict the scope of animal experience and make fundamental distinctions between even the perceptual capacities of rational and nonrational beings. In conjunction with these distinctions, the Stoics attribute to human beings a status of superiority over all nonrational beings in the cosmic scheme of things. In this respect, the Stoics take a decisive step beyond Aristotle, who stops short of seeing an overarching teleology in the cosmos as a whole. By the time of the later Stoics, particularly Epictetus, the notion of divine providence has become a central theme in Stoic thought and has been invoked as the basis for a cosmopolitan ethic according to which the highest beings in the ethical order are those capable of rational contemplation. Here, for the first time in the history of Western philosophy, human rationality is seized upon as the basis for a categorical claim to the moral superiority of human beings over animals.

The fact that this ethic comes to complete fruition only in the later Stoics reminds us that there is no one clear set of ideas or commitments that is canonically Stoic. Stoic thought ranges across numerous thinkers over four centuries, and it spans the divide between Greek and Roman civilization. The task of reconstructing Stoic doctrines is further complicated by the fact that we do not have whole texts written by early Stoic authors but instead have fragments and the reports of historians and philosophers such as Diogenes Laertius and Cicero. Yet another complication is posed by the fact that the broad range of Stoic thinkers and topics includes a variety of disagreements about such matters as the nature of perception in animals. Nonetheless it is possible to trace out a trajectory in the course of Stoic thought, in the course of which certain doctrines emerge as definitive of Stoicism as a movement. Central to that movement, and to an examination of Stoic views on animals, is the doctrine of *oikeiosis* (οἰκείωσις), the doctrine of belonging, community, or "loving devotion."[134] According to the Stoics, all animals exhibit a sense of belonging, but only human beings are capable of the specific sense of belonging that provides the basis for membership in the sphere of right or justice. Distinctive in the Stoics is the conviction that membership in this sphere is all or nothing, and that all and only rational beings enjoy membership in it. Although Aristotle comes close in the ethical and psychological texts to embracing such a position, the Stoics are the first to offer a systematic argument for the proposition that human beings owe no obligations whatsoever to animals.

This position follows in important part from the Stoics' views on the experiential capacities of animals. Like Aristotle, the Stoics deny rationality and the capacity for belief to animals. But the Stoics go even further by denying animals the capacity to withhold assent from their perceptual appearances. Animals cannot interrogate or hold back from appearances, but are moved immediately by them, whereas rational beings are capable of scrutinizing appearances and either assenting or withholding assent from them. All animals possess soul, and this means that they experience "impression [φαντασίαν, appearance] and impulse [ὁρμήν]."[135] From early Stoicism onward, appearance is conceived differently for rational and nonrational beings. "Another division of presentations [φαντασιῶν, appearances] is into rational and irrational, the former being those of rational creatures, the latter those of the irrational. Those which are rational are processes of thought, while those which are irrational have no name."[136] Irrational appearances, experienced by animals and human infants, are "pre-conceptual," whereas the appearances of mature human beings are cognitive in the sense that they have propositional content to which we can assent or withhold assent.[137] "One who has the cognitive appearance [καταληπτικὴν φαντασίαν] fastens on the objective difference of things in a craftsmanlike way, since this kind of impression has a peculiarity which differentiates it from other impressions."[138] Animals, due to their lack of rationality—they are ἄλογα (nonrational or nonlinguistic)—cannot seize upon the content of sensation in this way, but instead are lost in or enthralled by the perceptual appearances that they experience. Rational agents, on the other hand, experience perceptual impressions in a fundamentally different way. Their impressions are mediated through cognition so as to be accompanied by verbal expressions or λεκτα (lekta), by which the Stoics "mean that of which the content corresponds to some rational presentation."[139] In other words, "the lekton accompanying the presentation serves to spell out in linguistic form the content of the object presented."[140] This is possible because the object presented has cognitive content. As Long and Sedley put the point, "the mind's stock of conceptions is immediately activated when a sense-impression is received, with the result that the impression presents its object in conceptualized form."[141] This conceptualized form is distinctive of the content of human *phantasiai*. It is on the basis of this conceptualized content and its corresponding *lekton* that a rational agent can either assent to or withhold assent from a given presentation. Animals, in contrast, can neither assent nor withhold assent, because their experiences lack the requisite propositional content.[142]

The Stoic distinction between rational and nonrational perception also has implications for capacities such as emotion and memory. Where Aristotle equivocates on the question whether animals can legitimately be said to exhibit emotions, Stoics from Zeno to Seneca conceive of emotional states as involving rational assent and hence as states of which animals are incapable.[143] Rationality makes it possible for human beings to scrutinize the beliefs or judgments that ground their emotional states, and this puts us in a position to alter our emotional evaluations of things by refining our beliefs. Animals are incapable of this sort of modification, because they lack the requisite cognitive apparatus. Seneca says that "wild beasts have impulses, madness, fierceness, aggressiveness," but that none of these are properly classified as emotions because emotions such as anger are "born only where reason dwells." At most, animals have "traces" of emotions, which Seneca describes as "certain impulses similar to these emotions." Because animals lack reason, they are incapable of "love and hate . . . friendship and enmity, discord and harmony." For the same reason, they are also incapable of "wisdom, foresight, diligence, and reflection," which "have been granted to no creature but man."[144]

The Stoics' position concerning memory in animals is closely related to this reasoning. Animals can be reminded of a past event by the immediate presence of something that reminds them of the event, but they cannot recall the event in the absence of such a stimulus. For example, Seneca says that a horse can recall a familiar road when it is brought to the beginning of the road, but it cannot recall the road when it is standing in its stable. For Seneca, this is tied to the fact that "the dumb animal comprehends the present world through his senses alone." This in turn means that "animals perceive only the time which is of greatest moment to them within the limits of their coming and going—the present. Rarely do they recollect the past—and that only when they are confronted with present reminders," such as the horse's visual presentation of the road before it.[145]

The key difference between the actions of animals and human beings on this view is that human beings can scrutinize and choose from among different external objects with regard to their suitability, whereas animals cannot. Animals, as ensouled creatures, have their principle of movement within themselves. But all this really amounts to for the Stoics is that animals are strictly governed by the impulses that they generate internally in response to external presentations. "Ensouled things are moved 'by' themselves when an impression occurs within them which calls forth an impulse. . . . A rational animal, however, in addition to its impressionistic nature, has reason which passes judgement on impressions, rejecting some of these and accepting others, in order that the animal may be guided accordingly."[146] At most, animals exhibit a quasi-assent when they "yield" to the influence that external presentations exercise over them.[147]

The Stoics' characterization of the experiential capacities of animals culminates in a claim that places the Stoics in the company of Aristotle: that because animals lack rationality and the capacity for assent, they have no relationship to the good and hence no share whatsoever in virtue or vice. According to Seneca, "the Good . . . does not exist in dumb animals or little children" because it is "a matter of the understanding [intellectus]."[148] Understanding or intellect develops in children as they grow up, but animals are said to have no share whatsoever in it. That reason is the exclusive possession of adult human beings is Seneca's basis for seizing upon it as our sole good in life, for arguing that virtue consists entirely in the proper exercise of reason, and for arguing that our rational capacity makes us fundamentally superior to animals.[149]

The Stoics' minimalist interpretation of action in animals is difficult to reconcile with the story of a clever dog that Sextus Empiricus attributes to Chrysippus. Sextus argues, against the Stoics, that animals exhibit "acceptance of the familiar and avoidance of the alien, knowledge of the arts related to this, possession of the virtues pertaining to one's proper nature and of those having to do with the pathē [emotions]."[150] The dog, for example, who "guards his family and benefactors but wards off strangers and malefactors, would not be lacking in justice. And if he has this virtue, then in virtue of the unity of the virtues he has them all." The dog is likewise "valiant and smart in his defending," as is amply shown by Homer's depiction of Argus as the sole member of the household to recognize Odysseus.[151] Chrysippus himself supports this characterization of canine abilities, if only against his own intention:

> According to Chrysippus, who was certainly no friend of non-rational animals, the dog even shares in the celebrated Dialectic. In fact, this author says that the dog uses repeated applications of the fifth-undemonstrated argument-schema, when, arriving at a juncture of three paths, after sniffing at the two down which the quarry did not go, he rushes off on the third without stopping to sniff. For, says this ancient authority, the dog in effect reasons as follows: the animal either went this way or that way or the other; he did not go this way and he did not go that; therefore, he went the other.[152]

The dog is aware that two of three possible paths lack the scent of the animal it is pursuing. In order for the dog to head down the third path without checking for the scent, it must have drawn the logical inference that its quarry could only have gone down the third path. This interpretation confers upon the dog the full range of abilities possessed by rational beings. But Chrysippus himself denies rational capacity in animals, hence he would not accept Sextus's suggestion that this story confirms Chrysippus's acknowledgment of reason in animals. Chrysippus's commitment to a fundamental distinction between human beings and animals forces him to account for the dog's behavior in strictly nonrational terms.

The Stoics freely acknowledge all sorts of abilities in animals to care for themselves, but the Stoics deny that any of these abilities depend on reason. In contrast with Aristotle, who flirts with the possibility that animals possess at least "rudimentary concepts" and some sort of *phronesis*, the Stoics categorically deny animals these capacities and seek to explain animal behavior entirely on the basis of perception and impulse. This forces the Stoics onto the high ground of what later thinkers classify as instinct. Animals have an inborn relation to their own bodies. This relation is the basis for an animal's capacity for self-preservation. "An animal's first impulse, say the Stoics, is to self-preservation, because nature from the outset endears it to itself, as Chrysippus affirms . . . His words are, 'The dearest thing [οἰκεῖον] to every animal is its own constitution and its consciousness [λέγων, ability to pick out] thereof." Impulse enables animals "to go in quest of their proper aliment [τὰ οἰκεῖα, what is appropriate to them]."[153] In animals, the "use of external impressions" is sufficient "to eat and drink and rest and procreate, and whatever else of the things within their own province the animals severally do."[154] These impressions give rise to nonrational impulses that govern the behavior of animals.

In addition to eating, drinking, and procreating, animals possess an awareness of the constitution of their bodies sufficient for the purposes of self-defense. Hierocles says that "as soon as an animal is born it perceives [αἰσθάνεται] itself. . . . The first thing animals perceive is their own parts . . . both that they have them and for what purpose they have them." Moreover, "animals are not unaware of their equipment for self-defence. When bulls do battle with other bulls or animals of different species, they stick out their horns, as if these were their congenital weapons for the encounter. Every other creature has the same disposition relative to its appropriate end and, so to speak, congenital weapons."[155] Central to the Stoic view is the conviction that animals have an immediate, perceptual relation to their bodily parts, without any understanding.[156] They are possessed of this awareness "immediately at birth . . . they are born full-trained."[157] Evidence for the "naturalness" of animal skills is provided by the fact that animals manifest their distinctive skills and tendencies spontaneously and totally, without experience and without gradual development. An animal's aversion to dangers such as natural predators is "not reached . . . through experience," but instead "is because of an inborn desire for self-preservation. The teachings of experience are slow and irregular; but whatever Nature communicates belongs equally to everyone, and comes immediately."[158] Seneca gives as examples of naturalness an infant's struggle to stand erect and a tortoise's struggle to right itself when it has been placed on its back.[159] Equally natural are the characteristic skills exhibited by animals such as bees and spiders.

> Do you not see how skillful bees are in building their cells? How completely harmonious in sharing and enduring toil? Do you not see how the spider weaves a web so subtle that man's hand cannot imitate it. . . . This art is born, not taught [nascitur ars ista, non discitur]; and for this reason no animal is more skilled than any other. You will notice that all spider-webs are equally fine, and that the openings in all honeycomb cells are identical in shape. Whatever art communicates is uncertain and uneven; but Nature's assignments are always uniform.[160]

The fact that spider webs exhibit such uniform perfection, and that every spider achieves this perfection from the very first web that it spins, is evidence for Seneca that reason is not involved in any way in the spider's behavior. Strictly speaking, in fact, Seneca cannot properly say that the spider's weaving is an "art." As he himself intimates, true art is achieved through a process of practice and gradual improvement in the artist, whereas the spider's "art" is perfected at the moment of its birth.

This analysis of animal skills shows that, on the Stoic view, animals can act purposively, but only with regard to their self-preservation. Animals lack the ability of rational beings to scrutinize their perceptions and gain control over their impulses. In the cosmic scheme of things, this places animals in a fundamentally inferior position to human beings. Animals and human beings each have their respective good in this scheme. The immediate good of animals is self-preservation.[161] In human beings, reason makes a higher good possible, namely, virtue.[162] The respective goods of animals and human beings are derived from a cosmic holism that separates the Stoics from Aristotle, and according to which moral status is determined by a being's proximity to the gods. The Stoic conviction that animals exist for the sake of human beings (that is, that the ultimate good of animals is to satisfy the needs of human beings) is part of a larger set of commitments about the ideal order of the cosmos and the potential of rational beings to contemplate that order. Chief among these commitments are the Stoic ideal of "living in accordance with nature," the notion of providence, and the doctrine of *oikeiosis* or belonging. Taken together, these three commitments reflect the cosmic holism that ultimately separates the Stoics from Aristotle.

The ideal of living in accordance with nature is the guiding thread in the Stoic program for "situating human nature within the providential cosmic perspective."[163] Each natural being has a proper place in the scheme of the cosmos, and in each case this proper place gets characterized in terms of the capacities of the being in question and the relationship that the being has to the cosmic whole. "Our individual natures are parts of the nature of the whole universe."[164] Each part derives its sense and its proper aspirations from the sense of the whole, "for nor is there anything else besides the world which has nothing missing, and which is equipped from every point of view, perfect, and complete in all its measures and parts."[165] In his *Hymn to Zeus*, Cleanthes characterizes the sense of the whole in terms of the *logos* or rational plan that guides all events:

> (1) Most majestic of immortals, many-titled, ever omnipotent Zeus, prime mover of nature . . . (2) All this cosmos, as it spins around the earth, obeys you, whichever way you lead, and willingly submits to your

sway. Such is the double-edged fiery ever-living thunderbolt which you hold at the ready in your unvanquished hands. For under its strokes all the works of nature are accomplished. With it you direct the universal reason [κοινὸν λόγον] which runs through all things and intermingles with the lights of heaven both great and small. . . . (3) No deed is done on earth, god, without your offices, nor is the divine ethereal vault of heaven, nor at sea, save what bad men do in their folly.[166]

The cosmos is a rationally ordered totality. Nonrational beings such as plants and animals necessarily act in accordance with Zeus's *logos*. Rationality confers on human beings the power of assent or choice, which makes possible the folly of bad men. But it also makes it possible for human beings to live in accordance with the divine dictates of the *logos*. "Let us achieve the power of judgement by trusting in which you [Zeus] steer all things with justice, so that by winning honour we may repay you with honour, for ever singing of your works, as it befits mortals to do. For neither men nor gods have any greater privilege than this: to sing for ever in righteousness of the universal law [κοινόν ἀεί νόμον]."[167]

The possession of rationality thus confers on human beings a fundamentally different place in the cosmos and a fundamentally different sense of living in accordance with nature than that proper to animals. The cosmic scheme exhibits a hierarchy of perfection. The world itself is the highest perfection. Because this perfection is fundamentally rational, the Stoics suggest, rational beings are in a better position than nonrational beings to live in complete accordance with nature. Seneca draws out the significance of this notion of hierarchy for the respective places of human beings and animals. "The true Good is not found in trees or in dumb animals; the Good which exists in them is called 'good' only by courtesy. . . . The real Good cannot find a place in dumb animals. . . . Its nature is more blest and is of a higher class." Specifically, the true Good is such that only human beings and gods, in virtue of their rationality, are capable of participating in it. Rational beings are thus more perfect than beings such as trees and animals, which "are perfect only in their particular nature, and not truly perfect, since they lack reason. . . . That alone is perfect which is perfect according to nature as a whole, and nature as a whole is possessed of reason."[168]

The respective senses of living in accordance with nature proper to human beings and animals reflect this notion of a cosmic hierarchy. Lacking rationality, animals are determined by present experience and impulses; "for them it is sufficient to eat and drink and rest and procreate, and whatever else of the things within their own province the animals severally do." For human beings, however, "to whom [God] has made the additional gift of the faculty of understanding, these things are no longer sufficient. . . . For of beings whose constitutions are different, the works and the ends are likewise different."[169] Thus, "to preserve oneself in one's natural constitution" may be sufficient for animals to live in accordance with nature, but for humans to do so there must in addition be "choice fully rationalized and in harmony with nature."[170] For a human being, material welfare is a necessary but not a sufficient condition for living in accordance with nature. Moreover, any being for which bodily preservation is sufficient, is inferior in the order of nature to beings for which physical welfare is only part of living in accordance with nature. Rationality makes human beings capable of moral conduct, and such conduct "is the sole thing that is for its own efficacy and value desirable, whereas none of the primary objects of nature is desirable for its own sake."[171] Plants and animals are counted among such "primary objects," and they exist for the sake of human beings. "With the exception of the world everything else was made for the sake of other things: for example, the crops and fruits which the earth brings forth were made for the sake of animals, and the animals which it brings forth were made for the sake of men. . . . Man himself has come to be in order to contemplate and imitate the world."[172]

On its face, this statement looks indistinguishable from Aristotle's statement in the *Politics* that plants exist for the sake of animals and animals for the sake of human beings. The fundamental difference is evident in Cleanthes' appeal to the *logos* as a universal teleological principle and the accompanying ideal of living in accordance with nature. Chrysippus seizes upon Cleanthes' ideal and intensifies the emphasis on the significance of human beings in the cosmic scheme of things. "Cleanthes takes the nature of the universe alone as that which should be followed," whereas "Chrysippus understands both universal nature and more particularly the nature of man" under the rubric of living in accordance with nature.[173] Chrysippus thereby augments the anthropocentrism of the Stoic position, by assuming that "the rational order of a human being is part of the organization of the universe . . . in the sense that whatever fits with the one fits with the other."[174]

This intensification of anthropocentrism in Stoic thought has its fruition in Seneca's conception of the true good and Epictetus's interpretation of providence [προνοία]. Seneca considers the good for human beings to be that which they alone possess. "If there is no other attribute which belongs peculiarly to man except reason, then reason will be his one peculiar good." Seneca draws out the implications of Chrysippus's focus on the human when he says that reason is "a good that is worth all the rest put together."[175] This makes fully manifest the latent tendency of earlier Stoic thought to place a premium on the distinctiveness of human beings in the cosmic scheme, by asserting the fundamental superiority of virtue, the sole human good, over the goods of all nonrational beings in the cosmos, and by classifying the human good as the only *true* good. "A certain sort of good will be found in a dumb animal, and a certain sort of virtue, and a certain sort of perfection—but neither the Good, nor virtue, nor perfection in the absolute sense. . . . Good can exist only in that which possesses reason."[176]

The Stoic conception of the good for human beings is too complex to be done justice in the context of the present discussion. Several key elements, however, can be identified on the basis of the foregoing remarks. Bodily goods such as physical health are not part of the true good, because these are goods in which animals have a share. The Stoics do not repudiate such goods, but instead treat them as necessary preconditions for the pursuit of virtue, which is the true good. Virtuous conduct or "right action" includes "behaving prudently, moderately, justly, gladly, kindly, and cheerfully, and walking about prudently, and everything which is done in accordance with right reason."[177] At the same time, the good consists not in the acquisition of external goods but in our internal relation to those goods and the process of choosing them. "The good is not in the thing selected, but in the quality of the selection. Our actions are honourable, but not the actual things which we do. . . . If I have the choice, I shall choose health and strength, but . . . the good involved will be my judgment regarding these things, and not the things themselves."[178] The proper end of human conduct "is reasoning well in selections of things which have value in relation to reasoning well."[179] The body, that part of us that makes us like animals, is a mere "cloak" for the soul, and bodily goods such as "health, rest, and freedom from pain" are worth choosing "not because they are goods" but "because they are according to nature and because they will be acquired through the exercise of good judgment on my part."[180]

An important corollary of this emphasis on rational choice is the Stoics' characterization of the passions as threats to reason and hence to living in accordance with nature. The wise man exhibits a tranquility [ἀπάθεια, a state of lacking passion] and detachment [ἀταραξία, lack of disturbance] born of having achieved total independence from contingencies outside his complete control.[181] He has become indifferent to goods of fortune, so that his failure to acquire them cannot affect his happiness.[182] This dual discounting of external goods and the passions leaves the wise man in a position of self-sufficient detachment constitutive of "happiness."

The life of the human being is thus, when well led, at a great remove from the lives of animals. Animals are governed by impulse, confined within the present moment, and oriented exclusively on self-preservation and propagation. Moreover, animals exist entirely for the sake of human beings, who enjoy the luxury of being "indifferent" to the benefits that animals and other external things provide, even though human beings would be incapable of living a life of virtue in the absence of those benefits. This rarefied ideal of human potential is reinforced by the Stoic conception of providence, according to which human beings exist to contemplate God and His works and the world exists to satisfy the material needs of human beings so that they may be free for the task of contemplation. The more human beings free themselves from bodily needs and engage in acts of contemplation, the more they are like gods and less like animals.[183] Like Aristotle, the Stoics see human beings as standing between gods and animals. But the Stoics go an important step further by conceiving of the world (including animals) as existing for the sake of higher, rational beings. "Suppose someone asks for whose sake this vast edifice has been constructed. For the trees and plants, which although not sentient are sustained by nature? No, that is absurd. For the animals? No, it is no more plausible that the gods should have done all this work for the sake of dumb ignorant animals. Then for whose sake will anyone say that the world was created? Presumably for those animate creatures which use reason: that is, for gods and men."[184] As an object of contemplation, the world exists equally for gods and humans. But because the gods are inherently self-sufficient, the world, to the extent that it is an instrumentality available for the satisfaction of physical needs, exists for human beings.[185] From this perspective, animals and other nonrational beings are "destined for service," so humans may be freed for reflection on "the divine administration of the world."[186]

This capacity for reflection places humans in intimate company with the gods, in a rational community in which detached contemplation of the divine *logos* is the highest occupation. This notion of community with the gods comes to fruition in Epictetus's cosmopolitan ideal. Unlike animals, "destined for service," a human being can become "a citizen of the world" by achieving the requisite detachment from passions and worldly goods.[187] In this state, "all things are full of friends, first gods, and then also men, who by nature have been made of one household [ᾠκειωμένον] with one another."[188] A. A. Long notes the anthropocentric orientation of the cosmopolitan ideal. "World citizenship . . . involves the idea that the world is providentially organized to be the proper habitation of human beings, whose possession of divine rationality, construed as the prescriptions of *correct* reasoning, makes them participants with God in a shared law and therefore a shared community, irrespective of their local nationalities and interests."[189] Marcus Aurelius seems to have this sense of community in mind when he says that "the good of a rational being is community [κοινωία]."[190]

"Community" in this connection has a precise sense that distinguishes it from the sense in which animals live in communities. Aristotle and the Stoics freely acknowledge that many animals live in communities. But, with respect to political and moral associations, these thinkers categorically deny that animals have anything in common with human beings. The implications of this denial remain latent in Aristotle's writings because he seems intent on exploring the commonalities between humans and animals as well as the differences between them. The Stoics, on the other hand, by further restricting the notion of animal capacity beyond the limits Aristotle imposes on it, render moot the question of our commonalities with animals. The idea of a fundamental difference between humans and animals becomes axiomatic for the Stoics. This presupposition leads the Stoics, by way of the doctrine of *oikeiosis* or belonging, to the conclusion that human beings owe animals no duties of justice whatsoever.

The doctrine of *oikeiosis* is a doctrine of community with an "all or nothing" approach to the question of community membership: For a given community, a specific set of capacities is necessary and sufficient for community membership, and the nature of those capacities determines the purpose or highest form of action for the community. In the case of human community, the requisite capacity is rationality; the purpose of the community is the shared cultivation of virtue, which includes goods such as reciprocal justice. Ideally, the shared pursuit of virtue will render members of the human community suitable for participation in the cosmopolis of gods and men. The doctrine of *oikeiosis* is intended to show this community to be a fundamentally higher form of community than the form taken by animal associations.

The term "*oikeiosis*" signifies belonging, ownership, or relatedness. That which is "*oikeios*" is one's own, proper or fitting to someone, one's kin or relations, or domestic in the sense of being part of one's household. It signifies appropriation in the sense of making something one's own, or belonging in the sense of two things being naturally suitable or related to one another.[191] As a formal doctrine, *oikeiosis* is a natural process that occurs in stages, and all but the final stage are essentially the same in animals and human beings. The initial stage coincides with the beginning of life. "Immediately upon birth . . . a living creature feels an attachment for itself, and an impulse to preserve itself and to feel affection for its own constitution and for those things which tend to preserve that constitution; while on the other hand it conceives an antipathy to destruction and to those things which appear to threaten destruction."[192] For the Stoics pleasure is not an original motivation, but instead is a consequence or by-product of having acquired things in accordance with (one's) nature. For Chrysippus, living in accordance with nature means in the first instance for an animate being to live in accordance with its original "affection for its own constitution."[193] On the Stoic view, this self-affection is so primary as to precede even the impulse to self-preservation, which derives from it. This first stage of *oikeiosis* is a pure self-relation; the sense of "belonging" here is not social, but instead is a being-at-one with oneself and one's own interest. In the *Discourses*, Epictetus observes that "every living thing is to nothing so devoted [*okeiotai*, appropriated] as to its own interest. Whatever, then, appears to stand in the way of this interest, be it a brother, or father, or child, or loved one, or lover, the being hates, accuses, and curses it. For its nature is to love nothing so much as its own interest."[194]

The second stage of *oikeiosis* involves a broadening of the sphere of belonging to include other members of one's immediate family, specifically in the mode of affection to one's own offspring. "Nature creates in parents an affection for their children . . . it could not be consistent that nature should at once intend offspring to be born and make no provision for that offspring when born to be loved and cherished. Even in the lower animals nature's operation can be clearly discerned; when we observe the labour that they spend on bearing and rearing their young, we seem to be listening to the actual voice of nature."[195] The natural tendency to propagate and to broaden the scope of concern from one's own body to one's progeny unites us with animals so intimately that the self-affection and affection for offspring exhibited by animals serve as a lesson to us about our own nature and what is "appropriate" to it. "The actual voice of nature" speaks to us through the loving devotion that animals show for their young. "A sheep does not abandon its own offspring, nor a wolf: and yet does a man abandon his?"[196] The initial stages of *oikeiosis* hold up animals as a mirror in which we catch sight of ourselves as part of a larger cosmic whole.

These initial stages show that the Stoics conceive of *oikeiosis* in terms of a progression through increasingly inclusive circles of belonging, starting with the individual's self-relation and progressing to a relation to one's offspring as an extension of oneself.[197] The Stoics also recognize that members of certain species of animals form mutually beneficial social groupings that extend beyond immediate filial bonds, and that certain animals engage in cross-species symbiosis.[198] But here the capacity to extend the circles of belonging is sharply circumscribed in animals. Only human beings are able to extend the scope of *oikeiosis* beyond these limits, by employing their powers of reflection to recognize a higher potential hidden in the parental bond exhibited by animals. That bond "is the source to which we trace the origin of the association of the human race in communities. . . . We derive from nature herself the impulse to love those to whom we have given birth. From this impulse is developed the sense of mutual attraction which unites human beings as such; this also is bestowed by nature."[199] The Stoics conceive of the "mutual attraction" at work here to be different in kind than the kinship found in animals. For while there are certainly nonhuman animals that exhibit a sense of cooperation, in the case of human beings "this bond of mutual aid is far more intimate." Ants and bees are unusually social, and yet even they never recognize the common bee-ness or ant-ness of members of other colonies. Human beings, on the other hand, are capable of a "circle" of *oikeiosis* that includes all of humanity. "The outermost and largest circle [of *oikeiosis*], which encompasses all the rest, is that of the whole human race. . . . It is the task of a well tempered man, in his proper treatment of each group, to draw the circles together somehow towards the centre."[200] Unique to human beings, then, is a universal sense of belonging that makes it incumbent on each of us to try to treat strangers far removed from our inner circles as if they were personally related to us.

"The mere fact of their humanity requires that one man should feel another man to be akin to him."[201]

Cicero characterizes the terms of this humanity, which serves in the doctrine of *oikeiosis* as the basis for asserting a key boundary between human beings and animals. "Nature has endowed us with two roles [*personae*], as it were. One of these is universal, from the fact that we share in reason and that status which raises us above the beasts; this is the source of all rectitude and propriety [*decorum*], and the basis of the rational discovery of our proper functions. The second role is the one which has been specifically assigned to individuals."[202] Both *personae* are unique to human beings; both are requisite to the true good of which only human beings are capable.

Our universal persona enables us to care for humanity as a whole and become a citizen of the world. In the doctrine of *oikeiosis*, this capacity is the basis for the categorical exclusion of animals from the sphere of right. In accordance with the priority they place on the soul's virtue over external goods, the Stoics envision an ideal community in which all and only beings capable of virtue are owed duties of justice. Community, in the authentic sense of reciprocal acknowledgment and the shared pursuit of the good life, includes *rational* beings and excludes all others. "It is [the Stoic] doctrine that there can be no question of right [δίκαιον] as between man and the lower animals, because of their unlikeness."[203] Because of this lack of kinship, "men can make use of beasts for their own purposes without injustice."[204] The highest level of *oikeiosis* is reached by progressing through forms of *oikeiosis* exhibited by man and animal alike. But for the Stoics, our capacity to reach a level of *oikeiosis* based in reason signifies that we have no cosmic sense of belonging or relatedness to animals, precisely because animals are nonrational beings.[205] Because animals have no share in justice, nothing we do to them can be construed as an injustice.[206]

In denying a common connection with animals and excluding them from the sphere of justice, Aristotle comes close to saying the same thing as the Stoics. But he stops short of advancing the universal teleology that the Stoics employ to render this principle a pillar of their cosmology. By denying rationality in animals, Aristotle makes the first decisive step toward a categorical exclusion of animals from the sphere of moral consideration. By further restricting the notion of animal capacities and embracing the doctrine of providence, the Stoics complete the trajectory of anthropocentric thinking opened up by Aristotle. The extreme point of this trajectory is the categorical denial of duties of justice toward animals. Whether we owe other sorts of duties to animals, such as benevolence, is left open by the Stoics. The strong implication of their thinking is that we have no direct duties whatsoever toward animals: As sheer instrumentalities, animals have no inherent worth but exist merely to serve us in our ascent to the Olympian heights of the cosmopolis. Sorabji is right that "a crisis was provoked when Aristotle denied reason to animals."[207] The Stoic denial of duties of justice toward animals is the culmination of this crisis.

CLASSICAL DEFENSES OF ANIMALS
Plutarch and Porphyry

The Stoics leave us with a view of animals as possessing merely instrumental value in the cosmos. The experiential capacities of animals are fundamentally inferior to those of rational beings, and as nonrational beings animals exist only for the sake of rational beings. It follows from this cosmic principle that animals are excluded entirely from the sphere of right. When the later Stoic Seneca deplores the delight that people take in watching their dinner of surmullet die at the dinner table, his moral outrage is not due to any transgression against the dignity of surmullets; the canonical Stoic position is that one can do no wrong to an animal. Instead, Seneca's outrage is directed at "the ingenuity of excessive extravagance" exhibited by people who find pleasure in watching the surmullet squirm and change color as life leaves its body.[1]

Plutarch, a generation younger than Seneca, sees such conduct in a different light. Plutarch's Platonism leads him to advocate, at least in all but his later years, a vegetarian diet, on the grounds that "nature disavows our eating of flesh."[2] For Plutarch, what nature demands of us pertains both to our nature and the nature of the animals that many of us are accustomed to eat: our own spiritual purification demands that we avoid the savagery of meat eating, and the experiential capacities of animals are sufficiently rich that the use of animals for food is a patent injustice against animals. Like Seneca, Plutarch deplores the practice of selecting one's dinner from among live animals.[3] But Plutarch launches a vigorous attack on the Stoic conception of animal capacities, and this attack leads him in the direction of concern for the welfare of animals where Seneca's concern is exclusively with the integrity of human beings.[4] He goes to great lengths in outlining the various abilities of animals, which serve for him as clear evidence that animals are rational beings, even if they are not as rational as human beings. His perspective on the capacities of animals is the primary basis for his claim that we owe duties of justice to animals. In direct opposition to the Stoics, Plutarch maintains that animals have worth in their own right, that they were not created for our sake, and that their experiential capacities are sufficiently rich that when we kill them their cries signify that they are "begging for mercy, entreating, seeking justice."[5]

Two centuries later, the Neoplatonist Porphyry picks up the threads of Plutarch's arguments on behalf of animals and incorporates them into his text *On Abstinence from Killing Animals*, written in the last part of the third century AD. But Porphyry's guiding motivations for defending animals and for advocating a vegetarian diet are not identical with Plutarch's. Both thinkers offer a variety of grounds for their views on abstinence from meat, including religious, rational-prudential, and ethical arguments. Plutarch places primary emphasis on the argument that the abilities of animals are the basis of a justice relationship between human beings and animals.[6] Porphyry focuses primarily on a two-pronged religious argument that stresses both kinship with animals and the need to abstain from meat eating for the sake of human spiritual purity. Taken together, Plutarch's and Porphyry's writings on animals contain many if not all of the essential elements of the defenses of animals discussed in later philosophy and in contemporary debates.

Plutarch

Plutarch is best known for his *Lives*, but he also wrote a multivolume *Moralia* that includes three texts on animals: *Whether Land or Sea Animals Are Cleverer*, known as *The Cleverness of Animals*, a dialogue that attacks Stoic views on animals and details the wide range of animal capacities; *Beasts Are Rational*, a dialogue between the Odysseus of book 12 of the *Odyssey* and Gryllus, who, along with Odysseus's other men, has been turned into a pig by Circe and who argues eloquently why it is better to remain a pig rather than to be returned to human form; and *The Eating of Flesh*, a pair of fragmented discourses famous for having inspired Percy Shelley's *A Vindication of Natural Diet* (1813).[7]

In arguing that we owe duties of justice to animals, Plutarch criticizes the Stoic view that animals are fundamentally nonrational. The opening sections of *On the Cleverness of Animals* consist of a discussion between Soclarus, the exponent of the Stoic position, and Autobulus, Plutarch's father and the representative of Plutarch's position. In these sections, Soclarus advances three main claims on behalf of the Stoics. First, Soclarus rehearses the Stoic view that animals "are witless force and violence" (that is, irrational) and therefore "do not explicitly aim at virtue."[8] Second, Soclarus maintains that if all animals possessed reason, there could not be any justice; if we killed animals we would be acting unjustly, but by not killing them for food we would make life impractical or impossible.[9] By respecting the rights of animals we would deprive ourselves of the prerogative to kill them for food, thereby making our own survival difficult if not impossible. Soclarus considers this burden to constitute an injustice to humanity. Third, Soclarus argues that "those who know nothing of right action toward us can receive no wrong from us either."[10] In this connection, Soclarus appeals to Hesiod's story in the *Works and Days*, according to which Zeus gave justice only to human beings, whereas he gave animals license to eat one another.

Autobulus's response to Soclarus in the opening sections of *On the Cleverness of Animals* lays out Plutarch's view that we owe duties of justice toward animals. This view focuses primarily on the question whether it is permissible to kill and eat animals. Autobulus rejects Soclarus's suggestion that hunting is "an innocent spectacle" and characterizes it instead as "savagery."[11] Moreover, human beings first adopted the practice of meat eating not because of hunger "but for pleasure and as an appetizer. Thus the brute and the natural lust to kill in man were fortified and rendered inflexible to pity, while gentleness was, for the most part, deadened."[12] This account recalls the association made by Hesiod and Ovid between meat eating and the advent of violent culture. It likewise implies that our sensitivity to animals could be rekindled through an emulation of the vegetarian practices characteristic of the golden age described by Hesiod and Ovid. In *On the Eating of Flesh*, Plutarch questions the idea that necessity first moved human beings to eat meat. He treats the eating of animal flesh as incomprehensible barbarism. And regardless of humanity's original motivations for eating meat, it is madness today to engage in "the pollution of shedding blood," given the abundance that people enjoy.[13]

Having turned aside the claims that meat eating is necessary and a matter of right for human beings, Autobulus attacks the Stoic account of animal capacities. Animals are both rational and emotional creatures.

In the opening sections of *On the Cleverness of Animals*, Autobulus sketches the basic logic of the attribution of these capacities to animals; the remaining sections of the text present concrete examples of animal intelligence and emotion that recall Aristotle's zoological treatises. Autobulus first disputes the Stoic logic according to which the existence of rationality in human beings necessitates a corresponding irrationality in animals. Even if the existence of rationality makes it necessary that "the irrational must exist as its opposite and counterpart . . . there is a plentiful abundance of the irrational in all things that are not endowed with a soul [ψυχῆς]."[14] As ensouled creatures, animals share in rationality. "It is the nature of every creature with a soul to be sentient [αἰσθητικόν] and imaginative," and "nothing is endowed with sensation which does not also partake of intelligence [σύνεσις]," which includes the capacities for reason [λογισμὸς] and opinion [δόξα].[15] Where the Stoics are content to suppose that animals are able to provide for their well-being simply "by nature," Autobulus considers such a view to beg the question. "The acts of seizing or pursuing that ensue upon the perception of what is destructive or painful, could by no means occur in creatures naturally incapable of some sort of reasoning and judging [κρίνειν], remembering and attending."[16] Pursuit involves directedness, selection, and the ability to recognize and adapt to unanticipated contingencies, and all these capacities are signs of rationality. The ability to desire and seek out an object that is not currently present is a further sign of rationality in animals and an additional argument against the Stoics.[17]

Autobulus's claim that animals are rational enables him to argue against the Stoics that animals experience a range of emotions, much as human beings do. "Many things that animals do and many of their movements . . . show anger or fear or, so help me, envy or jealousy." One consideration in support of this notion is the fact that people who "punish dogs and horses that make mistakes" do so "not idly but to discipline them; they are creating in them through pain a feeling of sorrow, which we call repentance."[18] The latter sections of *On the Cleverness of Animals*, as well as the bulk of *Beasts are Rational* and *On the Eating of Flesh*, are devoted to a discussion of specific examples of intelligence and emotion in animals, and to a defense of the claim that animals exhibit many of the virtues that many people tend to associate exclusively with human beings, such as bravery, ingenuity, and sociability.[19] As a preliminary consideration in favor of this view, Autobulus observes that in ordinary discourse we attribute different degrees of intelligence or courage to animals, but we never do so with regard to trees or vegetables.[20] Even if we surpass animals in intelligence, this does not mean that animals are devoid of it. It simply means that, in comparison with human intelligence, the intellect of animals "is feeble and turbid, like a dim and clouded eye."[21] As a response to the Stoics, this means that animals differ from human beings only in degree, not in kind, with regard to the range of capacities requisite for moral considerability.

At the same time, Autobulus does not place animals on a moral par with human beings. In his concluding remarks in the first part of *On the Cleverness of Animals*, Autobulus states that our duties of justice to animals are not incompatible with the use of animals as beasts of burden. He invokes the name of Pythagoras to lend support to the proposition that "there is no injustice, surely, in punishing and slaying animals that are anti-social and merely injurious, while taming those that are gentle and friendly to man and making them our helpers in the tasks for which they are severally fitted by nature." Autobulus also cites Aeschylus's Prometheus regarding the permissibility of using animals "to serve us and relieve our labours," thus hinting that even a strict Pythagorean need feel no moral scruples about placing animals in the service of human beings.[22] "Nature disavows our eating of flesh," but it does not prohibit the prudent use of animals to satisfy human needs. What it does prohibit is the gratuitous or cruel mistreatment of animals. "Boys throw stones at frogs for fun, but the frogs don't die for 'fun', but in sober earnest. Just so, in hunting and fishing, men amuse themselves with the suffering and death of animals, even tearing some of them piteously from their cubs and nestlings. The fact is that it is not those who make use of animals who do them wrong, but those who use them harmfully and heedlessly and in cruel ways."[23] Implicit in Plutarch's thinking is a sense of "naturalness," according to which animals possess a right to live and prosper. This sense of naturalness confers on human beings the entitlement to use animals and the responsibility to respect the intrinsic worth and prerogatives of animals.

Plutarch builds a case for the worth and natural dignity of animals by amassing evidence of the intelligence, virtues, and emotional capacities of animals. Many of these stories exhibit an excess of undue anthropomorphizing, but this is one of the unavoidable dangers involved in the struggle to capture the senses in which animal experience is comparable to human experience.[24] One thinks immediately of Chrysippus's dog, and the difficulty of accounting for the dog's behavior.[25] Plutarch offers a similar example, also attributed to a Stoic thinker.

Cleanthes, even though he declared that animals are not endowed with reason, says that he witnessed the following spectacle: some ants came to a strange anthill carrying a dead ant. Other ants then emerged from the hill and seemed, as it were, to hold converse with the first party and then went back again. This happened two or three times until at last they brought up a grub to serve as the dead ant's ransom, whereupon the first party picked up the grub, handed over the corpse, and departed.[26]

Taken literally, this story comes across as flat-footedly fanciful. Taken figuratively, it conveys Plutarch's fascination with the elaborate sociability of creatures such as ants and bees, which was well known in the ancient world. Contemporary ethologists have demonstrated that ants do not seem to grasp death as such, but instead treat as "dead" anything they come across that emits oleic acid; they will eject from their domicile even a live ant if it is coated with oleic acid. It seems to me not implausible that Plutarch appreciated the fact that sociability in ants does not involve language and conceptual clarity, and that he used the ant ransom story as a provocation to readers (and Stoics) beset with the prejudice that creatures such as ants are utterly incapable of subjective awareness. Plutarch's interest seems not to be in showing that ants engage in diplomatic negotiations, but rather in opening human beings to the prospect that animal experience is a much richer mystery than the Stoics acknowledge. Plutarch's examples of ingenuity and virtue in animals are best read as invitations to the imagination, not as annals of cognitive ethology.

At the same time, many of the examples cited by Plutarch are relatively straightforward ones of the kind examined increasingly in contemporary cognitive ethology. Like many contemporary ethologists, Plutarch considers it obvious that many animals demonstrate a sense of "purpose and preparation and memory and emotions and care for their young and gratitude for benefits and hostility to what has hurt them." To this list, Plutarch adds the somewhat more controversial capacities for "courage and sociability and continence and magnanimity."[27] The evident purposiveness of animals such as bulls, wild boars, elephants, and lions is clear evidence of animal intelligence. Plutarch cites as an example of purposiveness and sociability in lions the efforts made by younger lions to alleviate the burden on the older lions in the pride while on the hunt.[28] Animals show "cleverness in attacking and catching prey," for example, some fish catch others by extending a tentacle, and the octopus sometimes changes color to lure its prey.[29] Symbiotic relationships between animals, such as the crocodile and the plover or the guide and the whale, are further evidence of the intelligence and purposiveness of animals.[30] Dolphins are cited for the assistance they render to endangered sailors, and it is said of them that they even love music and are "the only creature who loves man for his own sake."[31] Plutarch also details a number of stories about the intelligence of elephants, who are taught to perform complex actions that many human beings would find difficult to master; he tells of one elephant that was observed to practice its lessons alone at night.[32] Another elephant is said to have helped its master in battle, by using its trunk to remove javelins with which the man had been struck.[33] Elephants are cited for their cooperative behavior; for example, when one falls in a pit dug by hunters, the others help it out by filling the hole with debris.[34]

Animals are also credited with a number of other cognitive abilities, such as time-consciousness and mathematical awareness. Oryx and goats perform certain behaviors in synchronization with the rising of the Dog Star that "agrees most exactly with the tables of mathematical calculation."[35] Tunnies "apparently need arithmetic to preserve their consociation and affection for each other. . . . They always form the school into a cube, making it an altogether solid figure with a surface of six equal plane sides."[36] Plutarch tells of a herd of cattle "which have cognition of number and can count. . . . They irrigate the royal park with water raised in buckets by wheels, and the number of bucketfuls is prescribed. For each cow raises one hundred bucketfuls each day, and more you could not get from her, even if you wanted to use force. . . . The cow balks and will not continue when once she has delivered her quota, so accurately does she compute and remember the sum."[37] Other capacities attributed to animals include the use of medicines and surgery, the single-minded pursuit of thieves and murderers by dogs, various forms of deception behavior, and impressive problem-solving abilities (e.g., "Libyan crows . . . when they are thirsty, throw stones into a pot to fill it and raise the water until it is within their reach").[38] One particularly vivid illustration of animal cleverness offered by Plutarch is a story he attributes to Thales about a mule that was used to carry bags of salt across a river. One day the mule

> accidentally stumbled and, since the salt melted away, it was free of its burden when it got up. It recognized the cause of this and bore it in mind. The result was that every time it crossed the river, it would deliberately lower itself and wet the bags, crouching and bending first to one side, then to the other. When Thales heard of this, he gave orders

to fill the bags with wool and sponges instead of salt and to drive the mule laden in this manner. So when it played its customary trick and soaked its burden with water, it came to know that its cunning was unprofitable and thereafter was so attentive and cautious in crossing the river that the water never touched the slightest portion of its burden even by accident.[39]

This example brings together Plutarch's convictions concerning the cognitive abilities of animals and his belief that nature permits the use of animals within certain limits. He decries not Thales's use of the mule, but rather the mule's attempt to shirk his duty to serve Thales. The story also reflects Plutarch's belief that the ability of animals to learn is a clear sign of their intelligence.

Plutarch makes one of his most direct challenges to the Stoics in his attribution of linguistic abilities to animals. Against the Stoic doctrine, first tentatively proposed by Aristotle, that animals possess voice but not articulate speech, Plutarch offers a number of examples to show that animals possess linguistic intelligence. Plutarch shows an awareness of Aristotle's distinction in *History of Animals* between sound, voice, and articulate speech, and he invokes Aristotle's testimony about the nightingale's ability to teach its song to its young as evidence for rational ability in the nightingale.[40] Plutarch proclaims as a fact the possibility broached by Aristotle that some birds are capable of speech. "As for starlings and crows and parrots which learn to talk and afford their teachers so malleable and imitative a vocal current to train and discipline, they seem to me to be champions and advocates of the other animals in their ability to learn, instructing us in some measure that they too are endowed both with rational utterance [λόγος προφορικός] and articulate voice."[41] The implication is that the intelligence of a particular kind of animal is not to be inferred on the basis of its physiology; even animals lacking the tongue requisite for articulate speech are nonetheless linguistic beings. There are fish that "will respond to their own names" and crocodiles that "not only recognize the voice of those who summon them and allow themselves to be handled, but open their mouths to let their teeth be cleaned by hand and wiped with towels."[42] At the same time, feats of intelligence are more easily discerned in animals possessing articulate voice. Plutarch describes "a wonderful prodigy of a jay with a huge range of tones and expressions, which could reproduce the phrases of human speech and the cries of beasts and the sound of instruments—under no compulsion, but making it a rule and a point of honour to let nothing go unrepeated or unimitated." Upon the death of a beloved person, the jay ceased to utter articulate sounds and resumed doing so only after she had taught herself to mimic perfectly the funeral trumpets that had played at the man's burial. One of the conclusions that Plutarch draws from this story is "that self-instruction implies more reason in animals than does readiness to learn from others."[43]

The ascription of reason and linguistic facility to animals strengthens Plutarch's attack on the Stoic view that animals lack emotion. The Stoics maintain that emotion requires the capacity for rational assent, and that animals therefore lack emotional states. Plutarch counters this position by presenting a number of examples of emotion involving intelligence in animals. It is "extraordinary that [the Stoics] obviously fail to note many things that animals do and many of their movements that show anger or fear or, so help me, envy or jealousy."[44] Animals are also capable of love, not only for their own kind but for human beings. For example, an elephant at Alexandria made himself Aristophanes' rival for the affections of a particular flower girl, and a serpent fell in love with an Aetolian woman, took to sleeping with her at night, and became petulant when the woman moved away.[45] Plutarch offers concrete examples of indignation, sympathy, gratitude, and vengefulness in animals.[46] Closely related to these ascriptions of emotion to animals is Plutarch's attribution of particular virtues to animals, again in direct opposition to the Stoics. Animals are capable of vices such as foolishness, intemperance, and even injustice, which for Autobulus is evidence that animals suffer from an imperfection or weakness of reason rather than from an outright lack of it.[47] On the Cleverness of Animals offers instances of probity, courage, wisdom, fidelity, self-control, obedience, and sagacity in animals.[48] The chief aim of Beasts are Rational, the dialogue between Gryllus and Odysseus, is to argue that animals possess virtues such as courage and temperance in a degree superior to that of human beings, and that it is therefore preferable to be an animal—hence the desire of Gryllus and Odysseus's other men to remain pigs rather than to be returned to human form. Gryllus also praises animals for possessing more reasonable desires than human beings, whose desires for luxury and excess are clear signs of their inferiority.[49] Gryllus traces the human practice of meat eating to luxury and cruelty, denying that this practice is based on any real need. Man "pursues illicit food, made unclean by the slaughter [φόνος, murder] of beasts; and he does this in a much more cruel way than the most savage beasts of prey. Blood and gore and raw flesh are the proper diet of kite and wolf and snake; to man they are an appetizer."[50] To Odysseus's suggestion that it is wrong "to grant reason to creatures that have no inherent knowledge of God," Gryllus concludes the dialogue by obliquely gesturing toward the fact that Odysseus's own father was an atheist.[51]

Plutarch's attributions of intelligence, emotion, and virtue to animals converge on his statement in *On the Eating of Flesh* that animals "are entitled by birth and being" to the enjoyment and "duration of life."[52] Dierauer interprets this "polemical antithesis to Stoic anthropocentrism" to mean that animals, on Plutarch's view, exist for their own sake, not for the sake of human beings.[53] This interpretation brings into focus the crux of Plutarch's arguments against meat eating in *On the Eating of Flesh*. He offers the indirect duty argument, familiar from the Epic and pre-Socratic thinkers, that meat eating encourages the desire for war, and he further associates the practice with sexual lust and cruelty toward our fellow human beings.[54] But at a more fundamental level, Plutarch suggests, the problem with meat eating is that it is unjust toward animals, as Pythagoras and Empedocles argue.[55] So it is not surprising that when Plutarch deplores practices such as killing and eating surmullets, his reasoning differs from Seneca's: Whereas for Seneca the problem is human extravagance, for Plutarch it is that surmullets possess worth in their own right "as being friendly and life-saving creatures," and hence merit the "veneration" shown to them by initiates into the Eleusinian mysteries.[56] Plutarch expresses some uncertainty regarding the doctrine of metempsychosis, but argues that we should err on the side of conservatism in this matter. "Which would be the better course: to approve a false suspicion and spare your enemy as a friend, or to disregard an uncertain authority and kill your friend as a foe? The latter course you will declare to be shocking."[57]

Plutarch's ultimate position in *On the Eating of Flesh* is that meat eating is both "useless and unnecessary" and a transgression against our duties of justice toward animals.[58] Plutarch was a vegetarian, although he appears to have abandoned the practice later in life in accordance with a shift in his view regarding duties of justice toward animals. In his *Life of Marcus Cato*, Plutarch writes that "we know that kindness has a wider scope than justice. Law and justice we naturally apply to men alone; but when it comes to beneficence and charity, these often flow in streams from the gentle heart, like water from a copious spring, even down to dumb animals."[59] Helmbold considers the three texts on animals to be nothing more than "a foible of Plutarch's early manhood."[60] Whether or not this is an accurate assessment, these texts offer the first and most spirited defenses of the capacities and moral status of animals to be directed against the Stoics. Many of the arguments presented in them remain forceful in spite of Plutarch's reversal on the question of justice toward animals.

Porphyry

One thinker for whom Plutarch's reversal had no implications for the moral status of animals is Porphyry, whose *On Abstinence from Killing Animals* draws on many of Plutarch's observations and arguments. Like Plutarch, Porphyry advances two main lines of argument in defense of animals, one of them oriented on human spiritual purity and the other on the intrinsic value of animals. A Neoplatonist and student of Plotinus, Porphyry writes *On Abstinence* as a guide to philosophers who seek to minimize the interference of embodiment and earthly existence in the quest for spiritual enlightenment. "The Olympics of the soul" requires that we "put aside everything we have acquired from our mortal nature, and the attraction to those things which itself brought about our descent, and . . . recollect the blessed and eternal being and eagerly return to that which is without color or quality."[61] This rigorous asceticism demands not only a vegetarian lifestyle but also the least possible reliance on any kind of food or drink, as "a far more lethal effect is transmitted to the soul from these than from poisons which are made on purpose to destroy the body."[62] Such asceticism is required not for all people, but only for those interested in the practice of spiritual discipline. Soldiers and athletes, for example, may well need to eat ample amounts of food, and to eat meat in particular, to keep their bodies sufficiently strong and healthy.[63] The argument for religious asceticism outwardly predominates in *On Abstinence*, but Porphyry also presents a number of arguments and considerations whose cumulative force is to rekindle the controversy over the place of animals in the cosmic scheme, and to give new force to Plutarch's suggestion that animals exist for their own sake or at least not for the sake of satisfying human needs.

On Abstinence is addressed to Porphyry's friend Firmus Castricius, who has lapsed from vegetarianism. The text is divided into four books, in the course of which Porphyry attempts to persuade Castricius to return to vegetarian purity. In book 1, Porphyry reviews traditional arguments for and against vegetarianism. In book 2, he criticizes traditional justifications of animal sacrifice, and challenges the traditional assumption that the need for animal sacrifice makes it permissible to eat the sacrificed animals. In book 3, he picks up anti-Stoic themes from Plutarch's writings on animals, and argues for duties of justice toward animals. In book 4, Porphyry argues that spiritual purity demands a vegetarian diet, appealing to a variety of religious traditions as authority for his position. Porphyry demonstrates a significant debt to Plutarch in this text, although there are two key differences. First, Porphyry's arguments are considerably more systematic than Plutarch's often rambling and intuitive suggestions. Second, Porphyry appeals to few of the sorts of concrete examples of animal intelligence and emotion that dominate Plutarch's discussions. The force of these differences is to distill and give prominence to the logic of Porphyry's arguments for vegetarianism, where Plutarch seems to have been concerned primarily with mitigating the influence of Stoic prejudices about the experiential capacities of animals.

Among the traditional defenses of meat eating discussed in book I are the Stoic claim that we owe no duties of justice toward animals; the sorites ("slippery slope") argument that if killing animals is wrong, then killing plants would also be wrong; and the Epicurean claims that meat eating is advantageous, and that we owe no duties to animals because they are incapable of entering into contracts. Porphyry also examines the prejudices of "the ordinary man," which include the idea that eating (cooked) meat is "natural for humans," that "between us and the beasts there is a war which is innate and also just," that the use of animals for food and medicines is good for human health, and that refraining from animal food would lead to animal overpopulation and human starvation.[64] The ordinary man's prejudices also include doubts about the doctrine of metempsychosis, the claim to a right of self-defense against animals, and the sorites argument that if we abstain from meat, then we should likewise abstain from milk, wool, eggs, and honey.[65] The defense of common prejudice concludes with the suggestion that the gods demand that we sacrifice and eat the sacrificed animals, and the observation that the need for animal flesh is so well known that Pythagoras himself trained athletes on meat.[66]

The remainder of book I and the balance of the text of On Abstinence from Killing Animals are devoted to a point-by-point refutation of these claims. Porphyry prefaces his response by noting that he is not arguing for universal vegetarianism. "My discourse will not offer advice to every human way of life: not to those who engage in banausic crafts, nor to athletes of the body, nor to soldiers, nor sailors, nor orators, nor to those who have chosen the life of public affairs, but to the person who has thought about who he is and whence he has come and where he should try to go."[67] Porphyry thus opposes the life of the many, guided by written law, to the life of the few, which is "superior" because it "aims at the unwritten, divine law."[68] Here Porphyry invokes Aristotle's ideal of the contemplative life, which presupposes the satisfaction of bodily needs and values pure contemplation ($\theta\epsilon\omega\rho\iota\alpha$) above all else.[69] The few who pursue such a life will necessarily observe the duties of justice to animals that Porphyry later develops in the text. The many, on the other hand, will not observe these duties—nor are they, apparently, expected to. The prerogatives of the many stand in an irreconcilable tension with the obligations toward animals for which Porphyry builds a case in *On Abstinence*. Porphyry never confronts this tension, but instead focuses his attention primarily on the ideal of life appropriate for elite truth seekers such as his friend Castricius.[70]

One indication of this emphasis in the text is the fact that all the preliminary arguments against meat eating in the second half of book 1 (1.28–1.57) are Neoplatonist in character: they stress the ascendancy of intellect over bodily appetites and passions. An ascetic stance toward food, sex, and other objects of bodily desire facilitates bodily health, which in turn facilitates the health of the spirit and helps us to avert "an Iliad of evils."[71] The primary argument against meat eating offered in this part of the text is that the practice not only is not necessary, but is harmful to our physical health and precludes a proper relation to God.[72] The emulation of God demands the greatest possible renunciation of bodily goods and the greatest possible identification of holiness with the life of pure spirit.[73]

In book 2 of *On Abstinence from Killing Animals*, Porphyry presents a set of arguments against animal sacrifice. Porphyry begins by challenging some common conceptions about killing and eating animals. Killing wild animals that threaten us in no way justifies our eating those animals, any more than killing a human adversary justifies eating him. Moreover, even if we can justify killing wild, injurious animals, this provides no justification for killing domesticated animals. And even if some people, for example, athletes and soldiers, need to eat meat, this does not justify philosophers in eating meat.[74] These three observations form the background of Porphyry's critique of animal sacrifice, a practice in which animals were killed and some of their parts burned in tribute to the gods. Then, typically, the priests and select members of the spiritual elite would

eat the meaty parts of the sacrificed animals. Nussbaum, following Burkert, writes that this practice

> expressed the awe and fear felt by [the] human community towards its
> own murderous possibilities. By ritually acting out the killing of an
> animal, not a human victim, and by surrounding even this killing with
> a ceremony indicative of the killers' innocence and respect for life, the
> sacrificers . . . distance themselves from, and at the same time acknowl-
> edge, the possibilities for human slaughter that reside in human nature.
> By expressing their ambivalence and remorse concerning even an animal
> killing, by humanizing the animal and showing a regard for its 'will', the
> sacrificers put away from themselves the worst possibility: that they will
> kill human beings, and kill without pity, becoming themselves bestial.
> Their ritual actions assert their humanity and at the same time their fear
> of ceasing to be human.[75]

The "regard" for the animal's will was exhibited by obtaining its "consent" to be sacrificed, which was accomplished "by pouring water on it
to make it shake its head."[76] Porphyry's critique of animal sacrifice makes
it clear that he considers such expressions of concern for animals to be
inauthentic. Porphyry offers a history of the practice of sacrifice that
recalls the "golden age" stories told by Hesiod and Ovid. The earliest
sacrifices were of plants. Subsequently, sacrifices came to include trees,
grain, cakes, flowers, wine, honey, and olive oil.[77] Porphyry invokes the
authority of the Peripatetic Theophrastus in arguing that the advent of
blood sacrifices was savagery against which the gods retaliated by making
some people atheists and other people "mind-forsaken rather than
godforsaken, because they think the gods are base, no better than us in
nature."[78] The gods would never sanction the sacrifice of animals. "All
the reasons" given for animal sacrifice "are full of unholy explanations."[79]

Porphyry introduces his discussion of Theophrastus's critique of
animal sacrifice by arguing that people tend to sacrifice what they are going
to eat anyway, and that doing so can hardly be classified as an act of piety.
People determine what they will sacrifice on the basis of their material
needs, not on the basis of reverence. Porphyry then presents Theophrastus's argument that we should sacrifice crops rather than animals to the
gods.[80] Animals are valued by the gods and are not the possession of
human beings. We may properly sacrifice only what is ours. Of the things
we have been given by the gods, crops are the most valuable; hence we
should sacrifice these to the gods. Doing so causes no one any harm, since

harvesting fruit is not against the plant's will, nor does it kill the plant. (Porphyry does not address the case of plants that we do kill when we harvest them.) An additional consideration in favor of plant sacrifice is that the gods favor sacrifices of what is inexpensive and easy to get; animals are expensive and difficult to obtain, hence the gods prefer that we sacrifice plants.[81]

Porphyry presents an additional argument against animal sacrifice in book 2 that recalls Pythagoras and Empedocles. He argues that "when friendship and perception of kinship ruled everything, no one killed any creature, because people thought the other animals were related [oikeios] to them."[82] Even if we can justify killing harmful animals, it is unjust to kill other animals. The fact that we sacrifice tame animals makes the conclusion unavoidable that animal sacrifice is inherently unjust. Porphyry notes that the Pythagoreans were vegetarians, and that they ate only animals sacrificed to the gods. Porphyry goes even further than the Pythagoreans, maintaining that "the altars of the gods should not be stained with murder, and people should not eat such food, any more than their own bodies."[83]

His position regarding animal sacrifice has two basic components. First, we should not sacrifice animals, since they are beloved to the gods and are our kin. "Earth is the common hearth of gods and people, and everyone, leaning upon her as on a nurse and mother, must hymn her and love her as the one who gave us birth."[84] We should abstain from eating animals, and we should sacrifice to the gods what we do eat. Second, if we do sacrifice animals, we must nonetheless not eat them. Not only does the sacrifice of animals have no connection with eating them, but we will treat other human beings better if we do not eat meat.[85] The prohibition on animal sacrifice is primary here. The only gods who would demand animal sacrifices are bad *daimones*, who are responsible for all earthly suffering. Our goal should instead be to emulate the good *daimones*, who exercise self-control guided by reason.[86]

This association of divinity with reason is the background to Porphyry's argument in book 3 that we owe duties of justice to animals. Porphyry invokes the authority of Pythagoras and Plutarch in developing his argument, which he directs explicitly against the Stoic view of animal capacities. "Every soul is rational in that it shares in perception and memory. Once that is proved, we can reasonably . . . extend justice to every animal."[87] The Stoics are led by "self-love" to maintain that "all the other animals without exception are non-rational, meaning by 'non-rationality' complete deprivation of *logos*. But if we must speak the truth, not only can *logos* be seen in absolutely all animals, but in many of them it has the groundwork for being perfected."[88] Porphyry argues that animals possess *logos* in two fundamental senses. First, every animal with voice is capable of *logos* in the sense of language. Even if we do not understand an animal's language, this does not mean that the animal has no language, any more than a Greek's inability to understand "Indian" means that Indians are incapable of language.[89] Moreover, "there are those who are said to have heard and understood the speech of animals," and some animals evidently learn Greek.[90] The fact that many animals come when we call them, that many are calmed by music, and that some animals teach their young, are all marshaled as evidence of linguistic ability in animals.

The second form of *logos* in animals is internal. The perceptions and passions of animals are very much like those of human beings. Animals possess a rational soul and memory, and are capable of wisdom as well as virtue and vice.[91] Porphyry does not offer the sorts of detailed examples of these capacities that Plutarch offers; but he does note, for example, that animals do not exhibit the kind of sexual promiscuity common in drunken human beings, that certain animals exhibit "marital chastity," that many of them suffer if deprived of society with human beings, and that animals exhibit hostility toward human beings only when forced to do so by dire necessity.[92] Animals are also able to pursue useful things and avoid harmful ones, which is further evidence that they possess reason, judgment, memory, and perception.[93] This, in turn, means that animals belong to the sphere of belonging within which justice prevails. "Perception is the origin of all appropriation [*oikeiosis*] and alienation, and the followers of Zeno make appropriation the origin of justice."[94] Given the evident capacity of animals for both internal and external *logos* (for inner experience and linguistic expression), to exclude them from the sphere of right would be self-serving and indefensible.

Equally self-serving and indefensible is Chrysippus's claim "that the gods made us for themselves and for each other, and the animals for us." Porphyry demonstrates the absurdity of Chrysippus's logic by drawing out some of its more peculiar implications. If, as Carneades says, "everything nature brings into being benefits when it achieves the end for which it is naturally suited and came into being," and if "the pig is brought into being by nature to be slaughtered and devoured," then "in experiencing this it achieves the end for which it is naturally suited, and it benefits."[95] And even if we are content with this view of the *telos* of the pig, there are many other animals, such as "flies, mosquitoes, bats, dung-beetles, scorpions, and vipers," which seem not to be useful to human beings at all.[96] Yet another peculiar implication of Chrysippus's logic is that human beings could be said to exist for the sake of predatory animals. Such animals may commit an injustice when they kill us, but "need and hunger drives them to this," whereas "we murder most animals out of aggression, or for luxury, or often for fun in theatres and hunting."[97]

This is not to say, however, that animals are perfectly virtuous. Porphyry acknowledges that the rationality of animals is imperfect and lacks the benefit of care and education, hence "no animal has a manifest aim for, or progress in, or desire for, virtue." But animals nonetheless exhibit passions and particular virtues and vices. Porphyry follows Plutarch in noting that we discipline horses and dogs in order to make them repentant, and he argues that animals exhibit virtues such as courage and vices such as cowardice and malice.[98] He also follows Plutarch in observing that many animals surpass human beings in capacities such as strength and swiftness, even if animals "have weak and turbid *logos*, like blurred and disturbed vision."[99] And like Plutarch, Porphyry maintains that it is permissible to kill animals that threaten us, but that we nonetheless have duties of justice toward harmless animals.[100] Our relationship with animals "is not severed because some of them are savage," any more than our relationship with our fellow human beings is destroyed by the savagery of some.[101] Acknowledging that animals are part of our *oikeiosis* (our sphere of relatedness or belonging) is not inimical to justice. What *is* inimical to justice is the exclusion of animals from the sphere of right for the sake of human pleasure.[102]

In book 4 of *On Abstinence*, Porphyry returns to the anthropocentric argument of book I that meat eating has bad consequences for the health of the human soul and body. Meat eating is "motivated by lack of control and licentiousness." Those who claim that meat eating is advantageous for human beings are "corrupted by pleasure" and fail to acknowledge that the first human civilization was a golden age in which peace prevailed both among human beings and between humans and animals.[103] Porphyry characterizes this golden age in terms familiar from Hesiod and Ovid: There was abundance, leisure, health, friendship, and a complete absence of war. An increase in human desire led to "excess possessions and laying hands on animals," which in turn led to competition and war.[104] The ensuing discussion suggests that both the elimination of luxury from life and the return to a peaceful relationship with animals would facilitate human efforts to become temperate and just. Porphyry notes that when Lycurgus minimized Sparta's dependence on animal food and "expelled luxury," the people became "braver and more temperate and more concerned for the right than those who came from other societies and who were corrupted in soul and body. It is clear that complete abstinence is appropriate to such a society, whereas [meat] eating is appropriate to corrupt societies."[105]

Porphyry then appeals to the examples set by the Egyptians, the Jews, and several other societies that practiced abstinence or near-abstinence from meat eating and exhibited exemplary self-control and spiritual purity. He lauds the temple discipline in Egypt, which permitted the priests to devote "their whole life to contemplation and vision of things divine." This vision "puts one beyond all greed, restrains the passions, and makes life alert for understanding."[106] The requisite discipline included an extremely frugal diet, which for many of the priests included complete abstinence from animal food, for the Egyptians "realised that divinity is present not only in human beings, nor does soul dwell only in humans upon the earth, but it is almost the same soul which is present in all animals. For this reason they used every animal to represent the gods."[107] They also recognize that "certain animals are dearer to some of the gods than humans are," and "have philosophic interpretations . . . of every animal, so it is from intelligence and great wisdom about the gods that they have come to reverence for animals." Porphyry also notes that the Egyptians' reverence for animals is based on the belief that the souls of animals transcend their bodies and are capable of oracular powers as well as "everything that a human can do when liberated."[108] In a similar vein, Porphyry says that the Persian Magi believe in metempsychosis, but he says nothing to indicate whether he subscribes to this doctrine or not.[109]

After discussing the virtues of societies such as the Essene Jews, the Persians, and the Indian Brahmins, all of which observed strict dietary discipline including abstinence from many if not all animals, Porphyry concludes On Abstinence by relating the virtues of priestly discipline to the lives of ordinary people. Any "fully law-abiding and pious man should abstain from all [animal foods]; for if in particular cases some people abstain in piety from some foods, the person who is pious in all cases will abstain from all."[110] Some peoples, such as the nomads, are "constrained by necessity" to eat animal flesh, but the practice must be avoided at all costs because it "surely brings contamination and a stain on our soul."[111]

We should emulate neither those who eat animal flesh out of necessity nor those who do so out of savagery, "but those who are pious and inclined towards the gods."[112] This leaves people such as soldiers, who may need to eat meat, in the uncomfortable position of having to live an impious and impure life in order to discharge their duties to society. Instead of taking a hard line and demanding that society as a whole abstain from meat, Porphyry sets up total abstinence as an ideal and allows for exceptions in the case of need. He never addresses the possibility that the idea of need may involve some flexibility, for example, that soldiers might in fact not suffer from a vegetarian diet. Instead, true to his Neoplatonist convictions, Porphyry identifies a life of piety with pure contemplation, and he says that contemplation is facilitated when we minimize the influence of bodily needs and passions in our lives. Not only is nearness to the gods facilitated when we abstain from animal food, but in the ideal case we would not eat anything at all.[113] "Abstinence, both from meat and from contact with bodily pleasures and actions, is more appropriate for moral people."[114] Our fall from the golden age leaves us in a situation in which not every member of society can live a moral life. This life seems to be reserved for the few who can detach themselves from the demands of the practical realm, and whose security can be provided for by other members of society, much as ascetics in Jainism are "*utterly* dependent on the laity" but nonetheless set an inspirational example of piety to others in the society.[115]

THE STATUS OF ANIMALS
IN MEDIEVAL CHRISTIANITY

The Biblical Background and Contemporary Debates

In 1967 Lynn White initiated a firestorm of controversy when he published "The Historical Roots of Our Ecological Crisis." In that essay, White argues that the book of Genesis sanctions the wholesale exploitation of nature for the sake of human welfare. All of creation was made "explicitly for man's benefit and rule." Building on this anthropocentric commitment, Christianity "not only established a dualism of man and nature but also insisted that it is God's will that man exploit nature for his proper ends. . . . By destroying pagan animism, Christianity made it possible to exploit nature in a mood of indifference to the feelings of natural objects."[1] The "voluntarist orientation" of the Latin Church, in contrast with the "intellectualist orientation" of the Eastern Church, grounds salvation not in resignation and spiritual illumination but rather in active self-assertion in the name of God.[2] One corollary to this call to action is the conceptualization of nature as inert matter that may be used to satisfy human desires. "To a Christian a tree can be no more than a physical fact. The whole concept of the sacred grove is alien to Christianity and to the ethos of the West."[3]

John Passmore, writing several years after White, introduces several key nuances into this account of the appropriation of Genesis by Christianity. Prior to the Fall, the earth was subject to human dominion but was not yet reduced to the status of a mere physical fact. In Genesis 1:26 and 1:28 God grants Adam "dominion" over the earth; but in 1:29 (cf. 2:9 and 2:16) God assigns Adam a vegetarian diet, thereby suggesting that human dominion is not to be indifferent to animals but instead is to take the form of stewardship. This is the image of human-animal relations that Milton depicts in book 4 of *Paradise Lost*:

> More grateful, to their Supper Fruits they fell,
> Nectarine Fruits which the compliant boughes
> Yielded them, side-long as they sat recline
>
> . . . .
>
> . . . About them frisking playd
> All Beasts of th' Earth.[4]

The prelapsarian condition is one of peaceful coexistence with animals and all of nature. "After the Fall, in contrast, [human beings] had no choice but to play the tyrant, not only over animals but over plants and soil."[5] The story of the Fall in Genesis anticipates the golden age stories told by ancients such as Hesiod and Ovid: Human beings first found themselves in a pristine primeval state, a vegetarian one at that, and only subsequently lapsed into a state of barbarism that included cruelty to human and animal alike. At the same time, if Christianity views the postlapsarian human-animal relation as one of tyranny, the same does not hold for Jewish tradition. Passmore notes that Jewish philosophers such as Maimonides explicitly reject the notion that sublunary beings exist for the sake of humans. Passmore suggests that the Christian idea of human beings "as nature's absolute master" derives not from Hebrew teaching but rather from the Greeks, particularly from Aristotle and the Stoics.[6]

The controversy sparked by the publication of White's essay is focused on the question whether Christianity has the potential to reconceive the human-animal relationship in terms of stewardship rather than tyranny. Can Christianity make a fundamental contribution to contemporary efforts to address our environmental crisis? More specifically, do the terms of Christianity leave room for a sense of kinship with animals, or do they consign animals and the rest of nature to the status of instrumentalities for the gratification of human desires? The answers to these questions depend both on the interpretation of Scripture and on the question whether Christianity is a fixed set of canonical doctrines or a living phenomenon that can change with the times. The controversy over the human-animal relationship in Christianity devolves upon the interpretation of key texts in the Pentateuch, particularly of passages from Genesis. This is amply attested to by the fact that virtually all the key patristic and scholastic figures wrote commentaries or homilies on the book of Genesis. Whether these interpretations of Genesis are authoritative for establishing "Christian doctrine" depends on whether we consider Christianity, and hence the interpretation of Scripture, to be capable of historical evolution.

Two examples from the nineteenth century illustrate what is at stake in this question. First, during the papacy of Pius IX (1846–1878), the Vatican staunchly opposed the establishment of a Society for the Prevention of Cruelty to Animals in Rome. (In England, such a society had been established in 1824.) Second, in 1901, the English Jesuit Joseph Rickaby published the influential *Moral Philosophy*, in which he argued not only that animals can have no rights, but also that human beings have no greater duties of charity toward animals than we have toward "stocks and stones"— which is to say that we have no such duties whatsoever.[7] White argues that that this view toward animals is canonical and inalterable in Christianity. In recent years, however, a number of Christian environmentalists have challenged this position on the grounds that it fails to acknowledge the historicity of Christian tradition.

> It is a familiar fact that interpretations of the Bible tend to harden in the shape of existing social practices, whereas conscientious reappraisals of the status quo often suggest the arbitrariness of such interpretations and the plausibility of quite different ones. Thus animal liberation has been impeded by the Bible in much the same way that the abolition of slavery and the equalization of women's rights have been impeded by it, but in the long run all of those liberation movements have assisted Christians to read the Bible with more acute moral vision, and to draw from it inspiration to assist those very movements. Our ways of living and our ways of reading influence one another, reciprocally and progressively, for good or ill.[8]

This call to revise our interpretation of Scripture in accordance with contemporary moral sensibilities is at once liberating and dangerous. The goal is to disburden us of cultural prejudices that influenced church fathers such as Saint Augustine, who argued categorically that we have no moral obligations whatsoever to animals; at the same time, we are to loosen the standards for our own interpretation of Scripture, so that radically revisionist readings become possible. But this loosening threatens to undermine the very notion of a scriptural tradition by sanctioning the recreation of that tradition in our own image. By following the terms of such revisionism, we might be able to ignore or explain away, for example, God's approval of Noah's animal sacrifice in Genesis 8:20–

21, or God's transformation of our relation to animals from stewardship to abject subjection in Genesis 9, in which God ordains that animals will henceforth have "fear and dread" of human beings and in which he sanctions meat eating.

Passages such as these make it very difficult to substantiate the claim that Christianity contains the elements of an animal-friendly environmental ethic. The New Testament contains little that stands in conflict with Genesis on the question of postlapsarian human-animal relations. More typical is Paul's interpretation of Deuteronomy 25:4, in which it is written that "You are not to muzzle an ox while it is treading out the grain": Paul asks rhetorically, "Do you suppose God's concern is with oxen? Must not the saying refer to us? Of course it does: the ploughman should plough and the thresher should thresh in hope of sharing the produce" (1 Corinthians 9:9–10). But there are other biblical passages that lend at least some support to the ideal of compassion toward animals. In Genesis, after sanctioning animal sacrifice and a carnivorous diet, God states that his covenant with Noah is also a covenant "with every living creature that is with you, all birds and cattle, all the animals with you on earth, all that have come out of the ark" (Genesis 9:10). But this covenant signifies only that God will never again subject the earth to wholesale devastation as he had done in the flood. On the question of animal sacrifice, Scripture is not consistent. Isaiah 1:11 and 66:3 repudiate the practice. Hebrews 10:8–10 suggests that animal sacrifice is no longer necessary because "we have been consecrated, through the offering of the body of Jesus Christ once and for all." And Job 39 challenges the assumption that all animals were made for the sake of human beings.

What emerges from this brief survey is the fact that the Bible expresses conflicting views regarding human obligations toward animals. What also begins to emerge is the fact that even the most animal-friendly passages of Scripture stop far short of placing animals on anything like a moral par with human beings. Even when interpreted literally, passages such as Deuteronomy 22:6–7 ("When you come upon a bird's nest by the road, in a tree or on the ground, with fledglings or eggs in it and the mother bird on the nest, do not take both mother and young. Let the mother bird go free, and take only the young; then you will prosper and enjoy long life") do not establish moral obligations toward animals so much as obligations to live our lives in ways that promote longevity and merit God's favor. Indeed, the most influential interpretations of such passages in the Middle Ages bear the stamp of a rigid anthropocentrism. Efforts in the contemporary Christian community to establish an ethic of compassion toward animals must therefore focus on scriptural passages that were relatively uninfluential in the Christian Middle Ages. Such passages are found predominantly in the Torah rather than in the New Testament; this is why efforts in the contemporary Christian community place emphasis primarily on the Old Law rather than on the New, and on the Yahwist passages of Genesis rather than on the Elohist and Priestly passages.[9]

Narrow focus on these sorts of passages can help contemporary Christians in the endeavor to establish ethical obligations toward animals. But the price of such a narrow focus is high: It demands that they disregard the wealth of scriptural emphasis on human life and the wealth of emphasis in the New Testament on spiritual inwardness and the salvation of human beings.[10] Notwithstanding Paul's suggestion that "the created universe is waiting with eager expectation for God's sons to be revealed" and hopes "to be freed from the shackles of mortality" (Romans 8:18–21), the overwhelming focus of the New Testament is the path of inwardness to redemption, a path that is denied to animals because of their lack of understanding. In this regard, the New Testament reflects the influence of Stoic thought, which denies intellect to animals and argues that animals were created for the sake of human beings.

This strain of thinking is predominant not only in Scripture, but also in patristic and scholastic thought. Saint Augustine and Saint Thomas Aquinas are categorical in their subordination of animals to the interests of human beings and in their denial of direct moral obligations to animals. These convictions are maintained in the fourth century by Basil, Origen, and John Chrysostom, and they persist virtually unmodified in the Renaissance thought of Martin Luther. Even such putatively heterodox figures as Saint Francis do not advance an unqualified defense of animals. The writings of these authors merit close examination, because they pose a serious challenge to anyone who would seek to build a robust sense of moral obligations toward animals on the foundation of orthodox Christian tradition.

Saint Augustine

Writing in the fourth century, Augustine articulates a Christian dualism according to which spiritual beings are fundamentally superior to physical ones. "Among living things, the sentient are placed above those which do not have sensation: animals above trees, for instance. And, among the sentient, the intelligent are placed above those which do not have intelligence; men, for example, are above cattle. And among the intelligent, the immortal, such as the angels, are placed above the mortal, such as men."[11] Augustine's principle for ordering the hierarchy of natural beings is relative proximity to God: the more rational and less dominated by bodily impulses a being is, the closer it is to the divine. Rationality is the ability to perceive the truth, which is ever unchanging. Beings that are bodily in nature perceive only changing things, hence "no criterion for truth [resides] in the senses."[12] Rational beings enjoy "the inner light of Truth," which grants them contact with "the things themselves made manifest within when God discloses them."[13] "Whoever has understanding" is capable of grasping this truth, which "is God himself"; thus only beings possessing the faculties of faith and understanding are capable of attaining "the highest good."[14] At stake in human life is understanding, which is "the recompense of faith."[15]

Uniting this ideal of inwardness with the Greco-Roman orientation on reason and the Stoic conception of providence, Augustine develops a view according to which only human beings are subject to salvation and all other earthly beings were created to serve us in our quest for redemption. As beings limited to sense experience, "dumb animals" fundamentally lack "the power of reason" and hence are denied the prospect of participating in God's truth.[16] Animals are governed by "the pursuit of physical pleasures and the avoidance of pains," whereas human beings can render themselves "ordered" when "these impulses of the soul are ruled by reason."[17] For Augustine, this is sufficient for concluding that "human beings are superior [to animals] in a certain respect, and that animals are part of the "earth and water and sky" that God has given us "to serve us in our weakness."[18] Purely earthly beings, including animals, are "the lowest part of the world," so low that they "cannot be either blessed or wretched."[19] "Because there is in man a rational soul, he subordinates all that he has in common with the beasts to the peace of that rational soul."[20] This subordination of "beasts" to rational souls is ordained by divine law, according to which "every soul is better than every body."[21]

The essential superiority of human beings over animals is a corollary of Augustine's conviction that rational beings are closer to God than merely corporeal ones. His belief that animals "cannot be either blessed or wretched" is, however, not without qualification. All of God's creations reflect his divine beauty and participate in his goodness, even those creatures such as animals, which rank lowest on the scale of perfection.[22] One constant refrain in the *Confessions* is the wisdom of Romans 1:20 that we know God through his creatures.[23] The more we contemplate earthly creation, the more we learn about God's eternal truth. To this extent, one function of animals is to bring us closer to God. "The sight of [small animals]," for example, "inspires me to praise you for the wonders of your creation and the order in which you have disposed all things."[24]

At the same time, Augustine's views on animals are influenced by his view of earthly existence as fallen and his orientation on salvation as the end of human existence. Augustine does not advocate the unbridled exploitation of nature for the sake of gratifying human desires, but instead tempers his belief in human superiority with a *contemptus mundi* (contempt for the world) that is to keep our aspirations for earthly existence in check. Our time on earth is merely "a long, unbroken period of trial" that stands between us and the prospect of eternal salvation; earthly goods are to be pursued not for their own sake, nor simply for the sake of our earthly estate, but only for the sake of God.[25] When we give primacy to our private good in the realm of changeable things, we turn away from God and toward evil.[26] In turning away from God, we succumb to "the snare of concupiscence."[27] In turning back toward God, we acknowledge God's command "to control our bodily desires" and properly subjugate our bodily drives, which place us on a par with mere "beasts," to our recognition of the divine law.[28] In this connection, it is important to note that limits on our exploitation of animals are intended not to benefit animals but rather human beings: The problem with the lust for mastery in earthly affairs is not that it does violence to animals and other sublunary beings, but that he who "is avid for mastery surpasses even the beasts in the vices of cruelty and luxury."[29] Augustine's concern here is with the corruption of the human soul, not with the fortunes of beings such as animals. The problem with the unbridled will to mastery is not that it harms animals, but that it is born of "the intoxication which causes the world to forget you, its Creator, and to love the things you have created instead of loving you, because the world is drunk with the invisible wine of its own perverted, earthbound will."[30]

Augustine's views on human dominion over animals must be understood in these squarely anthropocentric terms. Augustine embraces the Stoic principle that all earthly beings exist for the sake of human beings. "Everything which is made is made for man's use, because reason, which is given to man, uses all things by judging all things"; the end or goal of all such use is the facilitating of our "enjoyment of God," of which animals are incapable.[31] Our spiritual nature renders us fundamentally superior to the corporeal nature of animals; this superiority grants us license to use animals in any way we choose, provided that our use is in accordance with the aim of glorifying God. Augustine cites Genesis 1:26 in support of the proposition that God granted human beings "lordship over . . . irrational creatures . . . man over the beasts."[32] The terms of this lordship include license to kill animals as we see fit. The commandment against killing does not "apply to the non-rational animals which fly, swim, walk or crawl, for these do not share [sociantur] the use of reason with us. It is not given to them to have it in common with us; and, for this reason, by the most just ordinance of their Creator, both their life and their death are subject to our needs."[33] "To refrain from the killing of animals and the destroying of plants is the height of superstition . . . there are no common rights between us and the beasts and trees."[34]

One corollary of this exclusion of animals from the sphere of right is that it is entirely permissible to eat meat, as is clear from the examples of Noah, Elias, and John the Baptist.[35] Moreover, the fact that animals suffer when we kill them is no cause for concern—again, because animals do not share in community with us: "We can perceive by their cries that animals die in pain, although we make little of this since the beast, lacking a rational soul, is not related to us by a common nature."[36] One may kill animals with impunity, subject to the condition that our killing is consonant with the ideal of earthly dominion prescribed by God in Genesis. If our infliction of suffering on animals is not to be gratuitous, we may nonetheless satisfy ourselves that their suffering and death are entirely in accordance with the divine law, as is the husbanding of animals for the sake of securing our material welfare.

Origen, Basil, John Chrysostom

Augustine's views on the metaphysical and moral status of animals are representative of the prevailing commitments in the Christian community in the third and fourth centuries. In Augustine's writings we find the distillation of convictions expressed in homilies on Genesis delivered in the third century by Origen and in the fourth century by Basil the Great and Saint John Chrysostom. If the Christian conception of divine providence is overtly the guiding principle in these homilies, the implicit subtext is the Stoic conception of providence, according to which earthly beings exist for the sake of human beings and are incapable of active

community with the divine. One does find proponents of a more edified view of the moral status of animals in the Middle Ages; for example,
in the seventh century Isaac the Syrian maintained that duties of charity
extend not only to the human community but to animals as well; but such
views are rare, heterodox, and uninfluential in the medieval Christian
world.[37]

Origen, who died one hundred years before the birth of Augustine,
develops a position on the human-animal relation that paves the way for
the views articulated by the Bishop of Hippo. Against Celsus, who maintains that "everything was made just as much for the irrational animals
as for men," Origen argues that "God made all things for man."[38] Origen's
argument closely follows the terms of the Stoic conception of providence.
Among created beings, only humans are rational. "He who looks from
heaven upon the irrational animals, even though their bodies may be
large, will not see any origin for their impulses other than irrationality,
so to speak. But when he looks at the rational beings, he will see reason
which is common to men and to divine and heavenly beings. . . . This
explains why he is said to have been made in the image of God; for the
image of the supreme God is His reason (Logos)."[39] In comparison with
human beings, even unusually social beings such as bees and ants "do not
act from reason."[40] All irrational beings, including animals, have been
created by God "to serve the rational being and his natural intelligence."[41]

In his providence, God "takes particular care of every rational being."[42] God gave us dominion over animals for two reasons: to satisfy our
material needs, and to serve as reminders of our inner struggle with
concupiscence. Animal husbandry, for example, the use of dogs to herd
flocks and the use of oxen to till fields, serves our bodily needs.[43] More
importantly, animals serve our spiritual needs as well. In *Homilies on Genesis*,
Origen states that this is the real meaning of human dominion in Genesis.
The creation of animals represents "the impulses of our outer man, that
is, of our carnal and earthly man."[44] But to be created in God's image is
not to be corporeal, like animals; instead, "it is our inner man, invisible, incorporeal, incorruptible, and immortal which is made 'according to the image of God.'"[45] To live a proper Christian life is to subjugate our carnal side to our inward relation to God. Our dominion over
animals has an allegorical as well as a literal meaning: It signifies the need
to subjugate the things "which are brought forth from bodily desires and
the impulses of the flesh" to "the things which proceed from the inclination of the soul and the thought of the heart."[46] Our dominion over

animals is symbolic of our soul's dominion over our bodily drives. Moreover, exercise of dominion over animals facilitates the development of
our virtues; for example, wild animals such as "lions and bears, leopards
and boars . . . are said to have been given to us in order to exercise the
seeds of courage in us."[47]

Basil the Great, bishop of Caesarea and brother of Gregory of Nyssa,
provides a comparable interpretation of the human-animal relationship
in his *Homilies on the Hexaemeron*. Basil composed the *Homilies* in 370, seven-
teen years before Augustine began writing the *Confessions*. They are "the
earliest work devoted exclusively to an interpretation of the six days of
Creation" to survive the Middle Ages."[48] Their central purpose is "to in-
struct their readers, inspire them with pride in their faith, give them love
of their Creator, bind them to their duty, and illustrate, with picturesque
examples, the obligations of the Christian life: in a word, to work toward
the edification of the Church."[49] As in Origen, this mission of edification is one in which animals play a merely instrumental role.

Basil reasserts the conviction that human beings are rational and
animals "irrational" and argues on the basis of this distinction that human beings are fundamentally superior to animals. Animals are "endowed
with neither reason [λόγου] nor voice [φωνῆς]."[50] There is a hierarchy
among animals, such that land animals behave "as if their life were more
perfect" than that of sea creatures; and yet "even land animals are irrational."[51] Land animals differ from sea creatures in possessing "a soul
governing [their] bodies"; but this soul, in contrast with the immortal
soul of rational human beings, is merely "blood . . . something earthly.
. . . Do not think that it is antecedent to the essence of their bodies or
that it remains after the dissolution of the flesh."[52] This fundamental
distinction between human and animal souls brings with it a denial of the
Pythagorean-Platonic doctrine of metempsychosis: "Shun the idle talk
of the proud philosophers, who are not ashamed to regard their own soul
and that of dogs as similar, who say that they were at some time women,
or bushes, or fish of the sea."[53]

The rationality and immortality of the human soul, its transcendence
over the body, grants us the ability to "have forethought for the salvation
of our souls." This capacity is unique to humans among created beings,
inasmuch as animals are irrational and act strictly in accordance with
"natural and inborn" forces.[54] God "has placed all things under us because we have been made in the image of the Creator"; a clear example
of our superiority over animals is the fact that we are able to subdue even

a large and powerful animal such as an elephant.[55] Not only are we entitled to secure our physical existence "through the service of animals," but we are able to develop our wisdom by observing the examples of animals.[56] The struggle of animals to preserve their lives teaches us about virtues such as courage and vices such as deceit.[57] By observing "much wickedness and plotting in weak animals," we learn "to avoid imitating the evildoers."[58] By "listen[ing] to the fish," we learn the importance of following the law and avoiding idleness.[59] "Nature itself," even more than "the teaching of men," reveals to us "natural virtues" such as self-control, justice, courage, and prudence. And the prognosticating abilities of animals, for example, as they prepare for the coming winter, teach us that "we should not cling to our present life but should preserve all our zeal for future time."[60] The lives of animals, in short, possess no value in themselves, but instead "are a proof of our faith."[61]

The legacy of Saint John Chrysostom on the human-animal relationship is less straightforward than that of Origen or Basil. Some contemporary commentators have seen him as an exponent of the view that a fundamental kinship exists between human beings and animals. Donald Attwater attributes to Chrysostom the conviction that "we ought to show kindness and gentleness to animals for many reasons, and chiefly because they are of the same origin as ourselves."[62] It is tempting to interpret this statement as a sign that Chrysostom is a heterodox defender of animals in a tradition that is overwhelmingly anthropocentrist. Even on its face, however, the statement is ambiguous: It can mean that we owe direct duties to animals on the grounds that they stand on a moral par with us, or it can mean that, as God's creatures, animals participate in divine goodness and thus merit gentle treatment as indirect reflections of the divine majesty. The latter interpretation is one that Augustine could have adopted but did not. Chrysostom, archbishop of Constantinople in the late fourth century, pursues the line of thinking that Augustine rejects: animals are inferior to human beings in the scheme of things, animals exist for the sake of humans, and yet some measure of compassion toward animals is called for by divine law.

Chrysostom states that "the human being is the creature more important than all the other visible beings, and for this creature all the others have been produced—sky, earth, sea, moon, sun, stars, the reptiles, the cattle, all the brute beasts."[63] Only human beings are capable of eternal salvation, and all other earthly creatures exist to serve us in our earthly

estate. Animals "were intended to come under the control of the creature soon to be created." Animals serve both our material and spiritual
welfare. Some animals "are useful for our food, others for serving us."
For example, "physicians get from them many things which they employ
as medications capable of promoting the health of our bodies."[64] But the
ultimate function of animals is to lead us "to the knowledge of God and
cause us to be amazed at the greatness of his loving kindness in freeing
the human race from the harm brought on itself. You see, it was not simply for our use that everything was created by him, but . . . that the power
of [the] Creator might be proclaimed."[65] The recognition of that power
is to lead us "to scorn all human affairs" and "only in regard to spiritual
things to be alive and take an active interest."[66]

Chrysostom's views on compassion toward animals come into focus
in his remarks on the Flood. God "did everything out of his esteem for
the human being: as in the case of the destruction of human beings in
the flood he destroyed along with them the whole range of brute beasts,
so in this case too [viz., in saving Noah from the Flood], when he intends
to show his characteristic love for the good man out of his regard for him,
he extends his goodness to the animal kingdom as well."[67] Not only does
God save some animals for the sake of Noah, but his covenant, which
extends not only to Noah but to the animals as well, is likewise extended
for the sake of humanity rather than for "brute" natures. "Since these
creatures had been created for the human for that reason they now share
the kindness shown humanity. While the covenant with the latter and with
the animals seems identical, in fact it is not. This too happens for the
human's consolation, you see, so that he may be in a position to know how
much esteem he enjoys, since not only is the favor bestowed on himself,
but also that all the animals have a share in enjoying the Lord's generosity
on his account."[68] The goal of including animals in the covenant is not
to promote the interests of animals, but rather "to induce confidence and
security in the human race."[69] Our concern should not be to achieve
community with animals—practices such as meat eating are perfectly
permissible—but instead to train young people to be "athletes for [God],
that we and our children may light on the blessings that are promised to
them that love Him."[70] Any compassion that we exhibit toward animals
redounds ultimately not on animals but on our own worthiness in the eyes
of God; such compassion is at best an allegorical expression of the compassion that we hope to receive from our Creator.

Saint Francis: A Heterodox Champion of Animals?

Among figures in the medieval church, none is appealed to more frequently than Saint Francis as a proponent of the moral worth of animals. Andrew Linzey suggests that "some Christians have celebrated a non-instrumentalist view of nature and animals in particular. Not only St. Francis of Assisi of course but also numerous others have championed the claims of animals."[71] That Linzey names among such champions of animals Basil the Great and John Chrysostom should give us pause; for Basil and Chrysostom do not give anything like a vindication of the rights of animals. Passmore notes that the case of Francis "is anything but a clear one," inasmuch as the primary sources "were for the most part deliberately designed to create a particular image of Francis, the image varying from chronicler to chronicler."[72] The vast majority of source texts we have on Francis are chronicles of his life written by Saint Bonaventure and others. Even the influential *Little Flowers of Saint Francis* was not written by Francis but by a Franciscan a hundred years after Francis's death. The extant texts and letters of Francis comprise a little over 150 pages; they contain only two direct references to animals, and neither of these establishes Francis's credentials as a champion of animal rights. Nor do the various chronicles of Francis's life paint an unequivocal picture of the saint as a champion of animals. The overwhelming focus, both in the chronicles and in Francis's own writings, is on the orthodox virtues of poverty, chastity, and humility, and on the importance of subordinating bodily existence to the life of the spirit.

Francis's credentials as an animal advocate rest primarily on the legend that he preached to the birds. This story is told by several of Francis's biographers and commemorated in a fresco by Giotto. Thomas of Celano's life of Saint Francis gives the most detailed version of the story. Francis had a "great tenderness toward lower and irrational animals" such as birds, and endeavored one day to preach to a flock. "Seeing that they were waiting expectantly for him, he greeted them in his usual way. But, not a little surprised that the birds did not rise in flight, as they usually do, he was filled with great joy and humbly begged them to listen to the word of God." Francis beseeched the birds "to praise [their] Creator very much and always love him," since God provided them with the necessities of life. "The birds, rejoicing in a wonderful way according to their nature, began to stretch their necks, extend their wings, open their mouths and gaze at him." Francis, "seeing that they had listened to the word of God with such reverence," reproached himself for "not having preached to the birds before. . . . [So] from that day on, he solicitously admonished all birds, all animals and reptiles, and even creatures that have no feeling, to praise and love their Creator."[73]

One of the puzzles with which this story presents us is how we are to understand the endeavor to preach to creatures seen to be irrational. A similar story in the *Little Flowers* tells of Saint Anthony preaching to fish. There, too, animals are said to lack reason. It is also stated in this story that Anthony's purpose was to "[rebuke] the foolishness of the infidels and the ignorant and the heretics," by creating the impression in such people that "animals lacking reason listen to [God's] word better than faithless men!"[74] In this respect, Francis bears fidelity to the orthodox view that the actions of animals have allegorical significance: Just as we learn about the virtues of prudence and self-control by observing the industry of animals as they prepare for the winter, so we can learn about our own indebtedness to God by contemplating the image of supposedly "wild" animals exhibiting fidelity to God. In his life of Francis, Bonaventure tells of an exhortation by Francis to a sheep "to give God praise . . . the sheep was careful to follow his instructions, just as if it realized the affection he had for it."[75] The "as if" in this story underscores the fact that we are not really to suppose that a creature lacking reason could recognize a human being's affection; by the same token, it seems that we are not to take these stories of exhortations to animals literally, but are to see in them the ways in which animals reflect the goodness of God.

The numerous references to Francis's compassion toward animals should be read in this light: Like Chrysostom eight centuries before him, Francis expresses compassion for animals, such as worms, bees, lambs, and fish.[76] But he does not stop there; he is said to have had particular affections for flowers, the moon, water, the sun, and fire.[77] We are even told that "fire and other creatures sometimes obeyed and revered him" and that "his spirit was stirred by such love and compassion for them that he would not allow them to be treated without respect."[78] Francis's call for compassion toward animals is of a piece with this call for compassion toward creatures such as fire: As God's creations, all such beings participate in the divine and for *that* reason merit respect. In his own writings, Francis never calls for love or compassion toward animals. Instead, he calls only for compassion toward one's neighbor and love of one's brother and one's enemy.[79] In the "Canticle of Brother Sun," Francis says that God merits praise through his creation of the sun, moon, stars, wind, water, fire, earth, flowers, and herbs, but he makes no mention of animals.[80] In the "Praises of the Virtues," Francis writes that

> Obedience subjects a man
> to everyone on earth,
> And not only to men,
> but to all the beasts as well
> and to the wild animals,
> So that they can do what they like with him,
> as far as God allows them.[81]

Through the vow of humility and the forsaking of earthly goods, in other words, we expose ourselves to the dominion of animals, just as a pious Christian should subject himself or herself to the earthly dominion of a pagan dictator. In the only other direct mention of animals in his writings, Francis sketches out regulations on, but not a prohibition of, meat eating.[82]

One final consideration lends additional support to the conclusion that Francis was less concerned with the fortunes of animals than with those of human beings. *The Little Flowers of St. Francis* contains the story of a man who wanted a pig's foot to eat. Out of charity for the hungry man, Brother Juniper cut a leg off a live pig and fed it to the man. Francis scolds Brother Juniper—not for harming the pig, but for committing an offense against the *man*. At Francis's behest, Juniper apologizes to the owner of the pig, who is so moved by Juniper's words of contrition that "he goes and kills [the pig], and having cut it up and cooked it, he bears it with much devotion and with many tears to St. Mary of the Angels, and gives it to the holy Brothers to eat in compensation for the abuse he had given them." Most revealing about this story is its conclusion: Francis expresses no concern whatsoever for the fate of the pig, but instead praises "the simplicity and patience under adversity of the said holy Brother Juniper" and exclaims "Would to God, my Brothers, that I had a whole forest of such Junipers!"[83]

The Apex of Medieval Anthropocentrism:
Saint Thomas Aquinas

Aquinas develops an elaborate cosmic teleology that draws on Aristotle, the Stoics, and Saint Augustine in placing animals in the service of human interests. Everything in the universe is "ordained toward God as its end." The "less noble" creatures exist "for the nobler, as those creatures that are less noble than man exist for the sake of man."[84] Beings that are "more noble" stand in closer proximity to God, in virtue of their rational capacity for self-determination. "That which is active is always more noble than that which is passive. Now, among superior creatures, the closest to God are those rational ones that exist, live, and understand in the likeness of God."[85] Rational creatures are more active and hence more noble than nonrational creatures such as plants and animals. "The intellectual agent acts for an end, as determining for itself its end; whereas the natural agent, though it acts for an end . . . does not determine its end for itself, since it knows not the nature of end, but is moved to the end determined for it by another."[86] Only rational beings are "immediately ordered to God" and capable of active self-determination through reflection on ends and deliberation on means to chosen ends. Nonrational beings lack the "freedom to follow or not to follow the impressions produced by heavenly agents."[87] For Aquinas, the greater nobility of rational beings entails the conclusion that nonrational beings exist expressly for our use. "The last end of all generation is the human soul, and to this does matter tend as its ultimate form. Consequently, the elements are for the sake of the mixed body, the mixed body for the sake of living things, and of these plants are for the sake of animals, and animals for the sake of man. . . . The end of the movement of the heavens is directed to man as its last end in the genus of things subject to generation and movement."[88]

Aquinas develops his conception of experience in animals under the influence of Aristotle. Human beings are rational and possess freedom, whereas animals are imprisoned in the particulars of sense experience. Even the most sophisticated animals lack the ability to recognize universals; at best, they can remember and make associations between particulars.

> For an experience arises from the association of many singular [intentions] received in memory. And this kind of association is proper to man, and pertains to the cogitative power (also called particular reason), which associates particular intentions just as universal reason associates universal ones. Now since animals are accustomed to pursue or avoid certain things as a result of many sensations and memory, for this reason they seem to share something of experience, even though it be slight.

But above experience, which belongs to particular reason, men have as their chief power a universal reason by means of which they live.[89]

Like Aristotle in *Posterior Analytics* 2.19, Aquinas is not entirely clear on the epistemic status of "particular reason." This capacity does not involve universals, but somehow takes the animal beyond an individual particular and enables the animal to make associations between particulars of like kind. Thus, for example, a squirrel can recognize an acorn in the present moment by associating it with an acorn that it previously ate; otherwise the squirrel would not be capable of providing for its well-being.

Aquinas never suggests, however, that an animal such as a squirrel recognizes an acorn *as* an acorn. To do so would require a capacity for abstraction that animals categorically lack. Animals do not attain to the universal "but only to something particular"; their cognitive abilities are confined to *"knowing singulars."*[90] This leaves a puzzle as to how animals are able to provide for themselves. Animals possess the *vis aestimativa*, the estimative power to apprehend things that are not currently present to the senses.[91] This power enables the sheep to run away when it sees a wolf, "not because of its color or shape, but as a natural enemy."[92] What is not disclosed to sensation here is the danger posed by the wolf. But if animals are confined to acquaintance with particulars and have no universal reason, how can the sheep "recognize" the danger latent in the sight of the wolf? Aquinas is fond of citing the wisdom of John of Damascus: animals "do not themselves have the mastery over their own inclination. Hence 'they do not act but are rather acted upon' [*non agunt sed magis aguntur*]."[93]

Aquinas does not fully specify the nature of this "imperfect volition" in animals, but he does say that animals are inclined by appetite and act "without making any choice."[94] In the actions of animals "we notice certain marks of sagacity," but what we are referring to as 'sagacity' is merely a simulacrum the like of which "may be seen in the movements of clocks [*in motibus horologiorum*]."[95] Whereas human beings are governed by reason, animals are governed by sensitive appetite, which "is determined to one particular thing by the order of nature."[96] Animals are bound to the future not by cognition, as in the case of humans, but instead are "moved by natural instinct [*ex instinctu naturali movetur*] to something future, as though it foresaw the future. This instinct is planted in them by the Divine Intellect [*instinctus est eis inditus ab intellectu divino*] that foresees the future."[97] This "as though" qualification recalls the "as if" in Basil and Francis, and it is decisive for understanding Aquinas's conception of animal volition: Determination of "intentions" such as what is advantageous or disadvantageous occurs in animals purely "by some sort of natural instinct, while man perceives them also by means of a certain comparison."[98] Animals act virtually automatically; hence they are subject to neither praise nor blame, and "there is no participation of the eternal law in them, except by way of likeness."[99]

Aquinas's view on "particular reason" in animals is best understood in terms of this notion of likeness. Aquinas has a serious problem making sense of the prudential actions of animals; they seem inexplicable without recourse to something like reason. And yet he follows Aristotle in categorically denying universal reason (conceptual abstraction) to animals. "Reason is found fully and perfectly only in man. . . . Brutes have a certain semblance of reason inasmuch as they share in a certain natural prudence." This "semblance of reason" is "the well-regulated judgment which [animals] have about certain things. But they have this judgment from a natural estimate, not from any deliberation, since they are ignorant of the basis of their judgment. . . . [Animals] are driven by passions."[100] If animals "do not act but are acted upon," and if their "judgment" involves no deliberation, then it is important to consider whether and to what extent animals participate in reason. Clearly Aquinas is attempting to draw on the continuity between animals and human beings that led Aristotle to characterize humans as rational animals. But what is the meaning of judgment that involves no deliberation and lacks freedom to do otherwise? Animals lack "freedom of judgment, since their judgment is naturally determined to a single pronouncement."[101] This is why animals are subject to neither praise nor blame. The reason why divine law subjects animals to punishment is "not because they have sinned themselves, but because the men who own them are punished by their punishment."[102]

The crux of Aquinas's conception of "natural" judgment in animals is consonant with his view of animal activity as analogous to the functioning of clocks. "Judgment about what is to be done is attributed to brute animals in the same way as motion and action are attributed to inanimate natural bodies. . . . Brutes do not judge about their own judgment but follow the judgment implanted in them by God. Thus they are not the cause of their own decision nor do they have freedom of choice."[103] The sheep's "decision" to run from the wolf is no different than the flower's "decision" to turn toward the sun or a stone's "decision" to roll downhill. In all such cases, the so-called decision is determined by God. As noted above, in animals this is a matter of "natural instinct . . . planted in them by the Divine Intellect." Thus when Aquinas attributes "experience" to some animals and states that "experience requires some reasoning about the particulars, in that one is compared to another," we must be cautious in drawing too close a parallel between experience in animals and in human beings.[104] Aquinas says that the functioning of "brute animals cannot occur apart from the body."[105] So again: what is the meaning of "experience" or a "comparison of particulars" that is automatic and entirely bodily? Aquinas seems to be confronted with the same problem faced by earlier Church figures who attribute "allegorical" significance to the conduct of animals. He recognizes the difficulty involved in accounting for their natural prudence, and yet his conviction that rational beings are fundamentally superior to "brute animals" forces him to ascribe an "as if" character to the apparent choices made by animals.

This "as if" character of animal judgment is placed in clear relief when we consider Aquinas's unequivocal assertions regarding the moral status of animals. As fundamentally nonrational beings, animals are "lower" and exist for the sake of "higher" beings. Higher beings are those created in God's image. Human beings, as so created, possess immortal souls, whereas "the souls of brutes are corrupted, when their bodies are corrupted."[106] As mortal, animals are instrumentalities to be used by human beings as we see fit. "Now all animals are naturally subject to man. . . . For the imperfect are for the use of the perfect: plants make use of the earth for their nourishment, animals make use of plants, and man makes use of both plants and animals. Therefore it is in keeping with the order of nature that man should be master over animals. . . . Since man, being made in the image of God, is above other animals, these are rightly subject to his government."[107]

The terms of this dominion are clear in Aquinas: From a purely rational standpoint "it matters not how man behaves to animals, because God has subjected all things to man's power."[108] In particular, there is no sin or impropriety in killing animals, "for by the divine providence they are intended for man's use according to the order of nature. Hence it is not wrong for man to make use of them, either by killing or in any other way whatsoever."[109] Aquinas invokes the authority of Aristotle's *Politics* 1.3 and Augustine's *City of God* 1.20, and he suggests that we must kill animals to use them for food. Such treatment of animals is perfectly permissible, inasmuch as "they are naturally enslaved and accommodated to the uses of others."[110]

Even though we have no direct duties to treat animals in particular ways, Aquinas holds what has come to be known as an "indirect duties" view toward animals. We have obligations to treat animals in particular ways not because we owe anything to brute beasts, but instead because our conduct toward animals has implications for our conduct toward other human beings. For example "he that kills another's ox, sins, not through killing the ox, but through injuring another man in his property. Wherefore this is not a species of the sin of murder but of the sin of theft or robbery."[111] The story of Brother Juniper takes on clear meaning against the background of this indirect duties conception. We need not concern ourselves for the lives or sufferings of animals, except insofar as this concern makes us better members of the human community. Thus, "since it happens that even irrational animals are sensible to pain, it is possible for the affection of pity to arise in a man with regard to the sufferings of animals." The value of such an affection is simply that "if a man practice a pitying affection for animals, he is all the more disposed to take pity on his fellow-men."[112] Aquinas interprets the various biblical passages expressing concern for animals in this light. Prohibitions such as "one shall not muzzle the ox when it is treading out the grain," just as Paul tells us, are not about animals at all; for Aquinas, "these prohibitions were made in hatred of idolatry."[113] They were also made in an allegorical spirit: "If any passages of Holy Scripture seem to forbid us to be cruel to brute animals, for instance to kill a bird with its young [Deut. 22:6], this is either to remove a man's thoughts from being cruel to other men, lest through being cruel to animals one become cruel to human beings; or because injury to an animal leads to the temporal hurt of man."[114]

Aquinas's views on animals are the culmination of a legacy that begins in Scripture and is solidified in the course of the Christian Middle Ages. This legacy persists virtually unmodified throughout the Middle Ages and in the Renaissance thought of Martin Luther.[115] This is the basis on which Lynn White made his unpopular, but essentially correct, assessment of the moral status of nature in Christian tradition. If Christian doctrine is capable of the kind of historical evolution that some contemporary voices suggest, then a transformation of Christianity might be possible that embraced a sense of direct duties toward animals. But the terms of the resulting "Christianity" would bear little if any resemblance to the tradition that placed animals fundamentally in the service of human beings.

DESCARTES ON THE MORAL
STATUS OF ANIMALS

For centuries a certain conventional wisdom prevailed concerning
Descartes's views about animals. He was long assumed to maintain not
simply that animals are morally inferior to human beings, but that they
are in fact due no moral obligations whatsoever. On this view, Descartes
was able to justify such practices as vivisection on the grounds that nonhuman animals are mere machines. Scientists need have no moral scruple
about cutting up live animals because animals have no souls, and their
shrieks of what would appear to be pain are nothing but purely mechanical
responses on the part of creatures with no experiential or perceptual
capabilities, and consequently no capacity whatsoever to feel pain. This
interpretation of Descartes's views about animals dates back to Henry
More's famous letter to Descartes in which he charged Descartes with "the
internecine and cutthroat idea that you advance in the *Method*, which
snatches life and sensibility away from all the animals."[1] In part 5 of the
Discourse on Method, Descartes developed his most explicit and systematic
argument for the essential difference between human beings and nonhuman animals. There he maintains that the latter lack reason and language, and he assimilates them to machines.[2] This rationale led not only
More but also such recent commentators as Boyce Gibson and Norman
Kemp Smith to endorse the view that Descartes considered animals to
have no moral status at all, Smith going so far as to call Descartes's position "monstrous."[3]

In the course of his writings, Descartes presents two additional criteria for distinguishing animals from human beings, although only one
of them proves to be decisive for the question of the moral status of ani-

mals.[4] One of these criteria is mentioned at the end of part 5 of the *Discourse* and is developed in some of Descartes's other writings, namely the criterion that animals lack immortal souls. The other is that animals are incapable of conscious perceptual states such as pain because they are mere machines, in contrast with human beings that, like all sentient beings, have the capacity to be aware of their bodily states. On the strongest readings of Descartes's "monstrous" thesis, Descartes's denial of feeling in animals is a fundamental basis for his denying that animals have moral worth.

The position taken by the likes of More and Smith was long considered to be unimpeachable. But in recent years a controversy has emerged regarding Descartes's views on animals. Several commentators have sought to overturn this conventional wisdom as a simple misreading of Descartes's views. For example, John Cottingham tries to demonstrate that Descartes never denies feeling to animals. Implicit in Cottingham's argument is the proposition that if Descartes acknowledges that animals do feel, then one cannot plausibly defend the traditional claim that Descartes was indifferent to the suffering of animals.[5] Peter Harrison takes a different tack to arrive at the same conclusion: On Harrison's view, not only does Descartes believe that animals possess souls, but in addition Descartes never denies that animals can think.[6] Harrison believes that these considerations lend support to Cottingham's claim that history has done an injustice to Descartes as regards his views about animals. And most recently, Stephen Gaukroger argues for the view that Descartes acknowledged the capacity for something resembling conscious perceptual states in animals. On Gaukroger's view, Descartes's awareness of such perceptual states in animals makes it impossible for Descartes to have believed that animals are mere unfeeling machines.[7] All three of these commentators take the position, either implicitly or explicitly, that Descartes had a much more enlightened view of animals than is generally recognized. Cottingham believes that Descartes "was not altogether beastly to the beasts," and Harrison goes so far as to maintain that whereas "Descartes is commonly portrayed as one whose view of animals is morally repugnant. . . . Such moral indignation is misplaced."[8] Naturally, if animals can be said to have (something like) consciousness of their experiences and particularly of perceptual states like pain, and if it can be shown that Descartes held such a view, it would be impossible to endorse the traditional view that Descartes was "a brute to the brutes."

How could such complete disagreement arise over the views of a philosopher known to have placed a great premium on clarity? One source of confusion over Descartes's views on animals is the fact that he never sets forth a definitive statement of his position concerning the rational and perceptual capacities of animals; instead his views emerge from a troubling ambiguity that can be dispelled only through a consideration of the overall spirit of Descartes's philosophy and the tradition of thinking about animals that forms the essential background of Descartes's views. In the end it is possible to form a clear conception of Descartes's views concerning the moral status of animals. Careful consideration of Descartes's writings, the overall mission of his philosophy, and the relevant philosophical antecedents of his thought point toward the conclusion that the views of thinkers like Cottingham, Harrison, and Gaukroger are based on a selective reading of Descartes's remarks about animals and tend to ignore the spirit of his philosophy and his call for human beings to render themselves "the masters and possessors of nature."[9] It must be granted that Descartes never formally and definitively declares that animals are mere resources that we may use as we wish; but he says enough to make it clear that he considers animals to be of an inferior rank to humans in the order of creation, and that he considers animal experimentation to be an acceptable practice. In the end I reaffirm the conventional wisdom about Descartes on animals, although not without some qualification.

Beyond the fact that Descartes never presents an unequivocal statement of his views about animals, determining what his position must have been is complicated by an additional problem. There is a troubling tendency in recent scholarship on the matter to conflate Descartes's views with certain current sensibilities about the nature of animal experience generally and about the proper moral status of animals in particular. It is as though current defenders of Descartes simply cannot believe that he held a view that is repugnant by contemporary standards, so they attempt to revise Descartes to make his views acceptable by those standards. In doing so, such commentators distort the views that Descartes explicitly advances in his writings, and they distort their readers' understanding of Descartes's place in an entire historical context of philosophical thinking about animals. Moreover, they make some fundamental mistakes concerning the nature of consciousness; to this extent, their revisionist reading of Descartes is founded not only on a historical misunderstanding but on a crucial systematic distortion as well.

The views of Aristotle, the Stoics, and Christian theology culminating in Aquinas are decisive for understanding Descartes's views about animals. Fundamental to Descartes's position on animals is the ontological status that he attributes to corporeality. In line with a commitment that extends at least as far back as Aristotle, Descartes presents an ontology according to which immaterial things are superior to material ones. Embodiment is a sign of imperfection; the less dependent a being is on corporeality, the more perfect the being is.[10] Any being that is wholly corporeal is of the lowest order of being; and given Descartes's appeal to mechanism as the means for representing or explaining corporeality, this means that any being that can be explained exhaustively in mechanistic terms is of the lowest order of being.

In the following discussion, I demonstrate the link between Descartes's commitment to the mastery of nature and his views on the moral status of animals: Nature is taken in its essence to be pure corporeality, which for Descartes is fully explicable in terms of inert mechanism. Whatever is pure corporeality or mechanism is not worthy of moral respect, and this allows human beings to treat nature as a storehouse of energy and raw materials that are available for the satisfaction of human desires. In this regard, if his appeal to the technological imperative of systematic mastery distinguishes Descartes from his philosophical forbears, the inferior ontological and moral status that he attributes to animals does not: To the extent that Descartes considers animals to be mechanism and nothing more, he is committed to the view that animals can be used like any natural resource, without moral scruple. Notwithstanding the distinctive contribution that Descartes's conception of mechanism makes to the historical project of using nonhuman beings for the satisfaction of human needs, Descartes's conviction that we have no duties toward animals is wholly in accordance with a tradition of thinking about animals that extends back to antiquity.

I have shown, however, that the tradition is not univocal in its denigration of animals to the status of instrumentalities for the satisfaction of human needs. This holds not only for antiquity but for the Renaissance and early modernity as well. As regards defenses of animals, the main point of connection between these historical periods is the thought of Plutarch, who influenced both Montaigne and Giovanni Battista Gelli. Montaigne and Gelli each articulate views that express what George Boas refers to as "theriophily," the position "that the beasts—like savages—are more 'natural' than man, and hence man's superior."[11] Boas states that it is to theriophilists such as Montaigne and Gelli that Descartes directs his mechanistic polemic concerning animals, and I consider the positions developed by these thinkers before turning to an examination of Descartes.

Six years after Copernicus published *De revolutionibus orbium coelestium*, Gelli published his own version of Plutarch's *Gryllus* under the title *Circe*.[12] Like Plutarch's dialogue, Gelli's is founded on the conceit of Odysseus's (Ulysses', in Gelli's version) demand that Circe return his men to human form after they have been turned into animals. But where Plutarch's dialogue follows the terms of the *Odyssey* in considering the men to have been turned into swine, Gelli imagines the men having been transformed into a loose hierarchy of animals ranging from an oyster to an elephant. Ulysses endeavors to persuade each of the animals that they are better off being changed back into human form. Only the elephant ultimately consents to become human again. All of the others offer reasons why they are better off as animals, citing the supposedly superior temperance, strength, happiness, and so forth of animals.

Only the elephant ultimately accedes to Ulysses' desire that he be returned to his prior human state. He does so on the grounds, offered by Ulysses, that animals act in naturally instinctive ways and lack the capacity for free self-determination that is unique to human beings and the hallmark of human superiority. Ulysses presents an account of animal instinct that closely resembles Aquinas's position, even citing the sheep-wolf example that Aquinas employs to argue for the principle *non agunt sed magis aguntur*, that animals do not move themselves but instead are moved instinctively by external objects of desire and aversion.[13] Human will, in contrast, is capable of genuine self-determination in virtue of rationality, which makes possible conceptual abstraction and logical inference. This enables human beings to pursue not only self-preservation but also "the happiness and perfection of [their] being."[14] Gelli lauds this capacity in the same humanist terms that Pico della Mirandola uses in his *Oration on the Dignity of Man* to argue that human beings are the envy even of the angels: Freedom makes us "just like a chameleon," in that a human being can, "like a new Proteus . . . transform himself into whatever form he elects" and "make of himself either a terrestrial or a divine creature by piercing through all the barriers to the state which his own free will most desires."[15] There is some controversy as to whether the elephant's endorsement of this humanist perspective is ironic; Adams suggests that Ulysses "extorts" the elephant's compliance, which is at best "very limited and conditional."[16] There is some evidence for this in the text; for example, at several points the elephant complains that it is unable to follow some of what Ulysses is saying.[17] But the overall thrust of Gelli's *Circe* is that human beings are the envy of the entire universe in virtue of their "chameleon-like" capacity for self-determination, just as the Renaissance humanists argue.[18]

Comparably ambivalent is Montaigne's attack on the traditional presumption of human superiority over animals. Writing a generation after Gelli, Montaigne maintains in several of the essays that the earthly estate of human beings is no better than that of animals and may in fact be inferior. Anticipating Rousseau, Montaigne argues that "there is nothing barbarous in what is under [nature's] guidance," and that we have "quite smothered" nature with our arts and various inventions.[19] Human civilization modeled on the ideal of Plato's *Republic* is far removed from the "common kinship" characteristic of the golden age.[20] Montaigne invokes numerous examples from Plutarch to counter the prejudice of "imaginary kingship" over animals that has predominated in the tradition.[21] But he stops conspicuously short of advocating equality and full reciprocity between human beings and animals, and argues instead that he "[does] not put much stock" in "that cousinship between us and the animals."[22] We do have "a general duty of humanity, that attaches us not only to animals, who have life and feeling, but even to trees and plants." Our duty, however, is one not of reciprocal justice, but simply one of benevolence, as for Plutarch in his *Life of Cato the Elder*. "We owe justice to men, and mercy and kindness to other creatures that may be capable of receiving it. There is some relationship between them and us, and some mutual obligation," but not so much that animals deserve to be accorded the rights due to a full-fledged (human) member of society.[23]

The limits of Montaigne's "theriophily" come into focus when we consider the motivation underlying the *Apology for Raymond Seybond*. The *Apology* is a key text in the revival of Pyrrhonian scepticism in the sixteenth century. Montaigne's aim is to argue that knowledge is ultimately powerless to grant us certitude in life. It is simply in virtue of "foolish pride and stubbornness . . . that we set ourselves before the other animals and sequester ourselves from their condition and society."[24] From the standpoint of our earthly capacities and condition, we are no better than animals, and in some respects we are arguably inferior. But unlike animals, we are not merely earthly creatures. Montaigne concludes the *Apology* with the observation that true certitude and eternal salvation depend entirely on Christian faith, which elevate us above that condition in which we are no better than animals.

Descartes agrees with Montaigne on the importance of faith and divine grace in the quest for eternal salvation. But he conceives of our earthly condition in terms that are clearly at odds with those of Montaigne or Gelli. By appealing to a strict dualism, Descartes reduces animals to pure mechanism and categorically rejects the idea that we have any kind of duties toward animals. For Descartes, human beings and animals differ not simply in degree but in kind, and humans are fundamentally superior to animals.

Descartes's Denial that Animals Possess Reason and Rational Souls

Like the tradition of philosophers before him, Descartes bases his commitment to the inferiority of animals on the fact that animals lack speech (λόγος) in the sense of rational discourse. Descartes, like his predecessors, believes that language use is a sign that the being in question is rational, and that conversely the inability to use language is a sign that the being in question is not rational. Descartes's remarks concerning the relationship between humans, machines, and animals in part 5 of the *Discourse on Method* make his commitments in this regard unmistakable: The human body is essentially a machine, but human beings are not reducible to machines because "our soul is of a nature entirely independent of the body, and consequently . . . it is not bound to die with it."[25] This distinguishes human beings not only from machines but also from animals, which for Descartes are pure mechanism; in fact, the same criterion distinguishes humans from both machines and animals, namely the possession of reason (understanding) and language: Machines "could never use words, or put together other signs, as we do in order to declare our thoughts to others. . . . It is not conceivable that such a machine should produce different arrangements of words so as to give an appropriately meaningful answer to whatever is said in its presence, as the dullest of men can do." And "even though such machines might do some things as well as we do them, or perhaps even better, they would inevitably fail in others, which would reveal that they were acting not through understanding but only from the disposition of their organs." Descartes concludes from this that machines lack the faculties that could make them "act in all the contingencies of life in the way in which our reason makes us act."[26]

In the *Discourse*, Descartes views animals exactly as he views machines: No nonhuman animals are capable of "arranging various words together and forming an utterance from them in order to make their thoughts understood." And if we consider such animals as parrots, we must acknowledge that they can utter words but they "cannot show that they are thinking what they are saying. . . . This shows not merely that the beasts have less reason than men, but that they have no reason at all."[27] By applying the same criterion to animals that he applies to machines, Descartes seeks to assimilate the two; he concludes his discussion of animals in part 5 of the *Discourse* by observing that the actions of animals are due entirely "to the disposition of their organs. In the same way a clock, consisting only of wheels and springs, can count the hours and measure time more accurately than we can with all our wisdom."[28]

Descartes reiterates his assimilation of animals to machines in a letter to Reneri, in which he considers the hypothetical case of a man who "had been brought up all his life in some place where he had never seen any animals except men; and suppose that he was very devoted to the study of mechanics, and had made, or helped to make, various automatons shaped like a man, a horse, a dog, a bird, and so on."[29] Knowing the criterion from part 5 of the *Discourse* that distinguishes machines from human beings, this man, upon encountering live animals for the first time, would think they were "automatons made by God or nature."[30] In other words, not only would this man not mistake live animals for anything like human beings, but he would conclude that they were essentially machines—organic machines, admittedly, but finally no more than mechanisms.

What Descartes is at pains to show here is precisely what certain of his contemporaries were not willing to accept: Descartes wants to argue that animals are different than human beings not simply in degree but in kind, in virtue of the fact that animals lack the faculty of reason or thought whereas human beings possess it. Gassendi, and others after him, endeavored to maintain that even if animals do not possess the capacity for thought to the same extent that humans do, the difference is nonetheless merely one of degree.[31] In response to Descartes's claim in the Second Meditation that thinking is proper to the self, Gassendi maintains that "it remains for you to prove that the power of thought is something far beyond the nature of a body that neither a vapour nor any other mobile, pure and rarefied body can be organized in such a way as would make it capable of thought. You will have to prove at the same time that the souls of the brutes are incorporeal, given that they think or are aware of something internal over and above the functions of the external senses."[32]

Here Gassendi presents a possibility that came to be associated with Hobbes, Locke, and Hume, namely the possibility that animals have some sort of internal states of awareness, even if these states are not identical with human states of awareness:

> You say that the brutes lack reason. Well, of course they lack human reason, but they do not lack their own kind of reason. So it does not seem appropriate to call them ἄλογα except by comparison with us or with our kind of reason; and in any case λόγος or reason seems to be a general term, which can be attributed to them no less than the cognitive faculty or internal sense. You may say that animals do not employ rational argument. But although they do not reason so perfectly or about as many subjects as man, they still reason, and the difference seems to be merely one of degree. You may say that they do not speak. But although they do not produce human speech (since of course they are not human beings), they still produce their own form of speech, which they employ just as we do ours.[33]

On Gassendi's view, there is a *logos* (λόγος, language or rational faculty) common to humans and nonhuman animals, such that if we are going to say that human beings make judgments in the process of choosing their actions, then we must say that animals make judgments as well. If we make certain judgments about unseen men when we see only their hats and coats, then we must say that "a dog, which you will not allow to possess a mind like yours, certainly makes a similar kind of judgment when it sees not its master but simply his hat or clothes."[34]

Gassendi offers no argument in support of his claim, and Descartes's response is noteworthy for its insistence on settling the question in an "a posteriori" manner, from the outward actions of animals, rather than from speculations on what might be the case in a realm of events (namely the subjective experience, if there is any, of the animals in question) to which we have no access.[35] In his reply to Gassendi, Descartes does not so much offer an argument as simply question Gassendi's claim: "I do not see what argument you are relying on when you lay it down as certain that a dog makes discriminating judgements in the same way as we do. Seeing that a dog is made of flesh you perhaps think that everything which is in you also exists in the dog. But I observe no mind at all in the dog, and hence believe there is nothing to be found in a dog that resembles the things I recognize in a mind."[36] Here Descartes reiterates a conviction that he had first expressed in the *Regulae*, where he had said that "we refuse to allow that they [viz. nonhuman animals] have any awareness [*cognitio*] of things."[37]

Despite Descartes's very clear statement to the contrary, Gaukroger maintains that in this passage Descartes "is not denying that animals have cognition; only that it is not the kind of cognition that he is interested in, namely human cognition."[38] Gaukroger attempts to add support to this untenable interpretation by appealing to a letter from Descartes to the Marquess of Newcastle in which Descartes says that "if [animals] thought as we do, they would have an immortal soul like us."[39] Gaukroger suggests that the qualification "as we do" leaves open the possibility that there are nonhuman ways of thinking; in other words, he argues that Descartes does not believe that animals lack thought altogether, but only "that they lack thought *of the kind that we have*."[40] In essence, Gaukroger is saying that Descartes and Gassendi are in complete agreement. But such a conclusion is simply incorrect, for Descartes goes on in the letter to the Marquess of Newcastle to state definitively that animals cannot use language meaningfully "as we do . . . not [because] they lack the organs but [because] they have no thoughts. It cannot be said that they speak to each other but that we cannot understand them; for since dogs and some other animals express their passions to us, they would express their thoughts also if they had any."[41] Descartes's conviction is unequivocal: animals have no thoughts, whereas human beings do.

Descartes's letter to the Marquess of Newcastle highlights the extent of Descartes's debt to his philosophical forbears. The statement that "if [animals] thought as we do, they would have an immortal soul like us" shows that for Descartes, as for the likes of Aristotle and Aquinas, possession of the faculty of reason is coextensive with the possession of a rational soul: to possess one is to possess the other. Nonetheless, like Gaukroger, Peter Harrison argues that Descartes does not deny thought to animals, and Harrison argues in addition that if Descartes does not deny thought to animals then he cannot deny that they possess souls. But in his letter to More, Descartes explicitly rejects the idea that animals have immortal souls by saying that "it is more probable that worms, flies, caterpillars and other animals move like machines than that they all have immortal souls [*animalia immortali*]."[42] Harrison notes that Descartes is careful to hold back from any definitive pronouncements as to whether animals can think and hence whether they possess rational souls: In his letter to More, Descartes grants that "we cannot prove that there is any thought in animals, [and] I do not think that it can be proved that there is none, since the human mind does not reach into their hearts"; by the same token, we "cannot at all prove the existence of a thinking soul [*animam cogitantem*] in animals."[43] For Harrison, Descartes's acknowledgment of the limits of human insight into the inner constitution of other creatures is a sign that Descartes "is cautiously agnostic on the whole question" of animal souls.[44]

Harrison is right that Descartes cannot *prove* that animals lack souls; Descartes is aware that his own method makes this impossible.[45] But to conclude that Descartes is "cautiously agnostic" on this question is to ignore the context of Descartes's argument in his letter to More. Descartes treats as a "preconceived opinion to which we are all more accustomed from our earliest years . . . the belief that dumb animals think." He states that the sole reason that might support such an opinion is the fact that animals have sense organs that are more or less like human sense organs; so it may seem natural to infer that if animals sense like we do, then perhaps they think like we do as well. Descartes then states "that there are other arguments, stronger and more numerous, but not so obvious to everyone, which strongly urge the opposite," and he concludes that his "opinion is not so much cruel to animals as it is indulgent to human beings . . . since it absolves them from the suspicion of crime when they eat or kill animals."[46]

This indulgence hardly smacks of agnosticism; on the contrary, it expresses a commitment about the *moral* status of animals vis-à-vis human beings. In this connection, I now consider the extent to which Descartes's dualism is informed by his Greek and particularly his Christian heritage; for even if animals can be said to possess souls, these souls are fundamentally so different from human souls that any comparison of the two is dangerously misleading. Among earthly beings, only those possessing immortal souls (namely human beings) are destined to enter the city of God; all other beings, even if they possess some kind of soul other than an immortal one, are consigned to the function of serving human needs. To this extent, Descartes argues that animals are just like any other natural resource. Just as did Aristotle, the Stoics, Augustine, and Aquinas before him, Descartes believes that human beings may kill and eat animals without any moral scruple whatsoever. Harrison's position (and Cottingham's) depends in important part on ignoring this portion of Descartes's letter to More.

In Descartes's letter to More, the influence of the historical background on Descartes's views about animal souls is quite evident. There Descartes says that the actions of animals are due exclusively to "the corporeal soul [anima corporea]," which "is purely mechanical and corporeal," whereas the actions of human beings depend on "an incorporeal principle" that is unique to "the mind [mentem] or that soul [animam] which I have defined as thinking substance [substantiam cogitationem]."[47] Descartes's position is that even though we cannot prove definitively that animals lack immortal souls any more than we can prove that they are incapable of thought, the fact that animal behavior can be explained adequately in terms of corporeal processes makes it unnecessary and implausible to attribute anything like rationality or a rational soul to animals.

What Descartes has in mind when he attributes to animals a "purely mechanical and incorporeal" soul is made clear in a letter to Plempius in which he says that "the souls of animals are nothing but their blood [animas brutorum nihil aliud esse quam sanguinem]"; he further states that "this theory involves such an enormous difference between the souls of animals and our own that it provides a better argument than any yet thought of to refute the atheists and to establish that human minds cannot be drawn out of the potentiality of matter." The difference here, as in Aristotle and Aquinas, is between "rational and sensitive souls."[48] And in the Sixth Replies, Descartes says "I accept that the brutes have what is commonly called 'life', and a corporeal soul and organic sensation."[49] Here Descartes denies that the human soul is "corporeal," and he appeals to thought as the faculty that distinguishes the human soul from the corporeal or sensitive "soul" of animals.[50] In the letter to Plempius and in the Sixth Replies, Descartes restates the position he articulates in his letter to More. These comments round out the wholly mechanistic view of animals that Descartes presents in the Fourth Replies to the *Meditations*: "All the actions of the brutes resemble only those which occur in us without the mind. . . . We know of absolutely no principle of movement in animals apart from the disposition of their organs and the continual flow of the spirits which are produced by the heat of the heart as it rarefies the blood."[51] To say that animals possess a corporeal "soul" is essentially to say no more than that they are alive.

The moral implications of such a view are clear. Descartes's remark

to More about the permissibility of killing and eating animals is crucial:
To say that animals possess corporeal souls is to attribute to them a moral
status akin to that of plants, which are also alive and which, according to
the Aristotelian-Thomistic tradition, themselves possess a certain kind
of "soul." The notion of a corporeal soul is entirely compatible with
Descartes's reduction of animals to pure mechanism, inasmuch as, for
Descartes, "animal souls [are] reduced to the configuration of the parts
of their bodies."[52] In principle, animals are simply part of a larger sphere
of mechanistic, material resources; only human beings with immortal
souls are due moral respect.

Descartes on the Question of Feeling in Animals

A commonsense reading of the question of moral obligations toward
animals might be to maintain that there are reasons for extending moral
obligations toward animals that have nothing to do with whether or not
animals are rational. In accordance with some current sensibilities, one
might say that if animals can suffer, then we have at least some moral
obligations toward them, for example, the obligation to avoid inflicting
(unnecessary) pain on them. And while one would expect that Descartes's
indebtedness to his philosophical forbears would lead him to the conclusion that the question of animal feeling is ultimately *irrelevant* to the
question whether we have moral obligations toward animals, Descartes's
views on the question turn out to be more complicated than this. For while
Aristotle, the Stoics, Augustine, and Aquinas all believe that we have no
moral obligations toward animals even though they are capable of feeling pain, Descartes goes to some lengths to make a fundamental distinction between the nature of pain in animals and in sentient beings.
Descartes and his forbears believed in some form of the Stoic principle
of *oikeiosis* (οἰκείωσις, belonging), and for all of them the moral dividing
line lies between rational and nonrational beings. Why, then, did
Descartes deem it necessary to establish a fundamental distinction between feeling in animals and in human beings, and just what sort of distinction is apparent in his writings?

Descartes appears to have believed that such a distinction was demanded not by the principle of *oikeiosis* but by the terms of his dualism.
His distinction between feeling in conscious (rational) and nonconscious
(nonrational) beings results from the application of strict dualism to the
traditional principle of *oikeiosis*. While he never explicitly links this dis-

tinction to the question of morality, his views about sensation and morality make it clear that his position is this: All and only those beings that are *reflectively aware* of their sensations or feelings are the kind of beings that belong to moral community. But it is not in virtue of this awareness of one's feelings that one is a moral being; rather, this awareness is ancillary to the more fundamental capacity for rational reflection generally. Hence even Descartes's views about feeling in animals as opposed to human beings return us to the criterion of rationality.

I consider Descartes's views about feeling by returning to Gassendi's objections to the *Meditations*. In developing the claim that nonhuman animals may be capable of thought in some sense, Gassendi offers the following challenge to Descartes: "You must consider whether the sense-perception which the brutes have does not also deserve to be called 'thought', since it is not dissimilar to your own. . . . The brutes have nerves, animal spirits, and a brain, and in the brain there is a principle of cognition that receives the messages from the spirits" in exactly the same way that it occurs in human perception.[53] According to Gassendi, human beings are simply a species of animal, and hence we must perceive in essentially the same way that mere brute animals perceive. For example, Gassendi says, the physiological processes in virtue of which we flee in the face of a stone that is about to be thrown at us are exactly the same as the processes in virtue of which an animal flees danger or moves toward a piece of food.[54] Gassendi's point is that any being that has a sensation (a visual image, a feeling of hunger, pain, or whatever) must in principle be *aware* of that sensation, or it simply would not *be* a sensation.

Both Cottingham and Gaukroger implicitly follow Gassendi's reasoning regarding feeling in animals. Cottingham maintains that even if animals are mechanisms, if they are capable of feeling in any sense then they must be aware of their feelings—they cannot, as Smith had maintained, be unfeeling machines and nothing more.[55] By continually emphasizing that Descartes never says definitively that a lack of thought entails a lack of feeling, Cottingham argues that Descartes never excludes the possibility that animals feel in something like the way in which human beings feel even though animals have no capacity for reflective awareness:

Descartes, either inadvertently or wilfully, failed to eradicate a certain fuzziness from his thinking about consciousness and self-consciousness. To say that X is in pain (angry, joyful) is certainly to attribute a conscious

state to X; but this need not amount to the full-blooded reflective awareness of pain that is involved in the term *cogitatio*. To be dogmatic for a
moment, I should certainly say that cats feel pain, but not that they have
the kind of full mental awareness of pain that is needed for it to count
as a *cogitatio*.[56]

Gaukroger goes even further than Cottingham in maintaining that for
Descartes, "animal automata . . . are able to have genuine perceptual
cognition, in the form of a grasp of representations of perceptual
stimuli."[57]

Cottingham and Gaukroger present us with contemporary versions
of Gassendi's claim that perceptual states, in their very nature, include
some kind of conscious awareness. Descartes, however, insists on a fundamental distinction between the nature of sensation in animals as pure
mechanisms and in human beings as a composite of mind (soul) and
body. Descartes makes explicit reference to this difference when he says
that "animals do not see as we do when we are aware that we see, but only
as we do when our mind is elsewhere. . . . In such a case we too move just
like automatons."[58] Descartes's point is that animals are never conscious
of seeing in the way a conscious being often is; nonhuman animals are
never conscious.

What Descartes has in mind here becomes clear when this statement
is read together with a similar statement in the Fourth Replies:

When people take a fall, and stick out their hands so as to protect their
head, it is not reason that instructs them to do this; it is simply that the
sight of the impending fall reaches the brain and sends the animal spirits
into the nerves in the manner necessary to produce the movement even
without any mental volition, *just as it would be produced in a machine*. And since
our own experience reliably informs us that this is so, why should we be
so amazed that the 'light reflected from the body of a wolf onto the eyes
of a sheep' should be equally capable of arousing the movements of flight
in the sheep?[59]

What we might call "fear" in the sheep here is nothing more than a mecha-
nistically induced behavioral response. Similarly, in the *Passions* Descartes
says that "when a dog sees a partridge, it is naturally disposed to run towards it; and when it hears a gun fired, the noise naturally impels it to
run away."[60] Descartes explains this by saying that where human beings
react to their sensations on the basis of conscious experience (as when

we are repulsed by bad food), in animals, under similar circumstances, there is nothing but "all the movements of the spirits and of the gland which produces passions in us."[61]

Here, as in the Fourth Replies and the letter to Plempius, Descartes maintains that sense experiences such as seeing, hearing, and tasting are very different for animals than for human beings, because animals are incapable of thought. In animals such experiences can be *nothing but* "the movements of the [material] spirits and of the gland which produces passions in us"; sensation in sentient beings is of a fundamentally different kind, inasmuch as it is a mode of thinking and hence is conscious. For Descartes, animals lack the capacity for any kind of awareness because they are incapable of thought. His characterization of animal sensation is of a purely corporeal, and hence mechanical, process. In sharp contrast with a human being that besides having this mechanical process in the sense organs and brain *also* "has the full range of conscious powers, and is capable of language and abstract thought as well as sensation and feelings of hunger," animals on Descartes's view are material automata, "with no experience of any kind."[62]

In contrast with animals, which do not have conscious sensations but rather only "movements similar to those which result from our imaginations and sensations," conscious sensation is proper to conscious beings.[63] "Willing, understanding, imagining, and sensing and so on are just different ways of thinking, and all belong to the soul."[64] To understand sensation as a "way of thinking" is to understand it as something more and other than, say, "light reflected from the body of a wolf onto the eyes of a sheep"; it is to understand sensation as a conscious intentional state, which includes what Marjorie Grene refers to as "self-reference."[65] Where, on Descartes's view, the flight of the sheep is essentially no different from, say, the rising of mercury in a thermometer in response to an increase in temperature, *my* flight in the face of a wolf includes an awareness of the wolf as a threatening object in relation to me as a subject.

Descartes applies this general distinction between unconscious mechanistic sensation in animals and conscious sensation in humans to the specific case of feeling. In a letter to Mersenne, Descartes says that "I do not explain the feeling of pain without reference to the soul. For in my view pain exists only in the understanding. What I do explain is all the external movements which accompany this feeling in us; in animals it is these movements alone which occur, and not pain in the strict sense."[66] For an animal to "feel" is for motion to take place in its animal spirits. "Feeling" is really a misnomer here: Descartes says that we tend to draw an analogy between the outward behavioral responses of animals and our own outward behavioral responses when we feel sensations such as pain, even though there are no inner experiences in animals that correspond to our inner states of pain and the like.[67] Because animals have no subjective awareness, they have no experience of pain or any other sensation. Animals do not feel anything; only human beings do. Animals are essentially automata, so we should not be misled into thinking that there is "any real feeling or emotion in them."[68]

Grene's contention that there is a shift in Descartes's thinking about animals, such that the later Descartes comes to acknowledge the role of feeling in animals, is born of her failure to take into account everything that Descartes says.[69] Even when Descartes makes what for him at first appears to be an incredible statement, namely that animals experience fear, hope, and joy, he goes on to reiterate the dual criterion that distinguishes human beings from animals in part 5 of the *Discourse*, namely thought and language, and stresses that we should not be misled into thinking that animals are ultimately like humans.[70] Grene concludes that Descartes's attribution of fear and the like to animals is a sign that "the doctrine of the *bête-machine* and, with it, the doctrine of the pure automatism of the bodies of all animals including ourselves, has clearly broken down."[71] But everything depends here on understanding what Descartes *means* when he states that an animal experiences fear, hope, or joy. Descartes attributes such passions to animals in connection with talk of training animals to perform; and he gives as an example the idea that a magpie will "hope" to receive a piece of food after performing a trick if it has always been given a piece of food after performing the trick. Descartes stresses that "hope" cannot mean the same thing for the magpie as it means for a human being: "It seems to me very striking that the use of words [such as fear, hope, and joy], so defined, is something peculiar to human beings."[72] In animals, expression of hope and the like "can be performed without any thought."[73] What we call expressions of pain, fear, hope, and so on in animals are nothing more than outward behavioral responses, whereas in sentient beings such expressions have conscious concomitants that render those expressions different in kind.[74]

Descartes's Theory of the Passions and His View of Morality

Any lingering doubts concerning Descartes's estimation of the moral status of animals can be laid to rest when the foregoing discussion of Descartes's views is considered against the background of his several proposals for experiments to be performed on the hearts of live animals. In 1638, Descartes details a set of experiments conducted on the hearts of live fish and rabbits. Writing to Plempius, he says that the hearts of fish, "after they have been cut out, go on beating for much longer than the heart of any terrestrial animal"; and he goes on to explain how he has refuted a view of Galen's concerning the functioning of cardiac arteries by having "opened the chest of a live rabbit and removed the ribs to expose the heart and the trunk of the aorta. . . . Continuing the vivisection [*Pergens autem in hac animalis viui dissectione*], I cut away half the heart."[75] And in the "Description of the Human Body," written in 1647–1648, Descartes says that certain of Harvey's views concerning blood pressure in the heart can be corroborated "by a very striking experiment. If you slice off the pointed end of the heart in a live dog, and insert a finger into one of the cavities, you will feel unmistakably that every time the heart gets shorter it presses the finger, and every time it gets longer it stops pressing it."[76] Descartes proceeds to discuss other observations that can be made in the course of this experiment, and he also says that there are certain advantages to be gained from performing the experiment on the heart of a live rabbit instead of a dog.[77] All this is reported by Descartes from the standpoint of one who has conducted the experiments himself; and given his explicit statement in the letter to Plempius that he has performed a similar experiment on a live rabbit, there is no reason to believe that he has not performed this experiment as well. Moreover, the tenor of his remarks is that of curiosity and excitement rather than one of admonition or disapproval; in keeping with the unbridled ambitions of Descartes's project of mastery, there is no trace of Augustine's treatment of theoretical curiosity as *concupiscentia oculorum*. In the face of these proposals, it is difficult to take much comfort in Harrison's observation that Descartes was a devoted dog owner, which for Harrison is supposed to signify that Descartes's behavior "was not [that] of one who considered [animals to be] unfeeling machines."[78]

Descartes's view of the moral status of animals is a consequence of some more basic commitments about morality expressed in his writings.

Descartes never articulates the systematic theory of morality anticipated by the "provisional morality" of the *Discourse*, a definitive morality that was to be the capstone of rational method.[79] Descartes makes further reference to such a morality in the preface to the *Principles of Philosophy*, where he speaks of a "highest and most perfect moral system [*Morale*], which presupposes a complete knowledge of the other sciences and is the ultimate level of wisdom."[80] Descartes presents his principal thoughts on such an ethics in *The Passions of the Soul* and in correspondence with Princess Elizabeth of Bohemia, Queen Christina of Sweden, and Hector-Pierre Chanut (French ambassador to Sweden) during the mid to late 1640s.[81]

The *Passions* and that correspondence contain a conception of moral status whose essence John J. Blom captures in the following observation: "According to Descartes, animals other than man are swept along to narrowly preordained reactions by sheer physiological mechanism and reflexivity. Passivity is their whole estate, not merely a symptom of an incompletely developed nature or lack of good fortune. Man, however, in virtue of his very capacity for reasonable loves, hates, and desires, will continue to suffer a passivity unnatural to himself until his reason learns not to misconstrue experience and begins to hit the mark in questions about values."[82]

One is reminded of the principle that guides Aquinas's view of animals: *non agunt sed magis aguntur*. Because animals are nonrational, their desires and their actions are determined by the effects that external objects have on their bodily organs. Rational beings, on the other hand, are capable of self-determination in virtue of the fact that they can have knowledge of external ends and of the means toward those ends. Hence human beings, as a composite of mind (soul) and body, are subject to the same sorts of bodily desires as animals, but are able to reflect on those desires and render them (or supplant them with) "reasonable loves, hates, and desires."

To give an account of how this is possible is essentially the program of *The Passions of the Soul*. The moral theory of the *Passions* is one according to which virtue consists in achieving "a firm and constant resolution" to do whatever one judges to be best.[83] The dividing line between beings that are worthy of esteem and beings that are not is "the exercise of our free will and the control we have over our volitions."[84] All and only those beings that possess free will, and hence possess the reason that enables the will to *be* free, have moral worth. Membership in moral community makes it incumbent on human beings, as a composite of soul and body, to struggle to overcome inappropriate influences that the body can exert over the soul, for example, the inclination to flee when one should stand and fight. Descartes states that the possession of reason can enable us to gain complete mastery over our passions through knowledge of the truth, whereas the lack of reason in animals prevents them from achieving any kind of self-mastery.[85]

The Passions of the Soul clarifies the relationship of the passions to the project of moral self-mastery. Descartes distinguishes between actions (volitions) and passions, and he further distinguishes between passions of the body and of the soul. He defines the passions of the soul as "the various perceptions or modes of knowledge present in us"; these may be perceptions of our own volitions, or they may be representations caused by our bodily states.[86] In either case, the passions of the soul are intentional states that take the form of conscious awareness, either of our own acting or of our being acted upon. It is in virtue of such passions that we are able to reflect on our desires and render them rational, which is the key to rendering our conduct morally worthwhile. Because animals, as mechanisms, do not experience passions of the soul (although they certainly manifest bodily passions) they are incapable in principle of rendering their desires rational; and to this extent, they are excluded from moral community. Hence the question whether animals can feel is not decisive for Descartes's view of the moral status of animals, although it is a question that the terms of his dualism required him to address; the basis for his exclusion of animals from the sphere of moral obligation is the same conception of moral oikeiosis that guided his philosophical forbears.

Descartes's application of strict dualism to the traditional principle of oikeiosis leads him to the conviction that we owe no moral obligations to nature as mechanism—not even to animal nature, which is the highest form of mechanism in the material world. To this extent the conventional wisdom first articulated by Henry More is correct, although More is wrong to imply that the denial of feeling in animals is the basis for Descartes's assessment of their moral status. The essence of Descartes's reasoning is not so much that animals are incapable of feeling pain as that they lack any kind of awareness. In the final analysis, animals are incapable of feeling precisely because they lack consciousness, and they lack consciousness because God did not give them immaterial souls. In contrast, the possession of consciousness, which for Descartes is coextensive with the possession of rationality, qualifies human beings as beings with moral worth. Even though human beings are embodied, their essential being as immortal soul-substance is separable from their corporeal being, so that from an *essential* standpoint human beings can be said not to exist within nature at all. This in turn grants human beings the license to manipulate nature in any way they wish, provided that their actions promote the welfare of mankind. By viewing animals as pure mechanism, Descartes reduces them to mere means for the end of human happiness. And in doing so, he makes his commitments regarding the moral status of animals unmistakable.

The problem with Descartes's thinking is not, as Cottingham says, a "fuzziness" concerning the relationship between consciousness and self-consciousness.[87] Descartes is unequivocal in denying consciousness to animals. His views on the nature of animal experience suffer not from "fuzziness" but from their implausibility by contemporary standards.[88] Those who attribute to Descartes the view that animals possess consciousness misrepresent his views and thereby fail to see why he categorically excludes nonhuman animals from moral consideration.

THE EMPIRICISTS, THE
UTILITARIANS, AND KANT

Descartes and the Christian medieval thinkers address the problem of animal suffering in different ways. The Christian tradition acknowledges animal suffering but sees it as an inevitable consequence of human dominion. Acts of cruelty are prohibited, but only on the grounds that such treatment is ultimately bad for human relations. Descartes treats animal suffering as a pseudoproblem by arguing that animals are mechanisms and therefore not sentient. The views of the leading philosophers in the eighteenth and nineteenth centuries reflect dissatisfaction with Descartes's strict dualism and recognition that Aquinas's views on animal capacities merit further consideration. These philosophers agree that animals are sentient and that their suffering demands some kind of moral consideration. But they disagree on the proper characterization of animal sentience and on the exact moral status of animal suffering.

The initial strain of thinking to emerge in the wake of Descartes is a utilitarianism developed by Jeremy Bentham and later elaborated by John Stuart Mill. These thinkers take their bearings from the empiricist trajectory of thinking initiated by Hobbes and completed by Hume. The empiricist standpoint derives all experience and all thought from sensation. A corollary of this empiricist starting point is that human beings and animals share the same basic capacities for sentience and hence differ only in degree, not in kind. The empiricists, like most figures in the Western tradition, distinguish humans from animals on the basis of abstract rational thought; but unlike many of their predecessors, they argue that animals are capable of reasoning about particulars. Thus reason per se is not the exclusive possession of human beings, and the capacity for abstract thought, while distinctive, does not make human beings absolutely superior to animals but only relatively superior. When Bentham and Mill take up the empiricist standpoint, however, they do not base their utilitarian moral judgments about humans and animals primarily on cognitive capacities. They conceive of "sentience" not in terms of capacities such as abstract thought, but in terms of sensation. They base all moral judgments on considerations of pleasure and pain, thereby making a place for animals in our moral considerations. Bentham and Mill set the terms for current debates concerning utilitarianism.

The terms of current debates about deontology take their bearings from Kant, who developed his views about morality and animals in the late eighteenth century. A contemporary of Bentham, Kant opposes the utilitarian program on the grounds that pleasure, pain, and happiness are fundamentally irrelevant to considerations of moral worth. Kant seeks a "pure" ground for determinations of moral worth that places all beings with moral worth on a par with one another. The problem with considerations of pleasure and pain is that they are born of selfish interest and distort our assessment of what is right. Like Aquinas, Kant sees our desire for pleasure and our aversion to pain as tendencies that make us like animals. What makes us distinctively human is our ability to rise above such inclinations and occupy an objective vantage point on right and wrong that is grounded in an absolute principle of morality. All and only "rational" beings are capable of occupying such a standpoint. Here, too, Kant disagrees with the utilitarians: To be rational is to be free in exactly the sense articulated by Aquinas; it is to be able to transcend the realm of sensation and assess our various inclinations. Animals are determined by their sensory inclinations, and as such they are fundamentally nonrational beings. This in turn means, as it does for Aquinas, that animals are never objects of direct moral obligations. In chapter I, I note that Tom Regan modifies Kant's deontology so as to treat animals as "moral patients." This is a modification that Kant would never accept. For Kant, all and only those beings that can contemplate the moral law are direct objects of moral respect. To all other beings we have, at best, indirect duties, which is to say that they have no moral value in themselves.

The dispute between Kant and the utilitarians comes down to the question whether we have direct duties toward animals or only indirect duties. It matters little that the discourse of the utilitarians does not include the rhetoric of duty; the utilitarianism of Bentham and Mill clearly points to the conclusion that animals figure in our moral calcu-

lus, that in many instances the happiness and suffering of animals create obligations on our part to treat animals in certain ways, and that these
obligations are directly to the animals in question rather than to
humanity. Thus the basic terms of utilitarianism appear to be less anthropocentric than those of deontology. But as a matter of historical fact this
difference has turned out to be insignificant: As I note in chapter I, the
conclusions of current utilitarians and deontologists are scarcely distin-
guishable from one another, even if their conceptual means for arriving at those conclusions are fundamentally different. Classical utilitarian doctrine, even though it proceeds from a basic kinship between human beings and animals, depends on some fundamental assumptions
about the nature of sentience that militate against this underlying sense
of kinship.

The Empiricist Background: Hobbes, Locke, and Hume

In Descartes's own time vigorous opposition was voiced to the idea that
human beings are fundamentally different from animals. In particular,
More insists that animals are more than mere mechanisms, and Gassendi
suggests that animals may possess some kind of linguistic capacity. The
most systematic philosophical attempt to deny fundamental differences
between humans and animals came from the empiricists, who consistently
maintained that all experience and thought originate in sensation, and
that the capacity for conceptual abstraction constitutes not a difference
in kind but simply one of degree between human beings and animals.

This line of thinking about the nature of animal experience comes
to fruition in Hume in the late eighteenth century, but its roots are in
Descartes's contemporary Hobbes. Against rationalists such as Descartes,
Hobbes advances an empiricist program according to which not only
human beings but also animals are capable of thought. In the "Third Set
of Objections" to Descartes's *Meditations*, Hobbes asserts that "it may be that
the thing that thinks is the subject [*subjectum*] to which mind, reason or
intellect belong; and this subject may thus be something corporeal."[1]
Hobbes assimilates animals to human beings, not by arguing that animals
have immortal souls but instead by arguing that all living beings, humans
included, are fundamentally corporeal. If human beings are fundamentally corporeal and can think, then, to the extent that animals are corporeal in ways that closely resemble human corporeality, animals too must
be capable of some kind of thought.

The basis of Hobbes's empiricism is the conviction that "life is but a motion of limbs." The heart is a spring, nerves are strings, and joints are "so many Wheeles, giving motion to the whole body."[2] Even the state is a mechanism.[3] Hobbes explains the capacity for thought in strictly mechanistic terms as well. Sensation, which is the origin of all thought, is caused "by the pressure, that is, by the motion, of externall things upon our Eyes, Eares, and other organs thereunto ordained."[4] Sensations are immediate and fleeting, but they are preserved in imagination, which is "decaying sense," a capacity "found in men, and many other living Creatures."[5] Imagination can take the form of simple memories or of manipulations of memories, as when we combine the memory of a horse with the memory of a man to produce the image of a centaur. Imagination is "decaying" in the sense that it is never as vivid as sensation. Understanding, in turn, is "the imagination that is raysed . . . by words, or other voluntary signes." This capacity "is common to Man and Beast."[6] Hobbes gives the example of a dog understanding its master's call: To "understand" is not to have a detached cognitive awareness of the master's intention; it is, upon hearing the master's command, to experience the image of going to the master. This image, in turn, is to produce a desire in the dog to approach the master. Desire is simply motion toward an object.[7] Similarly, aversion is nothing more than motion away from an object, so that if the master calls out a reproach, the dog will experience an image of receiving a beating and thereupon will form an inclination to move away from its master.

What distinguishes understanding in human beings is our "conceptions and thoughts, by the sequell and contexture of the names of things into Affirmations, Negations, and other formes of Speech."[8] Human understanding, in other words, is distinguished by its linguistic character, which facilitates the formation of abstract ideas and complex reasoning of which animals are incapable; speech enables humans to share knowledge and express our intentions to others in ways denied to animals.[9] Nonetheless, animals are capable of "ordered chains of thought," which are nothing more than chains of images of related causes and effects.[10] Thus animals, like human beings, can seek causes for effects that they have experienced, and can act prudentially, by anticipating the consequences of their actions; for example, the dog may hesitate to dig up its master's flower garden because the image of doing so gives rise to an associated image of being beaten. Animals, like human beings, are capable of deliberation, because "deliberation" is nothing more than a succession of desire and aversion to favorable and unfavorable consequences.[11] All thought is resolvable into successions of images.

In spite of these fundamental commonalities between human beings and animals, the human capacity for language is decisive in excluding animals from the sphere of right. Animals, like "fooles, children, [and] madmen," are not subject to the law of the commonwealth, "nor are they capable of the title of just, or unjust; because they had never power to make any covenant, or to understand the consequences thereof."[12] But whereas fools, children, and madmen are human and hence are due certain obligations as members, albeit deficient ones, of the human community, we have "dominion over animals" in virtue of our "natural strength and powers." One "may at discretion reduce to one's service any animals that can be tamed or made useful, and wage continual war against the rest as harmful, and hunt them down and kill them."[13] In contrast, the laws of nature demand that we seek peace among human beings and resort to violence only in cases in which our lives are at stake.[14] Relations among human beings are to be based on reciprocity, those between humans and animals on absolute dominion.

The views of Locke and Hume are essentially refinements of Hobbes's position. Locke, writing a generation after Hobbes, tells the story of a Brazilian parrot "that spoke, and asked, and answered common Questions like a reasonable Creature," all in impeccable French. Locke does not say whether he considers the story to be true, but simply states that if the parrot were able to "discourse, reason, and philosophize," it would have to be considered "a very intelligent rational parrot."[15] Locke's views on animal capacities, however, make it clear that he does not take the story seriously. Locke follows Hobbes in considering sensation to be the origin of all thought. He stresses, against Descartes, that not thought but rather sensation and passion are the core of experience. Animals share with human beings not only the capacity for sensation and passion, but also the capacity for thought. We cannot prove that animals think, any more than I can prove that another person thinks; but for practical purposes, animals exhibit "all the demonstration of [thought] imaginable, except only telling us, that they do so."[16] This is evident in the prudential capacities and the expressions of emotion that assimilate animals to human beings. But animals lack the capacity for abstraction. For Locke, as for Hobbes, all thoughts originate in particular, concrete experiences. Abstraction occurs when "the Mind makes the particular *Ideas*, received from particular Objects, to become general; which is done by considering them

as they are in the Mind such Appearances, separate from all other Ex-
istences, and the circumstances of real Existence, as Time, Place, or any
other concomitant *Ideas*."[17] The capacity for abstraction is the ability to
move from a group of particulars related by a common feature, to a conception of that common feature completely detached from the particular circumstances characterizing the various particulars in question. We
form an abstract idea of triangularity by moving from concrete experiences of particular triangular shapes, with particular locations and dimensions, to an idea that contains nothing but the essence shared in
common by all the particular triangles. General ideas are the sine qua non
of abstract reasoning and hence of sciences as diverse as physics and
politics.

For Locke, the capacity for abstraction is the clear dividing line between the mental capabilities of human beings and animals. "The having of general ideas, is that which puts a perfect distinction betwixt Man
and Brutes. . . . For it is evident, we observe no foot-steps in them, of
making use of general signs for universal *Ideas*; from which we have reason to imagine, that they have not the faculty of abstracting, or making
general *Ideas*, since they have no use of Words, or any other general
Signs."[18] Here Locke reproduces the thread of reasoning that persists
throughout the tradition from Aristotle to Descartes: Language and
abstract rationality are inseparable, so that any being lacking one must
necessarily lack the other. But Locke implicitly rejects Descartes's conception of animals when he states that "if [animals] have any ideas at all,
and are not bare Machins (as some would have them) we cannot deny them
to have some Reason. It seems as evident to me, that they do some of them
in certain Instances reason, as that they have sence; but it is only in particular *Ideas*, just as they receiv'd them from their senses."[19] This conception of reasoning draws on Hobbes's conception of reasoning in animals.
Animals are able to make associations between particular experiences, as
when the present impression of an event brings to mind the image of the
likely consequences of that event. Thus my cat can make an association
between the sight of a squirt gun (my last line of defense) and the prospect of getting wet, and she can make an association between the sight of
a garden hose and the same prospect; but she cannot generalize the notion
of objects that shoot water, that is, she cannot see the general relationship between squirt guns and garden hoses, nor between these objects and
yet other objects that shoot water.

Because animals "are tied up within these narrow bounds," they have little or no ability to scrutinize particular ideas "so as to perceive them to be perfectly different, and so consequently two, to cast about and consider in what circumstances they are capable to be compared."[20] Because animals are imprisoned in the concrete present and the immediate future, they cannot adopt the detached perspective from which ideas can be examined as such, and from which circumstances can be assessed according to general principles. Thus animals are incapable of certain knowledge, which is the perception of "the Agreement or Disagreement of any of our *Ideas*"; and they are incapable of certain real knowledge, the recognition that "those *Ideas* agree with the reality of Things."[21]

The inability of animals to engage in abstract reasoning excludes them from the social contract and subjects them to human dominion. Locke opens the *Essay Concerning Human Understanding* by stressing that "it is the *Understanding* that sets Man above the rest of sensible Beings, and gives him all the Advantage and Dominion, which he has over them."[22] In the treatises on government, Locke makes it clear that this dominion over animals is not simply a matter of fact but rather one of *right*. In the *Second Treatise*, he classifies animals as property and states that, unlike human beings, animals were made for our use; he bases both claims on the proposition that human beings are "all the Workmanship of one Omnipotent, and infinitely wise Maker," whereas animals are merely "the Servants of one Sovereign Master."[23] In the *First Treatise*, Locke justifies human dominion by appealing to Scripture. "God makes [man] *in his own image after his own Likeness*, makes him an intellectual Creature, and so capable of *Dominion*. . . . therefore David says in the *8th Psalm* . . . [that] *Thou hast made him little lower than Angels, thou has made him to have Dominion*."[24] Locke writes at length of Genesis 1:28, in which God gives Adam dominion over the earth. He notes further that after the Flood, God grants Noah prerogatives over animals that Adam did not enjoy, and he goes to some lengths to establish that Noah's prerogatives over animals were not private but extend to all of humanity. These prerogatives include "a Right, to make use of the Food and Rayment" with which God has provided us.[25] The focal point of the *Second Treatise* is the protection and cultivation of life, liberty, and property. Any consideration that animals merit in society is simply a corollary of Locke's law of nature, which "teaches all Mankind, who will but consult it, that being all equal and independent, no one ought to harm another in his Life, Health, Liberty, and Possessions."[26]

Animals are instrumentalities given to us by God to serve us in our pursuit of human welfare. It is our prerogative even to "destroy" such "Inferior Creatures . . . where need requires it."[27]

Hume, writing nearly a century after Locke, completes the trajectory of empiricist thinking about animals by affirming his predecessors' views about animal cognition and developing a theory of property rights that places animals on a par with plants and slaves. Unlike Hobbes and Locke, Hume does not address the question of human dominion over animals directly. His suggestion that "the life of a man is of no greater importance to the universe than that of an oyster" points toward the possibility that Hume had a different view of dominion than his forbears.[28] But Hume's writings on morals make it clear that he is ultimately unconcerned with the point of view of the universe. His sole concern is the standpoint of human relations and the need, recognized by the social contract theorists, to provide human beings with a motivation for respecting the principles of reciprocity and mutual respect.

Hume bases his interpretation of the experiential capacities of animals on analogy to human experience. Just as we may draw physiological analogies between animals with similar circulatory systems, "any theory, by which we explain the operations of the understanding, or the origin and connexion of the passions in man, will acquire additional authority, if we find, that the same theory is requisite to explain the same phenomena in all other animals."[29] On this basis, Hume argues that animals draw inferences and form beliefs, and that an animal's ability to do so improves with experience. Thus animals establish knowledge over time about such phenomena as fire and water.[30] When we think of the capacity to draw inferences and form beliefs in this connection, Hume stresses that we should not conceive of these operations as acts of detached cognition. Instead, in animals as in human beings, "belief is more properly an act of the sensitive, than of the cogitative part of our natures."[31] Inferences and beliefs are formed through a process of simple association: When we experience an immediate impression of an object or event with which we have prior familiarity (or that is similar to an object with which we have prior familiarity), our imagination immediately produces the image of an event that has commonly followed the present event in time.[32] If I brandish the water pistol at my cat, she will immediately associate this action with the image of getting soaked. The belief or inference is "sensitive" rather than cogitative in the sense that I *feel* an irresistible impulse to assume that the first event will be succeeded by the second event. The process is largely the same in animals as in human beings: In both, instinct functions to produce the association and the irresistible impulse.[33]

The difference between reasoning in animals and human beings is that the rationality of animals is limited to inferences about "matters of fact," which concern concrete and immediate causal relations, whereas in human beings the capacity for generalization enables us to reason about "relations of ideas" as well. This ability makes possible "abstract reasoning" in demonstrative sciences such as algebra, through "the discovery of the proportions of ideas, consider'd as such."[34] It also makes possible the formation of general considerations concerning the form of social organization that is most conducive to human welfare. When Hume turns to the question of social relations in book 3 of the *Treatise*, he says almost nothing about animals. But what he does say reveals a great deal about his view of the moral status of animals. Animals draw inferences and experience a range of passions, such as love, hate, sympathy, fear, courage, envy, and malice; they also exhibit a clear sensitivity to each other's pain and pleasure, as is evident from the play behavior of animals.[35] Animals exhibit particular virtues and vices. But unlike human beings, they have no capacity to "discover" virtues and vices as such, hence they are not subject to moral evaluation.[36] Nor are animals capable of participating in matters of justice or property, since their relations to things "must lie solely in the body; and can never be plac'd either in the mind or external objects."[37] Thus human beings "are superior to beasts principally by the superiority of their reason," which gives rise to general principles of prudence, right, property, and obligation.[38]

These general principles are established by convention among human beings to promote peaceful coexistence.[39] Hume implicitly believes that all and only those beings capable of establishing such conventions are entitled to be beneficiaries of them. Justice and the property rights founded upon justice are founded on reciprocity.[40] Animals are incapable of reciprocity and hence of justice, obligation, right, and property. They are mere instrumentalities, without rights or moral status. "The fruits of our garden, the offspring of our cattle, and the work of our slaves, are all of them esteem'd our property."[41] It is the "nature" of such "inferior beings" to be "*useful* and *beneficial*" to us.[42] Hume bases this conclusion not on detached reasoning about the structure of the universe, but rather on the tendencies of human sentiment. Morality, like belief, "is more properly felt than judg'd of."[43] In effect, animals have the status of property not because of any cosmic truth, but because human beings are generally content to treat them that way. The life of an oyster has a different importance to human beings than to the universe.

Utilitarianism: Bentham and Mill

The British empiricists all acknowledge that animals experience passions and feel pleasure and pain. But instead of basing moral judgments on considerations of pain and pleasure, they implicitly accept the traditional principle that the putatively inferior cognitive abilities of animals disqualify animals as direct objects of moral concern; at most, we should treat animals in certain ways because we are obliged to respect the property rights of their owners. Among the empiricists, Hume comes closest to overturning this conventional wisdom when he assimilates the process of deliberation and belief formation in animals and humans: in both, the process is "more sensitive than cogitative." The recognition that feeling plays a fundamental role in human choice brings with it a recognition that we are more like than unlike animals, and this in turn opens up the possibility of taking the fortunes of animals into account in our moral reflections. In particular, it points toward the prospect of incorporating considerations of animal suffering into a calculus of pleasures and pains. But Hume does not pursue this possibility. Instead he takes only the direct welfare interests of human beings into account in developing his moral and social ideals.

A utilitarianism that focuses on sentience as the capacity for feeling and incorporates considerations of the welfare of animals as well as human beings was first explored in a preliminary way by Jeremy Bentham, who published *An Introduction to the Principles of Morals and Legislation* in 1789, thirteen years after Hume's death.[44] Bentham follows Hume in conceiving of belief as a "sentiment" rather than an act of detached cognition.[45] He likewise conceives of moral deliberation as a process driven by feeling rather than by abstract reasoning: "Passion calculates, more or less, in every man."[46] In principle, "acts of the mind" just *are* sentiments.[47] Bentham argues that pleasure and pain are our "two sovereign masters," and that our moral choices should be based on the instructions of these masters. The principle of utility provides a "standard of right and wrong" according to which all our choices should promote "the greatest happiness of all those whose interest is in question."[48] One could develop an anthropocentric utilitarianism according to which only the pleasures and pains of human beings are taken into account; this, in effect, is what Hume does in book 3 of the *Treatise*. But Bentham goes another way. He maintains that the capacity for suffering, rather than the capacity for abstract reasoning or language, is the proper basis for a being's inclusion in moral calculations:

> The French have already discovered that the blackness of the skin is no reason why a human being should be abandoned without redress to the caprice of a tormenter. It may come one day to be recognized, that the number of the legs, the villosity of the skin, or the termination of the *os sacrum*, are reasons equally insufficient for abandoning a sensitive being to the same fate. What else is it that should trace the insuperable line? Is it the faculty of reason, or, perhaps, the faculty of discourse? But a full-grown horse or dog is beyond comparison a more rational, as well as a more conversable animal, than an infant of a day, or a week, or even a month, old. But suppose the case were otherwise, what would it avail? the question is not, Can they *reason*? nor, Can they *talk*? but, Can they *suffer*?[49]

Bentham derides "the ancient jurists," in whose eyes animals "stand degraded into the class of *things*."[50] But Bentham himself does not entirely escape the influence of this ancient prejudice. In the same passage in which he proclaims that the capacity for suffering is the proper basis for including a being in our moral calculations, Bentham states that there is nothing wrong with our killing animals to provide ourselves with food; he even implies that animals are better off dying at our hands rather than dying a natural death. When we kill animals for food, "we are the better for it, and they are never the worse. They have none of those long-protracted anticipations of future misery which we have. The death they suffer in our hands commonly is, and always may be, a speedier, and by that means a less painful one, than that which would await them in the inevitable course of nature. . . . We should be the worse for their living, and they are never the worse for being dead."[51] An animal's inability to engage in abstract reasoning makes it incapable of contemplating anything more remote than the extremely near term. Hence its awareness of what it has to lose by dying is dim by comparison to human awareness of such a loss; based on sheer calculations of pleasure and pain, the animal loses little because it is *aware* of losing little. Moreover, we do animals a favor by killing them for our food, since the alternative of dying in the adversity of nature would be considerably more painful.

Bentham never considers the possibility that an event such as death can be harmful even if the being in question is unaware of the extent of the harm. Instead he calculates the quality of a being's life on the basis of its ability to feel pleasure or pain, and he sees a direct correlation between a being's ability to prosper or suffer and its ability to contemplate its future. On this view, beings lacking contemplative ability are a fortiori inferior to beings possessing that ability. Bentham makes only a gesture toward this reasoning in *The Principles of Morals and Legislation*. But it gets developed by John Stuart Mill in the mid-nineteenth century, and thereafter it becomes canonical in utilitarian thought. This orientation is easy to overlook in Mill's thought because he devotes a great deal of energy to arguing that animals must be included in our utilitarian calculus. Against those, such as William Whewell, who maintain that the interests of animals should never be placed above those of human beings, Mill states that the central question must always be this: "Granted that any practice causes more pain to animals than it gives pleasure to man; is that practice moral or immoral?" Mill's answer is that it is unquestionably immoral.[52] If we reject this reasoning, we might as well say that feudal lords were right to place their own happiness above that of many serfs, and that slaveholders were right to refuse to promote the happiness of blacks at the expense of that of whites; the historical proclivity of whites to discount the interests of blacks and of humans to discount the interest of animals is due to the fact that we tend "to estimate the pleasures and pains of others as deserving regard exactly in proportion to their likeness to ourselves."[53] Instead of assessing our "likeness" to other beings on the basis of considerations such as physiognomy and skin color, we should focus on the ability to experience pleasure and pain. In this respect animals are very much like human beings. Hence the reasons that recommend legal intervention on behalf of children likewise recommend intervention on behalf of animals. In particular, animals deserve anticruelty laws, not because such laws are advantageous to human beings but because of "the intrinsic merits of the case itself."[54]

Mill's call for consideration of the fortunes of animals follows in part from his rejection of the traditional prejudice that earthly things were made for the sake of humanity. "The scheme of Nature regarded in its whole extent, cannot have had, for its sole or even principal object, the good of human or other sentient beings. What good it brings to them, is mostly the result of their own exertions."[55] But in spite of this rejection of Stoic–Christian dogma, Mill reasserts the human prerogative to master nature. "The ways of Nature are to be conquered, not obeyed. . . . All praise of Civilization, or Art, or Convenience, is so much dispraise of nature; an admission of imperfection, which it is man's business, and merit, to be always endeavoring to correct or mitigate."[56] Our goal should not be to harmonize with nature, but rather to exploit it for the sake of human community. Mill categorically rejects all idealized views of nature and instead reduces nature to instrumentality.

Mill is thus subject to the same ambivalence about animals exhibited by so many thinkers in the tradition. Animals are sufficiently like human beings in the relevant respects that we may not be indifferent to animals; but animals have a fundamentally inferior status in our moral considerations, which is to say that the interests of human beings ultimately take precedence over those of animals. Mill's utilitarianism, like Bentham's, requires us to take the likely suffering of animals into consideration in our moral reflections. But his account of the nature of animal suffering mitigates the force of this principle. In *Utilitarianism*, Mill makes a distinction between different kinds of pleasure and argues that human beings are capable of experiencing pleasures superior to the carnal pleasures enjoyed by beasts. "Human beings have faculties more elevated than the animal appetites, and when once made conscious of them, do not regard anything as happiness which does not include their gratification. . . . Pleasures of the intellect, of the feelings and imagination, and of the moral sentiments [have] a much higher value as pleasures than [do] those of mere sensation."[57] In calculations of pleasure and pain, "it would be absurd" to suppose that "the estimation of pleasures should be supposed to depend on quantity alone"; the quality of pleasures and pains is also of fundamental importance. The special quality of intellectual and moral pleasures is such that "few human creatures would consent to be changed into any of the lower animals, for a promise of the fullest allowance of a beast's pleasures."[58] What human beings possess and animals lack is "a sense of dignity . . . which is so essential a part of the happiness of those in whom it is strong, that nothing which conflicts with it could be, otherwise than momentarily, an object of desire to them."[59] This sense of dignity makes us desire and take satisfaction in morality, justice, and the "higher" pleasures to which "dumb" animals are entirely insensitive. Our "more developed intelligence . . . gives a wider range to the whole of [our] sentiments" and enables us to form a social bond with all human beings.[60]

Mill's conclusion regarding the relative worth of human beings and animals is that "it is better to be a human being dissatisfied than a pig satisfied; better to be Socrates dissatisfied than a fool satisfied. And if the fool, or the pig, is of a different opinion, it is because they only know their own side of the question. The other party to the comparison knows both sides."[61] Mill does not tell us exactly how much preference the "higher" interests of human beings should receive over the "brute" interests of animals. But his remarks about the imperative to "conquer" nature suggest that his views are very much like Bentham's: The lives of animals have worth in their own right, inasmuch as animals are capable of enjoyment and suffering; hence we have duties not to inflict gratuitous suffering on animals. But the fundamental superiority of "intelligent" human beings entitles us to give priority to our own welfare over that of animals, at least in cases in which the happiness enjoyed by humans is greater than the suffering imposed on animals. That happiness is to be reckoned not only quantitatively but also qualitatively, and given that the qualitative possibilities for happiness are much greater in humans than in animals, Mill intimates that the use of animals to satisfy human desires is entirely permissible as long as we find ways to minimize animal suffering. Given the differences in experiential capacities, humans are capable of greater suffering than animals, hence the lives of animals are worth less than the lives of humans.

Kant's Deontology

A contemporary of Bentham, Kant roundly rejects considerations of pleasure and pain in moral reflections and instead seeks an absolute rational principle to serve as the basis for morality. Kant shares Hume's concern that our natural sentiments lead us to give preference to ourselves and our loved ones over strangers; and like Hume, Kant sees the need for equality and reciprocity in considerations of morality and justice. But unlike Hume, Kant does not believe that prudent self-interest by itself can move us beyond partiality and make us respect strangers as we respect those close to us.[62] Where the utilitarians equate moral good with happiness, understood as the maximization of pleasure and the minimization of pain for the greatest number affected, Kant maintains that "making a man happy is quite different than making him good."[63] Considerations of pleasure and pain inevitably distort our judgments about what is right and good. Even feelings such as sympathy, which is the cornerstone of a viable utilitarianism, are fundamentally "pathological" because they cannot escape the influence of self-interest and partiality.[64] In place of a concern for consequences, Kant maintains that "the preeminent good which is called moral can consist in nothing but the representation of the law in itself, and such a representation can admittedly be found only in a rational being insofar as this representation, and not some expected effect, is the determining ground of the will."[65] The "law" is the moral law, which commands unconditional respect for rational beings, without regard to consequences.

To merit moral respect, a being must qualify as a "person" rather than a "thing." A person is a being "whose existence has in itself an absolute worth, something which as an end in itself could be a ground of determinate laws."[66] To be a ground of determinate laws is to be capable of adducing and contemplating the moral law for oneself; it is to be capable of legislating the law of respect and following the law that one has legislated. The capacity for legislation and voluntary subjection to the moral law is unique to rational beings, which "are called persons inasmuch as their nature already marks them out as ends in themselves, i.e., as something which is not to be used merely as means and hence there is imposed thereby a limit on all arbitrary use of such beings, which are thus objects of respect."[67] All nonrational beings, "whose existence depends not on our will but on nature have . . . only a relative value as means and are therefore called things."[68] A "thing" is "something to be used merely as a means," whereas a person "must in all his actions always be regarded as an end in himself."[69] Kant explicitly distances himself from the Christian view that human beings were made in God's image. By means of his transcendental turn, Kant argues that we cannot know the nature of things beyond our own experience, and this means that we can neither prove God's existence nor establish knowledge of his nature or intentions. But Kant nonetheless adheres to the traditional prejudice that nonrational beings are instrumentalities to be used by rational beings.

On Kant's view, human beings count preeminently as persons, and animals are unquestionably things. His account of the differences between humans and animals is strikingly reminiscent of Aquinas's view. Kant first appears to treat animals as Cartesian mechanisms. He considers animal existence to be subject to "*mechanical ordering*," in contrast with the capacity of rational beings for self-determination.[70] But Kant rejects the notion that animals are mere automata by arguing by analogy "from the similarity between animal behavior [*Wirkung*] (whose basis we cannot perceive directly) and man's behavior (of whose basis we are conscious directly) . . . that animals too act according to *representations* [*Vorstellungen*] (rather than being machines, as Descartes would have it)." Animals are "living beings" of "the same general kind as human beings."[71]

As living beings, animals are governed by instinct and bodily inclinations. Like Aquinas, Kant believes that "all animals have the capacity to use their powers according to choice [*nach Willkühr*]. Yet this choice is not free, but necessitated by incentives and *stimuli* [*durch Reitze und stimulos neceßitiert*]. Their actions contain *bruta necessitas*."[72] "Animals are necessitated *per stimulos*, so that a dog must eat if he is hungry and has something in front of him."[73] Even though animals are not mere machines, "their nature develops automatically [*von selbst*]." In human beings, on the other hand, our nature develops "by art, and so we cannot allow nature a free hand."[74] The nature of a human being is to be an end in itself, an end worthy of moral respect, and as such human beings must learn to subjugate their carnal nature to the pure demands of rationality. The key difference between human beings and animals is that human beings possess autonomy, which for Kant is the capacity to determine one's will in accordance with the dictates of reason rather than those of mere corporeal nature. Whereas animals are subject to mechanical ordering, "nature gave man reason, and freedom of will based upon reason, and this in itself was a clear indication of nature's intention as regards his endowments. For it showed that man was not meant to be guided by instinct or equipped and instructed by innate knowledge; on the contrary, he was meant to produce everything from out of himself."[75] Animals are strictly determined by their corporeal nature, whereas rationality makes human beings capable of progress. This ideal of self-improvement distinguishes human beings from animals, and underlies Kant's conviction that the only comprehensible final purpose in the world is "*man under moral laws*."[76]

In rejecting the Cartesian conception of pure mechanism in favor of a Thomistic recognition of animal instincts and passions, Kant acknowledges a continuity between humanity and animality. But he sets as his moral ideal the progressive transcendence of our animal tendencies toward a "kingdom of ends" in complete harmony with the dictates of rationality and the principle of respect for persons.[77] The realization of such a kingdom requires the progressive subjugation of subjective interest and inclination to the demands of universal reason. Animals are not capable of membership in such a kingdom because they are pure "nature," driven by instinct. But human beings are subject to nature (empirical will) and rationality (intelligible will), and we are capable of bringing our empirical inclinations under the authority of reason. Given our dual nature as animality and humanity, we possess two distinct types of value.

> In the system of nature, a human being (*homo phaenomenon, animal rationale*) is a being of slight importance and shares with the rest of the animals, as offspring of the earth, an ordinary value (*pretium vulgare*). . . . But a human being regarded as a person, that is, as the subject of a morally practical reason, is exalted above any price; for as a person (*homo noumenon*) he is not to be valued merely as a means to the ends of others or even to his own ends, but as an end in himself, that is, he possesses a *dignity* (an absolute inner worth) by which he exacts *respect* for himself from all other rational beings in the world.[78]

Kant gives a clear priority to intrinsic moral worth over the "ordinary value" of natural beings. Mere life becomes subordinated to the constellation of beings who can realize a "kingdom of ends." Human beings are part mere nature, but we are also part autonomous will. With a firm commitment to cultivating our rational nature, in the course of time we "will be ever more remote from nature," that is, we will progressively subjugate our "predisposition to animality" to our "predisposition to humanity."[79]

Against the background of Kant's conception of rational beings as ends in themselves, animals emerge as "things," mere means for the satisfaction of higher ends. "Man has, in his own person, an inviolability [*eine Unverletzlichkeit*]; it is something holy, that has been entrusted to us. All else is subject to man . . . That which a man can dispose over, must be a thing. Animals are here regarded as things [*Sachen*]; but man is no thing."[80] Our understanding gives us this disposition over animals. "Man is indeed the only being on earth that has understanding and hence an ability to set himself purposes of his own choice, and in this respect he holds the title of lord of nature; and if we regard nature as a teleological system, then it is man's vocation to be the ultimate purpose of nature."[81] The condition for viewing nature as a teleological system is that we be able to "give both nature and [ourselves] reference to a purpose that can be independent of nature, self-sufficient, and a final purpose"; that final purpose is "*civil society*."[82] Kant sketches a cosmopolitan ideal that, like the

Stoic ideal, elevates humanity above mere nature and entitles us to use natural beings to place ourselves in the position to let "our natural predispositions develop maximally."[83] From Kant's cosmopolitan standpoint, animal nature is "an instrument for satisfying desires and inclinations [ein Instrument die Begierden und Neygungen zu befriedigen]."[84] Kant's cosmopolitan perspective follows the terms of Stoic cosmopolitanism in many respects; in particular, Kant accepts the Stoic principle that all and only rational beings belong to the sphere of justice. Unlike the Stoics, however, who believe that animals can have community among themselves, Kant maintains that animals are utterly incapable of "community [Gemeinschaft]," not only with human beings but even among themselves.[85]

Kant is the first to use the term "indirect duties" in characterizing the moral status of animals. Like Aquinas, Kant believes that animals are inferior in principle to human beings, and that as a result animals have no direct moral worth of their own. We can experience feelings such as sympathy for animals, but we cannot relate to them as beings with moral worth in themselves. "Respect always applies to persons only, never to things. The latter can awaken inclinations, and even love if they are animals (horses, dogs, etc.), or fear, as does the sea, a volcano, or a beast of prey; but they never arouse respect."[86] Such inclinations to feel tenderly toward animals are not, however, moral obligations. Instead, such inclinations really refer to humanity: "Even gratitude for the long service of an old horse or dog (just as if they were members of the household) belongs indirectly to a human being's duty with regard to these [in Ansehung dieser] animals; considered as a direct duty, however, it is always only a duty of the human being to [gegen] himself."[87] Feelings of fondness and gratitude toward animals have no moral significance in themselves, but only as such feelings further our cultivation of our humanity. We treat faithful animals well because it would be less than fully human not to do so.

For comparable reasons, we refrain from destroying inanimate nature gratuitously and from engaging in acts of cruelty toward animals.

A propensity to wanton destruction of what is beautiful in inanimate nature (spiritus destructionis) is opposed to a human being's duty to himself; for it weakens or uproots that feeling in him which, though not of itself moral, is still a disposition [Stimmung] of sensibility that greatly promotes morality . . . .With regard to the animate but nonrational part of creation, violent and cruel treatment of animals is far more intimately opposed to a human being's duty to himself, and he has a duty to refrain from this; for it dulls his shared feeling of their suffering and so weakens and gradually uproots a natural predisposition that is very serviceable to morality in one's relations with other men.[88]

It is wrong to be cruel to animals, not because we transgress against a moral bond with animals but because we violate a principle of respect for *humanity*—it is degrading to human beings to exercise cruelty, just as it is degrading to be wasteful or to fail to cultivate one's talents. But killing and working animals does not infringe upon our humanity. "The human being is authorized to kill animals quickly (without pain) and to put them to work that does not strain them beyond their capacities (such work as he himself must submit to)."[89] And even though cruelty toward animals violates duties to humanity, Kant says that cruelty is permissible if it leads to useful results for human beings. "When anatomists take living animals to experiment on, that is certainly cruelty, though there it is employed for a good purpose [*zu was gutem*]; because animals are regarded as man's instruments, it is acceptable, though it is never so in sport [*als ein Spiel*]."[90] "Agonizing physical experiments for the sake of mere speculation, when the end could also be achieved without these, are to be abhorred."[91] But given that animals are mere "things" to be used for the sake of human lordship over nature, cruelty toward them is entirely justifiable if it is not gratuitous but promises material benefits for humanity.

For all his similarities to Aquinas—he makes a distinction in principle between rational and nonrational beings, reduces nonrational beings to the status of things, and denies any direct moral significance to animal suffering—Kant develops a position that is surprisingly close to that of the utilitarians. Even though the utilitarians stress the commonality of feeling in humans and animals and make the capacity to suffer a sufficient condition for inclusion in direct moral considerations, their distinction between "higher" and "lower" feelings significantly weakens their claim that we have obligations to treat sentient animals in certain ways. Whether the basis be feeling or rationality, Kant and the utilitarians both find ways to represent animals as fundamentally inferior to human beings. To this extent, both approaches reproduce the prejudices of the tradition.

CONCEPTIONS OF CONTINUITY
Schopenhauer, Darwin, and Schweitzer

The Romantic Background: Condillac, Rousseau, Herder

Kant's transcendental turn brings with it the denial that we can know the inner nature of reality, and this means that we cannot purport to *know* that the soul (or God, or anything outside the physical realm) exists. Kant treats notions such as the mind and human freedom as transcendental conditions for the possibility of experience and scientific knowledge, that is, these are the *forms* that the coherent experience of nature and ourselves always take. Thus, for example, we cannot prove that we are free, but instead freedom is the necessary presupposition of a viable ethics—freedom is the precondition for the possibility of moral responsibility.[1] The same holds for the human mind: Even if we cannot prove that the mind exists, for Kant the only viable epistemology is one that treats the mind *as if* it exists outside of nature, as the "subject" of experience. From this standpoint, both our knowledge of and our relationship to nature are to be understood as products of a bridge to nature established by a being that transcends nature.

Even before Kant's time, philosophers expressed serious misgivings about the sort of dualism that views the human soul or mind as fundamentally separate from and superior to nature and the body. Where Descartes and Kant both denigrate embodied experience on the grounds that it distorts our pursuit of knowledge, the empiricists and the utilitarians reject dualism and lay the foundation for a reassertion of the primacy of embodied experience. This sense of the primacy of the body, which figures so centrally in the thought of Aristotle (for whom, for example, soul is not separate from body but rather is the form of a body's activity), appealed to the sensibilities of a number of thinkers in the eighteenth and nineteenth centuries and culminated in Romanticism in the generations after Kant. The primary aim of the Romantics was not to arrive at an edified conception of animals. Instead, they sought to overcome the ways in which the dualist tradition had distorted our understanding of the human condition. An important if unwitting by-product of the Romantic revolution is the assertion of some key affinities between human beings and animals that could contribute to the development of an ethic of kinship. The Romantics were interested less in elevating the status of animals than in mitigating what Nietzsche later calls "the extreme overvaluation of man" produced by Christian dualism.[2] Nonetheless, a sense of continuity between human beings and animals lies at the root of Romantic thought and informs the views of the most important thinkers on animals in the nineteenth and early twentieth centuries: Schopenhauer, Darwin, and Albert Schweitzer.

Romanticism is notoriously difficult to define. Isaiah Berlin, in a series of lectures on Romanticism, deferred even the attempt to offer a definition.[3] Nonetheless, there are some key themes that connect the movement's central thinkers and make it possible to speak of Romanticism as a movement. Chief among these themes is the refutation of dualism, and the attempt to reinscribe human existence within the context of living nature without sacrificing human freedom. Cartesian dualism brought with it a remarkable capacity to represent nature in mathematical and mechanistic terms, with an eye toward predicting and controlling natural processes. But this capacity came at the price of leaving no room for human freedom. Because all natural processes are subject to strict causal determinism, either human freedom must be a fiction or it must reside in some supranatural realm. One of the goals of Romanticism is a "vitalist theory of mind" that traverses "a middle path between the extremes of a reductivistic materialism and a supernaturalistic dualism."[4] The inscription of mind within nature necessitates both a rejection of a purely mechanistic conception of nature and the search for a teleological-organic conception of nature that can account for the distinctiveness of human beings while still accommodating the insights of modern science.

A related Romantic theme is the primacy of feeling over cognition in human experience. The empiricist-utilitarian rejection of the ideal of detached cognition has its corollary in the ideal of a relationship to reality that is first of all felt and only derivatively grasped by intellect. The

Romantic conception of experience that emerges in the eighteenth and nineteenth centuries tends to characterize cognition as a modification of sense experience rather than as a faculty that supervenes upon sensation. This commitment to the priority of sensibility over understanding is born of the conviction that human beings, even if we are ultimately "superior" to animals and the rest of nature, are nonetheless part of nature and share much of our physical constitution and many of our experiential faculties with animals. The historical endeavor to see our intellect as separate from nature is the response to a need to see ourselves as different in kind than animals and other natural beings. The Romantic endeavor to see human beings as a special case of nature is a response to the sense of lostness and alienation produced by the attempt to remove the essence of human being from nature. For the Jena Romantic Novalis, "philosophy is really homesickness," an attempt to find our place in the midst of the totality of the world.[5] For his contemporary Schleiermacher, as for Novalis, it is through the affects of "love and hope" rather than through detached contemplation that we may eventually find our "distant home [der fernen Heimath]."[6]

Their commitments to organic holism and the primacy of the affects lead the Romantics to give a special place to the beauty and sublimity of nature. The priority given by many Romantics to literature over philosophy reflects the belief that "beauty [reveals] a more intuitive, emotionally marked, and even mystical path to reality's inner core" than does the cold speculation of detached reason.[7] This is the spirit that moves Wordsworth to write,

> Therefore am I still
> A lover of the meadows and the woods
> And mountains; and of all that we behold
> From this green earth; of all the mighty world
> Of eye, and ear,—both what they half create,
> And what perceive; well pleased to recognize
> In nature and the language of the sense
> The anchor of my purest thoughts, the nurse,
> The guide, the guardian of my heart, and soul
> Of all my moral being.[8]

The sense that human beings are part of a natural whole and that we find our moral bearings in relation to that whole is strictly opposed to the sense of nature that Kant articulates in the *Critique of Judgment*. Still wedded to a fundamentally Christian dualism, Kant sees the contemplation of nature as a vehicle to asserting and cultivating our transcendence of nature toward the perfection of our own moral natures. For the Romantics, we realize our potential to be moral beings not by elevating ourselves above nature, but rather by acknowledging our natural condition and seeking to find our proper place within the totality of nature. The cultivation of our humanity is founded on a recognition that we differ from natural beings not in kind but only in degree.

As Berlin and others amply demonstrate, the roots of Romanticism are diverse and extensive. For the purposes of establishing the background against which Schopenhauer, Darwin, and Schweitzer develop their ideas on animals, I confine my attention to three key thinkers: Condillac, Rousseau, and Herder.

By the time Condillac wrote his *Essay on the Origin of Human Knowledge* in 1746, thinkers such as Adam Smith and Jean-Baptiste Du Bos had established a school of thought that gave primacy to sympathy and natural sociability in human relations. Condillac develops this approach by making language and reason fundamentally dependent on sensation, emotion, and embodied action. Language originates in the spontaneous expression of natural emotions, as when an animal screams in fear. But language is not simply the expression of emotions. It is the deliberate use of conventional signs that have been produced in reflection. Thus there are two stages in the development of linguistic ability: the instinctive emotional response to an object or situation, and the deliberate representation of ideas by means of arbitrary signs. Many animals are capable of the first stage, but only human beings are capable of the second.

The use of conventional signs requires memory, which is the power "to recall signs of our ideas or the circumstances that have accompanied them."[9] Memory enables us to direct our attention to objects "away from those [things we have] before [our] eyes at the moment," so that we contemplate them at will and as such.[10] Memory and reflection give us deliberate control over the signs we have produced in reflection, so that we are not limited to the use of natural signs that have been produced accidentally; we can create associations between arbitrary, conventional signs and objects, states, and events in our experience. Conventional language, the connection of "some ideas to arbitrary signs," originates in "the language of action," the habitual association of natural cries with feelings and objects.[11] Condillac thus follows the empiricists in rejecting the Cartesian notion of innate ideas and in maintaining that "the simplest ideas" are those "that the senses supply"; for example, ideas such as solidity "come directly from the senses."[12] He also follows the empiricists in drawing a fundamental link between the evolution of language and concrete, embodied experience: the conventional language of abstract, arbitrary symbols develops out of the concrete "language of action."

The language of action is a capacity exhibited by human and animal alike. In his *Treatise on Animals* (1755), Condillac emphasizes the continuity between human beings and animals on the basis that animals share in sense and some intelligence even if they are deprived of reason and symbolic language.[13] The animal is capable of expressing its limited range of feelings through "a very imperfect language" of "inarticulate cries"; but because it lacks reflection and formal language, "the animal does not have it in its nature to become human."[14] Animals have a narrowly circumscribed range of needs, and are moved fundamentally by instinct and habit. Their lack of reflective capacity confines animals in the immediacy of concrete particulars.[15] The instinct that guides animals is "infinitely inferior to our reason," because reflection (*la réflexion*) enables human beings to perform "voluntary and free actions."[16] The superiority of human beings over animals is most evident in our capacity for cumulative progress over generations, and our capacity for morality and religion.[17] All of these "superior" human capacities depend on our rational and linguistic capabilities.

In the *Essay on the Origin of Human Knowledge*, Condillac presents a detailed account of the distinction between the cognitive and linguistic abilities of human beings and animals. Animals lack memory and therefore are incapable of using conventional signs. They "have only an imagination that they cannot direct. They represent something absent to themselves only to the extent that the image in the brain is closely connected with a present object."[18] Animals are guided not by reflection but simply by their feelings. For example, when an animal feels hunger, its imagination creates an association between the present feeling and the "perceptions of absent objects" that might satisfy the animal's hunger.[19] Animals are thus guided by "instinct," which is simply "an imagination which in the presence of an object revives the perceptions that are immediately connected with it and which by that means guides all kinds of animals without the assistance of reflection."[20] Even though they lack the capacity for reflection, animals can communicate with one another by using natural signs, such as cries that have become habitually associated with natural sentiments. In this connection there is no need to suppose that animals possess the "precise ideas" that memory and reflection permit human beings to form.[21]

For all the similarities between human beings and animals and Condillac's characterization of reason and language as natural phenomena, he still considers human beings to be superior to animals. "The similarity between animals and us proves that they have a soul; and the difference between us proves that it is inferior to ours. The matter is made evident by my analyses, for the operations of the animal soul are limited to perception, consciousness, attention, reminiscence, and to an imagination which is not at their command, whereas ours possesses additional operations."[22] Our ability to "attach ideas to [arbitrary] signs" gives us a mastery over our imagination that animals fundamentally lack: we can recall ideas at will and contemplate objects and ideas that are remote from us in space and time, whereas animals are locked in the immediacy of the present. For all that, however, animals are not, as Descartes maintains, "pure automatons."[23]

Condillac's contemporary Rousseau gives tremendous impetus to Romantic conceptions of human-animal kinship by sketching an ideal of natural existence in comparison with which civilization is an inferior condition. Social relations offer the advantage of cooperation in the endeavor to secure ourselves against the forces of nature, but they also introduce competition, resentment, and self-love. All of our vicious tendencies are attributable to the advent of social cooperation. The primary purpose of government is to provide citizens with as close an approximation as possible of the freedom that they would enjoy in a state of nature. Rousseau's characterization of the "savage" conveys the sense of health and freedom that has been lost in the socialization process. The natural virtues of the savage represent the highest potential of human nature; they remind us of our hidden essence lying beneath the veil of social relations, an essence that stands in an inner connection to the essence of animal life.

The savage lives in a state of nature that has never existed, but that stands as an image of what human life could be like in the absence of avarice and competition. The savage possesses a healthy self-esteem (amour de soi-même), is self-sufficient, and possesses no vices whatsoever.[24] Like animals, the savage "is wholly given over to the sentiment of its present existence, with no idea of the future." The savage's needs are entirely physical, immediate, and moderate; the savage exhibits no foresight or curiosity, and no desire to acquire more than is required by the needs of the moment.[25] The natural individual is robust, resilient, not particularly violent, and exhibits an innate compassion.[26] "This man cannot feel either hate or the desire for revenge," because he lacks the corrupt "self-love" (*amour-propre*) that results from the comparisons we make between ourselves and others in a social setting.[27]

Rousseau opposes this ideal of naturalness to the socialized condition of humanity, which is responsible for the vast majority of our suffering. In many respects the savage is like an animal, though Rousseau draws clear distinctions between human beings and animals. "Every animal has ideas because it has senses," and "even combines its ideas up to a certain point. . . . In this regard, man differs from beasts only in degree." But animals are moved entirely by instinct, whereas human beings possess the capacity to be free agents. "Nature commands every animal and the beast obeys. Man feels the same impulsion, but he knows that he is free to acquiesce or to resist; and it is particularly in the consciousness of this liberty that the spirituality of his soul is displayed."[28] Our freedom is tied to our capacity to form general ideas, which we are able to form in virtue of our linguistic ability. This capacity enables us to move beyond the primitive language that we share with animals, namely "the cry of nature," and to employ symbolic language founded on the use of "conventional signs."[29] But the activities and institutions that reason and language make possible are the very source of our misery. Thus when Rousseau notes that human beings but not animals are capable of self-improvement, he does not mean to compliment us; he means to point out that the capacities that distinguish us from animals place us at a disadvantage, and that we would be better off if we lived like the savage, whose life does not require any improvement.[30]

What we learn about the life of the savage holds clues to any redemption that we might seek as civilized beings. For Rousseau there is no possibility of simply returning to a natural state, but there is the prospect of emulating the natural virtues of the savage. It is in this spirit that Rousseau wrote *Émile*, an account of the upbringing of "an imaginary pupil" subject to the best possible influences. Rousseau's program for Émile's upbringing is designed to avoid the corrupting effects produced by the formal education of Rousseau's day.[31] Émile is a lover of peace, both among human beings and animals. He does not seek to dominate others, but exhibits the natural compassion of the savage; he "suffers when he sees suffering," and seeks never to inflict it.[32] In this respect, Émile is very much like animals, who themselves "sometimes give perceptible signs of [compassion]."[33] The absence in Émile of any desire to dominate others opposes him to the so-called "civilized" human being, who "will end by slaughtering everything until he is the sole master of the universe." Émile is like the savage, "to whom one would have great difficulty even explaining what servitude and domination are."[34]

This idealization of naturalness has implications for our relationship to animals. Rousseau links the advent of war and practices such as hunting and fishing to the increase of human population and the resulting need for industry. "As the human race spread, difficulties multiplied along with men. . . . Along the sea shores and the river banks they invented the hook and line and became fishermen and eaters of fish. In the forests, they made bows and arrows, and became hunters and warriors; in cold countries, they clothed themselves with the skins of beasts that they had slain."[35] But Rousseau is not consistent in treating practices such as hunting, fishing, and meat eating as by-products of civilization. When he describes the living conditions of the savage, he sometimes states that pre-civilized people would wear animal skins when necessary, and he paints a pastoral image of savages carving fishing boats, suggesting that the use of animals would be part of the savage's daily life.[36] But he also states that natural human beings would be "constantly engaged in obtaining their subsistence from trees and plants," thereby implying the naturalness of a vegetarian diet.[37] As regards the relationship between humans and animals, Rousseau says that it is wrong to suppose "that one species is destined by nature to serve as food for the other"; that is, we should no more suppose that animals exist as our food than that we exist as food for animals.[38] Consonant with this sentiment, the ideal rustic diet described in Émile includes fruits, vegetables, and dairy products.[39]

But Rousseau does not unequivocally call for a vegetarian diet, and moreover his remarks about diet are motivated more by an interest in the health of human beings than the welfare of animals. He states early in the Discourse on Inequality that, in virtue of their capacity for suffering, animals should be accorded at least "the right not to be needlessly mistreated."[40] And he maintains that practices such as hunting accustom us to cruelty, a passion unknown to the savage.[41] But his emphasis in regard to dietary practices is on moderation for the sake of bodily vitality.[42] At one point in Émile, Rousseau states that Émile's companion Sophie, while not a vegetarian, "eats very little meat."[43] Thus Wollstonecraft overstates the case when she claims that "Rousseau will not allow man to be a carnivorous animal."[44] His prohibition on meat eating is not categorical. His equivocations about the ideal diet notwithstanding, however, Rousseau appropriates the idea that human beings and animals differ not in kind but only in degree, and he sees the instinctual life of the animal and the savage as an ideal to be emulated to whatever extent possible within the confines of civilization.

Condillac and Rousseau offer naturalistic conceptions of human existence with opposing implications: Both see the human condition as an outgrowth of natural processes, and both see the difference between human beings and animals as one of degree rather than of kind. Even language emerges from out of concrete, embodied, natural processes. In this regard, Condillac and Rousseau are much more akin to Aristotle and his organic conception of life than to Descartes's dualism and his strictly mechanistic conception of nature. But Condillac sees the differences between human beings and animals as indicative of a difference in relative perfection: the scope of animal needs and capacities is strictly limited to survival (food, protection from the elements, and self-defense), whereas the scope of human needs is much greater in virtue of our capacities for language and reflection.[45] In turn, human beings, in virtue of the capacity for symbolic communication and the cooperation that it facilitates, are capable of cumulative progress over generations. Because we alone are "capable of discerning the truth and being aware of the good, [we] create the arts and sciences and raise ourselves up to divinity."[46] For Rousseau, on the other hand, our most desirable state is one that cannot be attained by a member of society, namely, the condition of the isolated individual who lives a life closely akin to that of a wild animal. Society is not only not superior to a state of nature, it is a perversion of nature.

Herder enters this debate in the late eighteenth century and takes a position that anticipates Wollstonecraft's criticism of Rousseau: "Based on a false hypothesis his arguments are plausible but unsound. I say unsound; for to assert that a state of nature is preferable to civilization, in all its possible perfection, is, in other words, to arraign supreme wisdom; and the paradoxical exclamation, that God had made all things right, and that error has been introduced by the creature, whom he formed, knowing what he formed, is as unphilosophical as impious."[47] Herder, like Condillac and Rousseau, sees a continuum between human beings and animals, and he considers distinctively human capacities such as speech as developing out of a natural language of action. Like Condillac, Herder places a great premium on human sociability and the capacities for advancement across generations that distinguish human beings from animals. Herder the philosophical anthropologist characterizes human culture as a genetic outgrowth of the natural condition that we share with animals. Herder the general superintendent of the Lutheran clergy at Weimar proclaims that, notwithstanding our continuity with animals, human beings stand in close proximity to the divine and are "the highest point attainable by terrestrial organization."[48]

The starting point of Herder's genetic account of language and history is the naturalistic insight that all understanding has its origin in sensation and that human beings share the roots of understanding with animals. "Beasts are the older bretheren of man. . . . The world, it is true, was given to man: but not to him alone, not to him first: animals in every element render his monarchy questionable. One species he must tame: with another he must long contend. Some escape his dominion: others wage with him eternal war. In short, every species extends its possession of the Earth in proportion to its capacity, cunning, strength, or courage."[49] Herder advances an organic conception of life according to which the physiological similarities between human beings and animals reflect an essential similarity. "The nearer they approach man, all creatures bear more or less resemblance to him in their general outline; and . . . Nature, amid the infinite variety she loves, seems to have fashioned all the living creatures on our Earth after one grand model of organization."[50]

Herder's account of the genesis of language shares Condillac's and Rousseau's bias against Cartesian dualism. Human beings are not metaphysically distinct from the rest of creation, nor is language absolutely unique to human beings. In his *Treatise on the Origin of Language* (1772), Herder attacks Süßmilch's thesis that language has a divine origin, arguing instead that language has its origin in natural cries, that animals share in language at this level (Condillac's "language of action"), and that symbolic language is a specifically human invention inspired by specifically human needs.[51] Herder's specific contribution to the evolution of thinking about language concerns the shift from animal language to human speech, a shift for which he criticizes Condillac and Rousseau for having failed to explain.[52] On Herder's account, the human essence is such that our understanding is linguistic from the very start. "Did people need a thousand generations to understand for the first time what language is? The first human being understood it when he thought the first thought."[53] It was "precisely the most human thing, to abstract words for oneself where one needed them. . . . Human reason cannot exist *without abstraction*, and each abstraction does not come to be *without language*."[54] Human language takes its first bearings from "the language of nature," but the capacity for speech is the focal point for potentialities that are absolutely unique to human beings.

Speech facilitates reflection, the formation of abstract ideas and arbitrary signs, self-reflective awareness [*Besonnenheit*], and the unification of experience [*Sammlung*]. Animals have a much more confined sphere of needs and activities than human beings, and thus each animal is confined to just one type of work; in comparison with human beings, an animal is "an infallible machine in the hands of nature." The human being has the "free space to practice in many things" and "can seek for himself a sphere for self-mirroring, can mirror himself within himself. . . . he becomes his own end and goal of refinement."[55] Human beings alone are free, rational, and capable of reflection; only a human being can "be conscious of its own awareness." This form of awareness "is essential to [the human] species." Reflective self-awareness enables us to distinguish different objects, contemplate them as such (as the objects that they are), isolate individual features of experience and "acknowledge one or several as distinguishing properties." *Besonnenheit* (self-reflective awareness) enables us to form distinct concepts and make judgments.[56] *Besonnenheit* enables us to be "the freely active, rational creature." Thus for Herder, what distinguishes human beings from animals is not the capacity for self-expression, but rather the kind of linguistic ability that gathers together those capacities patently lacking in animals: reason, reflection, freedom.[57] Only human beings can determine ends for themselves rather than having ends assigned to them by nature. Herder calls the ordering of experience and needs in terms of a chosen end "gathering" (*sammeln, Sammlung*).[58] Only human beings are capable of contemplating their experience and gathering it together as a cognitive and an ethical whole. "There thus arises through self-reflective awareness [*Besonnenheit*] '*a progressive unity of all conditions of life*.'"[59] Only human beings can establish scientific knowledge of the world, and only human beings can engage in the moral reflection that gives rise to a vision of the world as a whole and our special place in it.[60] Animals, in contrast, are incapable of reflection and hence of a sense of past and future.

The assignment to human beings of the special capacities for speech, self-reflective awareness, and free unification leads Herder to sketch a hierarchy of natural beings with humans at the apex of creation. He restates the Aristotelian-Stoic hierarchy of plant-animal-human, and asserts that "higher life must come to be from inferior life through sacrifice and destruction."[61] The unique cognitive and linguistic abilities of human beings show that only we "are created in God's image."[62] "The deeper, purer, and diviner our cognition is, then the purer, diviner, and more universal our efficacy is too, hence the freer our freedom."[63] Much as Adam's naming of natural beings in the garden signified his dominion over them, our ability to classify and unify things through language establishes in us "a right of property" over them.[64] Even though we share an underlying "grand model of organization" with the entire animal kingdom, human beings exhibit "the most perfect form, in which the features of all are collected in the most exquisite summary."[65] The relative perfection of the human form is evident especially in our erect posture, which facilitated the development of our hands and enables us to look up to heaven.[66] Our erect posture is also responsible for "the divine gift of speech," by which we "rule the Earth by the words of [our] mouth," cultivate our sense of truth and justice, and practice science and religion.[67] By contrast, animals "are but stooping slaves" that stand irretrievably below us in the natural hierarchy.[68] We have no "fraternity" with animals, not even apes.[69] The only reason to exhibit "humanity" to animals is that doing so makes them more "useful" in fulfilling "the purposes of man."[70] "From stones to crystals, from crystals to metals, from these to plants, from plants to brutes, and from brutes to man, we have seen the form of organization ascend." With the human being "the series stops: we know no creature above man, organized with more diversity and art: he seems the highest point attainable by terrestrial organization."[71]

Condillac and Herder acknowledge the natural continuity between human beings and animals, but they hold fast to the traditional prejudice that reason and language elevate us above animals. Herder provides crucial background for the emergence of Schopenhauer's and Darwin's ideas by arguing for a fundamental link between physiological development and the extent of a being's capacities for intellect and language. Rousseau takes the idea of natural continuity to the opposite extreme by maintaining that animals and savages have fundamental advantages over human beings and that language and reason have done little more than cause mutual interdependence and enmity among human beings. When the leading thinkers on animals in the nineteenth century take up this debate, the terms of their discussions reflect the deep influence of the anti-Cartesianism and organicism that characterized the eighteenth-century debates about language and the place of human beings in the cosmos. In their discussions they also reproduce the old debate and the old ambivalence over whether human beings share a spark of the divine, or whether we are instead what Nietzsche would call "clever beasts who have to die."[72]

Schopenhauer

In his conception of the human condition, Schopenhauer unites Condillac's and Herder's insights into the natural origin of language and intelligence with the cynicism of Rousseau's assessment of society. Schopenhauer places fundamental emphasis on the sameness of understanding in human beings and animals by arguing that human beings differ from animals only in degree, in virtue of the ability to engage in acts of rational abstraction from concrete experience. He characterizes the shared experience of animals and human beings as manifestations of one indivisible, anonymous world will, and argues that the will is not a thing or faculty but rather an endless process of striving and suffering. The experience of any particular living being is simply a reflection of this process, and has in itself no real significance. Nor is there any ultimate significance to the eternal process of striving and suffering, although human beings, endowed with reason, are capable of contemplating the essential features of the process.[73] Given that the process is inalterable and lacks an ultimate meaning, Schopenhauer implies that there is an underlying futility to existence: nothing can be changed, nothing can be securely grasped, and human beings have no special place in the cosmic scheme of things. Schopenhauer develops his views as a polemical response to Kant, who ascribes a privileged place to rational beings and expresses a clear optimism about the prospects for genuine progress in human life. Schopenhauer is deeply influenced by Buddhist and Vedic philosophy, and develops his ethic of resignation and releasement in accordance with these traditions. Given that willing is an endless cosmic process, and given that willing unavoidably causes suffering, the only prospect for gaining satisfaction in life is to suspend the will—in Schopenhauer's words, to "affirm and deny the will," that is, to acknowledge its permanence and on the basis of that acknowledgment to retreat into the passivity of contemplation. As far as affirmative acts of one's individual will are concerned, the only legitimate acts are those aimed toward ameliorating the suffering of living beings.

Schopenhauer's starting point in describing experience is embodied perception. "Our own body . . . is the starting point for each of us in the perception of the world. . . . The body is for us the immediate object, in other words, that representation that forms the starting-point of the subject's knowledge."[74] Different bodies in the world act on each other, and some of those bodies act on the bodies of perceiving subjects such as human beings and animals. The cause-and-effect relationships between bodies are such that the effects in perceiving subjects are "representations" of the actions in question. These representations constitute knowledge. Hence all animals, not just human beings, possess the faculty of understanding, which establishes knowledge of causal relations through perceptual experience. "All animal bodies are . . . starting-points in the perception of the world . . . *Knowledge* . . . is the proper *characteristic of animal life*, just as movement consequent on stimuli is the characteristic of the plant. . . . The understanding is the same in all animals and all men."[75] The capacity for perception, shared by all animals, makes possible "the identity of a consciousness" and "movement consequent on motives."[76] To this extent, "in all essential respects, *the animal* is absolutely identical with us and . . . the difference lies merely in the accident, the intellect [*Intellekt*], and not in the substance which is the will."[77]

The nature of this "accident" is that, in addition to possessing understanding, human beings also possess reason and self-reflective awareness. Schopenhauer, like Herder, believes that the crux of human rationality or reflection is "that *sober reflectiveness* [*Besonnenheit*] which is wanting in the animal."[78] The animal knows individual cause-and-effect relationships through its concrete perceptual encounter with things, but "the absence of reason restricts the animals to representations of perception immediately present to them in time, in other words to real objects. We, on the other hand, by virtue of knowledge in the abstract, comprehend not only the narrow and actual present, but also the whole past and future together with the wide realm of possibility."[79] Human intellect transcends the immediacy of the present in virtue of the rational capacity to form abstract concepts. Because human beings are "determined by abstract concepts independent of the present moment," we are capable of language, deliberation, consciousness of ourselves and the world as such, and cooperation and deliberate planning.[80] This means that human beings have individual character, whereas "in the animals this individual character as a whole is lacking."[81] Moreover, "the animals have infinitely less to *suffer* than we have, because they know no other sufferings than those directly brought about by the *present*."[82] Animals cannot recall past suffering, nor can they anticipate future suffering; in particular, an animal "learns to know death only when he dies, but man consciously draws every hour nearer to his death."[83]

Given that animals are imprisoned in the present, Schopenhauer's assertion that animals can act on motives must be qualified. Animals, like human beings, engage in acts of willing; as perceiving and feeling beings, animals are not mere machines. Schopenhauer's conception of willing in animals is very much like Aquinas's. Animals cannot reflect on motivating circumstances, but instead are determined by them; animals "choose," but not freely. Whereas the human being "has an actual choice between several motives" in virtue of the capacity to *reflect* on different motives and weigh them against one another, "the animal . . . is determined by the present impression."[84] The animal is a less highly organized form of life than the human being, hence its experiential capacities are less extensive. Nonetheless, both human beings and animals are phenomena that emerge from out of material processes. "Each more highly organized state of matter succeeded in time a cruder state. Thus animals existed before men, fishes before land animals, plants before fishes, and the inorganic before that which is organic."[85]

This sense of a hierarchy reflects an inner tension in Schopenhauer's thought between the idea that human beings are simply a more highly organized manifestation of the world will and the idea that human beings are somehow "higher" than animals. The problem that Schopenhauer faces is on what basis he can argue for "higher" and "lower" in specifically ethical terms, given that he abandons and severely criticizes both dualism and the Christian worldview that gave birth to it. A thinker such as Herder can argue for the superiority of human beings on the grounds that capacities such as language, even if they do not have a divine origin, show human beings to stand in close proximity to the divine intelligence. But the denial of a Platonic intelligible world hovering above the phenomenal world of concrete, embodied existence deprives Schopenhauer of the grounds for making this sort of value judgment, and this has significant consequences for the ethical status that he ultimately attributes to animals.

The animal's inability to engage in reflection gives it an advantage over human beings: animals enjoy an "enviable tranquillity and placidity," whereas "by means of reflection and everything connected therewith, there is developed in man from those same elements of pleasure and pain which he has in common with the animal, an enhancement of susceptibility to happiness and unhappiness which is capable of leading to momentary, and sometimes even fatal, ecstasy or else to the depths of despair and suicide."[86] Given his fundamental conviction that willing is inseparable from suffering, Schopenhauer places little stock in our prospects for happiness. Instead he focuses on the problem of suffering and devotes his ethical concerns to the task of minimizing suffering. In this connection, he considers the suffering of beings with greater experiential capacities to take precedence over those with "cruder" capacities. Nonetheless, he considers all suffering to be the proper object of our moral concern.

Against Kant, who appeals to abstract rational principle, Schopenhauer appeals to concrete compassion as the true basis of morality. The core of moral obligation "is the everyday phenomenon of *compassion*, of the immediate *participation*, independent of all ulterior considerations, primarily in the *suffering* of another, and thus in the prevention or elimination of it; for all satisfaction and all well-being and happiness consists in this. It is simply and solely this compassion that is the real basis of all voluntary justice and genuine loving-kindness."[87] In this connection "the mere concept is as unfruitful for genuine virtue as it is for genuine art"; Kant's mistake is in failing to see that a "pure, i.e., disinterested affection for others" is the only legitimate basis for morality, that "what can move [us] to good deeds and to works of affection is always only *knowledge of the suffering of others*, directly intelligible from one's own suffering, and put on a level therewith."[88] The basis of morality is not any kind of abstract concept nor a rational conception of duty, but rather the *felt* connection we have with all living beings capable of suffering. This sense of a direct affective relationship with other suffering beings places us on a cosmic par with animals, so much so that Schopenhauer approvingly cites Larra's suggestion that "whoever has never kept a dog does not know what it is to love and be loved."[89]

By shifting the basis of morality from a Kantian conception of duty to compassion, Schopenhauer gives animals the status of direct beneficiaries of moral concern. He excoriates Kant for proposing "that beings devoid of reason (hence animals) are things and therefore should be treated merely as means that are not at the same time an end." On Kant's view, animals are nothing more than "the pathological phantom for the purpose of practicing sympathy for human beings."[90] Because the true moral incentive is compassion, and because animals and human beings alike suffer, "*animals* are also to be taken under [the] protection" of direct moral concern. In this connection we should follow the example of Pythagoras, who recognized that "compassion for animals is so intimately associated with goodness of character."[91] The fact that animals, deprived of reflective awareness, have no consciousness of morality is irrelevant to their status as objects of direct moral concern.[92]

Thus we owe animals "not mercy but justice." Once Europe recognizes "that animals are in all essential respects identical with us and that the difference lies merely in the degree of intelligence, i.e., cerebral activity," animals will "cease to appear as creatures without rights." In this respect Europe has much to learn from "the higher morality of the East, since Brahmanism and Buddhism do not limit their precepts to 'one's neighbor', but take under their protection 'all living beings.'"[93] A central fault of Christianity is that "it has most unnaturally separated man from the animal world" and "regards animals positively as things; whereas Brahmanism and Buddhism, faithful to truth, definitely recognize the evident kinship [*Verwandtschaft*] of man with the whole of nature in general and the animals in particular."[94] By viewing the world as "a piece of machinery and animals [as] manufactured for our use," Christianity maintains that animals are beings "without any rights" and thus may be subjected to "the revolting and outrageous wickedness with which our Christian mob treat animals, laughing as they kill them without aim or object, maiming and torturing them. . . . It might truly be said that men are the devils of this earth and animals the tortured souls. These are the consequences of that installation scene in the Garden of Paradise." Inasmuch as the Judeo-Christian tradition "regards the animal as something manufactured for man's use," "we should give up crediting [Christianity] with the most perfect morality."[95]

One particular focal point in Schopenhauer's critique of Christianity is the practice of vivisection. "Christian morality leaves animals out of account. . . . They can therefore be used for vivisection, hunting, coarsing, bullfights, and horse racing, and can be whipped to death as they struggle along with heavy carts of stone."[96] Vivisection is on a par with these other practices. "Every quack . . . now considers himself entitled to carry out in his torture-chamber the cruellest tortures on animals," even "in order to settle purely theoretical and often very futile questions." In carrying out such practices, we "put nature on the rack in order to enrich [our] knowledge."[97] But Schopenhauer does not call for a categorical prohibition on vivisection. In discussing the practice, Schopenhauer invokes the wisdom of Blumenbach, his physiology professor at Göttingen, who counseled that vivisection "should very rarely be resorted to and only in the case of very important investigations that are of direct use."[98] The acknowledgment of an essential kinship between human beings and animals entails an acknowledgment of animal rights, but it does not entail that animals have a right not to be experimented upon. The rights of animals are simply such that it should "not be open to any medical quack to put to the test every odd and eccentric caprice of his ignorance by the most horrible tortures on numberless animals, as happens at the present time."[99]

In a similar vein, Schopenhauer stops short of a categorical prohibition on meat eating. "Sympathy for animals should not carry us to the length of having to abstain from animal food, like the Brahmins; for in nature the capacity for suffering keeps pace with intelligence, and thus man would suffer more by going without animal food, especially in the North, than the animal does through a quick and always unforeseen death—which should, however, be made even easier by means of chloroform."[100] In virtue of our capacity for reflective awareness (*Besonnenheit*), we are related not only to the immediacy of the present but also to past and future. Hence "man's innumerable mental and physical sufferings have a much stronger claim to compassion than have the sufferings of animals, which are only physical and themselves less acute."[101] If Schopenhauer had appealed to a deontological principle such as respect for all sentient beings, where 'all' includes moral patients as well as moral agents, he would not be able to argue for such a conclusion. But because he appeals to a notion of compassion, and believes that the extent of our duties of compassion is directly proportional to the sufferings of the being that is the object of our concern, he effectively projects a hierarchy of moral desert according to which human beings merit greater moral consideration than animals. We may not act capriciously with regard to animals. But provided that we can point to some potential material benefit for human beings that outweighs the suffering inflicted upon animals, our practices are completely justified. The fact that we can kill animals painlessly (Schopenhauer omits to note that we can do the same to human beings) and the belief that animals are fundamentally less capable than humans of suffering give rise to an ethic whose implications for the fortunes of animals do not differ significantly from the views of Aquinas, Mill, or Kant.

Darwin

Darwin, a younger contemporary of Schopenhauer, takes up the same Romantic ideas that guided Schopenhauer. *The World as Will and Representation* had a lukewarm response and went virtually unnoticed when it was first published in 1818. By the time the second edition was published in 1859, the same year as the first edition of Darwin's *Origin of Species*, Schopenhauer's ideas had become highly influential. Schopenhauer's thought, together with the teleological-organic views of nature developed by Blumenbach, Reil, Kielmeyer, Goethe, and Schelling in the late eighteenth and early nineteenth centuries, set the stage for the emergence of Darwin's theory of species continuity.[102]

The key implications of Darwin's "theory of descent with modification through variation and natural selection" are that "man is descended from some less highly organized form," that human beings and animals share "a common progenitor," and that human beings and animals are subject to "the same general causes" and "obey the same laws" of mental and physical development.[103] Darwin seeks an explanation for the growth and development of animal species, which he considers to be "utterly inexplicable on the theory of creation."[104] He also seeks a scientific account of the myriad similarities between the physiology and the cognitive abilities of human beings and "the lower animals." By comparison with the theory of natural selection, the theory of creation lacks the power to explain the obvious developmental affinities between human beings and animals.

As regards the moral status of animals, Darwin's views on the shared emotional and cognitive capacities of humans and animals are of the greatest significance. Darwin stresses that "there is no fundamental difference between man and the higher animals in their mental faculties."[105] Nor is there any fundamental difference between the mental faculties of humans and the lowest animals; there is only a difference of degree. The reality of shared emotions in humans and animals serves to illustrate this fact. Even though the lower animals do many things on the basis of sheer instinct, "without any conscious intelligence . . . the lower animals are excited by the same emotions as ourselves."[106] In *The Descent of Man* (1871), Darwin cites examples of courage, timidity, revenge, jealousy, ennui, curiosity, sympathy, and love in animals, and he states that "all animals feel Wonder."[107] In *The Expression of the Emotions in Man and Animals* (1872/1889), Darwin argues that similarities in the expression of the emotions in humans and animals lend support to "the conclusion that man is derived from some lower animal form."[108] In this text, Darwin discusses the survival advantages posed by the communication of emotions among members of a colony or a species. He traces a variety of gestures that humans use to express emotions to more primeval conditions that link us with animals. "With mankind some expressions, such as the bristling of hair under the influence of extreme terror, or the uncovering of teeth under that of furious rage, can hardly be understood, except on the belief that man once existed in a lower and animal-like condition" and is descended along with animals "from a common progenitor."[109] This common ancestry makes it easier to accept the proposition that "the lower animals are excited by the same emotions as ourselves," and that "even insects express anger, terror, jealousy, and love by their stridulation."[110] Darwin argues for the genesis of human language from rudimentary animal communication, thus echoing Herder's belief that human speech has its origin in the imitation of natural sounds. Darwin "cannot doubt that language owes its origin to the imitation and modifications of various natural sounds, the voices of other animals, and man's own instinctive cries, aided by signs and gestures."[111]

Darwin's theory of descent from a common progenitor entails that "the mind of man . . . has, as I fully believe, been developed from a mind as low as that possessed by the lowest animals."[112] Darwin recognizes that emotions are part of the mental makeup of animals, and he sees the connection between the expression of emotions and the other cognitive capacities that contribute to survival and development of species.[113] Darwin shows the influence of thinkers such as Hume in his characterization of intelligence in terms of the association of ideas. Darwin sees that intelligence is not an all-or-nothing affair but has gradations leading from the simple making of associations to the full-fledged rational and linguistic apparatus of human beings. Dogs and monkeys, for example, establish knowledge of the meaning of human gestures through habitual associations; this knowledge "certainly is not instinctual," and is comparable to the habitual associations that young children learn to make between their elders' expressions of emotions and the meaning behind the expressions.[114] "Dogs, cats, horses, and probably all the higher animals, even birds . . . possess some power of imagination." Moreover, "animals possess some power of reasoning. Animals may constantly be seen to pause, deliberate, and resolve. . . . Some animals extremely low in the scale apparently display a certain amount of reason."[115]

In his account of the ability to deliberate and choose, Darwin follows the general terms of the empiricist conception of knowledge and choice. Animals produce ideas from sense experience, and their actions are reactions to what they experience in their sensible environment. These reactions "are due to instinct, or to reason, or to the mere association of ideas."[116] Human beings have "the same senses as the lower animals" and "some few instincts in common [with animals], as that of self-preservation, sexual love, the love of the mother for her new-born offspring," and so on. But animals possessing more highly developed mental powers are less dependent on instinct than the lower animals.[117] The more highly developed the animal, the greater the role played by associations, which are "intimately connected with reason." The full apparatus of reason in the higher animals includes "the power of association, . . . drawing inferences and . . . observation." The difference between the abilities, say, of a pike and a monkey to make associations is simply one of degree, as is that between human beings and any animal; the differences between human beings and animals by no means imply "the possession of a fundamentally different mind."[118]

Darwin illustrates the lack of a fundamental difference with the example of a dog and a human being each encountering water at a low level. "A cultivated man would perhaps make some general proposition on the subject; but from all that we know of savages it is extremely doubtful whether they would do so, and a dog certainly would not. But a savage, as well as a dog, would search in the same way, though frequently disappointed; and in both it seems to be equally an act of reason, whether or not any general proposition on the subject is consciously placed before the mind."[119] Even the dog makes inferences and exhibits ingenuity in its search for water. These are reasoning skills and do not depend on the ability to make generalizations. As Schopenhauer suggests, animals are confined to the present and immediate future, and thus have neither the need nor the capacity to form general propositions whose application extends beyond the present case.

But in spite of their inability to form general propositions, which presuppose the apparatus of predication, Darwin suggests that higher animals such as dogs can employ general concepts. "When a dog sees another dog at a distance, it is often clear that he perceives that it is a dog in the abstract. . . . It is a pure assumption to assert that the mental act is not essentially of the same nature in the animal as in man. If either refers what he perceives with his senses to a mental concept, then so do both." How else, Darwin asks, can his family dog understand that the utterance "hi, hi, where is it?" signifies that "something is to be hunted" and immediately rush off into a thicket in search of a bird or a squirrel?[120] Darwin offers the capacity for abstract concepts as a hypothesis rendered plausible by the evolutionary continuity between human beings and animals. He offers no other evidence in support of this particular hypothesis; nor does he consider whether, as Vygotsky would later argue, complex associations perform a function in animals and children comparable to the function performed in adults by abstract concepts. On Darwin's view, evolutionary continuity is a sufficient basis for concluding that the only barrier to fully developed language in animals is the degree of brain function, which in human beings facilitates an advanced "power of associating together the most diversified sounds and ideas."[121] Animals exhibit linguistic facility. For example, dogs understand many sentences; this places them on a par with infants. Parrots make extensive associations between words, things, and events. Ants communicate with their antennae. And Paraguayan monkeys articulate six distinct sounds to communicate their emotions, "which excite in other monkeys similar emotions."[122] Examples such as these confirm that the "half-art, half-instinct" of language is not the property of human beings alone.[123]

The continuity between human and animal mental capacities is so great that it "seems extremely doubtful" that capacities such as self-consciousness are unique to human beings.[124] "That animals retain their mental individuality is unquestionable."[125] Each animal, possessing sensation, emotion, and at least rudimentary reason, is a subject of experience with a sense of both the relationship and the difference between itself and other beings. Animals possess linguistic ability, and some even appreciate beauty.[126] The basic difference between human beings and animals is not conceptual or linguistic ability, but rather the human being's "almost infinitely larger power of associating together the most diversified sounds and ideas; and this obviously depends on the high development of his mental powers."[127]

Darwin's views on morality in general and the moral status of animals in particular emerge against the background of his conviction that humans and animals differ only in degree. The origin of morality, which is unique to human beings, is the social instincts, which humans share with animals. "It can hardly be disputed that the social feelings are instinctive or innate in the lower animals; and why should they not be so in man?"[128] The essential difference between these instincts in animals and human beings is that the more sophisticated cognitive-linguistic abilities of humans facilitate the development of social instincts into "the moral sense or conscience."[129] That social instincts are present in even the lower animals is evident from the various ways in which they warn and assist one another. Darwin details examples of cooperation among rabbits, birds, horses, fish, and various other animals; he further states that "it is certain that associated animals have a feeling of love for each other."[130] At least some animals exhibit sympathy, heroic actions on behalf of their companions, and noble fidelity.[131] Starfishes, spiders, and some earwigs exhibit the parental affection that the Stoics identify as the second stage of *oikeiosis* (belonging).[132] It even seems to be the case that "dogs possess something very like a conscience."[133]

Darwin's account of the origin of sociability in instinct follows from his theory of natural selection. Acts of social concern promote the survival of the group. Darwin notes, as Hume had done, that sympathy is much stronger toward loved ones than toward strangers; Darwin infers from this fact that sociability does not promote the welfare of the entire species but only that of the group of which the sympathetic individual is a member.[134] As instinctive, acts of sympathy produce feelings of pleasure. As these acts become habitual, they stop producing pleasure. Habitual acts of sociability can be passed from generation to generation. The resulting welfare of the group "may be attributed in part to habit, but chiefly to natural selection."[135] While this may sound like the sort of utilitarianism advanced by Bentham or Mill, it is not. Darwin argues that what is promoted by instincts such as sociability is not overall happiness but rather overall good or material welfare. "Darwin's theory . . . postulated that nature both selected impartially and had impartiality as the trait selected for: those communities whose members utterly failed to regard the common good would have perished from the earth." In contrast with the utilitarians, Darwin maintains "that group selection gave rise to the biologically unselfish moral sense."[136]

Just as human beings differ from animals merely in degree, human morality is simply an elaboration of the social instincts that promote survival even in the lower animals. In effect, Darwin asserts a "fundamental identity between the moral good and the biological good."[137] Inasmuch as "the social instincts both of man and the lower animals have no doubt been developed by nearly the same steps, it would be advisable, if found practicable, to use the same definition in both cases, and to take as the standard of morality, the general good or welfare of the community."[138] Darwin characterizes the faculty of conscience in terms of "an inward sense of possessing certain stronger or more enduring instincts . . . so that there would often be a struggle as to which impulse should be followed. . . . An inward monitor would tell the animal that it would have been better to have followed the one impulse rather than the other. The one course ought to have been followed, and the other ought not; the one would have been right and the other wrong."[139]

Darwin thereby reduces the "ought" of morality to imperatives of group survival. There is no absolute "ought," as in Aquinas or Kant; there is only the biological imperative. Darwin refers to Kant several times in his reflections on morality, and when he does so he suggests that the Kantian ideal of the dignity of humanity is fundamentally no more than a modification or elaboration of the social instincts.[140] A corollary of Darwin's view that social instincts are exercised not for the sake of the entire species but only for the group is that there is no such thing as a universal moral standpoint that regulates actions between species. In particular, there is no absolute moral imperative for members of one species to treat members of another species in a particular way; the only moral justification for treating members of another species in certain ways is that such treatment has consequences for the survival of one's own group. Darwin recognizes, as the Stoics had, that the human capacity for reflection enables us to transcend the present and contemplate our relationship to humanity as a whole. Human beings, unlike animals, can compare their past and future actions and motives, and approve or disapprove of them. In virtue of this capacity, "the judgment of the community" plays a significant role in the moral evaluations of human beings.[141]

Notwithstanding the rootedness of morality in biological imperatives, Darwin recognizes the tendency of human reflection to broaden the scope of our sympathies with other beings. "As man gradually advanced in intellectual power, and was enabled to trace the more remote consequences of his actions . . . his sympathies became more tender and widely diffused, extending to men of all races, to the imbecile, maimed, and other useless members of society, and finally to the lower animals—so would the standard of his morality rise higher and higher."[142] Darwin's grounding claim that morality is a modification of survival instincts stands in a peculiar tension with his conclusion that "disinterested love for all creatures" is "the most noble attribute of man."[143] He never explains how sympathy toward animals promotes the survival of any human group, and the terms of the theory of natural selection prevent him from making universal claims about morality that transcend considerations of material welfare. At one point he even suggests that if animals were capable of morality, the moralities of different animal groups might well differ in fundamental ways; for example, if "men were reared under precisely the same conditions as hive-bees, there can hardly be a doubt that our unmarried females would, like the worker-bees, think it a sacred duty to kill their brothers, and mothers would strive to kill their fertile daughters; and no one would think of interfering."[144] Darwin implicitly relies on the well-established philosophical insight into the capacity of human reflection to occupy a universal standpoint in arguing that human beings can transcend the relativity of the moral standpoints that animals would occupy if they were capable of morality. But he never addresses the seeming contradiction between his appeal to such a universal standpoint and his basic claim that human morality is simply a more highly developed version of the social instincts exhibited by animals, except to note on several occasions that the theory of natural selection is not incompatible with a belief in God.[145]

Notwithstanding this unresolved tension in his viewpoint, Darwin maintains that "humanity to the lower animals" is "one of the noblest [virtues] with which man is endowed." This virtue "seems to arise incidentally from our sympathies becoming more tender and more widely diffused, until they are extended to all sentient beings."[146] In his *Autobiography*, Darwin deplores the unnecessary suffering caused animals by vivisection, and he recounts his efforts to have a bill passed in Parliament to place restrictions on animal suffering caused by the practice.[147] But like Schopenhauer, Darwin stops clearly short of calling for a categorical prohibition on vivisection. "I fear that in some parts of Europe little regard is paid to the sufferings of animals, and if this be the case, I should be glad to hear of legislation against inhumanity in any such country. On the other hand, I know that physiology cannot possibly progress except by means of experiments on living animals, and I feel the deepest conviction that he who retards the progress of physiology commits a crime against mankind."[148] Darwin notes here that the study of physiology promises benefits for animals as well as humans, but his central focus is on the crime against mankind that would be committed if we abandoned vivisection altogether. In statements such as this one, Darwin retreats from his universal moral standpoint and returns to the anthropocentric standpoint. He notes that "savages in all parts of the world easily succeed in taming wild animals," and he states that the value of domesticating animals lies in their "service to man."[149] Even though he argues that universal sympathy is among our most noble capacities, he ultimately holds to the conclusion that "man may be excused for feeling some pride at having risen, though not through his own exertions, to the very summit of the organic scale; and the fact of his having thus risen, instead of having been aboriginally placed there, may give him hope for a still higher destiny in the distant future." Even though "man still bears in his bodily frame the indelible stamp of his lowly origin," our "god-like intellect" gives us a special place at the apex of creation, and this fact seems to entitle us to certain prerogatives in the husbanding of and experimentation upon nonhuman animals.[150]

Schweitzer

Another thinker who attempts to reconcile our "god-like intellect" with our "lowly origin" is Albert Schweitzer. Writing in the early twentieth century, Schweitzer develops an ethic of reverence for all life that proceeds from a Schopenhauerian recognition of the universality of willing to an affirmation of the special status of the human individual in the cosmic scheme of things. In part 2 of *Civilization and Ethics*, delivered as the Dale Memorial Lectures in 1922, Schweitzer states that he seeks "a basis in thought for the world- and life-affirming world-view" that Western philosophy has so far failed to establish.[151] The philosophical tradition to date has failed to realize an ethic of reverence for all life, in some cases because the tradition has embraced a false optimism and in other cases it has succumbed to a life-denying pessimism. For the most part, traditional philosophers have embraced an "optimistic-ethical interpretation of the world" in accordance with which they seek to attribute a specific meaning to existence and believe that genuine progress can be made in the realization of that meaning.[152] Wherever there is this kind of optimism in the tradition, "a belief is embraced in a general purposiveness, ruling in the world and directed to perfection, in which purposiveness the efforts of man and humanity toward spiritual and material progress find both sense and meaning, and at the same time become secure of ultimate success."[153] Conspicuous examples of such optimism in modernity are Descartes, who posits an ideal of progress in the mastery of nature, and Condorcet, one of the preeminent exponents of the Enlightenment's faith in historical progress. In both cases, Schweitzer believes, faith in progress is founded "on a crude interpretation of the world."[154]

The crudeness of the "optimistic-ethical" interpretation consists in its failure to acknowledge Schopenhauer's insight into the universality of the world will and the inalterability of the inner nature of things—in short, exponents of the optimistic-ethical interpretation fail to recognize that suffering is an insuperable condition, and that we overestimate ourselves when we believe that human industry can change the nature of things. By acknowledging the lack of an ultimate meaning or goal in the cosmos, we will abandon our pretensions to work toward the realization of that goal. Then we will be in a position to cultivate an ethics that does justice to the inner nature of things. "We can discover no trace in the world of any purposive development which might lend significance to our actions. No ethical element of any sort is observable in the world-process. . . . as far as we are affected the objective world is in every respect an enigmatical phenomenon of the general will-to-live."[155]

Schweitzer sees the endeavor to establish "lordship of the spirit over the forces of nature" to be an unethical "egoism" born of metaphysical dualism.[156] The central failing of dualism is that it is "unconnected to any form of nature-philosophy."[157] Schweitzer endorses the nineteenth-century reaction against dualism and follows the general terms of Schopenhauer's and Darwin's monistic characterizations of life. Human beings are fundamentally part of nature. The ethical position that Schweitzer articulates proceeds from this conviction, and places fundamental emphasis on the inner connectedness of all living beings subject to suffering. But unlike Schopenhauer, who retreats into resignation and ultimately counsels the quietistic endeavor to "suspend" the will, Schweitzer seeks a "true optimism" that consists in "conceiving and willing the ideal, as this is inspired by profound and self-consistent affirmation of life and of the world."[158] Ethics must pass through a phase of resignation; it must acknowledge that human beings are ultimately powerless to alter the inner nature of things, which consists in endless willing and consequent suffering. But to stop at this point is "an incomprehensible impoverishment of moral ideas."[159] In this connection, we have much to learn from later Stoics such as Seneca, who "caught sight . . . of the idea of humanity" and exhibited an "optimistic-ethical monism" in place of the tragic resignation of Schopenhauer and the early Stoics.[160]

The central failing of a thinker such as Schopenhauer is that his pessimism, like that of the early Stoics, permits "only an ethic of purification, but no ethic of action."[161] Because his worldview is ultimately life-denying, Schopenhauer leaves no room for the human individual to engage in actions with genuine ethical significance.

> All ethical activity becomes illusory because of the negative attitude toward the world which it necessarily pre-supposes. Schopenhauer's sympathy is only the sympathy of passive reflection. He cannot know, any more than the Indian thinkers, the meaning of that kind of sympathy which involves active assistance. This last has no more meaning for him than has any sort of active effort in the objective world. He is unable to alleviate the wretchedness of other creatures since this wretchedness itself is really rooted in the will-to-live—which always involves irremediable sorrow. Thus the one and only thing which sympathy can really affect is to explain to the will-to-live everywhere the kind of snare in which it is caught, and to bring it to the quietness and peace of world- and life-negation. Schopenhauer's sympathy is at bottom, like that of the Brahmins and the Buddha, only theoretical. It can make use of expressions coined by the religion of love, but it remains far behind this in reality. The ideal of non-activity stands in the way of a real ethic of love in his case just as in that of the Indian thinkers.[162]

Schopenhauer neutralizes the capacity of human individuals to accomplish something in the world, even if our accomplishments do not alter the course of nature. Schweitzer agrees with Schopenhauer that ethics needs to become "universal and cosmic," but he rejects Schopenhauer's contention that the individual is nothing more than a particular phenomenon of the world will.[163] Life and the world must be affirmed; what is at stake in ethics is "the exaltation and perfection of life." It is imperative that we demonstrate "an optimistic-ethical world-view" that is "inherent in the intrinsic nature of things" and does not permit us to commit the traditional mistake of considering human beings to be above nature.[164] "The meaning of human life must be sought for" not in the ideal of a transcendent Platonic world but "in the meaning of the objective world" that confronts us concretely.[165] Once we reorient our reflections on the one world of which we are a living part, we will become capable of "world-affirmation," in which "my individual existence becomes attuned to the aims and purposes of the great hidden universal will-to-live, of which I am one among many phenomenal expressions."[166]

Paradoxically, we can become "attuned" to these aims and purposes even though it is impossible to recognize any "purposive element" in objective facts about the world.[167] This attunement is not a matter of knowledge, but instead one of religious inspiration. The ethic of reverence for all life ultimately derives from an "active mysticism" that discloses the universal will-to-live and the imperative to revere all life.[168] "The will-to-live is stronger than the pessimistic intellect. There is in us an instinctive awe in the presence of life, for we ourselves are sparks of the will to live. . . . All pessimism is thus illogical."[169] Schweitzer's "optimistic ethical" standpoint calls not simply for a resigned sense of compassion for suffering beings, but for the combination of self-sacrifice and self-fulfillment, both of which are ultimately "cosmic" ideals. On the side of self-sacrifice, we must extend compassion to all living beings, placing the interests of other living beings above our own interests when the circumstances warrant it; in particular, we must be willing to engage in acts of self-sacrifice on behalf of animals.[170] Self-sacrifice is founded on the recognition that "there is really no such thing as an essence or content of existence, but only eternal existence in eternal phenomena."[171] This recognition inspires us to revere and preserve life, and to avoid the destruction of life.[172] Our participation in one indivisible cosmic process along with animals, that is, our essential kinship with animals as with other living beings, makes it incumbent upon us to act with reverence toward animals.

But how are we to reconcile reverence for life with the destruction and suffering that seem inevitable in the cosmic course of events? Schweitzer's answer to this question is that each individual must decide for himself or herself how to apply the ethic of reverence for life and determine ad hoc how the demands of one's own individuality are to be balanced with the suffering of other beings.[173] This is where self-sacrifice must be balanced with the ethical dimension of self-fulfillment. The ethic of reverence for life calls not only for compassionate regard for other beings such as animals, but also for the cultivation of "the inner perfection of the individual."[174] The ethic of reverence for life "demands that man should strive . . . to be true to himself and to take part in all the life around him as a bringer of sympathy and help."[175] Schweitzer's solution to the problem posed by pessimism is to give a special priority to the individual, hence to human beings, in the midst of the will-to-live: he secures his "optimistic-ethical" viewpoint against the ravages of pessimism by asserting a special priority of creatures capable of being individual selves. The ground of Schweitzer's ethics is reverence for life, but its culmination is faith "in the spiritual progress of man and of humanity."[176]

Thus it is no surprise that Schweitzer believes that, in the course of history, "only Jesus has really constructed a genuinely complete ethic" that incorporates both passive and active self-fulfillment.[177] At bottom, the "ethic of reverence for life is the ethic of Jesus Christ brought to philosophical expression."[178] One implication of this ethic is that killing animals is necessary for the provision of human food; Schweitzer treats the killing of animals as a lamentable but unavoidable corollary of individual self-realization.[179] Schweitzer thereby imports into his ethics the same anthropocentric prejudice that informs the ethical views of so many thinkers in the eighteenth and nineteenth centuries: that even though human beings are products of nature and share an essential kinship with animals, the experiential capacities distinctive of human beings give us a special priority over other beings in the constellation of moral values. However, Schweitzer seeks to impose limits on the exercise of the human will by inscribing human individuality within a comprehensive worldview that imposes stewardship responsibilities on human beings with regard to the rest of creation. In endeavoring to unite "the ethic of Jesus Christ" with an ethic of direct concern for animals and other natural beings, Schweitzer raises an aporia that remains unresolved to this day.

POSTMODERN CONCEPTIONS OF
THE HUMAN-ANIMAL BOUNDARY

The confrontation between the liberal humanist and Romantic conceptions of animals poses a central problem for contemporary environmental
ethics: The tension between human self-assertion and the sense that we
are part of a larger cosmic whole seems irreducible; and yet as long as this
tension remains unresolved, the moral status of animals will remain
critically problematic. On the one hand, we have the claims of liberal
thought, according to which, following the trajectory initiated by Aristotle
and the Stoics, animals at best possess inferior moral status vis-à-vis
human beings (Mill), and at worst no intrinsic moral status whatsoever
(Kant). On the other hand, we have the Romantic aspiration to situate
human beings within the scope of a larger cosmic framework that is itself a source of meaning and value and that alone confers a sense of proper
limits and legitimacy on human action. The confrontation between the
liberal and Romantic conceptions reflects a profound ambivalence between two seemingly incommensurable ways of conceiving of value: one
that makes human valuations the source of all value, and another according to which value has a cosmic source that transcends human experience.

The claims of liberalism are significant, for they embody not only an
ethic of human self-assertion against nature, but also a set of values that
are definitive for the task of what Freud calls "regulating human beings'
relations with one another."[1] Liberal society takes as axiomatic the values of equality, reciprocity, and respect. The sacrifice of these values
brings disastrous consequences of the kind seen on an epic scale in Nazi
Germany and Stalin's Soviet Union, where liberal ideals were rejected in

the name of totalitarianism and the "virtues" of centralized planning.[2] Against this background, Romantic appeals to "homecoming," wholeness, totality, and belonging threaten to undermine the ideals of civility that champions of the Enlightenment fought to secure. And yet the anthropocentric terms of liberalism virtually *define* human beings as superior to animals. To this extent, liberalism fails animals precisely where it vindicates human beings. As a theory for "regulating human beings' relations with one another," liberalism is inextricably linked to that other key value of society lauded by Freud, "the protection of human beings from nature."[3] Liberal values are the modern form of the Stoic doctrine of *oikeiosis* or belonging, according to which all and only rational beings possess full moral worth. All other beings are viewed either as potential means to human security and happiness or as threats to be neutralized. Even if we acknowledge that animals, unlike trees and streams, suffer, their suffering nonetheless counts less than human suffering, because according to the anthropocentric logic of liberalism only human beings possess the highest and purest moral status.

Unless limits are placed on liberalism, animals in our society will invariably be sacrificed for the sake of promoting human interests in all except those uncontroversial cases in which the recognition of the interests of animals does not interfere with the promotion of human interests. As Kant recognized, to subject a discipline to critique is not to condemn it but rather to explore its nature *and its limits*. But Kant never performed a critique on liberalism; instead, he took the basic terms of liberalism for granted and turned his critical eye toward the faculties of understanding and reason, which together address three anthropocentrically posed questions: what can I know, what ought I to do, and what may I hope for?[4] This anthropocentric orientation pervades Kant's conception of morality and is responsible for his classification of duties toward animals as "indirect" at best. It seems, then, that only a genuine critique of liberalism holds the promise of establishing a coherent and substantial sense of the moral status of animals.

The purpose of a critique of liberalism is not to dispense with liberal ideals, but rather to recognize the inability of liberal ideals to do justice to the moral status of animals. Democratic notions such as equality, reciprocity, and duty are not by themselves well suited to the task of establishing human obligations to animals and the environment, because these notions are designed to regulate relations between rational, self-conscious human beings. What is needed is a way of seeing how liberal notions can function within a broader understanding of the relationship between human beings and the rest of nature.

Heidegger: "The Animal Is World-Poor"

Some preliminary indications of how human relations might be located within a larger cosmic framework are provided by Martin Heidegger, a pioneer of the phenomenological movement and a notorious member of the Nazi Party. Heidegger's writings, lectures, and speeches contain a troubling mix of insight into the human condition and insensitivity to the ideals of liberal society. While some critics dismiss Heidegger's thought in its entirety on the grounds that it is fundamentally poisoned by the philosopher's personal political convictions, others recognize that Heidegger's reflections contribute significantly to our understanding of the human-animal boundary and the moral status of animals.

Heidegger's primary concern is not the nature and fate of animals, but rather the nature and place of human beings in the cosmic scheme of things. In this respect Heidegger is, as his student Karl Löwith notes, still working within an essentially Christian framework in which a higher value is placed on spirit than on matter or merely embodied beings.[5] Heidegger's focal point is human Dasein, the human being understood as a historically conditioned process of interpretation. Like other figures in the Western philosophical tradition, Heidegger tends to focus on the ways in which animals lack the capacities and characteristics that make human beings distinctive. Human Dasein is distinctive primarily in virtue of two potentialities that animals and other nonhuman beings lack: the ability to engage in acts of interpretation or the development of meaning, and the encounter with death that makes interpretation possible in the first place. Heidegger's view of the distinction between human beings and animals appears at first to be entirely in line with the tradition that he is at pains to critique. But Heidegger's insights into phenomenology open a possibility long buried in the origins of our culture's encounter with animals.

Heidegger is known—and excoriated—for maintaining that "existence" is a capacity reserved exclusively for human beings. Heidegger uses the term "existence" to characterize the historical, linguistic, self-referential cultivation of meaning that is distinctive of human beings. "The being that exists [*das in der Weise der Existenz ist*] is the human being. Rocks are, but they do not exist. Trees are, but they do not exist. Horses are, but they do not exist. Angels are, but they do not exist. God is, but he does not exist."[6] Only a being that encounters its own finitude *in the way in which human beings do so* can be said to "exist." That mode of encounter is "an open standing that stands [*offenstehende Innestehen*] in the unconcealedness of Being, which is to say that human beings encounter and ponder the limits of their own experience in a way that no other being does—not animals, and not God. This is "the reason why human beings can represent beings as such, and why they can be conscious of such representations."[7] Heidegger's qualification "as such" anticipates the distinction between perceiving an *X* and perceiving something *as* an *X* that I discuss in chapter I: Animals, as even Kant recognizes, have representations, but most do not appear to relate to their representations "as such"; that is, all but the few boundary cases such as the language-using primates seem to be completely immersed in their experiences and to be incapable of establishing cognitive-linguistic distance from those experiences. Human Dasein, in contrast, is "claimed by Being" in such a way that it is granted the possibility of language "as the home that preserves its essence."[8] Language enables us to preserve and contemplate our encounter with our own limits, just as Kant says that reason enables us to contemplate—to think, but not to know—our encounter with the thing-in-itself.

For Heidegger, this very encounter makes language possible. He characterizes our encounter with the limits of meaning as an encounter with the "Nothing" [*das Nichts*]: To be finite is to be immersed in something irreducibly nonfinite; all our attempts to grasp or make sense of this something, like the Kantian attempt to think the thing-in-itself, are essentially partial, provisional, and subject to revision precisely because of the irreducibility of that which we seek to grasp. Language represents beings as such; it cannot represent that which is fundamentally unrepresentable, and thus the unrepresentable presents itself to language as the "Nothing."

We encounter the Nothing, hence the possibility of meaning, in the defining mood of anxiety. In this mood, the comforts of the familiar and worldly "slip away" and the existential threat to coherence posed by the Nothing comes to the fore.[9] "Readiness for anxiety is a Yes to assuming a stance [*Inständigkeit*] that fulfills the highest claim, a claim that is made upon the human essence alone. Of all beings, only the human being, called upon by the voice of being, experiences the wonder of all wonders:

that beings *are*."[10] It is solely in virtue of our encounter with the Nothing, with the limits of our own finitude, that we can encounter beings "as such," that is, only in virtue of this encounter can we step outside what would otherwise be an animal-like immersion in the midst of beings. Because we encounter these limits, we find ourselves "called" to pose questions about our own nature, the nature of other creatures, and the relationship between the two. "If in the ground of its essence Dasein were not transcending, which now means, if it were not in advance holding itself into the nothing, then it could never adopt a stance toward beings nor even toward itself" and it would be incapable of selfhood and freedom.[11] The capacity for responsibility, in other words, depends fundamentally on an encounter with the Nothing and the ability to encounter beings through language.

In *Being and Time*, Heidegger characterizes the anxiety experience and our encounter with our own limits as a confrontation with death. Existentially conceived, death is not the demise of the body or the termination of life but instead is the freedom to choose oneself on the basis of the possibilities that have been handed down by one's tradition. This freedom, and the responsibility to make a choice that gathers one's life into a totality, are disclosed in anxiety. "Anxiety makes manifest in Dasein its *Being towards* its ownmost potentiality-for-Being—that is, its *Being-free for* the freedom of choosing itself and taking hold of itself. Anxiety brings Dasein face to face with its *Being-free for* (*propensio in . . .*) the authenticity of its Being, and for this authenticity as a possibility which it always is."[12] The distinctive capacity of the human being, on Heidegger's view, is the ability to be called to the moment of deciding on one's "ownmost potentiality for Being," that is, that understanding of oneself that reveals and establishes the totality of one's life and thereby makes incumbent on the individual a certain life task or set of choices. Until this fundamental decision is made, a person's life exhibits a "lack of totality," which lack is overcome in the confrontation of one's death in anxiety.

Death in the existential sense is not a ceasing to be or a perishing of the body, but instead is an active relation to oneself and one's freedom that human beings are constantly confronting. "The 'ending' which we have in view when we speak of death, does not signify Dasein's Being-at-an-end, but a *Being-towards-the-end* of this entity. Death is a way to be, which Dasein takes over as soon as it is."[13] Death *as a way of being* is unique to human Dasein, inasmuch as "in [Dasein's] Being, that Being is an *issue* for it."[14] What is at issue in one's life becomes most pressing in the moment of anxiety, in which "Dasein finds itself *face to face* with the 'nothing' of the possible impossibility of its existence. . . . Being-towards-death is essentially anxiety."[15] "Possible impossibility" refers to all the fundamental paradoxes of existence that we confront when we engage in the act of pure wonder that is the origin of all philosophical thinking. One of these paradoxes is that I must gather my life into a totality and make a fundamental choice even though anxiety has disclosed to me the sheer contingency that underlies my existence and the possible choices that I might make, that is, to be human is to be charged with the responsibility to confer a sense of necessity on one's life while at the same time recognizing that one's life is grounded in sheer contingency. Another of these paradoxes is expressed in the fundamental question of metaphysics: "Why are there beings at all, rather than nothing?"[16] Heidegger distinguishes human beings as the beings that confront such paradoxes in the activity of questioning, which constitutes "the piety of thinking."[17] Human existence is a process of questioning or interrogating the human condition, one's individual life in particular, the nature of beings, and the "ontological difference" between Being and beings.

In contrast with human Dasein, animals neither exist nor have any relation to death in the existential sense. As with the term "existence," Heidegger reserves the term "death" for Dasein, and says that living beings "perish" (*verendet*).[18] Living beings, including animals, lack language, which "brings beings, as what is extant, into the Open for the first time."[19] The "Open" is the space of intelligibility that is unique to human beings, in which we have an active sense of "nearness" or proximity to beings.[20] This sense of nearness is distinguished from the way in which animals relate to things by the "as such"—only human beings, in virtue of our linguistic, questioning relation to the world and to ourselves, can relate to beings as the beings that they are. In comparison, animals relate to beings and to their environment, but they do not relate to these "as such" because they have no linguistic, questioning distance from things or from themselves. Such distance is characteristic of a specific kind of being, which Heidegger in his later writings refers to as the mortal. "Mortals are those who can experience death as death. Animals are not capable of this. But the animal also cannot speak."[21]

Because they are incapable of speech—in the language of the Greeks, they are *aloga* (ἄλογα, lacking in rational speech)—animals do not relate to their own finitude as such, and hence they do not relate to possibility and impossibility as such, and in this specific sense they do not inhabit a world as a space of intelligible and articulable interrelationships. To lack a relation to the "as such" is to lack the "as-structure" that makes it possible for human beings to disclose and hold in present awareness the objects, concerns, projects, and interrelationships that make the world a space of meaningful interrelationships. Heidegger's conviction that only human beings are "worldly" in this sense, which is inseparable from his conviction that only human beings "exist" and are subject to death in the existential sense, recalls Saint Augustine's distinction between memory as recollection in human beings and memory as mere recall of sensible particulars in animals. These convictions also shed light on Löwith's interpretation of Heidegger as a philosopher in the Christian tradition. Given the rigid distinction between animals and human beings maintained by the Christian philosophers, it is not surprising that Heidegger appears to maintain fidelity to Christian ontology.

But Heidegger's affinities with Christian tradition have clear limits, as is evident in his reflections on the relationship between Dasein and the "living." In the "Letter on 'Humanism',," he observes that "of all the beings that are, presumably the most difficult to think about are living creatures [das Lebe-Wesen], because on the one hand they are in a certain way most closely akin [am nächsten verwandt] to us, and on the other they are at the same time separated from our ek-sistent essence by an abyss."[22] Heidegger's anthropocentrism is clear in his assertion that "plants and animals are lodged in their respective environments but are never placed freely into the clearing of being which alone is 'world.'"[23] His basic concern is not the nature or fate of animals, but rather that of human Dasein and the proper exercise of our freedom, which is made possible by our encounter with the Nothing.[24] For all that, however, Heidegger explores the question of the living, and specifically the question of the animal, at length in a lecture course held in 1929–1930, almost two decades before he wrote the "Letter on 'Humanism.'"

In that course, Heidegger situates the experience of animals somewhere between the inert being of things such as stones and the interpretive activity of human beings. In attempting to explore the character of human worldliness, Heidegger draws a distinction between humans, animals, and nonliving beings. He advances the following three theses: "The stone is worldless," "the animal is world-poor [weltarm]," and "the human being forms or develops world [ist weltbildend]."[25] To say that animals are world-poor is not to say that they have no relationship to things in their environment, but rather that they "have less"; they suffer under a comparative lack of world that is finally no more than a "difference of degree" in comparison with the worldliness of human beings.[26] Heidegger, like Aristotle before him, has a tendency in his different writings sometimes to draw a distinction in kind between humans and animals (in denying existence, death, and freedom to animals) and at other times merely a difference of what Aristotle called "more or less." The 1929–1930 lecture course is the one place where Heidegger explores the extent and significance of the animal's participation in world, and this text stands in the same relationship to Heidegger's other writings that Aristotle's zoological writings stand to his ethical and psychological writings. In this lecture course, Heidegger acknowledges that animals have ways of relating to their environments. Bees, for example, have to be able to distinguish between different sorts of flowers and must be able to find and return to them; what is distinctive about these ways of relating to the environment is that animals such as bees relate to a strictly limited domain characterized by food, potential enemies, and potential prey.[27] The domain of things to which animals can be actively related is not something fixed, but instead possesses a certain "mobility." Such mobility is a basic feature of the way in which animals are "captivated" (benommen) by their environment, that is, they are enthralled in an immediate relation to the environment that does not permit any interpretive distance from things. The mobility of the animal's surroundings reflects the fact, of which Heidegger offers no acknowledgment in his other writings, that "to [the animal's] essence belongs an openness to . . . , which pervades its behavior"; here a "leeway [Spielraum] is created, within which what is encountered can be encountered in such and such a manner, i.e., it can affect the animal by means of a freeing-up [Enthemmens]."[28] The "kinship" between humans and animals, to which Heidegger refers in the "Letter on 'Humanism'," consists in our shared capacity to have an active, open relationship to our environment, that is, beings can show up for animals. But the gulf or "abyss" that divides us from animals is evident in the different ways in which human beings and animals can relate to their respective surroundings.

The key to this difference lies in the fact that the environment is "open" to animals in a fundamentally more limited way than it is open to human beings. Whereas human beings confront a "world" in the sense of a space of meaningful interrelationships that can be grasped "as such," animals do not inhabit a world in this precise sense. "World signifies not the accessibility of beings, but instead means among other things the

accessibility of beings as such." To this extent, "the animal, in its captivation [*Benommenheit*] in the sense of being deprived [*Genommenheit*] of the
openness of beings, can in principle have no world, even though that to
which it is related can always be experienced in *our* experience as beings."[29]
Strictly speaking, the animal, in its captivation, relates not to a worldly
environment (*Umwelt*) but instead to its "surroundings" (*Umring*).[30] The
precise nature of the "openness" of things to the animal's awareness is,
for Heidegger as for all of his predecessors, a question. Heidegger attempts to provide a phenomenologically clarified account of the fact that
animals lack human language (λόγος, *logos*). Part of Heidegger's clarification comes in his extensive efforts to correct the ancient Greek misunderstanding of *logos* in terms of strings of words and declarative statements; he wants to draw out the sense in which the articulation of meaning
occurs at a more fundamental and less formalized level than that of logic
and predication.[31] But for Heidegger, even that more fundamental level
still involves the idea of the "as such." Thus the articulation of meaning
cannot be attributed to animals on Heidegger's view, and this in turn leads
Heidegger to a second step of phenomenological clarification: he attempts
to capture the sense in which beings can be "open" for animals, without
the dimension of the "as such." Like his forebears, Heidegger encounters the limits of language in his attempt to characterize this sense of
openness, and is hard pressed to get beyond the point of stating that
"openness in captivation is an essential possession [*Habe*] of the animal.
On the basis of this possession, it can lack, be poor, be defined in its being
by poverty. Of course, this possession is not the having of a world, but
rather a being given over to the range of what has been freed up
[*Enthemmungsring*]."[32] The animal lacks a world in the narrow sense that
"world" is, for Heidegger, possible only for beings that can hold specific
meanings in openness, retrieve them at will, and form interpretations
that have the uniquely human character of self-referentiality. Unlike
other beings, humans form and develop interpretations *about* interpretations, as part of the questioning activity that defines human beings and
that animals lack. Animals possess something analogous to world, but it
lacks the dimension of meaning because it lacks the elusive "as such";
animals, for example, never attend to the fact that they are confronted
by an environment, by beings, in the first place.[33]

The central problem on which Heidegger focuses in his discussion
of animals is how the openness characteristic of the animal's experience
is to be characterized. To say that the animal is "world-poor" is not to

condemn the animal to an inferior status vis-à-vis human beings. "The thesis of the animal's world-poverty is thus not an interpretation of what is essentially proper to animals, but rather merely a comparative illustration."[34] Heidegger's larger concern is to reflect on the human phenomenon of world. His discussion of animals is meant to help establish a dividing line between the human and the nonhuman. Thus Heidegger acknowledges that his reflections on animals are merely provisional, and that the thesis about the animal's world-poverty "must remain in place as a problem."[35] At the same time, it must be acknowledged that, in comparison with the world-forming capacities of human beings, animals are fundamentally lacking. For one thing, the lack of an ability to relate to beings *as* beings, as opposed to simply relating to them in the mode of immediate captivation, means that the bee seeking nectar in a field of flowers "does not know the stamens of these blossoms as stamens, it does not know the roots of the plants, it does not know such a thing as the number of stamens and leaves. In comparison with this, the world of human beings is rich."[36] This lack, in turn, reflects the poverty of the animal's experience in relation to the following features of Dasein's "existence": "1. the openness of beings as beings, 2. the 'as', 3. the relation to beings as a letting-be and a not-letting-be, conduct toward . . . , attitude and selfhood. None of this is found in animality or in the living generally."[37]

With these conclusions, Heidegger shows his analysis of animal life to be of a piece with his remarks about the uniquely human character of existence, death, and the ability to articulate meaning. Animals do not relate to the world as a totality of significations that can be altered or called into question, and animals do not take into consideration the relationship of part (individual reference or sign) to whole (totality of reference or signification that constitutes the world). The "openness of beings" that human beings possess and animals lack is the very openness that Heidegger appeals to in "On the Essence of Truth" when he characterizes the freedom of human beings to "let beings be" and to engage themselves with the disclosedness of beings; this engagement is the "eksistence" that Heidegger refers to in "What Is Metaphysics?"[38]

For Heidegger, the contrast between human beings and animals is ultimately that between a being that is free for meaning, questioning, selfhood, and responsibility, and a being that is *comparatively* limited in the ways in which it is able to relate to its environment. Animals are "world-poor" in the sense that they are deprived of the experience of meaning

as such, of the possibility of contemplating life and the totality of meaning, and hence of making distinctions between a freely self-chosen existence ("authenticity") and an existence determined by the authority of
one's cultural background ("inauthenticity"). This deprivation translates
directly into an inability to take part in ethical relations: "An animal can
never be 'evil' . . . For evil presupposes spirit [Geist]. The animal can never
get out of the unity of its determinate rank in nature. . . . The animal
is not capable of dealing with principles."[39] The contrast between human
freedom and the "captivated freeing-up" that Heidegger attributes to
animals recalls the distinction between a Hobbesian-Humean sense of
freedom as a lack of external impediments, and the Kantian notion of
an autonomy that can transcend the realm of inclination. Only a being
that possesses the capacity for Kantian autonomy is capable of historical reflection and authentic selfhood.

At best it would be far fetched to attribute such capacities to animals.
This does not mean, however, that animals are eo ipso inferior to human beings. Heidegger acknowledges that

> this comparison between animals and humans in terms of world-poverty
> and world-formation does not give license to estimations and evalua-
> tions of perfection and imperfection—quite apart from the fact that such
> estimations are hasty and inappropriate. For we encounter the great-
> est difficulty when we pose the question which are the higher and which
> the lower kinds of access to beings, e.g., when we compare the ability of
> the falcon's eye to grasp things with that of the human's eye, or the dog's
> ability to smell with that of the human. However quick we may be to
> estimate the human as a higher being than the animal, such an evalu-
> ation is questionable, particularly when we consider that the human can
> sink lower than the animal; an animal can never become corrupted as
> a human can. . . . From everything that has been said, it is clear that talk
> of world-poverty and world-formation is, from the very start, not to be
> taken in the sense of a disparaging rank-ordering. Of course, a relation-
> ship and difference are expressed here, but in a different sense. In what
> sense? This is exactly what we are looking for. In this connection, it is
> necessary that we give an adequate definition of poverty.[40]

The question of the difference and the relationship between humans and
animals devolves upon the question of the meaning of the animal's
"poverty," because this poverty is not an absolute characteristic of the
animal but rather a comparative characteristic of the animal. Only in the

specific sense that animals lack certain human capacities are animals "poor." In other respects, animals may well be superior to human beings, assuming that we can make sense of the notions of superiority and inferiority at all in comparisons between humans and animals—an assumption that Heidegger calls into question. This questioning challenges even Heidegger's own classification of animals as "world-poor." Hence we cannot declare definitively that animals are inferior to human beings, and we can say only provisionally that their poverty "signifies a lack [*Entbehren*]," not simply with regard to *what* but ultimately with regard to the *how* of their lacking in comparison with human beings.

Heidegger attempts to shed light on this lack by hyphenating *Armut*, the German word for "poverty," as "Ar-mut," so as to place emphasis on "mut," which is found in various words and expressions signifying state of mind.[41] The "how" of the animal's lack is to be understood in terms of "how things seem" to it ["wie *es ihm dabei* zu Mute *ist*"] subjectively: The precise character of that "how" remains fundamentally obscure, but it is clear that human beings act in distinctive ways—questioning, engaging in historical reflection, cultivating a sense of the "as such"—that are foreign to the subjectivity of animals. The animal is that being among nonhuman beings that lies closest to the boundary between the human and the nonhuman. But the animal ultimately lies on the other side of the boundary. Notwithstanding our kinship with animals, to which Heidegger alludes in the "Letter on 'Humanism'," our ability to conceive of animal subjectivity is fundamentally limited by that boundary. The best that we can do in our attempt to grasp the nature of the animal, at least from within the framework of the Western philosophical tradition, may be to acknowledge that the animal has *some* sort of subjective relation to world— it is not merely present among things in its environment the way a stone is, but has a relation to its environment that is, in comparison with human worldliness, strictly circumscribed. Beyond acknowledging that animals possess their own kind of subjectivity and studying the outward behavioral effects of this subjectivity, we may ultimately never be in a position to answer Thomas Nagel's question "What is it like to be a bat?"[42] One might even say that "we cannot really image [*sic*] what [the animal's] world looks like without reverting to anthropomorphism," and that "this is *our* poverty."[43]

Our encounter with the human-animal boundary recalls Kant's reflection on our encounter with the bounds of sense and his appeal to transcendental ideas of reason as regulative notions to help us conceptualize our encounter with what lies beyond those bounds. Heidegger's analysis returns us to the prospect, acknowledged continually in the history of Western philosophy, of *thinking* our kinship relation with animals even though we can never *know* that relationship. Like his forebears in the tradition, Heidegger does not explore this prospect but simply attests to its *possibility* as a human calling. As noted at the beginning of this chapter, in exploring the possibilities opened up by Heidegger's views on animals, we will do well to be on guard against conflating those views with other aspects of Heidegger's thought that have rightly been found to be pernicious. It is in this spirit that we must approach the critiques of Heidegger's views of animals and the environment developed by Levinas and Derrida. Both of these thinkers shed important light on the nature and limits of Heidegger's views about animals, but neither maintains a rigorous distinction between Heidegger's positive contribution to our understanding of animals and the totalitarian implications of his thought. In particular, both thinkers, implicitly if not explicitly, see Heidegger's views about animals and the environment as inseparable from his fidelity to the aims of National Socialism.

The Call of the Other: Levinas's Critique of Heidegger

Like so many philosophers before him, Heidegger seizes upon linguistic ability as the sine qua non of ethical responsibility. As the only beings capable of questioning, only human beings are capable of *responding* to the call of conscience and ethical obligation.[44] But does this mean that animals, as beings presumably incapable of questioning, are thereby excluded from the realm of ethical community? Even if animals cannot be moral agents, are they not capable of entering into some kind of ethical relationship with human beings?[45] This is the question that Emmanuel Levinas takes up in "The Name of a Dog, or Natural Rights," which concerns his encounter with a particular dog while he was interned in a Nazi labor camp. Having been reduced by the Nazis to the status of a "subhuman . . . gang of apes," the prisoners were deprived of the dignity of an ethical encounter with others, and hence with themselves, until "a wandering dog entered [their] lives. . . . He would appear at morning assembly and was waiting for us as we returned, jumping up and down and barking in delight. For him, there was no doubt that we were men."[46] This dog, whom the prisoners affectionately called "Bobby," functioned as the "other" that is, on Levinas's view, the essential condition for an ethical relation. Against Kant, who sees ethical responsibility as a task for each rational individual to constitute from out of his or her isolated rationality, Levinas believes that a sense of the other, and the possibility of subordinating one's own interests to those of the other, are the essential ground of ethics. Deprived of human others who could function in this capacity, the Jewish prisoners were blessed to encounter Bobby, who acknowledged their humanity and who, in an odd sense, "was the last Kantian in Nazi Germany"—odd because he lacked "the brain needed to universalize maxims and drives."[47]

The paradox that Levinas illuminates with this reminiscence is that "there is transcendence in the animal!" even though the animal cannot cognize and contemplate its own transcendence. Levinas sees nobility in an animal such as Bobby, or the ability to relate to human beings in a way that can confer on or restore to us our sense of authentic humanity. "There is enough, there, to make you a vegetarian again."[48] Levinas's reflection on Bobby invites the conclusion that Levinas is interested in cultivating an ethical relation between human beings and animals on the basis of kinship. Levinas points toward "the radical possibilities that can be opened up when the reach of the ethical question *who is my neighbor?* is widened to include nonhuman acquaintances. If animals are also murdered, if their deaths are no longer denegated as merely being put to death, then to whom or what am I answerable? The unstated analogy between the murder of the Jews and the killing of animals in effect creates a *rhetorical* neighborhood in which humans and animals dwell and summon each other into responsibility."[49] But Levinas does not explore this "rhetorical neighborhood" beyond noting the sense of transcendence conveyed to him by his encounter with Bobby. Levinas is horrified by Heidegger's equation of "the manufacture of corpses in gas chambers and death camps" with "the motorized food industry" for trivializing the systematic dehumanization of Jews and other victims of the Nazi regime.[50] In his reflections on animals, Levinas implies that there is a parallel between the Nazi treatment of the Jews and human treatment of animals. Clark states that Bobby's silence in the face of the prisoners doubles the prisoners' silence in the face of their captors.[51] Thus we might expect Levinas to develop his reflections on Bobby into a sense of ethics that encompasses the animal as well as the human, thereby distancing himself not only from Heidegger's silence regarding the Final Solution but also from Heidegger's exclusion of animals from the ethical sphere. And yet this is precisely what Levinas does *not* do.

Instead, in the larger framework of his writings on ethics, Levinas implicitly treats the silence of an animal such as Bobby as a mere simulation of the capacity for silence that is uniquely human and lies at the core of ethics. "What distinguishes human language from animal or child expression, for example, is that the human speaker can remain silent, can refuse to be exposed in sincerity. . . . This ability to keep silent, to withhold oneself, is the ability to be political. . . . Language as *saying* is an ethical openness to the other."[52] Levinas follows Heidegger in seeing silence as a necessary condition for the possibility of meaningful utterance, and in conferring on humans alone the possibility of authentic speech. To this extent, Bobby is not "the last Kantian in Nazi Germany," but simply a *simulation* of the last Kantian in Nazi Germany, a reminder of the prisoners' humanity from just beyond the boundary of that humanity.

In many respects, Levinas's account of ethics follows the terms of Heidegger's account; in particular, both seize upon the figure of death as an essential category of the ethical, as the focal point for the call to responsibility. But "whereas for Heidegger death is *my* death, for [Levinas] it is the *other's* death." For Levinas, ethics "is a form of vigilant passivity to the call of the other" that places the other higher than oneself.[53] Ethics requires us to subordinate our freedom to the freedom of the other. This possibility is founded on a relation to God, traces of whose fundamental absence come to presence in our moments of ethical self-sacrifice. The possibility of ethics also depends on the ability to relate to a self as a self, be this oneself or another. Presumably Bobby's lack of a "brain needed to universalize maxims and drives" makes him unable to relate to a self as a self, hence unable to witness the traces of the divine as they come to presence and unable to subjugate his own freedom to that of another.

In Levinas's terminology, Bobby does not possess a "face." The face represents the claim exerted by another's existence over my own so as to make me sense my ethical responsibility toward the other. Only a being with a face can take part in an ethical relation. It is clear to Levinas that human beings have faces, but the question of the animal face is more obscure. "I cannot say at what moment you have the right to be called 'face'. The human face is completely different and only afterwards do we discover the face of an animal. I don't know if a snake has a face. I can't answer that question."[54] Levinas equivocates in his writings on the question of the animal face. On the one hand, he associates the face with "alterity, the unencompassable, the transcendent" and he sees transcendence in the animal.[55] But on the other hand, he characterizes ethics as a specifically human project:

> I do not know at what moment the human appears, but what I want to emphasize is that the human breaks with pure being, which is always a persistence in being. This is my principal thesis. A being is something that is attached to being, to its own being. That is Darwin's idea. The being of animals is a struggle for life. A struggle for life without ethics. It is a question of might. . . . With the appearance of the human—and this is my entire philosophy—there is something more important than my life, and that is the life of the other.[56]

Ethics is specifically human, because ethics depends on language. "The beginning of language is in the face. In a certain way, in its silence, it calls you."[57] To say that Bobby lacks a face is to say that he cannot remain authentically silent, cannot speak, cannot confer on me a sense of ethical responsibility toward *him*. There may be "enough, there, to make you a vegetarian again," but there is no *ethical* obligation to become one. Levinas is moved by his revulsion to Heidegger's silence about Nazism to establish distance from Heidegger's philosophical stance. Levinas's account of alterity (the ethical claim of the other), and his characterization of ethics as "an essentially religious vocation" that seeks to bring to presence the traces of an absent God, show the extent of this distance. But when it comes to animals, Levinas does not get a single step beyond Heidegger. "The moral priority of the other . . . [is] motivated by something beyond nature. The ethical situation is a human situation," whereas animals are ultimately no more than a part of living nature.[58] Levinas leaves us at the same point as Heidegger: wondering what sort of "transcendence" constitutes animality.

Much Ado about (the) Nothing: Derrida's Critique of Heidegger

Derrida intensifies the terms of the critique of Heidegger initiated by Levinas by calling into question the boundary between human and animal that Heidegger presupposes. Like Levinas, Derrida seeks the elements in Heidegger's philosophy that led him to embrace National Socialism. This leads Derrida to call for a rethinking of the notion of responsibility articulated by Heidegger. Such a rethinking demands above all a radical questioning of the "who" of responsibility and obligation. Derrida accepts Levinas's proposition that this "'who' . . . is a singularity that dislocates or divides itself in gathering itself together to answer to the other, whose call somehow precedes its own identification with itself."[59] Derrida takes Levinas's conception of alterity one step further, by making central the question of the boundary between self and other: the "who" of responsibility can be conceived, if only provisionally, only by thinking it in relation to the other that precedes it. Derrida seeks "that *Urform* [original or primordial form] of the transcendental experience [in which] the subject conjoins with nonsubject."[60] Like Heidegger, Derrida seeks to overcome the traditional notion of the human self as a stable, ahistorical, autonomous "subject" in the Cartesian sense; he seeks a nonmetaphysical sense of the "subject" that calls into question the proposition that only human beings can *be* subjects. Nonetheless he posits the task as an endeavor to think the relation between humanity ("subject") and nonhuman living beings ("nonsubject"). The task of rethinking human subjectivity devolves upon the task of thinking the boundary between the human and the nonhuman "other." This task takes us "back to the question of the animal."[61]

Like Heidegger and Levinas, Derrida recognizes that "the *alter ego* cannot present itself, cannot become an originary presence for the *ego*."[62] If we are to conceive of ourselves and our sense of responsibility on the basis of our encounter with the other, this does not mean that the other can be reduced to conceptual clarity. Derrida follows Heidegger in recognizing that this limitation pertains especially to our encounter with animals. But Derrida is severely critical of Heidegger for taking it for granted that animals cannot be Dasein, that they cannot take part in the enterprise of intersubjectivity. Derrida calls for a "deconstruction" of the notion of subjectivity that will open up a sense of primordial "responsibility toward the living in general."[63]

Heidegger fails, in Derrida's estimation, to acknowledge such a sense of responsibility because his thesis about the world-poverty of the animal is irretrievably "anthropo-teleological."[64] Heidegger's thesis confers an absolute superiority on humans over all other beings, and subtly incorporates the Stoic prejudice that all nonhuman beings exist for the sake of humanity. Heidegger's anthropocentrism regarding animals is a "carno-phallogocentrism," that is, it asserts the primacy of meat-eating, male, linguistic beings in the cosmic scheme of things, thereby effectively excluding all other beings from the bond of ethical responsibility.[65]

Derrida challenges Heidegger's exclusion of animals from the ethical sphere by challenging his distinction between the death of Dasein and the mere perishing of living beings. "What [Heidegger] places at the origin of moral conscience (or rather *Gewissen*) is obviously denied to the animal. *Mitsein* [Being-with other Dasein] is not conferred, if we can say so, on the living in general, no more than is *Dasein*, but only on that being-towards-death that also makes *Dasein* into something else, something more and better than a living [thing]."[66] By denying animals a share in death, not only do we exclude them from the ethical sphere, but we also prejudice all of our judgments regarding the "just" and "unjust" treatment of animals as well: "If we wish to speak of injustice, of violence or of a lack of respect toward what we still so confusedly call animals—the question is more topical than ever, and so I include in it, in the name of deconstruction, a set of questions on carno-phallogocentrism—we must reconsider in its totality the metaphysico-anthropocentric axiomatic that dominates, in the West, the thought of just and unjust."[67]

Heidegger's existential conception of death marks "an absolute limit between the living creature and the human *Dasein*" that forecloses a sense of openness and responsibility toward animal others.[68] Derrida seeks to challenge (deconstruct) this limit by subjecting Heidegger's existential conception of death to critique. He challenges the very idea of an existential conception of death, and asks whether a conception of death higher than the "vulgar" one is not simply "impracticable, nonviable, and impossible."[69] This is to ask whether Heidegger's appeal to Dasein's "death" is nothing more than a fanciful gesture that seeks to transfigure the mundane fact of "perishing."[70] It is to challenge Heidegger's "anthropo-teleological" conviction that the death of Dasein is higher than the mere demise of living beings.

But at the same time, Derrida expresses an appreciation of the fact, acknowledged by both Levinas and Heidegger, that death is a unique and irreducibly transmundane phenomenon. One must remain mindful of

the indeterminacy of the word "death." Fundamentally, one knows perhaps neither the meaning nor the referent of this word. It is well known that if there is one word that remains absolutely unassignable or unassigning with respect to its concept and to its thingness, it is the word "death." Less than for any other noun, save "God"—and for good reason, since their association here is probably not fortuitous—it is possible to attribute to the noun "death," and above all to the expression "my death", a concept or a reality that would constitute the object of an indisputably determining experience.[71]

In challenging the proposition that death can mean something higher than what is signified by its "vulgar" concept, Derrida seems to want to say two things. First, "any border between the animal and the *Dasein* of speaking man [is] unassignable."[72] The very idea of such a boundary must be deconstructed. Second, Heidegger has not placed too low a value on the death of animals, but rather too high a value on that of humans. The deconstruction of the putative boundary between animal and human leads to a devaluation of humanity in relation to nonhuman living beings. But in drawing an intimate association between death and the divine, Derrida shows another side to his thinking that recalls not only Levinas's association of death and God, but also the fundamental premium that Heidegger places on death in *Being and Time* and on mortality and divinity in his later writings. Death, Derrida concludes, "is neither entirely natural (biological) nor cultural."[73]

This returns us to the question of the *animal* in Derrida: To what extent does Derrida want to place animals on a par with human beings, to explore an inner kinship between the two, to confer on animals the profound alterity that Levinas hints at but never fully embraces? David Wood observes that "Derrida's attitudes to other animals are ambivalent."[74] Apart from his enticing assertion that the primordial call of responsibility ultimately "is not 'human'," Derrida does little to explore or acknowledge the terms of animality and the place that animals might have in the ethical sphere.[75] He notes with disapproval Aristotle's and Heidegger's exclusion of animals from the sphere of friendship, and their denial that we "have a responsibility toward the living in general." He calls into question the notion of "a noncriminal putting to death" and speaks of the "monstrosity" of killing, though he is not clear as to whether he is mortified by the killing of animals as much as he is by the killing of human beings. But he brings closure to these remarks by stating that he is "not recalling this in order to start a support group for vegetarianism, ecologism, or for the societies for the protection of animals."[76] To do so would be to bring to reductive closure a process of questioning that must remain forever *open* and hence capable of genuine responsibility.

Here is a good test analogy: Try to imagine Derrida saying the same thing about efforts to memorialize or avert a massive *human* tragedy. The reason such a possibility cannot be taken seriously is that Derrida's entire critique of Heidegger is motivated primarily (if not entirely) by his mortification at Heidegger's silence about the Nazi death camps. It is conspicuous that in his discussions of animals, Derrida almost always incorporates references to this mortification. In "Eating Well," Derrida articulates his concern about the commandment against killing not ultimately in terms of animals, but in terms of the "unthinkable" horror of Auschwitz, and he effectively treats reflection on animality as a means to thinking this unthinkable.[77] In "On Reading Heidegger," Derrida concludes his reflection on "*life* and *animality* in Heidegger's ontology" not with an expression of concern for kinship with animals, but, again, with Heidegger's "monstrous" silence about the Holocaust.[78] And the entire motive force of Derrida's *Of Spirit* is to challenge the legitimacy of Heidegger's conception of human spirit by locating that conception at the center of a regime of thinking that sought to extinguish all opposition in a "furnace of spirit."[79]

This leaves Derrida in the ironic position of embracing, if only unwittingly, a position that is not far removed from the humanism with which he charges Levinas and Heidegger.[80] Perhaps we should be "mortified" by the killing and eating of animals, but we should not do anything about it, at least not if we seek to ground our actions in any kind of determinate principle. The "ghost, flame, and ashes" of the Holocaust are quite another matter for Derrida; these were the consequences of a Nazi conception of spirit that "was not born in the desert" but "had grown like a mushroom in the silence of a European forest . . . an immense black forest."[81] That Derrida is unwilling to speak in comparable terms of the "ghost, flame, and ashes" that rise up from our treatment of animals is a sign of his humanist orientation. In the end, Derrida makes no more place in the ethical sphere for animals than does Heidegger or Levinas.

If, however, none of these thinkers admits animals into the ethical sphere, each nonetheless makes an inchoate gesture toward the possibility of doing so. All three thinkers, implicitly if not explicitly, adhere to the classical formula according to which language opens up the possibility of ethical responsibility. For Heidegger, "plant and animal do not will because, muted in their desire, they never bring the Open before themselves as an object."[82] Willing in the full sense of the term is possible only for a being capable of the "as such" that opens up a distance between the self and its world and makes willing as such a project or "venture." Language makes human beings "the more venturesome ones," who "must dare the venture with language" and thus enter into the realm of responsibility.[83]

Derrida gives a comparable primacy to language. He says that the process of questioning is inextricably bound up with "a responsibility it has not chosen and which assigns it even its liberty."[84] To be claimed by language and the call of responsibility is, for Derrida as for Heidegger and Levinas, the distinctive capacity of the human.

But all three thinkers also confront the boundary between the human and the animal in a way that merits further exploration. Heidegger denies that the human-animal distinction is ultimately a value judgment. Levinas attempts to see the alterity of a dog that lacks the capacity to universalize maxims. And Derrida sees the need to radicalize the "question of the very origin of responsibility."[85] If our inherited sense of responsibility is a product of the way in which language has disclosed its claim on us, then a radicalization of language might open up the possibility of reconfiguring our ethical relation to animals.

> The idea according to which man is the only speaking being, in its traditional form or in its Heideggerian form, seems to me at once undisplaceable and highly problematic. Of course, if one defines language in such a way that it is reserved for what we call man, what is there to say? But if one reinscribes language in a network of possibilities that do not merely encompass it but mark it irreducibly from the inside, everything changes. I am thinking in particular of the mark in general, of the trace, of iterability, of *différance*. These possibilities or necessities, without which there would be no language, *are themselves not only human*.[86]

The task with which Heidegger, Levinas, and Derrida leave us—if we allow ourselves to be claimed by it—is how to rethink the notions of language and responsibility so as to illuminate the sense of kinship with animals that moved Plutarch and Porphyry. The problem with which we are left, and to which the polemic between Heidegger, Levinas, and Derrida attests, is how we are to undertake such a radical rethinking without sacrificing the achievements of liberal political theory. How are we to realize a sense of belonging together with animals in the whole of nature, without committing the Jacobin excesses of a romanticism that sacrifices the individual for the (supposed) good of the whole? The aporia that confronts us is how we are to reconcile the seemingly irreducible conflict between individual human liberty and the ethical claim imposed on us by the animal other.

RETHINKING THE MORAL STATUS OF ANIMALS

In the history of Western philosophy, capacities play a primary role in reflections on the moral status of animals. Expressions of a sense of kinship with animals recur throughout that history as well. A combination of the capacities and kinship approaches provides a basis for overcoming the limitations and confusions in the contemporary debates about animals.

Near the end of *Animal Minds and Human Morals*, Richard Sorabji asks whether any one philosophical theory or viewpoint is capable of adequately grounding our sense of the moral status of animals. After discussing the views of Regan, Singer, and others, Sorabji concludes that "from a philosophical point of view, I do not think we have to adopt any moral theory at all, and certainly not any moral theory of [the] unifying type which seeks, as far as possible, to boil down all considerations to one." Sorabji finds neither "the two ancient theories of useful contract or of belonging (*oikeiosis*)," nor "the two modern ones of preference satisfaction or inherent value," to be satisfactory.[1] He concludes that we would do best simply to dispense with moral theories altogether.

This proposition merits further consideration, but I think it will be more fruitful in the long run to develop a sense of the necessary complementarity of the capacities and kinship approaches. Neither of these theories alone is sufficient to ground a viable animal ethic, but each is necessary. There are two reasons that a combination of approaches is superior to the wholesale abandonment of moral theories.

First, if we abandon theory, we are forced to rely too much on intuitions that are susceptible to subjective viewpoints and acculturation. Both

Regan and Sorabji appeal to intuition in thinking about the moral status of animals. Regan bases his case for animal rights on the claim that animals have beliefs and desires. His "cumulative argument" for this conclusion includes an appeal to ordinary language and common sense, which are themselves dependent upon intuitions that embody cultural and personal bias.[2] Sorabji, instead of arguing for the viability of intuition as a basis for reflections on the moral status of animals, challenges the idea that "invoking a moral theory" could overcome disagreements in debates about animals, and observes that on his approach "agreement on moral relevance will [not] always be possible."[3] Sorabji is right to suggest that no theory is guaranteed to convert opponents automatically, but that is not a reason to abandon theory altogether. At their best, theories—particularly moral theories—guide us as we reflect on and seek to develop our intuitions. Theory does not solve all problems, but it is a basis for overcoming the perspectival character of pre-reflective intuitions.

The second reason for pursuing the complementary approach rather than abandoning theory altogether is found through a reflection on the historical unfolding of thought about animals examined in this book. Even if some of the contemporary approaches are ramified through the classical liberal notion of the autonomous individual or that of a calculus of pleasures and pains, every one of these views is deeply rooted in positions that were devised and explored long before the modern age. Thus, for example, even if Sorabji is right that the Greeks could not have had a conception of human or animal *rights*, it remains the case that the Stoic doctrine of belonging (*oikeiosis*) lays the fundamental groundwork for the rights approach as it is realized in thinkers such as Kant and Rawls.[4] Moreover, the historical debates about animals show not only that each position has its problems, but also that a number of philosophers tend to move back and forth between the two main views. Appeals to the capacities of animals as a basis for evaluating moral status implicitly presuppose some kind of kinship between human beings and animals. By the same token, appeals to a kinship relation presuppose shared capacities—if not the capacity for cognition, or to feel pleasure and pain, then at least the capacity to flourish and to realize "ends" in the Aristotelian sense of the highest and best point of development in a being. Taken in isolation, each of the main views I examine in this book leads to absurdities or to significant problems. The rights approach privileges those beings most capable of asserting their own rights. Utilitarianism makes the pleasures and pains of more sentient beings count more in the social calculus. And appeals to kinship threaten to place creatures such as oysters, which lack even a central nervous system and hence the capacity for any cognition or sentience, on a moral par with human beings.

At bottom, the idea of kinship is based not on *experiential* capacities but rather on the shared struggle of different natural kinds to realize their potential for growth or development. On the kinship view that is part of a complementary approach to moral status, it is not necessary that a being be conscious of its struggle for life and growth. In this respect, I therefore disagree with Tom Regan, who believes that *"kinship theories . . .* grow out of the idea that beings resembling humans in the quite fundamental way of being conscious, and thus to this extent kin to us, have moral standing."[5] I agree with Regan that "the presence of inherent value in a natural object is independent of any awareness, interest, or appreciation of it by any conscious being."[6] One task in the endeavor to incorporate a sense of kinship into a complementary theory of the moral status of animals is defining inherent value and deciding whether the interests of certain beings with inherent value should be privileged over the interests of other beings with inherent value, as when Regan proposes in the lifeboat dilemma that the dog should always be sacrificed for the humans.[7] Only on a kinship view as Regan conceives of it—that is, only on a view that bases kinship on shared experiential capacities—is the solution to such a dilemma as straightforward as Regan suggests. The path to a solution becomes much more difficult to envision once we base kinship on the capacity for realizing a *telos* or end in life. This basis, however, is a double-edged sword: On the one hand, it enables us to cultivate a sense of kinship even with nonanimal living beings such as mountain ecosystems and giant sequoias; it allows us to retrieve an ancient sense of belonging to a larger cosmic whole referred to in the golden age myths. But on the other hand, this conception of kinship has implications that are problematic by the standards of contemporary sensibilities. For example, it can appear to put us in the position of giving preference to the interests of nonhuman living beings over those of "people living in extreme poverty" in the third world, who are frightened by "the romanticism of nature that [they] find in many American and European visitors."[8] What is needed, as Nussbaum recognizes, is an approach that acknowledges the uniqueness of human beings while not giving humanity an absolute priority over nonhuman natural beings.[9] On the complementary approach that I propose, one can resolve these difficulties by articulating the relative significance of experiential capacities and kinship in a theory of the moral relationship between human beings and animals.

Ferry's Challenge to Romantic Holism

When Luc Ferry wrote *The New Ecological Order* in 1992, he chose these words by Robert Musil as the book's epigraph: "Our times are characterized by extraordinary intellectual romanticism: we flee the present to take refuge in the past, any past, seeking the starry-eyed romance of a lost security. . . . And what I wish to show is precisely that this fearfulness is unfounded. To my mind, the European spirit is not decadent at present, but in transition; it is not in excess, but insufficiently mature." Musil's words echo Edmund Husserl's sentiment that romantic flights into irrationalism are in reality "the rationality of 'lazy reason', which evades the struggle to clarify the ultimate givens of experience [*letzten Vorgegebenheiten*] and the goals and directions which they alone can rationally and truthfully prescribe."[10] Ferry's epigraph likewise recalls Freud's appeal to "the claim of reason [*den Anspruch der Vernunft*]" in *The Future of an Illusion*.[11] Like Freud, Husserl, and Musil before him, Ferry appeals to the power of reason to address concrete human problems. Moreover, he gives a special place to specifically *human* problems as the proper object of rational inquiry and concern. He derides the entire environmental ethics movement as a set of efforts to replace "a humanistic vision of law [with] a cosmic one" that establishes the moral status of nature at the cost of human dignity. On Ferry's view, any approach to animals or the environment based on a cosmic kinship between humans and nonhuman beings proceeds on the assumption that anthropocentrism is "arrogant." In dismissing the achievements of liberalism, such approaches manifest dangerous affinities with neo-fascism.[12] Therefore we must be suspicious of any viewpoint that celebrates a premodern ethos—think, for example, of the golden age stories of Hesiod and Ovid—inasmuch as all such viewpoints seek to recapture an idealized sense of rootedness that overcomes the modern sense of homelessness. To this extent, such viewpoints are tantamount to fascism. In Ferry's words, any such approach is "a bit khaki in its green."[13] Even if only against their own intentions, and perhaps consonant with them, members of movements such as deep ecology express a hatred of humanity, by subordinating humanity to the cosmos.[14]

The basis of Ferry's critique of movements such as deep ecology, which proceed on the basis of a sense of kinship with the natural environment, is a Kantian affirmation of the uniquely human capacity for freedom. Unlike nonhuman animals and other natural beings, only humans possess the capacity for constant self-improvement; unlike any other beings, only we are capable of *perfecting* our nature.[15] At the same time, the price of this capacity for perfectibility is precisely the sense of belonging sought by romantic thinkers who assert the kinship of, and the subordination of the human will to, the cosmos as a whole. "What concrete form will [human] freedom take if not the destruction—the perpetual uprooting—it seems to invite? To be 'authentic', faithful to his essence (which is to have no essence), mustn't the human being *destroy* all content that would risk determining him? Is he not forced to affirm his freedom by dissolving any individual determination, by permanently rejecting all past tradition as well as any present incarnation?"[16] On Ferry's view, Kant's insight into the nature of human freedom is fundamentally at odds with any commitment or approach that would impose limits on human freedom by giving priority to any sort of nonhuman interest or concern. Like Kant, Ferry sees in human freedom a value and a dignity that must not be allowed to be compromised by any purportedly nonhuman interests—precisely because nonhuman beings may not properly be said to *have* interests. Human beings govern themselves, whereas animals are "governed by natural codes."[17] Ascribing inherent dignity to beings governed by such "codes" expresses a yearning for wholeness that is unattainable in principle and founded on a failure to appreciate the nature of human freedom. "The aporias of absolute freedom" demand not such flights of fancy but rather a "nonmetaphysical humanism" whose primary goal is to let the freedom of human individuals flourish.[18]

The central problem with holistic, cosmos-centered views such as deep ecology is that they privilege the "richness and diversity" of life generally over the specific interests of self-conscious, autonomous beings. Ferry sees a "radical opposition" between the ascription of autonomous rights to nature and "the legal humanism that dominates the modern liberal universe."[19] The liberal ideals of equality, reciprocity, and justice are irretrievably sacrificed if we cede to nature anything like inherent dignity or value. Here Ferry makes the connection between environmental holism and fascism clear: Any view that expresses "love of the native soil"—this rhetoric is found repeatedly in Nazi discourses—is inextricable from a "hatred of modernity."[20] Rather than seeing dislocation as liberating, environmental holists blame modern liberalism and the ascendancy of the individual for the loss of a sense of community with nature. "The love of nature . . . is accompanied . . . by a certain penchant for deploring everything in culture that results from . . . [the very] 'separation'" on which the Enlightenment ideals of individual moral and political autonomy are founded.[21] These ideals become replaced with the conservative romantic program for social reform advocated in the early twentieth century by Ludwig Klages, Oswald Spengler, Carl Schmitt, and Ernst Jünger.[22] These thinkers see modernity as a progressive decline (a *Verfallsgeschichte*) from a prior sense of wholeness that must be regained at the cost of the individual. Deep ecology in particular "continually hesitates between conservative romantic themes and 'progressive' anticapitalist ones. . . . Some of deep ecology's roots lie in Nazism."[23]

This assertion recalls Levinas's and Derrida's charge that Heidegger's views on animals are founded on fascist sensibilities. This is not surprising, given that Heidegger's political thought places him squarely within the conservative romantic tradition that is the object of Ferry's critique. But is Ferry's assertion a fair one? Is environmental holism necessarily a form of crypto-fascism? Ferry offers the following considerations in support of an affirmative answer to this question. The Nazis adopted a romantic sentimental view of nature and sought a "unity of nature and culture."[24] At the same time that they sought to persecute non-Aryans such as Jews and Gypsies, the Nazis enacted a series of environmental protection laws regulating hunting, cruelty to animals, and the conservation of nature. In particular, the Nazis enacted laws, orders, and decrees regulating animal slaughter and animal protection in 1933; hunting and animal protection in 1934; protection of nature in 1935; animal breeding, the protection of plants and animals in the wild, disposition of feral cats, and slaughter and the holding of fish and other cold-blooded animals in 1936; and animal transport in 1937. An expanded version of the 1933 animal protection law (*Tierschutzgesetz*) was promulgated in 1938. Subsequent laws and decrees regulated such matters as the inspection of meat and the shoeing of horses, and a decree prohibiting Jews from keeping pets was issued in 1942.[25] That the Nazis could express such profound concern for animals and the natural environment while inflicting unprecedented terror on large segments of humanity is a sign, Ferry seems to say, of an indissoluble connection between holistic environmental concern and the sacrifice of the liberal ideal of the individual.

Ferry's charge should not be dismissed blithely. As Sax observes, even though Nazism was ultimately an incoherent mixture of romantic holism, suspicion of modernity, critique of capitalism, and Aryan self-assertion, certain identifiable tenets lie at its core. One of these tenets is that nature is "a realm of absolute order, opposed to the anarchy brought on by civilization. In imposing inflexible authoritarian rule, the Nazis believed that they were restoring natural order to society. . . . By extending centralized control almost without limits, the Nazis thought they would become nature itself, harsh and implacable yet always orderly."[26] According to the Nazi logic, nature is harsh and unforgiving, and favors the victor over the vanquished. Like the Platonic formula according to which art imitates nature, the Nazis sought to make politics an art that imitates nature by elevating strength and solidarity at the expense of individuality and weakness. "By replacing the murky complexities of parliamentary democracy with a single structure, the Nazis sought to restore a putative primal simplicity in human relationships. This hierarchic structure, embracing not only people but all living things, defined their conception of the natural world. Every individual creature would have a rank and a place, and those that did not fit in could be destroyed."[27]

Ferry's concern is that all forms of environmental holism, whether their exponents realize it or not, are inextricably linked with nationalism and communalism—tendencies that Friedrich Hayek showed to be absolutely incompatible with individual autonomy.[28] "The affirmation of the rights of nature . . . implies the rejection of a certain type of democracy."[29] The tradition of legal humanism that Ferry appeals to is a Kantian-Rawlsian one according to which rational, self-conscious beings enjoy pride of place in social and legal considerations. On Ferry's view, it is not even clear that we can attribute interests to animals, regardless of whether they are sentient. "All valorization, including that of nature, is the deed of man and . . . consequently all normative ethic is in some sense humanist and anthropocentrist." Animals and nature "always remain *objects and not subjects of law*. In other words, the idea of creating a normative, antihumanist ethics is a contradiction in terms" because it is impossible to "project into the universe itself an 'intrinsic value.'"[30] By treating animals and nature as beings with intrinsic value, we impose a totalizing view on the world that silences individual appeals to reason and conscience, thereby effectively destroying the liberal humanist individual that Ferry sees as the crowning achievement of the Enlightenment.

Hence for Ferry "the sacralization of nature is *intrinsically* untenable," both because it falsely projects inherent value into nature and because it

subjects human individuals to an oppressive regime of romantic conservatism whose dangers are amply demonstrated by the example of National
Socialism. Nonetheless, Ferry is not insensitive to the ideal of environmental concern. He recognizes that there are legitimate reasons to seek
a balance between the rootlessness of the modern mind and our sense of
belonging to nature. In our endeavor to seek such a balance, "the moment of separation from inherited codes must ultimately prevail over
tradition."[31] These inherited codes include both the "natural codes" that
guide the actions of animals and the cultural practices that constitute a
national tradition. To give priority to the moment of separation is to
subordinate nature and specific cultural traditions alike to the prerogatives of detached, autonomous, human individuality.

Löwith's and Jonas's Challenges to Liberal Individualism

Approaches to the moral status of animals that give an absolute priority
to the prerogatives of human beings over nonhuman nature run the risk
of relegating animals to the status of mere instrumentality. Even though
the Stoics embrace a conception of cosmic wholeness, they effectively
reduce animals to this status through the doctrines of belonging
(οἰκείοσις) and providence (πρόνοια). The liberal conception of humanity
as detached from nature that guides Ferry is the contemporary correlate
of the Stoic exclusion of animals from the sphere of right. Thus the liberal
conception is open to a line of critique that has its origins in ancient
critiques of the Stoics. The significant achievements of modern deliberative democracy are not to be underestimated, nor are they to be swept
aside in the name of environmental integrity. And yet these achievements
pertain exclusively to human relations; concern for animals or the nonhuman environment is not an object of liberal political theory, as is made
clear by John Rawls.[32]

    Can anthropocentric and nonanthropocentric ethics be brought
into harmony with one another? Is there a middle position between the
extremes of unrestricted liberalism and unrestricted cosmic holism?
Could a middle position balance the claims to existence and well-being
made by or on behalf of human beings and nonhuman beings such
as animals? A balance or harmony between the liberal and holistic
approaches on the side of ethics corresponds to the harmony between
capacities and kinship approaches that I propose on the side of ethology.
The two sides of this project are linked by the endeavor to do justice

to animals without losing sight of those qualities that are distinctively human.

Hans Jonas and Karl Löwith provide clues to the establishment of a balance between liberalism and holism. Both were students of Heidegger, and both express a profound desire to recapture the sense of human belonging to nature expressed in the ancient world. Like Heidegger, Jonas and Löwith consider the dislocation at the core of modern liberalism to be the problem rather than the solution; where Ferry sees this dislocation as radically liberating, these thinkers see in it the sacrifice of authoritative standards or measures for human conduct. A primary focus of Löwith's critique is the ideal of inevitable progress in history in the Enlightenment philosophies of history. Hegel envisions history in eschatological terms, as a rational, linear progression toward a crowning point of fruition. Comte modifies Hegel's notion of progress so that "history is no longer the temporal unfolding of an absolute truth and the providential fulfillment of an eternal design but a secular history of civilization, the truth of which is 'relative' by being related to changing conditions and situations."[33] Henceforth history is understood as the unfolding of inevitable progress, even if it is not a progression toward a transmundane Christian end point. On Löwith's view, such thinking is the historical product of a detachment of human reflection from a prior sense of belonging to a cosmos whose basic structure assigns human beings a sense of limits and a sense of proper place. He seeks to retrieve this ancient sense of belonging by rehabilitating the Stoic view according to which human existence has its roots in the eternal cycles of nature. Löwith abandons the linear conception of time taken by the Enlightenment philosophers from Christian eschatology, and replaces it with the Stoic cyclical conception of time. In accordance with this Stoic orientation, Löwith favors the cultivation of tranquility (ἀπάθεια) and calm or equanimity (ἀταραξία) through the contemplation of the eternal order exhibited by nature.

In pursuing this line of thinking, Löwith at first appears to be open to the criticism so often lodged against Heidegger: that by subjugating the insights of human reason to a cosmic totality that is ultimately inscrutable, he deprives reason of its authority and thereby opens humanity to the extreme dangers of irrationalism and totalitarianism.[34] Löwith, however, is sensitive to the dangers of a total critique of reason, and he criticizes Heidegger for having "managed to give a generation of students new measures and to persuade them that 'logic' and 'reason' must dissolve in the whirl of a more primordial questioning."[35] Related to this criticism is Löwith's criticism of Heidegger's "remarkably precarious and undeveloped" appropriation of the ancient Greek sense of nature as *physis*.[36] By reducing nature to "a ubiquitous emergence into the Open and a retreat into what is closed off," Heidegger condemns history to "[losing] all definite and demonstrable meaning."[37] In place of Heidegger's irrationalism and his conception of *physis* as an irretrievable hiddenness, Löwith seeks to preserve the Stoic sense of a divine *logos* in nature that can be the object of human contemplation and the basis for a meaningful and articulable way of life.

In developing this ideal, Löwith follows Jakob Burckhardt in "counseling resignation concerning ultimate meaning" in history.[38] Meaning is to be found not in the human affairs of any particular time, but rather in the recognition that "what is 'interesting' in history is what is seemingly uninteresting, namely that which is constant and repeats itself in all change, because humans are as they always already were and always will be."[39] The study of history does not disclose any primordial truths, for it yields only "a sober insight into our real situation: struggle and suffering, short glories and long miseries, wars and intermittent periods of peace." Historical reflection makes us sensitive to "some kind of permanence in the very flux of history, namely its continuity," which can serve "as the common standard of all particular historical evaluations."[40] In becoming attuned to this permanence, we find ourselves simultaneously within and beyond history.

For Löwith, this simultaneity is the point of connection between specifically human concerns and the standpoint of the cosmos so valued by the Stoics. Writing in a post-Nietzschean world that has witnessed the putative death of God, Löwith does not seek a return to the Stoic ideal of human beings dwelling in special proximity to the gods in virtue of our rational capacities. Löwith follows Nietzsche in seeking to cultivate a sense of human belonging to *this* world instead of aspiring to some transcendent "higher" world. But unlike Heidegger, who envisions the return of a sense of belonging through the advent of a god who can replace the gods who have disappeared in the course of time, Löwith does not frame his ethical ideal in terms of gods at all.[41] In this respect, Löwith parts company with Heidegger and the ancient Stoics alike: He seeks a return to nature and its eternal cycles, but he does not privilege human beings over other natural beings on the basis of our putative proximity to the gods.

"When we achieve complete insight, the mountain again becomes simply a mountain and the river simply a river. In this final acknowledgment of being-thus-and-not-otherwise, the world and human beings show up primordially and once and for all."[42] The world as such is more primordial than the specifically human world. "This pre- and supra-human world of heaven and earth, which stands and maintains itself utterly on its own, infinitely eclipses the world that stands and falls with human beings."[43] It is this supra-human world within which we ultimately find ourselves and from which we must take our bearings in a reconceptualization of the tasks of ethics and dwelling.

Löwith's inscription of the human world within a larger, nonanthropocentric cosmos leads him to stop short of ascribing an absolute privilege to humans over nonrational beings. Löwith does not explore the precise relationship between human and nonhuman beings in his writings. Instead he makes the provocative suggestion that we cultivate a "cosmopolitical" perspective in which we counter the specter of hubris by imposing fundamental limits on the prerogatives of human reason and willing to alter nature.[44] The terms of Löwith's cosmo-political ideal remain to be developed, but one thing is clear: It differs from the cosmopolitanism of the Stoics and Kant in denying human beings a privileged place in the larger scheme of things. We are subject to the same inalterable laws of fate that govern other natural beings, and in this respect we share a basic kinship with all beings that suffer or struggle. Viewed from this standpoint, the fact that we are rational in ways that make us different from other beings begins to lose its moral relevance, even if it retains a clear relevance from the standpoint of the specifically human world.

Hans Jonas's reflections on the relationship between what Löwith calls "world" and "human world" shed light on the way in which liberalism and holism might be brought into harmony with one another, and his reflections further clarify the reason why such a coordination of viewpoints is needed at this point in history. The focal point for Jonas is the metaphysical dualism that underlies modern technological consciousness. Like Heidegger before him, Jonas recognizes that technology fundamentally degrades nature by representing it as an object of exploitation rather than as a cosmic whole of which we are a part. This reduction of nature is traceable principally to Bacon and particularly to Descartes, who eliminated Aristotelian teleology from nature and used mathematics to arrive at a characterization of nature as a nexus of sheer mechanistic instrumentalities. In doing this, Bacon and Descartes denude nature of inherent value and elevate human concerns above nature.[45] But this approach "by itself, that is, under its own management, has at the height of its triumph revealed its insufficiency in the lack of control over itself, thus the impotence of its power to save not only man from himself but also nature from man."[46] In the shift from the medieval to the modern, God is abandoned as the ultimate arbiter and measure for the proper exercise of the human will; in its place, human will itself becomes the absolute standard for the exercise of technological power in the modern age.

Along with this abandonment of divine measures for human action comes a fundamental shift in the very idea of theory. Aristotle understood theory as the highest human activity: the contemplation of the eternal, which has no practical application. Modern theory, on the other hand, has as its end practical application. Both Bacon and Descartes explicitly marshal theory in the service of the conquest of nature. Where ancient theory takes its bearings from "an objective transcendence," which implies "objects higher than man," modern theory "is about objects lower than man." Henceforth even the stars, which the ancients considered to be of a fundamentally higher order than earthly things, are now simply "common things."[47] By eliminating Aristotelian final causes from nature, modern theory renders all natural things value-free and hence subordinate in significance to human beings. Corresponding to this conception of nature as an objective, neutral given in dualism is a conception of human beings as fundamentally superior to nature and entitled to manipulate nature in any way they see fit.

The result of the shift to modern technological consciousness is that there are no inherent limits on the uses to which we put theory, nor on the uses to which we may put nature.

> What has neither will nor wisdom and is indifferent to itself solicits no respect. Awe before nature's mystery gives way to the disenchanted knowingness which grows with the success of the analysis of all things into their primitive conditions and factors. The powers that produce those things are powerless to impart a sanction to them: thus their knowledge imparts no regard for them. On the contrary, it removes whatever protection they may have enjoyed in a prescientific view. The implication this has for man's active commerce with the equalized manifold is obvious. If nature sanctions nothing, then it permits everything. What-

ever man does to it, he does not violate an immanent integrity, to which it and all its works have lost title. . . . There is only the extrinsic necessity of causal determination, no intrinsic validity of results.[48]

In the history of Western thought, dualism develops through antiquity and the Christian Middle Ages, in which nature exists for the sake of human beings, and comes to fruition in a modern conception of human self-reliance in which the universe is thought to have no ultimate purpose and may be used for whatever ends the human will posits. Nature is denuded of any connection to divinity and thereby is reduced to the status of mute instrument.

This development of our relationship to nature is at once liberating and seriously problematic. It deprives humanity of any authoritative measures or standards above the human will, and thereby reduces nature to a space of resources to be used to satisfy human needs and desires. The idea of respect for nature is incompatible with this dualist conception— it is a contradiction in terms, given the claims of liberal thinkers such as Kant and Rawls that nonrational beings cannot properly be conceived to be worthy of respect. Jonas recognizes the inability of the liberal model to address the problem of environmental concern at a fundamental level. To overcome this limitation of liberalism and the dualism on which it is founded, Jonas seeks a nondualistic conception of our place in nature that promises to restore a sense of dignity and authority to nature. Such a conception offers "the prospect of a new cosmic harmony."[49]

At the same time, Jonas is sensitive to the threat posed to humanity by the sacrifice of liberal ideals. As a Jew exiled from Nazi Germany who lost his mother at Auschwitz, Jonas devoted a great deal of his work in philosophy to the effort to reconcile the demands of political philosophy with the problem of reintegrating humanity into nature.[50] Like Löwith, Jonas sees a need to ground ethics in a philosophy of nature, rather than in the liberal (Kantian) conception of human autonomy. Between the Scylla of human self-assertion and the Charybdis of unbridled cosmic holism, Jonas seeks a middle course that would do justice to humanity and nature alike:

The disruption between man and total reality is at the bottom of nihilism. The illogicality of the rupture, that is, of a dualism without metaphysics, makes its fact no less real, nor its seeming alternative any more acceptable: the stare at isolated selfhood, to which it condemns man, may wish to exchange itself for a monistic naturalism that, along with the rupture, would abolish also the idea of man as man. Between that Scylla and this her twin Charybdis, the modern mind hovers. Whether a third road is open to it—one by which the dualistic rift can be avoided and yet enough of the dualistic insight saved to uphold the humanity of man—philosophy must find out.[51]

Jonas sees the ascendancy of human reason and willing in the modern age as the source of a sense of ultimate meaninglessness. By extinguishing any sense of a connection to eternal truths that disclose themselves to us through our experience of nature, modern dualism—the very dualism celebrated by Ferry—is inseparable from a state of moral groundlessness that can be overcome only through an attempt to ground ethics in ontology, that is, in a philosophy of nature. Such grounding is needed for the human world as well as for the relationship between the human world and the world as such.

Jonas's claim is extremely controversial. Not only does he attribute a fundamental primacy to nature over strictly human concerns, but he also stands open to the charge of totalitarianism. Ferry notes that the task that Jonas sets for humanity, "to again master the mastery of nature . . . seems impossible, or at least infeasible, according to Jonas, within the framework of a democratic society. We must have recourse to force . . . to State constraint, for example, which Jonas cannot help but admire and encourage in Asia and formerly in the Soviet Union."[52] Jonas advocates a "heuristics of fear" that places stress on the unpredictable nature of technological activity and calls for conservative restrictions on technology for the sake of future generations.[53] Jonas sees such a heuristics of fear as imperative "to preserve the integrity of [the human] essence, which implies that of his natural environment."[54] Ferry sees environmentalist programs such as Jonas's (and Aldo Leopold's) as driven by "blatantly nationalist and communalist" sensibilities.[55] On one level, such a claim seems exaggerated and polemical; Ferry seems to dismiss Jonas as a crypto-fascist, just as Levinas and Derrida dismiss Heidegger. But on another level, Ferry's concern is warranted. Richard Wolin has warned that the future envisioned by Jonas would be ruled by "paternalistic, antidemocratic" forces with close affinities to fascism.[56] Wolin bases this claim on Jonas's acknowledgment that "only an elite can assume, ethically and intellectually, the kind of responsibility for the future which we have postulated."[57]

Jonas recognizes that, at least from the standpoint of contemporary dualist consciousness, the task of environmental stewardship can be conceived only in terms of autocracy. But he expresses the hope that a new philosophy of nature would give rise to a new, "true consciousness" for which "empirically there is little ground for . . . faith," though "neither is there a veto against it."[58] Jonas calls on us to retrieve a sense of belonging to nature that has manifested itself episodically in the history of Western philosophy and would have the power to give us a sense of measure and propriety in adjudicating conflicts between human welfare and that of the natural environment. The task that Jonas sets for humanity is one for which detached liberal consciousness is not yet prepared, and which liberal consciousness naturally treats with fear and suspicion. In this regard, modern liberal consciousness employs its *own* "heuristics of fear," that is, it gives primacy to worst-case scenarios when it contemplates the subordination of liberal prerogatives to a philosophy of nature. And yet at the same time it criticizes thinkers such as Jonas for invoking a heuristics of fear in their endeavor to impose limits on liberalism and technological rationality.

At this point in the historical development of thinking about humanity and our relationship to the natural world, this problem remains unresolved. Notwithstanding our current inability to think through its resolution, the virtue of Jonas's call to inscribe individualism within a philosophy of nature is that it returns us to the ancient wisdom that human will is and ought not to be considered supreme in the world. It reminds us that beings can fare well or ill even if they possess no consciousness of doing so, and that we as rational beings have a responsibility toward beings that are nonrational (or nonconscious, or less rational or conscious than ourselves). Ferry and Wolin warn of the dangers of an unbridled cosmic holism that would autocratically force antidemocratic values on human individuals. Löwith invites us to envision the retrieval of a sense of belonging to the world rather than celebrating our uprootedness. And Jonas sketches the broad outlines of a program for the harmonization of the two sides of this seemingly irreducible conflict. At the core of his vision is the establishment of a philosophy of nature that would restore to human beings a sense of the dignity of nature, a sense that is conspicuously absent from the liberal model of individual autonomy.

At stake in the endeavor to harmonize the principles of liberal individualism with the imperatives of environmental crisis is the imposition of limits on an anthropocentrism that historically gave rise to liberal ideals in the first place. But this need not come at the sacrifice of liberal ideals themselves. Instead, the inscription of liberalism within a philosophy of nature would allow liberal ideals to prevail as principles governing human relations, while denying ultimate authority to such ideals in matters bearing upon human relations with nature. As Jonas recognizes, it is not clear how such an inscription is to be achieved. But my examination of some leading examples from the annals of cognitive ethology shows what is at stake *for animals* in the endeavor to make Jonas's dream a reality.

Cognitive Ethology and the Task of Rethinking the Moral Status of Animals

Studies in cognitive ethology tend to place such great emphasis on the study of capacities for intelligent thought and communication that it is easy to overlook the fact that ethology's greatest contribution to our understanding of animals may be to awaken a sense of our *kinship* with members of other species. Often the debates about animal capacities get stuck on questions such as whether apes can master the syntax of human language, rather than considering the possibility, noted by Sorabji, that the apparent inability of apes to master anything more than rudimentary human syntax is completely irrelevant to considerations of moral worth.[59] What is more important is that apes can participate in meaningful linguistic exchanges with human beings, and that even if the nature of the apes' orientation on language is not the same as the human orientation, it is nonetheless clear that we can have meaningful interrelationships with apes. Sue Savage-Rumbaugh acknowledges that

> certainly these creatures cannot plan ahead as we do, organize large societies, or produce complex tools, calendars, and religions. Yet for me, there is more to being human than such abstract intelligent actions. There is a kinship I recognize when I interact with young children that does not depend on these abstract skills. It is a kinship of awareness that others share some of my feelings and I theirs. I know, at least in part, how other people feel, and they know how I feel.
>
> With bonobos, I experience a similar two-way understanding. I know how they feel and they know how I feel. This is possible because of the expressions that emanate from their faces, the way they interpret the feelings of others, the depth of their commitment to one another, and

the understanding of one another that they share. Their sharing of emotional perspective is of a peculiarly human sort.[60]

Savage-Rumbaugh frames kinship in anthropomorphic terms because she studies the bonobo, a species whose cognitive abilities are much more like those of humans than are the abilities of most (perhaps all) other non-human animals. But the annals of cognitive ethology contain ample evidence of forms of kinship between humans and animals, even if it becomes more difficult and speculative to attribute knowledge to animals whose cognitive abilities are much less sophisticated than those of apes. Dogs, for example, do not exhibit any of the linguistic abilities of higher primates, and this may entail that dogs cannot form cognitions of the abstract form "X is the case." Yet the emotional lives of dogs, and their emotional bonds with human beings, are well known. Savage-Rumbaugh bases her acknowledgment of kinship with bonobos on the fact that complex intelligent actions are only part of the ways in which we relate to our environment. We also relate to the world through our emotions, and this opens up the prospect of conceptualizing kinship as a bond that relates us not only to higher primates but to a wide variety of other animals as well. At the extreme, it might even be possible to conceive of kinship not simply in terms of reciprocal relationships with animals that can relate to us emotionally, but also in terms of a sense of commonality with beings that have no awareness whatsoever. At this extreme, it might be possible to cultivate a sense of kinship with a being such as Hume's oyster, which appears to possess no sentience whatsoever, but does share with us the struggle for life and flourishing.

Cases of ape language and problem solving, while controversial, are the best starting point for exploring the idea of kinship because the cognitive abilities of apes are the most similar among animals to those of human beings. Much has been written about Koko, Kanzi, Nim, and other apes who have mastered certain aspects of language. Savage-Rumbaugh has been working with apes for decades and has shown that "they can learn words spontaneously and efficiently, and they can use them referentially for things not present . . . they can learn words from one another . . . they can learn to use words to coordinate their joint activities and to tell one another things not otherwise known . . . they can come to announce their intended actions . . . and they are spontaneous and not necessarily subject to imitation in their signs."[61] The chimpanzees Sherman and Austin, for example, learned to select their own lexigrams to name objects that they could then request or give to one another; they also developed "spontaneous indicative ability," that is, the ability to initiate the process of selecting and naming objects on their own, without prompting from the human researchers.[62] Sherman and Austin also exhibited the following sort of complex ability: "The chimpanzee came to the door, looked at the five objects in the tray, walked back into the room, used the keyboard to announce which object he was going to get, then returned and gave the teacher the named object."[63] On one occasion, Austin went to the keyboard to name objects outside the scope of training tasks. In the midst of play, he would sometimes stop, run to the keyboard, hit the key for "tickle" or "chase," and then go back to tickling or playing.[64] Savage-Rumbaugh also conducted experiments in which Sherman and Austin learned to select tools cooperatively to obtain food, which they then shared with another—an impressive feat, given that "primates, at least nonhuman primates, are not distinguished by their willingness to share food. Indeed, they are notorious for not sharing food even with offspring."[65]

Savage-Rumbaugh's work with the bonobo Kanzi shows that he responds to requests and solves problems posed in human language. "For example, when he heard 'Would you put some grapes in the swimming pool?' he got out of the swimming pool, walked over to where a number of foods were placed on a towel, and picked up the grapes and tossed them in the water. When he knew we were playing a game of surprises, and he heard a clue such as 'I hid the surprise by my foot' or 'Rose hid the surprise under her shirt', he immediately raced to the correct location and retrieved his surprise." Savage-Rumbaugh concluded that "Kanzi really did understand sentences as well as a two-and-a-half year old human child."[66] Savage-Rumbaugh acknowledges the need for scepticism regarding such claims as a scientist's responsibility, and she likewise acknowledges the resulting dilemma: Because we cannot examine the inner mental states of the experimental subjects directly, we cannot say definitively that apes "understand" linguistically. Instead we must proceed on the basis of analogy to human experience. Moreover, we must approach questions of animal mentation as "explanatory" rather than as "evidential" ones.[67] Savage-Rumbaugh borrows this strategy from Markl by way of Cheney and Seyfarth, who approach cognition as "the ability to relate different unconnected pieces of information in new ways and to apply the results in an adaptive manner. This definition is useful to those who study animals because it enables them to examine cognition in terms of what individuals *do* without specifying or being limited to any particular mental mechanisms that might underlie behavior."[68] This "operational strategy" shifts *"the onus of proof from the ape language researcher*—who affirms the metalinguistic claim [that communicative utterances are semantically significant to the apes]—*to the skeptic, who denies that that affirmation is justified."*[69]

This approach has an important advantage over the "evidential" approach. By focusing on what animals *accomplish* rather than on the endeavor to prove anything about their inner states, it helps to overcome the threat to ethology posed by Nagel's challenge that we cannot know what it is like to be another animal because the nature of each animal's perceptual encounter with the world is ultimately unique. This in turn enables us to think less about how much the cognitive capacities of certain animals approximate or approach those of human beings, and more about the ways in which those animals are engaged in life projects that make them our kin. We will never know exactly how Sherman and Austin see the world and experience the relationship between their computer keyboard and the problems that they endeavor to solve together. Nonetheless we get a very good sense from the work of Savage-Rumbaugh and others that life is significant for apes such as Sherman, Austin, and Kanzi, and that they are able to interact in productive, innovative ways with human beings that testify to this significance.

Savage-Rumbaugh's work also shows that higher primates such as Sherman and Austin are able to communicate with each other symbolically in ways that enable them to solve problems collaboratively. The capacity for intraspecies communication is not limited to bonobos. Such communication is an important part of the struggle for survival in vervet monkeys, rhesus macaques, and a number of nonprimate species as well. In the late 1960s, Struhsaker established that vervets emit at least three distinct types of alarm call, depending on whether the approaching threat is posed by a flying predator (typically a martial eagle), a carnivorous mammal (such as a leopard), or a low-lying ground predator (a python).[70] The responses of the vervets who have been warned likewise fall into three distinct categories. When they hear the eagle alarm call, they move into thick vegetation, which protects them from eagles but would make them vulnerable to ground predators. When they hear the leopard alarm call, vervets climb a tree and move out to the outermost branches, which a leopard cannot reach but an eagle could. And when vervets hear a snake alarm call, they stand on their hind legs, look around at the ground, and prepare to run away when they spot the python. Each of the alarm calls is distinct, and each of the responses is tailored to the specific type of predator that has been announced. Subsequent research has also shown that vervets emit other sorts of distinct utterance (grunts) in the course of ordinary social interactions, though the specific meaning of each type of grunt has not been established.[71] Cheney and Seyfarth conclude that monkeys "use calls—alarm signals and close-range vocalizations—in a manner that effectively represents, or denotes, objects and events in their environment. The use of these calls seems to be under relatively voluntary control, since call production can be conditioned in the laboratory and animals in the wild routinely give specific vocalizations only in particular circumstances. Primates make subtle acoustic discriminations when distinguishing between calls, and one well-studied case provides evidence of left hemispheric specialization in vocal perception."[72] Cheney and Seyfarth note that the linguistic capabilities of vervet monkeys are similar to those exhibited by young children at specific stages of linguistic development.[73]

Rhesus macaques also emit distinct meaningful utterances. Gouzoules, Gouzoules, and Marler studied screams emitted by young males in the context of fighting or exchanging threats with other members of their group.[74] These males emit five distinct types of agonistic scream, which differ on the basis of the social status of the opponent. Gouzoules, Gouzoules, and Marler have also determined that macaque mothers respond differently to the screams of their own sons than to those of other members of the group.[75] These screams, and the responses of the mothers, are part of a complex network of needs, emotions, and social interactions—in short, they reflect an engagement with the struggle for existence and flourishing that makes monkeys kin to human beings, regardless of whether we believe that monkeys are capable of self-consciousness, reflective thought, and other capacities traditionally thought to be unique to human beings.

The significance of kinship as a complement to capacities in our thinking about the moral status of animals becomes clearer when we consider that animal species other than primates exhibit linguistic abilities. Cockerels emit distinct alarm calls to indicate aerial versus ground predators; they also give food calls that vary with the nature of the food and the presence and nature of an audience of other cockerels.[76] African gray parrots, long known for their ability to learn and utter words and phrases, are able to learn to ask for particular foods by name. Pepperberg has done extensive work with an African gray named Alex, who can correctly answer questions about the color, shape, and material of objects; he also answers questions regarding the sameness or difference of objects with a high degree of accuracy. Alex has "learned the functional use of a vocabulary of over 80 words, and his ability is comparable to that shown by the great apes—an amazing demonstration of unsuspected cognitive ability in a bird! Alex's use of 'want' followed by the object or activity desired demonstrates a rudimentary syntax."[77] Pepperberg's work with Alex is controversial, not least because this research has been confined to one specific parrot; therefore caution is needed when evaluating Griffin's claim that there is a "strong indication that Alex thinks about colors, shapes, sameness and so forth. . . . In short, he gives every evidence of meaning what he says."[78] But in accordance with the operational or explanatory approach, we need not attribute such full-fledged anthropomorphic capacities to Alex to come to the conclusion that his interaction with his environment is rich, complex, and much more than merely mechanical or "instinctual."

As we proceed along the human-animal continuum away from animals such as apes and monkeys, which are very similar to human beings, and toward animals such as cockerels and parrots, which are comparatively unlike human beings, the importance of the explanatory or operational approach becomes increasingly clear. Dogs, for example, exhibit behavior that strongly suggests rich emotional lives and complex ways of negotiating their environments. Young dogs are initiated into the practices of defense and hunting through play behavior. Bekoff has shown this behavior to be an intricate set of practices with subtle nuances of which dogs must become aware not only if they are to become adept hunters and defenders, but also in order to maintain successfully their place in the structured hierarchy of relations within their group.[79] In particular, dogs must learn to appreciate the fine but crucial line between aggressive play and actual fighting. Like human beings, dogs must negotiate this line by making subtle discriminations that are extremely difficult to account for through appeals to instinct; the ability to make such discriminations improves with age and experience, whereas instinctual responses do not in general improve with experience. Research in recent decades has shown play behavior in a wide variety of animals, such as birds, rats, and kangaroos. This research suggests that play behavior gives animals pleasure, promotes fitness, and teaches animals "codes of social conduct that influence how they interact with other animals."[80]

That dogs have rich subjective lives explicable in terms of struggle and flourishing is further attested to by studies conducted on their emotional makeup. In the most famous of these studies, Seligman and his colleagues induced "learned helplessness" in dogs (and rats) to show the connection between a sense of helplessness and feelings of depression in both humans and animals. Dogs are confined in hammocks and receive shocks with no possibility of escape. Then they are placed in a shuttle box, a device with a barrier down the middle that the dogs are capable of jumping over. When they receive shocks in the shuttle box, the dogs can escape the shock by jumping over the barrier; they "can also prevent or *avoid* shock altogether if the jump occurs before the shock begins. We intended to teach the dogs to become expert shock avoiders," but what the researchers discovered "was bizarre": Dogs that had not been conditioned to shock in the hammock learned to jump the barrier and avoid shock. But dogs that had previously been confined in the hammock and had learned that they could do nothing to avoid shock now made no effort to avoid shock in the shuttle box, even though they were no longer confined in a hammock.[81] Seligman focuses on the trauma induced by the recognition that escape is futile. In the case of animals as well as human beings, the experience of trauma is based in part on a "cognitive representation of the contingency (learning, expectation, perception, belief)" in question.[82] In the case of the learned helplessness experiments, the representation is "the expectation that responding and relief are independent."[83] Helplessness is traumatic because it frustrates the "drive for competence," which is a central goal for any creature capable of the sorts of cognitive representation that Seligman makes central to his theory.[84] Dogs seek competence in their life activities and projects, and they exhibit frustration and depression when they fail to achieve competence—not unlike human beings. The lives of dogs are structured in terms of motivations to achieve goals such as competence, and their emotional well-being is significantly impaired when their sense of competence is undermined by the experience of helplessness. At the extreme, feelings of depression turn to a sense of "hopelessness," even in rats.[85]

One of the most significant implications of Seligman's work is that many if not all animals with cognitive lives also have emotional lives. Clark has proposed that "the attribution of emotion to another [be it animal or human] does involve that other in a definite moral universe."[86] Thus the recognition that dogs, rats, and a variety of other animals have complex emotional lives lends support to the idea that we must look beyond the terms of liberal political discourse (Löwith's "human world") if we are to accommodate the moral status of animals in the larger framework of a philosophy of nature (Löwith's "world" as such). As Clark notes, the key difference between humans and animals as regards emotions is that we can "tame" our passions "through speech and reasoned discourse," whereas few if any nonhuman animals can do so.[87] But this difference, while it signifies a lesser degree of agency in animals than in humans and hence a lesser degree of moral responsibility for their actions, has no clear implications for our moral obligations toward animals. We still populate a "moral universe" along with animals, hence "we need a cosmology" that can accommodate and motivate a sense of responsibility toward animals.[88]

The further along the human-animal continuum we proceed, the more significant the implications of this proposition. A reflection on the complex abilities of honeybees is a case in point, for, among all animals, we are least inclined to think of invertebrates as possessing consciousness and thought. But much has been learned about the sophistication of bee communication. Leaders in this area of research state that "the dance-communication of honey bees . . . appears to have no counterpart in the insect world and is exceeded in complexity and information-carrying capacity only by human speech"; it is "the most remarkable nonhuman communication system known."[89] On Griffin's view, the communicative capacities of bees by means of the "bee dance" are so sophisticated that "we may infer that . . . worker bees think about food sources [and potential locations for the establishment of new hives], according to the needs they have perceived at the time." Honeybees "communicate about what appear to be simple beliefs," which presupposes the capacity for "explicitly entertained mental representations."[90] On the other hand, Gould and Gould, two of the leading apiary ethologists, raise the distinct possibility that the dance language of bees "requires no conscious grasp of the problem," inasmuch as "some of the most impressively complex examples of behavior we see are known to be wholly innate."[91] And even if bees demonstrate the ability to learn from experience and modify their behavior accordingly, an information-processing approach to intelligence need not attribute any conscious awareness to bees at all.[92]

The controversy over the mental lives of bees concerns the "dance language" that honeybees employ to communicate information to other workers about direction, distance, and the type of desired object found. That object can be pollen, nectar, water, or the location for the establishment of a new colony. A central issue in apian ethology is whether the ability of bees to convey complex information about objects remote in space and time (for some time has elapsed since the dancing bee located the desired object, and the bee is now at some distance from the object) is to be construed as a sign of inner mental states such as belief or of programmed information-processing more along the lines of a computer than a human being. Thomas Nagel's challenge to cognitive ethology, that we cannot answer such questions because the perceptual encounter that a bee has with the world is so fundamentally different than our own, need not be considered crippling in this connection. Nagel acknowledges that many animals whose perceptual encounters with the world are very much unlike our own nonetheless have subjective experiences of the world, that is, "there is something it is like to *be*," say, a bat or a bee.[93] Nagel's argument poses a challenge to the method of analogy to human experience, on which ethologists rely in interpreting animal behavior.[94] But as Griffin notes, Nagel's is not an insuperable challenge: "While [Nagel] may be quite correct that we cannot hope for perfect, total descriptions, we can make substantial progress" in understanding animal behavior through interpretation by analogy.[95]

In particular, the method of "heterophenomenology" provides some insight into animal behavior, including the behavior of bees. This method interprets behavior by way of analogy, on the basis of facts known about the specific physiological constitution of the animal in question. "One describes how the world would appear to the organism if it had sensory experiences (third-person perspective), or how it would appear to me if I had certain features in common with it (first-person perspective), to explain or predict some aspect of the organism's sensory systems or of its recognition of objects in the environment."[96] In the case of hearing calls, for example, "the heterophenomenologist wants to know how the call sounds to another subject. . . . [This question] is answered with the aid of calculations involving head size, transduction properties of the middle ear bones [in the case of a hawk or an owl], and any other factors that might be considered relevant."[97]

Heterophenomenology has proved useful in gaining insight into the nature of bee color vision. Bee vision is composed of "facets," a large number of small lenses that create a composite image for each eye.

> Worker bees have about 4500 facets, or *ommatidia*, in each eye; queens (who have little use for vision) about 3500; and drones (who must spot the queen at a considerable distance if they are to win the ensuing race to be the first to mate with her) about 7500. Each facet is an independent

eye aimed at a unique part of the visual world, but no image is formed in an ommatidium; instead, the picture is pieced together from the thousands of individual ommatidia. As a result, the world for a bee must have a very grainy appearance, rather like a needlepoint canvas. For a rough comparison, the bee's brain receives about one percent as many connections as our eyes provide.[98]

Early in the twentieth century, von Frisch established that bees possess color vision; we now know that the physiology of the bee's eye permits perception of green, blue, and ultraviolet, but not red. Based on this knowledge, von Frisch and his student Daumer were able to establish, for example, that ultraviolet vision makes bees see as purplish ("bee purple") what human beings see as yellow, and they were able to establish the nature and limits of bee color vision in circumstances that vary with the percentage of ultraviolet energy present in the visual field.[99] This information, found in the endeavor to answer the heterophenomenological question "how do flowers look to a bee?" has proved to be very useful in the investigation "not only of honey bee vision, but also of the co-evolution of plants and their pollinators."[100]

Just as heterophenomenology can help us understand bee vision, it may help us gain some insight into the ways that bees experience the bee dance. This endeavor has two components—the way that the dancing bee seeks to convey information to the bees in the hive, and the way that the other bees grasp and act on the basis of the information. Worker bees must be able to find sources of pollen and water, as well as possible locations for the establishment of new colonies. They must also be able to communicate to other workers the locations of these desired objects. Thus one question is how a worker bee that has found a desired object finds its way back to the hive, and how it is able to relocate the desired object. Research suggests that bees use a "cognitive map," which is "a record in the central nervous system of macroscopic geometric relations among surfaces in the environment used to plan movements through the environment."[101] Bees "have a metric large-scale map, a representation of the approximate location of a food source in terms of the angle one must fly relative to large-scale features of the terrain around the nest and the distance one must cover."[102] Bees sometimes use cognitive maps to revise their flight direction; for example, when the researchers have moved the location of the hive at night the bees are still able to find the previous day's desired object by orienting their flight to the line of trees rather than to the previous day's compass direction.[103] The question left by these experiments is whether the bees have a subjective, conscious experience of any of these factors, or whether their behavior is essentially programmed.

The same question is central the controversy over the bee dance. Honeybees that have found desired objects return to the hive and perform one of two types of dance, a "round dance" that conveys information about nearby desired objects and a "waggle dance" about more distant objects.[104] In each case, the goal of the dancing bee is to recruit other workers in the foraging effort, and to provide information that enables the others to locate the desired object. The dance language has been shown to be extremely effective in communicating all the needed information, so much so that Gould and Towne consider the dance language of the honeybee to be the most sophisticated form of language known other than human language. As to the question whether the foraging and communicative abilities of honeybees serve as a basis for concluding that bees possess inner awareness that has at least some affinities with human consciousness, views in the ethological community are mixed. Griffin argues that "dancing is not something the bees do mechanically and automatically, but only as part of the larger nexus of communication." The fact that "the bees communicate about something displaced in both time and space from the immediate situation where the communication takes place" leads Griffin to urge the conclusion that bees possess some kind of consciousness, including the capacity "to communicate about what appear to be simple beliefs."[105] Further, Griffin argues that if creatures such as bees possess perceptual consciousness, which means that they have "memories, anticipations, or thinking about nonexistent objects or events as well as immediate sensory input," then "denying them some level of self-awareness would seem to be an arbitrary and unjustified restriction."[106] In other words, to the extent that bees can identify and communicate about objects that are remote in time and space, they must possess not only the ability to entertain beliefs but also some kind of self-awareness.

At the other extreme in this debate, critics argue that all the behaviors observed in bees can be explained as instinctual or programmed, and no appeal to subjective awareness is needed in accounting for the behavior of animals such as bees. Gould and Gould are cautious on the question of inner awareness in bees, but they lean toward the information-processing view of animal mentation, a view that renders the notion of subjective awareness superfluous. They infer from the present state of research that

> either bees are not very good at forming concepts, or we are incompetent at teaching them; from long experience, we take the latter alternative very seriously. At present, then, we regard the question of whether bees are capable of concept formation as unanswered. Even if the answer is yes, the question still remains whether concept formation involves any intelligence. After all, if pigeons are so adept, it cannot require much mental sophistication. Perhaps concept formation is an innate and automatic process, requiring no comprehension on the part of the animal.[107]

Nor is it clear to Gould and Gould "that the 'planning' that animals engage in with the use of their mental maps requires any personal intelligence or comprehension."[108]

One problem with such an account is that it loses sight of the sense that there is something it is like to *be* a honeybee, even if we must be cautious in attributing cognitive abilities such as self-awareness to such animals. Bees may not possess the "personal intelligence" of a human being, which includes abstraction (Aristotle's "calculative imagination") and a clear sense of oneself as a self among other selves, but this does not mean eo ipso that bees have no subjective awareness; it simply means that the resources of heterophenomenology would need to be marshaled to construct a conception of apian subjectivity that is not overly anthropomorphic. What it is like to be a bee is undoubtedly vastly different than what it is like to be a human being. But it is by no means clear that information-processing models and the like can do justice to the sophistication of the bee's encounter with its environment. Even if such models can provide operational accounts of apian problem solving and communication, it is worth questioning whether they grasp the whole truth about the lives of bees. For they treat bees and other animals in exactly the same way that Descartes did: as pure organic mechanism.

More importantly, it is not clear that the question of the moral status of animals such as bees ultimately depends on whether they possess self-consciousness, have beliefs, and so forth. Just as Descartes was aware that there is no way to prove definitively whether or not animals possess immortal souls, there is no way to prove whether or not they have subjective experiences. But the fact remains that bees are purposive creatures engaged in the struggle for survival and prosperity. They can fare well or ill, regardless of whether they are "subjectively aware" of their fortunes, and regardless of how much their awareness (if they have any) resembles our own. In this respect, invertebrates such as bees are *like* many other creatures, from dogs and cats to apes and monkeys to human beings. It is here that the capacities and kinship views meet: Capacities are not confined to capacities for subjective awareness (cognition, self-consciousness, sentience) but include capacities for growth and flourishing. Beings with either of these sorts of capacities have a fundamental kinship with human beings. On the basis of this complementary conception of capacities and kinship, the doctrine of belonging (*oikeiosis*) could be reconceived so as to constitute a sphere of kinship among *all* beings that struggle for life and well-being, not simply among all beings that are rational and linguistic in the specifically human sense.

A particularly promising approach to this task has been proposed by Paul W. Taylor. Taylor proceeds from a biocentric outlook that recognizes that human beings are part of a shared community of life with other living beings; that living beings are part of a web of interdependence; that "all organisms are teleological centers of life in the sense that each is a unique individual pursuing its own good in its own way; and that "humans are not inherently superior to other living things."[109] His ideal is "a world order on our planet where human civilization is brought into harmony with nature."[110] The realization of this ideal requires "an *inner* change in our moral beliefs and commitments."[111] Taylor's biocentrism directly counters the anthropocentrism of the leading traditional approaches by making the principle of respect for persons subject to the principle of respect for nature. The idea of human superiority is "an irrational and arbitrary bias" whose abandonment gives rise to the possibility of cultivating virtues such as compassion and impartiality as part of an environmental ethic.[112] Taylor develops a complex approach to the problem of conflicts between human beings and nature. His view requires us not only to acknowledge but also *to make restitution* to nature for the wrongs that we commit against it.[113]

Taylor's biocentric view has the potential to move discussions of the moral status of animals beyond the limitations of anthropocentric approaches by enabling us to inscribe those approaches within a cosmic holism without sacrificing the achievements of liberal political theory.[114] The "moral universe" of which Clark speaks would ultimately take precedence over the sphere of liberal political relations among human beings. The biocentric outlook proposed by Taylor would impose limits on the exercise of individual human freedom as regards the natural environment, in the interest of respecting and protecting nonhuman beings and establishing a sense of harmony with nature.[115] At the same time, liberal ideals would be maintained in the interest of regulating relations between human beings. Such an integration of liberal individualism into cosmic holism is difficult to envision today because the needed cosmological framework remains undeveloped. It is in this connection that a reflection on the history of Western thinking about animals will prove to be decisive. That history not only set the terms for the subjugation of animals, but it also contains clues to the establishment of a cosmology that would assert the essential dignity of animals without losing sight of what is uniquely human.

NOTES

Introduction

1. G. S. Kirk and J. E. Raven, *The Presocratic Philosophers: A Critical History with a Selection of Texts* (Cambridge: Cambridge University Press, 1979), frag. 15, p. 169.

2. Immanuel Kant, *Critique of Judgment*, trans. Werner S. Pluhar (Indianapolis: Hackett, 1987), sec. 83, p. 318 (Ak. 431).

Chapter 1: Contemporary Debates on the Status of Animals

1. Martha C. Nussbaum, "Animal Rights: The Need for a Theoretical Basis" (review discussion of Steven M. Wise, *Rattling the Cage: Toward Legal Rights for Animals*, Cambridge, Mass.: Perseus Books, 2000), *Harvard Law Review* 114 (2001): 1548.

2. Richard Sorabji, *Animal Minds and Human Morals: The Origins of the Western Debate* (Ithaca: Cornell University Press, 1993), 217.

3. Ibid., 219.

4. Ibid., 218.

5. David Hume, "Of Suicide," in *Essays Moral, Political, and Literary*, 2 vols., new edition, ed. T. H. Green and T. H. Grose (London: Longmans, Green, and Co., 1882), vol. 2, p. 410.

6. Peter Singer, *Practical Ethics*, 2d ed. (Cambridge: Cambridge University Press, 1993), 12, 14.

7. Peter Singer, *Animal Liberation*, 2d ed. (London: Jonathan Cape, 1990), 171.

8. Singer, *Practical Ethics*, 113–15. Cases of deceptive behavior in chimpanzees are examined by Franz de Waal in *Chimpanzee Politics* (London: Jonathan Cape, 1982). A catalogue of deceptive behavior in different species of animals is provided by Donald R. Griffin in *Animal Minds* (Chicago: University of Chicago Press, 1994), ch. 10. I show in chapter 3 below that in his zoological writings, Aristotle exhibits a clear awareness of deceptive behaviors in various species.

9. Singer, *Practical Ethics*, 277.

10. Peter Singer, "Utilitarianism and Vegetarianism," *Philosophy and Public Affairs* 9 (1980): 328.

11. Ibid., 329: "So utilitarians can do much to revise moral theory in favor of animals, merely by defending the claim that no being should have its interests disregarded or discounted merely because it is not human."

12. Ibid., 327.

13. Cora Diamond, "Eating Meat and Eating People," *Philosophy* 53 (1978): 472.

14. Singer, "Utilitarianism and Vegetarianism," 327–28.

15. John Stuart Mill, *Utilitarianism*, in *On Liberty and Other Essays*, ed. John Gray (Oxford: Oxford University Press, 1998), 138.

16. Tom Regan, *The Case for Animal Rights* (Berkeley: University of California Press, 1983), 205–6.

17. Stuart Hampshire, "Morality and Pessimism," in *Public and Private Morality*, ed. S. Hampshire et al. (Cambridge: Cambridge University Press, 1978), 2.

18. Regan, *The Case for Animal Rights*, 81.

19. Ibid., 78. When Regan speaks of "animals" in this text, he explicitly says that he is referring only to healthy mammals one year or older.

20. Ibid., 84–85, 75.

21. Ibid., 279 (where Regan refers to the arbitrariness of granting respectful treatment to moral agents but not to moral patients such as animals); see also p. 260. On the ability of animals such as dogs to engage in acts of abstraction, see p. 74.

22. Ibid., 294–95.

23. Ibid., 243.

24. Ibid., 236, 245–46.

25. See Tom Regan, "The Nature and Possibility of an Environmental Ethic," *Environmental Ethics* 3 (1981): 19–34.

26. Regan, *The Case for Animal Rights*, 285–86.

27. Ibid., 324.

28. Ibid., 351. For the same reason, "in lifeboat cases . . . the obligation to be vegetarian can be justifiably overridden."

29. Jamieson, "Rights, Justice, and Duties to Provide Assistance: A Critique of Regan's Theory of Rights," *Ethics* 100 (1990): 359. See also Gary L. Francione, *Introduction to Animal Rights: Your Child or the Dog?* (Philadelphia: Temple University Press, 2000).

30. Theodore Roethke, "The Lizard,"in *The Collected Poems of Theodore Roethke* (Garden City, N.Y.: Doubleday, 1966), 226.

31. David DeGrazia, *Taking Animals Seriously: Mental Life and Moral Status* (Cambridge: Cambridge University Press, 1996), 252.

32. For a complete discussion of this argument, see Daniel A. Dombrowski, *Babies and Beasts: The Argument from Marginal Cases* (Urbana: University of Illinois Press, 1997).

33. Rosalind Hursthouse, *On Virtue Ethics* (Oxford: Oxford University Press, 1999), 230.

34. See Aristotle, *Nicomachean Ethics* 2.4 at 1105a30–1105b1, in *The Complete Works of Aristotle*, 2 vols., ed. Jonathan Barnes (Princeton: Bollingen/Princeton University Press, 1995), 2:1746.

35. Hursthouse, *On Virtue Ethics*, 9.

36. Ibid., 13.

37. Ibid., 227.

38. See Plato, *Republic* 2 at 372a–c.

39. Hursthouse, *On Virtue Ethics*, 229.

40. *Nicomachean Ethics* 2.7 at 1107b4, in *The Complete Works*, 2:1748.

41. *Nicomachean Ethics* 3.10 at 1117b32–1118a32; 2.7 at 1107b7–8.

42. Hursthouse, *On Virtue Ethics*, 226.

43. DeGrazia, *Taking Animals Seriously*, 43.

44. Nussbaum, "Animal Rights," 1535–36.

45. Ibid., 1538.

46. S. F. Sapontzis, *Morals, Reason, and Animals* (Philadelphia: Temple University Press, 1987), 43.

47. Ibid., 44.

48. Ibid., 46; cf. pp. 27–28.

49. Martha C. Nussbaum, *Upheavals of Thought: The Intelligence of Emotions* (Cambridge: Cambridge University Press, 2001), 91, 128. Cf. pp. 136–37: "Desire contains considerable intentionality and selectivity, even when we are talking about nonhuman animals. . . . We may deliberate not only about how to get to ends that are already fixed, but also about the ends themselves. . . . This sort of deliberation takes place in animals as well."

50. Griffin, *Animal Minds*, 3.

51. Ibid., 114–15, 155, 169.

52. Ibid., 122, 140.

53. DeGrazia, *Taking Animals Seriously*, 132, 138, 148–49, 155.

54. Thomas Nagel, "What is it like to be a bat?" in *Mortal Questions* (Cambridge: Cambridge University Press, 1979), 165–80 (originally published in *Philosophical Review* 83, no. 4 [October 1974]: 435–50).

55. Colin Allen and Marc D. Hauser, "Concept Attribution in Nonhuman Animals: Theoretical and Methodological Problems in Ascribing Complex Mental Processes," *Philosophy of Science* 58 (1991): 227.

56. Colin Allen, "Mental Content and Evolutionary Explanation," *Biology and Philosophy* 7 (1992): 8 (referring to experiments conducted by Seyfarth, Cheney, and Marler).

57. Allen and Hauser, "Concept Attribution in Nonhuman Animals," 234–37.

58. For useful summaries of these three examples, see Griffin, *Animal Minds*, 217–24 (ape language), 198–210 (deception in fireflies, birds, snakes, chimpanzees, and other animals), 128–36 (pigeon discrimination tasks).

59. De Waal, *Chimpanzee Politics*.

60. See R. J. Herrnstein, D. H. Loveland, and C. Cable, "Natural Concepts in Pigeons," *Journal of Experimental Psychology: Animal Behavior Processes* 2 (1976): 285–302; R. J. Herrnstein, "Objects, Categories, and Discriminative Stimuli," in *Animal Cognition: Proceedings of the Harry Frank Guggenheim Conference, June 2–4, 1982*, ed. H. L. Roitblat, T. G. Bever, and H. S. Terrace (Hillsdale, N.J.: Lawrence Erlbaum Associates, 1984), 233–61.

61. Allen and Hauser, "Concept Attribution in Nonhuman Animals," 225–26.

62. John Searle, "Animal Minds," unpublished manuscript, cited in DeGrazia, *Taking Animals Seriously*, 132, 134. See also John Searle, "Intentionality and Its Place in Nature," *Synthese* 61 (1984): 14—15.

63. See for example, DeGrazia, *Taking Animals Seriously*, 148, where DeGrazia argues that the explanatory power of the intentional stance is evidence that it is true; cf. p. 150n, where DeGrazia advocates an information-processing approach to concepts by maintaining that "consciousness plays no crucial role in classifying types of representation and, therefore, concepts." See also Nussbaum, *Upheavals of Thought*, 91, where Nussbaum rejects the suggestion "that animals are incapable of intentionality, selective attention, and appraisal"; see also pp. 125—26, where Nussbaum claims that all emotion, in animals as well as in humans, "will always involve some sort of combination or predication," and p. 136, where Nussbaum states that "emotions are judgments" with "evaluative content" and that "desire contains considerable intentionality."

64. Norman Malcolm, "Thoughtless Brutes," *Proceedings and Addresses of the American Philosophical Association* 46 (1972—73): 13.

65. Donald Davidson, "Rational Animals," in *Actions and Events: Perspectives on the Philosophy of Donald Davidson*, ed. Ernest LePore and Brian McLaughlin (Oxford: Basil Blackwell, 1985), 480 (originally published in *Dialectica* 36 [1982]: 318—327).

66. Ludwig Wittgenstein, *Philosophical Investigations*, 3d ed., trans. G. E. M. Anscombe (New York: Macmillan, 1968), 174.

67. Davidson, "Rational Animals," 480.

68. Steven Stich, *From Folk Psychology to Cognitive Science: The Case against Belief* (Cambridge, Mass.: M.I.T. Press, 1983), 104—5.

69. See Steven P. Stich, "Do Animals Have Beliefs?" *Australasian Journal of Philosophy* 57 (1979): 17—18.

70. Daniel C. Dennett, *Content and Consciousness* (London: Routledge and Kegan Paul, 1969), 85. See also R. G. Frey, *Interests and Rights: The Case against Animals* (Oxford: Clarendon, 1980), 55—112.

71. Colin Allen, "Mental Content," *British Journal for the Philosophy of Science* 43 (1992): 544—45. Cf. p. 552: The prospect of specifying the content of animal concepts is one of Allen's hopes for "a more sophisticated cognitive science."

72. Regan, *The Case for Animal Rights*, 54.

73. In the case of the Stoics, this claim as regards desire needs some qualification. The Stoics attribute "impulse" (ὁρμή) to animals, but they distinguish this capacity from desire in human beings, which involves an evaluative dimension.

74. See James L. Gould and Carol Grant Gould, *The Honey Bee* (New York: Scientific American Books, 1988). I discuss the case of bees in detail in chapter 10 below.

75. Griffin, *Animal Minds*, 18, 138—39, 131.

76. Ibid., 232.

77. Davidson, "Rational Animals," 473.

78. Konrad Lorenz, *Studies in Animal and Human Behavior*, 2 vols., trans. R. Martin (Cambridge, Mass.: Harvard University Press, 1970—71), 1:252. Emphasis in original.

79. "Thought and word are not connected by a primary bond. A connection originates, changes, and grows in the course of the evolution of thinking and speech." Lev Vygotsky, *Thought and Language*, trans. and ed. Alex Kozulin (Cambridge, Mass.: M.I.T. Press, 1986), 210–11.

80. Ibid., 80.

81. Ibid., 106.

82. Ibid., 98 (where Vygotsky builds on Rimat's conclusion "that true concept formation exceeds the capacities of preadolescents").

83. Ibid., 131.

84. Ibid., 133.

85. Ibid., 113.

86. Ibid., 116.

87. Ibid., 87.

88. Ibid., 119.

89. Ibid., 121.

90. Ibid., 123.

91. Ibid., 49 (following Claparède and Piaget).

92. Ibid., 106–7.

93. Ibid., 124.

94. Ibid., 68, 71.

95. Ibid., 71 (citing Köhler in the first part of the passage and summarizing Henri Delacroix in the latter part).

96. Ibid., 76.

97. Ibid., 77. I discuss Savage-Rumbaugh's work in chapter 10. On the tool-using capabilities of chimpanzees in problem solving, see Daniel J. Povinelli, in collaboration with James E. Reaux, Laura A. Theall, and Steve Giambrone, *Folk Physics for Apes: The Chimpanzee's Theory of How the World Works* (New York: Oxford University Press, 2000).

98. Vygotsky, *Thought and Language*, 78.

99. See Sorabji, *Animal Minds and Human Morals*, 216 (referring to the apparent inability of apes to master human syntax).

100. Vygotsky, *Thought and Language*, 72.

101. Ibid., 135, 137.

102. Ibid., 138.

103. Ibid., 139.

104. Whether higher primates such as Kanzi or Koko are capable of inner speech is a problem that remains to be explored fully and may never be answered.

105. Vygotsky, *Thought and Language*, 139.

106. Ibid., 94.

107. Noam Chomsky, *On Nature and Language*, ed. Adriana Belletti and Luigi Rizzi (Cambridge: Cambridge University Press, 2002), 48–49. Cf. p. 46: Thus Darwin was wrong to characterize language as the ability to make associations.

108. Noam Chomsky, "Linguistics and Philosophy," in *Language and Philosophy: A Symposium*, ed. Sidney Hook, 51–94 (New York: New York University Press; London: University of London Press, 1969), 80. Chomsky's claim that language

258 ■ NOTES TO PAGES 35–40

capacity is innate has been accepted by many scientific researchers. See for example Laura Ann Petitto and Paula F. Marentette, "Babbling in the Manual Mode: Evidence for the Ontogeny of Language," *Science* 251 (1991): 1493 (citing Chomsky): "There is general agreement that humans possess some innately specified knowledge about language" that is "brain-based."

109. Noam Chomsky, *Rules and Representations* (Oxford: Blackwell, 1980), 239.

110. Ibid., 239–40, 57.

111. Noam Chomsky, *New Horizons in the Study of Language and Mind* (Cambridge: Cambridge University Press, 2000), 3. See also Noam Chomsky, *Reflections on Language* (New York: Pantheon, 1975), 40–41: "It is reasonable to surmise, I think, that there is no structure similar to UG [Universal Grammar] in nonhuman organisms and that the capacity for free, appropriate, and creative use of language as an expression of thought, with the means provided by the language faculty, is also a distinctive feature of the human species, having no significant analogue elsewhere. The neural basis for language is pretty much of a mystery, but there can be little doubt that specific neural structures and even gross organization not found in other primates (e.g., lateralization) play a fundamental role."

Chapter 2: Epic and Pre-Socratic Thought

1. Carol J. Adams, *The Sexual Politics of Meat: A Feminist-Vegetarian Critical Theory* (New York: Continuum, 1990), dedication page.

2. F. Barbara Orlans et al., *The Human Use of Animals: Case Studies in Ethical Choice* (New York: Oxford University Press, 1998), 255.

3. Jeremy Rifkin, *Beyond Beef: The Rise and Fall of the Cattle Culture* (New York: Dutton, 1992), 154.

4. J. A. Philip, *Pythagoras and Early Pythagoreanism* (Toronto: University of Toronto Press, 1966), 154.

5. See Bernard Knox's introduction to Homer, *The Iliad*, trans. Robert Fagles (New York: Penguin, 1990), 6–7.

6. *Iliad*, bk. 3, lines 16–40, p. 129. (Subsequent page citations to *The Iliad* refer to the Fagles edition.)

7. *Iliad*, bk. 5, lines 332–36, p. 174.

8. *Iliad*, bk. 5, lines 151, 158, pp. 168–69.

9. *Iliad*, bk. 7, lines 264–65, p. 222; Heracles is also characterized as "lionheart" at bk. 5, line 735, p. 185. Cf. bk. 20, lines 194–204, p. 509, where Achilles confronts Aeneas "rearing like some lion out on a rampage," teeming with "magnificent pride and fury." In the *Odyssey*, the epithet "lion heart" is also used to describe Odysseus; see *The Odyssey*, trans. Robert Fitzgerald (Garden City, N.Y.: Doubleday, 1961), bk. 4, lines 724, 814, pp. 78, 80; cf. bk. 11, line 267, p. 183, where Heracles is characterized as "lionish." (Subsequent page citations to *The Odyssey* refer to the Fitzgerald edition.)

10. *Iliad*, bk. 11, lines 201–2, p. 302; cf. bk. 11, line 451, p. 309, where the Trojans are compared to "bleating goats before some lion."

11. On the significance of this symbol in ancient Asia and Egypt, see Karl Sälzle, *Tier und Mensch. Gottheit und Dämon. Das Tier in der Geistesgeschichte der Menschheit* (Munich: Bayerischer Landschaftsverlag, 1965), 332–53.

12. On the significance of the image of the lion in Dutch history, see Simon Schama, *The Embarrassment of Riches: An Interpretation of Dutch Culture in the Golden Age* (New York: Knopf, 1987).

13. *Iliad*, bk. 13, lines 545–49, p. 356.

14. *Iliad*, bk. 22, lines 112–14, p. 544.

15. *Iliad*, bk. 20, lines 458–62, p. 516.

16. The comparison between human beings and animals, even lions, is not always favorable. In his desecration of Hector's dead body, Achilles is compared to "some lion / going his own barbaric way, giving in to his power, / his brute force and wild pride, as down he swoops / on the flocks of men to seize his savage feast." *Iliad*, bk. 24, lines 48–51, p. 589. Consider also the many comparisons made between men of poor character and animals such as dogs.

17. *Odyssey*, bk. 9, lines 105–15, p. 142.

18. *Odyssey*, bk. 9, lines 291–93, p. 147.

19. *Odyssey*, bk. 18, lines 140–42, p. 316.

20. *Odyssey*, bk. 18, lines 131–32, p. 316.

21. *Odyssey*, bk. 20, lines 9–13, p. 347. Cf. bk. 21, lines 129–41, p. 365, where Telemachus, on a sign from Odysseus, checks his pride, refrains from stringing Odysseus's bow, and pretends to be angry that he has failed.

22. *Odyssey*, bk. 17, lines 294–303, pp. 297–98.

23. *Odyssey*, bk. 17, lines 304–5, p. 298.

24. *Odyssey*, bk. 17, lines 331–33, p. 298.

25. Sextus Empiricus *Outlines of Pyrrhonism* 1.14.68, *The Skeptic Way: Sextus Empiricus's Outlines of Pyrrhonism*, trans. Benson Mates (New York: Oxford University Press, 1996), 98. Sextus says here that dogs possess justice and all the other virtues.

26. See, for example, *Odyssey*, bk. 14, line 426, p. 244, where a sacrificed bull's soul [ψυχή] is said to leave him when he dies. Here I follow Dierauer in rejecting Snell's claim that in Homer, animals typically lose passion or spirited desire [θυμός] at death, whereas only human beings lose soul [ψυχή]. According to Snell, "people were averse to ascribing the *psyche*, which a human being loses when he dies, also to an animal. They therefore invented the idea of a *thymos* which leaves the animal when it expires." Bruno Snell, *The Discovery of the Mind in Greek Philosophy and Literature* (New York: Dover, 1982), 11–12. Dierauer cites passages from the *Iliad* and the *Odyssey* that support the conclusion that both human beings and animals lose both passion (θυμός) and soul (ψυχή) at death. Urs Dierauer, *Tier und Mensch im Denken der Antike: Studien zur Tierpsychologie, Anthropologie und Ethik* (Amsterdam: Grüner, 1977), 9n.

27. Hesiod, *Works and Days* 276–79, in *Hesiod*, trans. Richard Lattimore (Ann Arbor: University of Michigan, 1959), 51. (Subsequent page citations of *Works and Days* refer to the Lattimore edition.) Porphyry cites this story in *De abstinentia* 1.5.3.

28. *Works and Days* 280–81, p. 51.

29. *Works and Days* 42, 47–49, p. 23. Hesiod explains Prometheus's deviousness in the *Theogony*: Prometheus "cut up / a great ox, and set it before Zeus, to see if he

could outguess him. / He took the meaty parts and the inwards thick with fat, and set them / before men, hiding them away in an ox's stomach, / but the white bones of the ox he arranged, with careful deception, / inside a concealing fold of white fat, and set it before Zeus." *Theogony* 536–41, in *Hesiod*, trans. Lattimore, p. 155.

30. *Works and Days* 57–58, p. 25. The story that I recount here is in *Works and Days* 40–105, pp. 23–31.

31. Plato, *Protagoras* 321c–322c, in *The Collected Dialogues of Plato Including the Letters*, ed. Edith Hamilton and Huntington Cairns (Princeton: Bollingen, 1961), 319–20.

32. *Works and Days* 105–201, pp. 31–43.

33. See *Paradise Lost*, bk. 5, lines 303–7.

34. *Works and Days* 207–11, p. 43.

35. Compare *Works and Days* 213 with 275.

36. See Ovid, *Metamorphoses*, bk. 1, lines 90–162, in *Metamorphoses*, 2 vols., Latin with English trans. by Frank Justus Miller (Cambridge, Mass.: Harvard University Press, 1977/1984), 1:9–13. (Subsequent page citations of *Metamorphoses* refer to this edition.)

37. See Porphyry, *De abstinentia* 3.27.10, in *On Abstinence from Killing Animals*, trans. Gillian Clark (Ithaca: Cornell University Press, 2000), 100; and chapter 4 below.

38. Diogenes Laertius 8.14, in *Lives of Eminent Philosophers*, vol. 2, Greek with English trans. by R. D. Hicks (Cambridge, Mass.: Harvard University Press, 2000), 353. (Subsequent page citations refer to this volume.) Long confirms that the doctrine of metempsychosis in Greece originates with Pythagoras, and he argues that the Orphics got their doctrine of metempsychosis from the Pythagoreans. See Herbert Strainge Long, *A Study of the Doctrine of Metempsychosis in Greece from Pythagoras to Plato* (Princeton: n.p., 1948), 11, 90.

39. Ovid, *Metamorphoses*, bk. 15, lines 72–3, 2:369.

40. Diogenes Laertius acknowledges this controversy at 8.13.

41. Plato, *Phaedrus* 248c–e, in *Collected Dialogues*, 495.

42. Iamblichus, *On the Pythagorean Life*, trans. Gillian Clark (Liverpool: Liverpool University Press, 1989), sec. 108, p. 48.

43. Ibid., sec. 168, p. 75.

44. Diogenes Laertius 8.4, 8.45, pp. 323–25, 361 (on Pythagoras's claim to prior human incarnations); 8.36, p. 353 (Xenophanes' story of the dog). Kahn notes that Xenophanes is making fun of Pythagoras when he relates this story. See Charles H. Kahn, *Pythagoras and the Pythagoreans: A Brief History* (Indianapolis: Hackett, 2001), 148.

45. Ovid, *Metamorphoses*, bk. 15, lines 165–67, p. 377.

46. Ibid., bk. 15, lines 127–29, p. 373.

47. Ibid., bk. 15, line 462, p. 397.

48. Sextus Empiricus, *Adversus mathematicos* 9.127–8, in *Sextus Empiricus*, vol. 3, Greek with English trans. by R. G. Bury (Cambridge, Mass.: Harvard University Press, 1936), 69. Cf. Diogenes Laertius 8.28–32, where the implication is made that, because not only men but sheep and cattle receive "dreams and signs of future disease and health," at least those animals if not all animals possess soul (ψυχή).

49. Plutarch, *De esu carnium* 997E, in *Moralia*, vol. 12, Greek with English trans. by Harold Cherniss and William C. Helmbold (Cambridge, Mass.: Harvard University Press, 1995), 569. Plutarch notes that Empedocles also held this view. On duties of justice toward animals, cf. Iamblichus, *On the Pythagorean Life*, sec. 229, p. 96: Pythagoras counseled "friendship of all for all, including some of the non-rational animals, through justice and natural connection and association."

50. As reported by Diogenes Laertius; see 8.37 and 8.44, pp. 353, 361.

51. Diogenes Laertius 8.23, p. 341.

52. Diogenes Laertius 8.22, p. 339. At 8.13, p. 333, Diogenes notes that Aristotle attributes this view to Pythagoras in his *Constitution of Delos*.

53. Diogenes Laertius 8.12, p. 331.

54. Iamblichus, *On the Pythagorean Life*, sec. 85, p. 38.

55. Porphyry, *De abstinentia* 2.28.2, *On Abstinence from Killing Animals*, p. 66. Elsewhere, Porphyry says that Pythagoras sacrificed primarily grain, cakes, and incense, and that he sacrificed animals such as hens and piglets "only occasionally." Porphyry, *Life of Pythagoras*, sec. 36, in *Vie de Pythagore. Lettre à Marcella*, Greek with French trans. by Édouard des Places, S. J. (Paris: Société d'Édition 'Les belles lettres,' 1982), 52.

56. Diogenes Laertius 8.12, 19, 23; pp. 331, 337, 341.

57. Diogenes Laertius 8.20, p. 339.

58. Diogenes Laertius 8.13, p. 333.

59. Diogenes Laertius 8.33–34, p. 349. On moderation, see 8.9, 18, pp. 329, 337.

60. Sorabji, *Animal Minds and Human Morals*, 173.

61. See Long, *A Study of the Doctrine of Metempsychosis*, 27: "It is difficult to believe that Pythagoras would have enunciated a non-moral doctrine of metempsychosis, for we know that the Pythagorean societies were concerned with the proper ordering of a man's or woman's daily life."

62. The evidence is not entirely clear about plants. But the implication is relatively straightforward that, at most, some plants have soul. "All things live which partake of heat—this is why plants are living things—but not all have soul, which is a detached part of aether, partly the hot and partly the cold, for it partakes of cold aether too. Soul is distinct from life; it is immortal, since that from which it is detached is immortal." Diogenes Laertius 8.28, p. 345. The only plant other than beans that Pythagoras is said to have prohibited killing or injuring is "trees that are not wild." Diogenes Laertius 8.23, p. 341.

63. Diogenes Laertius 8.24, p. 341.

64. Diogenes Laertius 8.39, 45, pp. 355, 361. In Iamblichus's version of the story, a group of Pythagoreans are pursued by Eurymenes and his men. Iamblichus, *On the Pythagorean Life*, 189–94, 82–84. In Porphyry's version, Damon and Phintias refuse to cross the bean field. *Life of Pythagoras*, sec. 61, in *Vie de Pythagore*, p. 66.

65. Iamblichus, *On the Pythagorean Life*, sec. 61, p. 25.

66. Iamblichus, *On the Pythagorean Life*, sec. 60, pp. 24–25.

67. Aristotle, *Rhetoric* I.13 at 1373b14–16, in *Complete Works of Aristotle*, 2:2187.

68. Diels and Kranz, *Die Fragmente der Vorsokratiker*, 3 vols., Greek with German trans. by Hermann Diels, ed. Walther Kranz (Zurich: Weidmann, 1964), 28 A 45.

69. DK frag. 31 B 110, *Die Fragmente der Vorsokratiker*, 3:353. Cf. Sextus Empiricus, *adversus mathematikos* 8.286 and 9.127–8. For a more detailed discussion of Empedocles' belief that thought pervades the universe, see Dierauer, *Tier und Mensch im Denken der Antike*, 43–44.

70. Porphyry, *De abstinentia* 2.21.2–3 (DK frag. 31 B 128); Kirk and Raven, *The Presocratic Philosophers*, 349.

71. Sextus Empiricus, *Adversus mathematikos* 9.129, in *The Presocratic Philosophers*, 350. Kirk and Raven note that although this passage does "not describe the primal sin but contemporary sin, there can be little doubt that this contemporary sin is a repetition of the primal sin." *The Presocratic Philosophers*, 351.

72. Porphyry, *De abstinentia* 2.31, in Kirk and Raven, *The Presocratic Philosophers*, 351.

73. Diogenes Laertius 8.53, p. 369.

74. Diogenes Laertius 8.77, p. 391.

75. Plutarch, *De exilio* 17 at 607D, in Kirk and Raven, *The Presocratic Philosophers*, 359.

76. Haussleiter argues that metempsychosis is the sole basis for Empedocles' ethic of abstinence. Johannes Haussleiter, *Der Vegetarismus in der Antike*, Religionsgeschichtliche Versuche und Vorarbeiten, vol. 24 (Berlin: Alfred Töpelmann, 1935), 163.

77. Diels and Kranz, *Die Fragmente der Vorsokratiker*, 1:358n (following the Persian philosopher Shahrastani's suggestion that this is "the Kalâm of Empedocles").

78. See in particular DK frag. 31 B 115 and 146, Diels and Kranz, *Die Fragmente der Vorsokratiker* 1.356–58, 369–70; in Kirk and Raven, *The Presocratic Philosophers*, pp. 351–52, 354: 31 B 115 states that demigods who have sinned must endure a series of mortal incarnations, "changing one baleful path of life for another. The might of the air pursues him into the sea, the sea spews him forth on to the dry land, the earth casts him into the rays of the burning sun, and the sun into the eddies of air." 31 B 146 states that "at the end they come among men on earth as prophets, bards, doctors, and princes; and thence they arise as gods mighty in honor, sharing with the other immortals their hearth and their table, without part in human sorrows or weariness." Long takes these two fragments and Diels's footnote as clear evidence that "in Empedocles, the soul goes from δαίμον to plant, to animal, to human being, to god." *A Study of the Doctrine of Metempsychosis*, 22.

79. Diogenes Laertius 8.60, p. 375.

80. Plutarch, *De sollertia animalium* 964D, *de esu cranium* 997E, in *Moralia*, 351, 569.

Chapter 3: Aristotle and the Stoics

1. Sorabji, *Animal Minds and Human Morals*, 7.

2. As reported by Theophrastus in *de sensu* 25–26, DK 24 A 5, in Kirk and Raven, *The Presocratic Philosophers*, 233. Diogenes Laertius 8.83 reports that Alcmaeon was a disciple of Pythagoras. Kirk and Raven believe that Alcmaeon "flourished, probably, in the early fifth century BC" (*The Presocratic Philosophers*, 232), while Sorabji places him in the "late sixth century BC" (*Animal Minds and Human Morals*, 9). Either

way, Alcmaeon is a predecessor to Aristotle, as is evident from Aristotle's several references to him (see, e.g., *Metaphysics* 1:5 at 986a29).

3. Dierauer, *Tier und Mensch im Denken der Antike*, 41.

4. Diogenes Laertius 8.83, p. 397.

5. Dierauer, *Tier und Mensch im Denken der Antike*, 43. Thinkers such as Protagoras, Xenophon, and Anaxagoras contribute to the emergence of this new scale of values. See Sorabji, *Animal Minds and Human Morals*, 9; and Dierauer, *Tier und Mensch im Denken der Antike*, 44–52.

6. For excellent discussions of the place of Plato's thinking in the ancient discussions of animals, see Sorabji, *Animal Minds and Human Morals*, 9–12 and Dierauer, *Tier und Mensch im Denken der Antike*, 66–80, 89–96. On Plato's influence on Aristotle, see William W. Fortenbaugh, "Aristotle: Animals, Emotion, and Moral Virtue," *Arethusa* 4 (1971): 137–39, 144–46, 150, 156.

7. *Philebus* 20e–21d, in *Collected Dialogues of Plato*, 1097–98.

8. *Statesman* 261c–e.

9. *Phaedrus* 2449b, in *Collected Dialogues of Plato*, 496.

10. *Phaedrus* 248c–d, in *Collected Dialogues of Plato*, 495. Cf. the myth of Er at the end of the *Republic* (620a–d), where some human individuals are said to have chosen the forms of animals for their next incarnations (Orpheus, for example, chose the form of a swan because he did not want to be born of woman again after having been killed by the Maenads, the women of Thrace), while in other cases there were all sorts of movements between animal and human form. On the ideal of transcending the body altogether, see *Phaedo* 80d–81b, in *Collected Dialogues of Plato*, 64.

11. *Phaedo* 81d–82b, *Timaeus* 42b–c, in *Collected Dialogues of Plato*, 64–65, 1171. Cf. *Timaeus* 91d–92c, in *Collected Dialogues of Plato*, 1210–11, where animals are said to have been created from deficient human beings.

12. At most, the welfare of the body is good as a means to the welfare of the embodied soul. At worst, the pursuit of goods pleasing to the body simply interferes with the soul's attempts to contemplate the truth, so Socrates says that it is best if "the philosopher frees his soul from association with the body, so far as is possible." *Phaedo* 64e–65a, in *Collected Dialogues of Plato*, 47. The Neoplatonist Porphyry uses this reasoning as one of his main arguments in favor of vegetarianism.

13. *Laws* 961d, in *Collected Dialogues of Plato*, 1506.

14. *Philebus* 11b–c, in *Collected Dialogues of Plato*, 1087.

15. *Republic* 376a–b, in *Collected Dialogues of Plato*, 622–23. There is evidently some irony here, as Socrates bases this assessment entirely on dogs' ability to discriminate between friends and enemies.

16. *Republic* 441a–b, in *Collected Dialogues of Plato*, 683. See also *Menexenus* 237d: Among animals, "man . . . is superior to the rest in understanding, and alone has justice and religion." In *Collected Dialogues of Plato*, 189–90.

17. *Phaedo* 82b.

18. *Symposium* 207b–c.

19. *Cratylus* 399c, in *Collected Dialogues of Plato*, 436: animals neither contemplate nor look up at what they see. *Laches* 197a–b, in *Collected Dialogues of Plato*, 140: Nicias says that animals cannot properly be said to be courageous, because their fearless-

ness is due to a lack of understanding of the dangers they face; but cf. *Laws* 963e, in *Collected Dialogues of Plato*, 1508, where the Athenian says that courage does not require reason but can be based entirely on temperament, and thus that animals and infants are capable of courage.

20. *Republic* 586a–b, in *Collected Dialogues of Plato*, 813–14. Cf. 571c, p. 798, where physical desires are called "beastly and savage," in contrast with the rational part of the soul, which is "gentle and dominant."

21. Sorabji's remarks on this point are particularly helpful; see *Animal Minds and Human Morals*, 10–11.

22. *Republic* 573d, in *Collected Dialogues of Plato*, 800; cf. 538c, in *Collected Dialogues of Plato*, 770.

23. *Republic* 442b–c, in *Collected Dialogues of Plato*, 684.

24. *Republic* 430b, in *Collected Dialogues of Plato*, 672.

25. Dombrowski notes that the diet in the ideal city sketched by Socrates in the *Republic* is vegetarian. Daniel A. Dombrowski, *The Philosophy of Vegetarianism* (Amherst: University of Massachusetts Press, 1984), 62; cf. *Republic* 372a–c. It is unlikely that Socrates recommends a vegetarian diet out of consideration for animals; he seems to shun meat as part of a general warning against luxuries, which soften people and divert them from the pursuit of the truth.

26. See Fortenbaugh, "Aristotle: Animals, Emotion, and Moral Virtue."

27. *Politics* 1.8 at 1256b15–21, in *Complete Works of Aristotle*, 2:1993–94.

28. Martha Craven Nussbaum, *Aristotle's De Motu Animalium* (Princeton: Princeton University Press, 1978), 96. Of course, one should not employ this interpretive principle indiscriminately. Aristotle also expresses a number of considered theoretical commitments in the first book of the *Politics*, some of which are examined below.

29. Dierauer, *Tier und Mensch im Denken der Antike*, 155, 240.

30. *Physics* 2.1 at 192b14–16, in *Complete Works of Aristotle*, 1:329.

31. *Physics* 2.1 at 193a29–30, 193b14, in *Complete Works of Aristotle*, 1:330.

32. *Physics* 2.3 at 194b30–33, in *Complete Works of Aristotle*, 1:332.

33. *Physics* 2.3 at 195a24–25, in *Complete Works of Aristotle*, 1:333.

34. Porphyry, *De abstinentia* 3.20.1, in *On Abstinence from Killing Animals*, 91.

35. See Nussbaum, *Aristotle's De Motu Animalium*, 95–97, and Balme's commentary in *Aristotle's De Partibus Animalium I and De Generatione Animalium I (with Passages from II.1–3)*, trans. D. M. Balme (Oxford: Clarendon, 1972), 98. At one point in the *Metaphysics*, Aristotle does say that "all things are ordered together somehow, but not all alike,— both fishes and fowls and plants; and the world is not such that one thing has nothing to do with another, but they are connected. For all are ordered together to one end." Aristotle here draws an analogy to the ordering of an army, whose parts are ordered to one highest good. "For the good is found both in the order and in the leader, and more in the latter; for he does not depend on the order but it depends on him." *Metaphysics* 12 at 1075a11–19, in *Complete Works of Aristotle*, 2:1699. But these statements do not clearly entail that animals exist specifically for the sake of human beings; the army analogy suggests not that soldiers exist for the sake of

their leader, but rather that they exist for the sake of a good that they share with the leader and which is more in the leader than in the organization of the army.

36. *Physics* 2.8 at 199a17—20, in *Complete Works of Aristotle*, 1:340; on plants, see 199a24—25.

37. *Physics* 2.8 at 199a26, 20—21, in *Complete Works of Aristotle*, 1:340. Among Aristotle's examples here are the production of leaves in a plant, the swallow's construction of its nest, and the spider's spinning of its web. All of these processes occur "by nature."

38. *Nicomachean Ethics* 10.8 at 1178b22—29, in *Complete Works of Aristotle*, 2:1863.

39. *Eudemian Ethics* 1.7 at 1217a24—25, in *Complete Works of Aristotle*, 2:1926.

40. *Politics* 1.2 at 1253a19, in *Complete Works of Aristotle*, 2:1988.

41. *Politics* 1.2 at 1253a26—27, in *Complete Works of Aristotle*, 2:1988.

42. *Politics* 1.2 at 1253a7—8, in *Complete Works of Aristotle*, 2:1988.

43. *Politics* 1.2 at 1253a9—11, in *Complete Works of Aristotle*, 2:1988. See also *On the Soul* 2.8 at 420b13, in *Complete Works of Aristotle*, 1:669: "Voice is the sound made by an animal."

44. *Politics* 1.5 at 1254b23, in *Complete Works of Aristotle*, 2:1990.

45. *Politics* 1.5 at 1254b21—25, in *Complete Works of Aristotle*, 2:1990.

46. On the responsibilities of the citizen, see *Politics* 3.1 at 1275a19—25, in *Complete Works of Aristotle*, 2:2023.

47. See *Nicomachean Ethics* 1.9 at 1099b30—31 and 10.9 at 1181b20—22, in *Complete Works of Aristotle*, 2:1867.

48. *Nicomachean Ethics* 2.6 at 1106b36—1107a2, in *Complete Works of Aristotle*, 2:1748.

49. *Nicomachean Ethics* 3.2 at 1111b6—10, 6.5 at 1140a25—30, and 7.6 at 1149b34—35, in *Complete Works of Aristotle*, 2:1755, 2:1800, 2:1816.

50. *Eudemian Ethics* 2.10 at 1225b26—27, in *Complete Works of Aristotle*, 2:1941: "But anger and appetite belong also to brutes while choice does not." See also *Nicomachean Ethics* 3.2 at 1111a22—1111b3.

51. Nonetheless, children and animals are subject to praise and blame even though they are not capable of virtue and vice. For a discussion of Aristotle's logic on this point, see Martha C. Nussbaum, *The Fragility of Goodness: Luck and Ethics in Greek Tragedy and Philosophy* (Cambridge: Cambridge University Press, 1987), 284. In *History of Animals*, Aristotle says that the soul of a human being in childhood "has practically no difference from that of wild animals." *History of Animals* 7 (following Balme's ordering of books) at 588b30—31, in *History of Animals, Books VII–X*, ed. and trans. D. M. Balme (Cambridge, Mass.: Harvard University Press, 1991), 61.

52. *Nicomachean Ethics* 8.11 at 1161b2—3, in *Complete Works of Aristotle*, 2:1835.

53. *Politics* 1.2 at 1253a10—15, in *Complete Works of Aristotle*, 2:1988; *Nicomachean Ethics* 2.1 at 1103b14—15, 5.1 at 1129b31—1130a1, in *Complete Works of Aristotle*, 2:1743, 2:1783.

54. *Nicomachean Ethics* 7.6 at 1149b30—35, in *Complete Works of Aristotle*, 2:1816.

55. *Nicomachean Ethics* 7.3 at 1147b4—5, in *Complete Works of Aristotle*, 2:1812.

56. Ibid.

57. *On the Soul* 3.3 at 428a21, in *Complete Works of Aristotle*, 1:681.

58. *De interpretatione* 16a1—10, in *Complete Works of Aristotle*, 1:25.

59. *On the Soul* 3.3 at 427b5–10, 428a5–21, in *Complete Works of Aristotle*, 1:680–81.

60. *Eudemian Ethics* 2.10 at 1225b27, *Nicomachean Ethics* 3.8 at 1116b24–1117a5.

61. On the three types of object of desire, see *Nicomachean Ethics* 2.3 at 1104b29–1105a1, in *Complete Works of Aristotle*, 2:1745. Here I can provide only a brief summary of these modes of desire in human beings. An excellent overview is provided by John M. Cooper in "Reason, Moral Virtue, and Moral Value," in *Rationality in Greek Thought*, ed. Michael Frede and Gisela Striker, 81–114 (Oxford: Clarendon, 1996).

62. *Nicomachean Ethics* 3.2 at 1111b8–9.

63. *On the Soul* 2.6 at 418a17–18, 3.1 at 425a14–15, in *Complete Works of Aristotle*, 1:665, 1:676.

64. *On the Soul*, 3.2 at 426b12–13.

65. Richard Sorabji, "Rationality," in *Rationality in Greek Thought*, ed. Michael Frede and Gisela Striker, 311–34 (Oxford: Clarendon, 1996), 314; see also Sorabji, *Animal Minds and Human Morals*, 12.

66. *On the Soul* 3.2 at 425b12, *Nicomachean Ethics* 3.3 at 1113a1–2, in *Complete Works of Aristotle*, 1:677, 2:1757.

67. *Movement of Animals* 7 at 701a32–33, in Nussbaum, *Aristotle's De Motu Animalium*, 42; see also *Nicomachean Ethics* 7.6 at 1149a35.

68. *Nicomachean Ethics* 3.10 at 1118a19–24, in *Complete Works of Aristotle*, 2:1765.

69. Nussbaum, *Aristotle's De Motu Animalium*, 257n.

70. Nussbaum, *Aristotle's De Motu Animalium*, 259.

71. *On the Soul* 3.3 at 429a2–3.

72. *On the Soul* 3.3 at 428a11–17, in *Complete Works of Aristotle*, 1:680–81.

73. *On the Soul* 3.3 at 428b2–4, in *Complete Works of Aristotle*, 1:681.

74. In *On the Soul* 3.10 at 433a12, Aristotle attributes imagination to all animals, but in 3.3 at 428a10–11 he says that it is not found in ants, bees, or grubs.

75. *On the Soul* 3.10 at 433b28–30, in *Complete Works of Aristotle*, 1:689.

76. Nussbaum, *Aristotle's De Motu Animalium*, 249.

77. *On the Soul* 3.11 at 434a5–9, in *Complete Works of Aristotle*, 1:690.

78. Nussbaum, *Aristotle's De Motu Animalium*, 248n.

79. See *Metaphysics* 6.4 at 1027b20ff., 9.9 at 1051b3–1052a3; *De Interpretatione* 16a4–11.

80. Juha Sihvola argues that, at least in an instance such as Aristotle's example of the sun appearing a foot wide, *phantasia* "clearly involves combination and predication and even admits propositional content." "Emotional Animals: Do Aristotelian Emotions Require Beliefs?" *Apeiron* 29 (1996): 117.

81. *Metaphysics* I.1 at 980a28–30, 981a15, in *Complete Works of Aristotle*, 2:1552.

82. *On Memory* 449b19–23.

83. *On Memory* 450a13–18, in *Complete Works of Aristotle*, 1:715.

84. *On Memory* 453a8–13, in *Complete Works of Aristotle*, 1:720.

85. *On Memory* 449b10–11, in *Complete Works of Aristotle*, 1:714.

86. *Posterior Analytics* 2.19 at 99b35–100a6, in *Complete Works of Aristotle*, 1:165–66.

87. *Posterior Analytics* 2.19 at 100a15–100b3, in *Complete Works of Aristotle*, 1:166.

88. Dierauer, *Tier und Mensch im Denken der Antike*, 122; cf. 147–48.

89. Sorabji, *Animal Minds and Human Morals*, 35.

90. Jean-Louis Labarrière, "De la *phronesis* animale," in *Biologie, logique et métaphysique chez Aristotle*, ed. Daniel Devereux and Pierre Pellegrin, 405–28 (Paris: Éditions du Centre National de la Recherche Scientifique, 1990), 418, 420.

91. *Posterior Analytics* 2.19 at 100b4–5, in *Complete Works of Aristotle*, 1:166.

92. *Metaphysics* 1.1 at 980b26–981a1, in *Complete Works of Aristotle*, 2:1552.

93. *Nicomachean Ethics* 6.5 at 1140b4–6, in *Complete Works of Aristotle*, 2:1800. Cf. 1140b26–27, in *Complete Works of Aristotle*, 2:1801: Practical wisdom is the virtue "of that part [of the soul] which forms opinions."

94. *Nicomachean Ethics* 6.7 at 1141b8–9, in *Complete Works of Aristotle*, 2:1802. Cf. 1141b14–15: *Phronesis* depends on the ability to recognize both particulars and universals.

95. *Nicomachean Ethics* 6.9 at 1142b12–15, in *Complete Works of Aristotle*, 2:1804.

96. *Nicomachean Ethics* 6.9 at 1142b35, in *Complete Works of Aristotle*, 2:1804

97. *Metaphysics* 9.10 at 1051b33–1052a3; *On Interpretation* 9 at 18a34–40.

98. *Metaphysics* 1.1 at 980b22.

99. *On the Soul* 3.3 at 427b7–9, in *Complete Works of Aristotle*, 1:680.

100. *Nicomachean Ethics* 6.7 at 1141a27–29, in *Complete Works of Aristotle*, 2:1802.

101. Fortenbaugh, "Aristotle: Animals, Emotion, and Moral Virtue," 143.

102. *Movement of Animals* 6 at 700b10–11, in Nussbaum, *Aristotle's De Motu Animalium*, 36.

103. *Movement of Animals* 6 at 701a31–33, in Nussbaum, *Aristotle's De Motu Animalium*, 42.

104. *Movement of Animals* 6 at 701a28–29, in Nussbaum, *Aristotle's De Motu Animalium*, 40.

105. *Nicomachean Ethics* 7.7 at 1149b31–32, in *Complete Works of Aristotle*, 2:1816.

106. Aristotle is not entirely clear on the question whether emotions depend on beliefs. Fortenbaugh and Nussbaum argue that they do; Sihvola argues that Aristotle makes some emotions dependent on belief, while characterizing other emotions as dependent on *phantasia* rather than on belief. Compare Fortenbaugh, "Aristotle: Animals, Emotion, and Moral Virtue," 143; and Martha C. Nussbaum, *The Therapy of Desire: Theory and Practice in Hellenistic Ethics* (Princeton: Princeton University Press, 1994), 78–91; with Sihvola, "Emotional Animals," 116–17, 140–42.

107. *Nicomachean Ethics* 3.8 at 1116b24–25. This raises the question what the end of spirited desire or *thymos* is in animals. In human beings, the object of *thymos* is the noble; but the noble is an object of contemplation, and hence cannot be the "end" of *thymos* in animals. Aristotle never answers this question. Aristotle's remark in the discussion of courage that "brave men act for the sake of the noble, but passion aids them; while wild beasts act under the influence of pain" even leaves open the possibility that the attribution of *thymos* to animals is itself merely metaphorical, at least in the *Ethics* if not in the zoological texts. *Nicomachean Ethics* 3.8 at 1116b31–32, in *Complete Works of Aristotle*, 2:1763.

108. *History of Animals* at 588a25–31, in *History of Animals, Books VII–X*, 59–61.

109. See Balme's remarks in *History of Animals, Books VII–X*, 7–8.

110. See Dierauer, *Tier und Mensch im Denken der Antike*, 137–48, 212–19.

111. *Parts of Animals* 3.6 at 669a18–20, in *Parts of Animals, Movement of Animals, Progression of Animals*, trans. A. L. Peck and E. S. Forster (Cambridge, Mass.: Harvard University Press, 1998), 257.

112. Aristotle gives clear expression to the value he places on the study of animals when he says that "we ought not to hesitate nor to be abashed, but boldly to enter upon our researches concerning animals of every sort and kind, knowing that in not one of them is nature or beauty lacking. . . . If, however, there is anyone who holds that the study of the animals is an unworthy pursuit, he ought to go further and hold the same opinion about the study of himself, for it is not possible without considerable disgust to look upon the blood, flesh, bones, blood-vessels, and suchlike parts of which the human body is constructed." *Parts of Animals* 1.5 at 645a23–31, in *Parts of Animals, Movement of Animals, Progression of Animals*, 101.

113. *History of Animals* 8 at 610b22, in *History of Animals*, Books VII–X, 235, 235n. See also 7 at 589a1–2, where different animals are said to have different degrees of understanding or sagacity (σύνεσις).

114. *History of Animals* 8 at 612a3–10, 611a16–18. See also 488b15 and 618a26.

115. *History of Animals* 8 at 616b20–31.

116. *History of Animals* 8 at 620b10–25, where Aristotle gives examples of fish that use cunning to catch other fish; 7 at 596b20–597b10, where Aristotle discusses the skill exhibited by various animals in dealing with changes in the weather; 8 at 615a15–20 and 616a5, where Aristotle calls the trochilos and the acanthylis "ingenious" (τεχνικός); and 8 at 622b23–24, where Aristotle remarks on the ingenuity of the spider. See also *Metaphysics* 1.1 at 981a.

117. *Parts of Animals* 4.5 at 679a4–7 (sepia and other cephalopods), *History of Animals* 8 at 621b29–622a14 (cuttlefish and octopus). Aristotle notes that the octopus also changes its color when hunting fish.

118. *History of Animals* 8 at 627b9–15; 1.1 at 487a11.

119. *History of Animals* 8 at 620a29–33.

120. *History of Animals* 8 at 630b32–631a8. The camel killed the man who had deceived it; the horse ran away and threw itself off a cliff.

121. *History of Animals* 8 at 608a20–21, in *History of Animals, Books VII–VI*, 215.

122. *History of Animals* 4 at 535a28–535b12, in *History of Animals, Books IV–VI*, trans. A. L. Peck (Cambridge, Mass.: Harvard University Press, 2002), 73–77.

123. *Parts of Animals* 2.17 at 660a17–25, in *Parts of Animals, Movement of Animals, Progression of Animals*, 201.

124. *Parts of Animals* 2.17 at 660a35–660b2, in *Parts of Animals, Movement of Animals, Progression of Animals*, 201–2. See also *History of Animals* 2.12 at 504b1; 4.9 at 536a20–22 and 536b11–20 (voice comes naturally, but nightingales specifically teach their young to sing); 7 at 597b27–30 (the parrot is "human-tongued" and "becomes even more outrageous after drinking wine"); 8 at 608a17–21.

125. *History of Animals* 8 at 631a15–20.

126. On jealousy, see *History of Animals* 8 at 619b27–31 (eagle). On fear, see 8 at 608a16, 609a31–35 (birds), 609b16–17 (ass), 618a25 (cuckoo is aware of its own cowardice), 622b14–15 (nautilus), 627a16–18 (bees), 629b20–22 (lions), 630b8–13 (bison). On courage, see 7 at 588a21; 8 at 608a15, 610b20, 629b6.

127. *Parts of Animals* 3.6 at 669a18–20, in *Parts of Animals, Movement of Animals, Progression of Animals*, 257.

128. *History of Animals* 8 at 608b4–8, in *History of Animals, Books VII–X*, 219.

129. *History of Animals* 7 at 588b7–12.

130. *On the Soul* 2.1 at 412a20–22, in *Complete Works of Aristotle*, 1:656.

131. *On the Soul* 2.1 at 412b10–11, in *Complete Works of Aristotle*, 1:657.

132. *On the Soul* 2.3 at 414a31–415a12.

133. *On the Soul* 1.4 at 408b19–20, 3.5 at 430a22–23.

134. This last characterization is Dierauer's. See *Tier und Mensch im Denken der Antike*, 199. Gisela Striker proposes "recognition and appreciation of something as belonging to one" as a working definition of the Stoic sense of *oikeiosis*. Gisela Striker, "The Role of *Oikeiosis* in Stoic Ethics," in *Oxford Studies in Ancient Philosophy* 1, ed. Julia Annas, 145–67 (Oxford: Clarendon, 1983), 145. Long and Sedley speak of "an affective disposition relative to the thing which is owned or belongs." A. A. Long and D. N. Sedley, *The Hellenistic Philosophers*, 2 vols. (Cambridge: Cambridge University Press, 1990), 1:351.

135. Philo, *Allegories of the Laws* 2.22–3 (SVF 2.458), in Long and Sedley, *The Hellenistic Philosophers*, 47P.

136. Diogenes Laertius 7.51, p. 161.

137. Cicero, *Academica* 1.40–1 (SVF 1.55, 61), in Long and Sedley, *The Hellenistic Philosophers* 40B; see also Long and Sedley's commentary, *The Hellenistic Philosophers* 2:240.

138. Sextus Empiricus, *Against the Professors* 7.51–2 (SVF 2.65, part), in Long and Smedley, *The Hellenistic Philosophers* 40E (translation altered). Cf. Diogenes Laertius 7.54: As such, cognitive impressions function as an authoritative measure of truth; Diogenes notes that the Stoics disagree on the question whether cognitive impressions are the only such authoritative standard, or whether there are others as well. The important point in the present discussion is that animals have no access to truth.

139. Diogenes Laertius 7.63, p. 173.

140. Brad Inwood, *Ethics and Human Action in Early Stoicism* (Oxford: Clarendon, 1985), 57.

141. Long and Sedley, *The Hellenistic Philosophers*, 1:240.

142. See Sextus Empiricus, *Against the Professors* 7.151–7, in Long and Sedley, *The Hellenistic Philosophers* 41C, p. 255: "Assent occurs not in relation to an impression but in relation to language." Benson Mates makes the important observation that the noncognitive character of animal presentations does not make them "irrational" in the everyday sense of the term: "Obviously there is nothing irrational about [animal] *phantasia*; it merely lacks a content that can be expressed in speech (*logos*). The 'irrational' (*alogoi*) animals are not crazy; their deficiency is that their *phantasiai* are not fit to be expressed in words." Sextus Empiricus, *The Skeptic Way: Sextus Empiricus's Outlines of Pyrrhonism*, trans. Benson Mates (New York: Oxford University Press, 1996), 37 (commenting on Diogenes Laertius 7.51; cf. Sextus, *Against the Mathematicians* 8.275).

143. See Diogenes Laertius 7.111, p. 217: The Stoics "hold the emotions to be judgements [κρίσεις]." Here Diogenes has Chrysippus in mind. Other Stoics, such as Zeno, appear to have considered emotions to be predicated on judgments, rather than being judgments; on the specific differences between Zeno's and Chrysippus's conceptions of emotion, see Nussbaum, *The Therapy of Desire*, 372, 381–82. For a succinct summary of the Stoics' views on emotion, see Sorabji, *Animal Minds and Human Morals*, 58–61.

144. Seneca, *On Anger* 1.3.4–7, in *Moral Essays*, vol. 1, Latin with English trans. by John W. Basore (London: Heinemann; New York: G. P. Putnam's Sons, 1928), 115.

145. Seneca, *Ad Lucilium Epistulae Morales*, vol. 3, Latin with English trans. by Richard M. Gummere (London: Heinemann; New York: G. P. Putnam's Sons, 1925), 124.16–18, pp. 445.

146. Origen *On Principles* 3.1.2–3 (SVF 2.988, part), in Long and Sedley, *The Hellenistic Philosophers*, 53A.

147. This reading of Diogenes Laertius 7.51 is tentatively proposed by Inwood. See *Ethics and Human Action in Early Stoicism*, 76–77.

148. *Ad Lucilium Epistulae Morales* 124.1–2, in *Ad Lucilium Epistulae Morales*, vol. 3, 437.

149. *Ad Lucilium Epistulae Morales* 76.11, 76.15–16, 76.9, in *Ad Lucilium Epistulae Morales*, vol. 2, Latin with English trans. by Richard M. Gummere (London: Heinemann; New York: G. P. Putnam's Sons, 1930), 153, 155–56, 151.

150. *Outlines of Pyrrhonism* 1.65–66, in Sextus Empiricus, *The Skeptic Way*, 97.

151. *Outlines of Pyrrhonism* 1.67–68, in Sextus Empiricus, *The Skeptic Way*, 98.

152. *Outlines of Pyrrhonism* 1.69, in Sextus Empiricus, *The Skeptic Way*, 98. Dierauer notes that there are two versions of this story, one according to which the dog must choose from among three paths, and one according to which the dog comes to a hole in the ground in the course of the pursuit, does not detect the scent of its quarry to the left or to the right, and immediately jumps over the hole. *Tier und Mensch im Denken der Antike*, 222.

153. Diogenes Laertius 7.85–6, pp. 193–95.

154. Epictetus, *Discourses* 1.6.13–14, in *The Discourses as Reported by Arrian, Books I–II*, Greek with English trans. by W. A. Oldfather (Cambridge, Mass.: Harvard University Press, 2000), 43.

155. Hierocles 1.34–39, 51–57, 2.1–9, Long and Sedley, *The Hellenistic Philosophers*, 57C.

156. See Epictetus, *Discourses* 1.6.12–13, in *The Discourses as Reported by Arrian, Books I–II*, p. 43: "You will, indeed, find many things in man only, things of which the rational animal had a peculiar need, but you will also find many possessed by us in common with the irrational animals. Do they also, then, understand what happens? No! for use is one thing, and understanding another."

157. Seneca, *Ad Lucilium Epistulae Morales* 121.6, vol. 3, p. 399. At 121.6 Seneca calls this awareness *scientia*, but the larger discussion in the letter makes it clear that he does not mean this literally; his remark at 121.9 that all animals have a *sensus* of their constitution better reflects the Stoic position.

158. Seneca, *Ad Lucilium Epistulae Morales* 121.20–21, vol. 3, p. 409.

159. *Ad Lucilium Epistulae Morales* 121.8. Here Seneca is challenging the Epicurean view, according to which all animals act on the prospect of pleasure and to avoid or minimize pain; both the infant and the tortoise are struggling *in spite* of pain, which for Seneca demonstrates that there are motivations more fundamental than pleasure. Cicero makes the same point in *On Ends* 3.16; for the Epicurean view, see 1.29–30.

160. Seneca, *Ad Lucilium Epistulae Morales* 121.23, vol. 3, pp. 409–10.

161. Hierocles 9.3–10, in Long and Sedley, *The Hellenistic Philosophers* 57D.

162. Seneca, *Ad Lucilium Epistulae Morales* 76.11, 76.15–16.

163. A. A. Long, *Epictetus: A Stoic and Socratic Guide to Life* (Oxford: Clarendon, 2002), 182.

164. Diogenes Laertius 7.87–88, p. 195.

165. Cicero, *On the Nature of the Gods*, 2.37, in Long and Sedley, *The Hellenistic Philosophers* 54H.

166. Cleanthes, *Hymn to Zeus* (SVF 1.537), in Long and Sedley, *The Hellenistic Philosophers* 54I.

167. *Hymn to Zeus*, in Long and Sedley, *The Hellenistic Philosophers* 54I.

168. Seneca, *Ad Lucilium Epistulae Morales* 124.13–14, vol. 3, pp. 443–44.

169. Epictetus, *Discourses* 1.6.14–17, in *The Discourses as Reported by Arrian, Books I–II*, p. 43.

170. Cicero, *On Ends* 3.20, in *De Finibus Bonorum et Malorum*, Latin with English trans. by H. Rackham (Cambridge, Mass.: Harvard University Press, 1999), 239. (Subsequent page citations refer to this edition.) Cf. 4.16–17, p. 319: The Stoics "extolled the soul as infinitely surpassing the body in worth, and accordingly placed the virtues also of the mind above the goods of the body."

171. Cicero, *On Ends* 3.21, pp. 240–41.

172. Cicero, *On the Nature of the Gods* 2.37–39, in Long and Sedley, *The Hellenistic Philosophers* 54H. Cicero attributes this view to Chrysippus. See also Epictetus, *Discourses* 1:6.18, 1:16.1–5, 2:8.6–8.

173. Diogenes Laertius 7.89, p. 197.

174. Nicholas P. White, "The Basis of Stoic Ethics," *Harvard Studies in Classical Philology* 83 (1979): 175.

175. Seneca, *Ad Lucilium Epistulae Morales* 76.11, vol. 2, p. 153.

176. Seneca, *Ad Lucilium Epistulae Morales* 124.20, vol. 3, p. 447.

177. Stobaeus 2.96, 18–97, 5 (SVF 3.501), in Long and Sedley, *The Hellenistic Philosophers* 59M.

178. Seneca, *Ad Lucilium Epistulae Morales* 92.12–13, vol. 3, p. 455. See also Cicero, *On Ends* 3.22.

179. Plutarch, *On Common Conceptions* 1072E–F (SVF 3 Antipater 59, part), in Long and Sedley, *The Hellenistic Philosophers* 64D (reporting the Stoic view).

180. Seneca, *Ad Lucilium Epistulae Morales* 92.11, vol. 3, p. 453. It is controversial whether the Stoics admit that external goods are really good at all. For a discussion of the controversy (and a defense of the view that they are not really goods), see Nussbaum, *The Therapy of Desire*, 360–66.

181. Epictetus, *Discourses* 3.15.12, in *The Discourses Books III–IV. Fragments. Encheiridion*, Greek with English trans. by W. A. Oldfather (Cambridge, Mass.: Harvard University Press, 2000), 103. See also Seneca *Ad Lucilium Epistulae Morales* 92.3, vol. 3, pp. 448–49: "Quid est beata vita? Securitas et perpetua tranquillitas [What is the happy life? It is peace of mind and lasting tranquillity]."

182. Cicero, *Tusculan Disputations* 5.40–1, 5.81–2.

183. Epictetus, *Discourses* 1.3.1–3; see also 2.9.1–3.

184. Cicero, *On the Nature of the Gods* 2.133, in Long and Sedley, *The Hellenistic Philosophers* 54N. See also Diogenes Laertius 7.138, pp. 242–43: Posidonius sees the cosmos as "a system constituted by gods and men and all things created for their sake."

185. See Epictetus, *Discourses* 1.16.1–5, p. 107: "The animals other than man have furnished them, ready prepared by nature, what pertains to their bodily needs. . . . Nature has made animals, which are born for service, ready for use, equipped, and in need of no further attention."

186. Epictetus, *Discourses* 2.10.3, pp. 268–69. An obvious challenge to the Stoic notion of providence is that some things appear *not* to exist for the sake of human beings, such as dangerous animals and diseases. See Porphyry, *On Abstinence* 3.20 and Lucretius, *De Rerum Natura* 5.218–21. This forces the Stoics to take the position (a "clumsy" one, Lactantius notes) that "among plants and animals there are many whose usefulness has up to now gone unnoticed; but . . . this will be discovered in the course of time, just as numerous things unknown in earlier centuries have been discovered by necessity and use." Lactantius, *On the Anger of God* 13.9–10 (SVF 2.1172), in Long and Sedley, *The Hellenistic Philosophers* 54R.

187. Epictetus, *Discourses* 2.10.3, p. 269; see also 1.9.2 and Cicero, *On Ends* 3.64.

188. Epictetus, *Discourses* 3.24.11, p. 187.

189. Long, *Epictetus*, 233–34.

190. Marcus Aurelius 5.16, in Long and Sedley, *The Hellenistic Philosophers* 63K.

191. The Stoics are not the first to use the term *oikeiosis*. On the meanings of *oikeiosis* in ancient philosophy, see S. G. Pembroke, "Oikeiosis," in *Problems in Stoicism*, ed. A. A. Long (London: University of London/Athlone Press, 1971), 115, 135.

192. Cicero, *On Ends* 3.16, pp. 232–33. Cicero's translations of *oikeiosis* are *commendatio* and *conciliatio*. See, e.g., *On Ends* 3.63.

193. Diogenes, Laertius 7.85, pp. 192–93.

194. Epictetus, *Discourses* 2.22.15–16, p. 387.

195. Cicero, *On Ends* 3.62, pp. 281–82.

196. Epictetus, *Discourses* 1.23.8, p. 147.

197. This characterization of the relationship between oneself and one's offspring is also offered by Plato (*Symposium* 207a–208b) and Aristotle (*On the Soul* 2.4 at 415a26–b2 and *Nicomachean Ethics* 8.12 at 1161b21–29).

198. See Cicero, *On Ends* 3.63, pp. 283–84, where Cicero discusses the symbiotic relationship between the sea-pen and the pinotes, and animals such as "the ant, the bee, the stork, [which] do certain actions for the sake of others besides themselves." The sea-pen is a mussel and the pinotes is a small crab that lives on the sea-pen and retreats into the sea-pen's shell in order to warn it of impending danger.

199. Cicero, *On Ends* 3.62–3, p. 283.

200. Hierocles (Stobaeus 4.671, 7–673,11), in Long and Sedley, *The Hellenistic Philosophers* 57G.

201. Cicero, *On Ends* 3.63, p. 283. Cf. 3.65, pp. 285–86: "We are born for society and intercourse, and for a natural partnership with our fellow men. Moreover nature inspires us with the desire to benefit as many people as we can, and especially by imparting information and the principles of wisdom."

202. Cicero, *On Duties* 1.107, in Long and Sedley, *The Hellenistic Philosophers* 66E.

203. Diogenes Laertius 7.129, p. 233 (referring to the views of Chrysippus and Posidonius).

204. Cicero, *On Ends* 3.67, p. 287 (describing Chrysippus's view).

205. Sextus Empiricus, *Against the Mathematicians* 9.131, in *Sextus Empiricus*, vol. 3, 70–71.

206. Sorabji points out that this does not really amount to a rejection of animal *rights*, because the Stoics do not possess the notion of a "right" in the modern sense. See *Animal Minds and Human Morals*, 134–57.

207. Ibid., 7.

Chapter 4: Classical Defenses of Animals

1. Seneca, *Natural Questions* 3, 18.3, in *Naturales Quaestiones I* (Seneca in Ten Volumes, vol. 7), Latin with English trans. by Thomas H. Corcoran (Cambridge, Mass.: Harvard University Press; London: William Heinemann, 1971), 243. See also 18.7, p. 245: Such people "are not content with their teeth and belly and mouth at the eating place; they are also gluttonous with their eyes [*oculis quoque gulosi sunt*]."

2. Plutarch, *On the Eating of Flesh* I, 995A, in *Moralia*, 551.

3. See *On the Eating of Flesh* 993C, 995A–B.

4. Charles Kahn notes that Plutarch's arguments against the Stoics "seem to have been originally developed by Carneades, in his skeptical attack on the Stoic dogma that animals are deprived of reason and therefore cannot belong to a moral community with human beings." *Pythagoras and the Pythagoreans*, 150–51.

5. Plutarch, *On the Eating of Flesh* I, 994E, in *Moralia*, 550.

6. See Max Schuster, *Untersuchungen zu Plutarchs Dialog "De sollertia animalium" mit besonderer Berücksichtigung der Lehrtätigkeit Plutarchs* (Augsburg: J. P. Himmer, 1917), 66; see also Haussleiter, *Der Vegetarismus in der Antike*, 227–28.

7. On the link to Shelley, see translator's preface to *On the Eating of Flesh*, in *Moralia*, 538. On several additional texts in which Plutarch discusses animals, see Damianos Tsekourakis, "Pythagoreanism or Platonism and Ancient Medicine? The Reasons for Vegetarianism in Plutarch's 'Moralia,'" in *Aufstieg und Niedergang der Römischen Welt: Geschichte und Kultur Roms im Spiegel der neueren Forschung* 2.36.1, ed. Wolfgang Haase, 366–93 (Berlin: De Gruyter, 1987).

8. *On the Cleverness of Animals* 959C, 962A, in *Moralia*, 321, 335.

9. Ibid., 963F–964A, in *Moralia*, 347.

10. Ibid., 964B, in *Moralia*, 349.

11. Ibid., 959C–D, in *Moralia*, 321.

12. Ibid., 959E-F, in *Moralia*, 323. See also *On the Eating of Flesh*, 995D-E, in *Moralia*, 555: "Note that the eating of flesh is not only physically against nature, but it also makes us spiritually coarse and gross by reason of satiety and surfeit." And 996D, p. 563: "It is indeed difficult, as Cato remarked, to talk to bellies which have no ears."

13. *On the Eating of Flesh* 994A, in *Moralia*, 545. See also 996A–B, p. 565: "It is not for nourishment or need or necessity, but out of satiety and insolence and luxury that they have turned this lawless custom [of meat eating] into a pleasure."

14. *On the Cleverness of Animals* 960C, in *Moralia*, 325–26.

15. Ibid., 960D, *Moralia*, 327–28. At 961A, Autobulus cites the Peripatetic philosopher Strato as authority for the view that "it is impossible to have sensation at all without some action of the intelligence." *Moralia*, 329. See also *Beasts Are Rational* 992D (in *Moralia*, 531) where Gryllus states that possession of soul is the basis for intelligence; hence animals are endowed with reason and intellect, whereas trees are not so endowed because they lack soul.

16. *On the Cleverness of Animals* 960E–F, in *Moralia*, 329.

17. Ibid., 961B–C, in *Moralia*, 331.

18. Ibid., 961D, in *Moralia*, 333.

19. Ibid., 962D, in *Moralia*, 339.

20. Ibid., 962F–963A, in *Moralia*, 341. Cf. 963D–E: Our willingness to speak of mad dogs or horses is a sign that we recognize a difference between healthy and unhealthy rational functioning in such animals. Rabies, for example, is "an affliction of [a dog's] natural organ of judgement and reason and memory." *Moralia*, 345–46.

21. *On the Cleverness of Animals* 963B, in *Moralia*, 343.

22. Ibid., 964F–965A, in *Moralia*, 353.

23. Ibid., 965B, in *Moralia*, 355. Plutarch presents some troubling examples of cruelty to animals in *On the Eating of Flesh* 997A.

24. Stephen R. L. Clark implicitly makes a strong case for this conclusion in "The Reality of Shared Emotions," in *Interpretation and Explanation in the Study of Animal Behavior*, vol. I, *Interpretation, Intentionality, and Communication*, ed. Marc Bekoff and Dale Jamieson, 449–72 (Boulder: Westview, 1990).

25. Plutarch argues that the dog does not draw an inference, but simply determines by scent the direction in which the prey ran. *On the Cleverness of Animals* 969B–C.

26. *On the Cleverness of Animals* 967E–F, in *Moralia*, 369–70.

27. Ibid., 966B, in *Moralia*, 361.

28. Ibid., 972C–D. This account of cooperation among lions is considerably more conservative, it should be noted, than the story told by Donald Griffin of an apparently remarkable case of cooperation among lions on the hunt. See Griffin, *Animal Minds*, 64–65.

29. *On the Cleverness of Animals* 978B–F, in *Moralia*, 433–37.

30. Ibid., 980A–981A.

31. Ibid., 984A–C, in *Moralia*, 469–73. The latter part of *On the Cleverness of Animals* takes the form of two discourses, one asserting the superiority of land animals and the other the superiority of sea animals. The attribution of such capacities to dolphins as the singular ability to "love man for his own sake" occurs in the latter set of arguments, hence its exaggerated character. The dialogue ends without any resolution of the question which type of animal is more intelligent.

32. *On the Cleverness of Animals* 968C–D, in *Moralia*, 373–75. Here Plutarch says that elephants exhibit a spontaneity of feeling and movement that reflects their understanding [σύνεσις].

33. Ibid., 970C–D, in *Moralia*, 385–87.

34. Ibid., 972B, in *Moralia*, 395–97. Here elephants are said even to pray to the gods; this suggestion is part of the argument for the superiority of land animals, so, like the remark cited above about dolphins, it must be treated with caution.

35. Ibid., 974F, in *Moralia*, 411.

36. Ibid., 979E–F, in *Moralia*, 443.

37. Ibid., 974D–E, in *Moralia*, 411.

38. Ibid., 974B, D (medicine and surgery); 969D–F, in *Moralia*, 379–83 (one dog identified his master's murderers, another pursued a thief at length); 971C–D, 978A–B, F, in *Moralia*, 391–93, 431–33, 437 (deception in partridges, hares, cuttlefish, and octopus); 967A, in *Moralia*, 365 (ingenuity of Libyan crows).

39. *On the Cleverness of Animals* 971B–C, in *Moralia*, 389–90.

40. Ibid., 973A–B; cf. Aristotle, *History of Animals* 4 at 536b17 and chapter 2 above.

41. *On the Cleverness of Animals* 973A-B, in *Moralia*, 401. This enables birds to "cherish the beautiful in their utterance rather than the useful."

42. Ibid., 976A–B, in *Moralia*, 417–18.

43. Ibid., 973A–E, in *Moralia*, 402–3.

44. Ibid., 961D, in *Moralia*, 333. See also 961E–F, p. 335, where Autobulus rejects as "contrary to plain evidence" the Stoic claim that animals simply behave "as if" they had perception and emotion.

45. Ibid., 972D–F, in *Moralia*, 397–99.

46. Ibid., 968D–E, in *Moralia*, 375 (indignation); 970A–B, in *Moralia*, 383 (sympathy); 966B, in *Moralia*, 361 (gratitude); 969D–F, in *Moralia*, 379–83 (vengefulness).

47. Ibid., 962D, in *Moralia*, 339.

48. Ibid., 970E, in *Moralia*, 387 (probity); 977B, in *Moralia*, 425 (courage); 982F, in *Moralia*, 461–63 (wisdom); 983A, in *Moralia*, 463 (fidelity); 969C, in *Moralia*, 379 (self-control, obedience, and sagacity).

49. *Beasts are Rational* 989C, 989F, in *Moralia*, 513–17.

50. Ibid., 991C–D, in *Moralia*, 525.

51. Ibid., 992E, in *Moralia*, 531–32. Cf. p. 532n: Helmbold notes that this may not actually be the end of the dialogue, but that the end of the dialogue may have been lost.

52. 994E, in *Moralia*, 549; see also 994B, p. 547: "Nature appears to have produced [animals, at least tame ones] for the sake of their beauty and grace."

53. *Tier und Mensch im Denken der Antike*, p. 274.

54. *On the Eating of Flesh* 997B–D, in *Moralia*, 565–69.

55. Ibid., 997E; see also 998B.

56. *On the Cleverness of Animals* 983F, in *Moralia*, 467–68.

57. Ibid., 998D, in *Moralia*, 575.

58. Ibid., 999A, in *Moralia*, 579.

59. Plutarch, *Life of Marcus Cato* 5.2, in *Plutarch's Lives*, vol. 2, Greek with English trans. by Bernadotte Perrin (Cambridge, Mass.: Harvard University Press; London: William Heinemann, 1985), 317.

60. Introductory notes to *On the Eating of Flesh*, in *Moralia*, 537.

61. *On Abstinence from Killing Animals* 1.31.3, 1.30.4, pp. 42–43. Cf. Saint Augustine, *City of God* 10.29, in *The City of God Against the Pagans*, ed. and trans. R. W. Dyson (Cambridge: Cambridge University Press, 1998), 437: Porphyry "teaches that the soul must leave behind all union with a body in order that the soul may dwell in blessedness with God," a view with which Augustine disagrees on the grounds that it incorrectly devalues God's creation and contradicts Scripture.

62. *On Abstinence from Killing Animals* 1.34.5, p. 44. Cf. 1.38.1, pp. 45–46, where Porphyry implies that, ideally, we would not eat any food at all.

63. See ibid., 1.27.1, 2.4.3, pp. 40, 55.

64. Ibid., 1.13–24, pp. 36–39. On the naturalness of meat, see 1.13.2, p. 36; on war between man and beast, see 1.14.1, p. 36.

65. Ibid., 1.19–21, p. 38.

66. Ibid., 1.25.1, 1.26.1–2, pp. 39, 40. Diogenes Laertius (8.12) reports that Pythagoras is said to have been the first to train athletes on a diet of meat.

67. *On Abstinence from Killing Animals* 1.27.1, p. 40.

68. Ibid., 1.28.4, p. 41.

69. Ibid., 1.28.3; cf. Aristotle, *Metaphysics* 1.1–2 at 981b14–983a23 and *Nicomachean Ethics* 10.8 at 1177b15–1178a7.

70. Haussleiter notes that this ideal "towers above all other motivations" offered in the text for dietary discipline. *Der Vegetarismus in der Antike*, 326.

71. *On Abstinence from Killing Animals* 1.47.2, p. 50.

72. Ibid., 1.51.6–1.52.1, 1.57.2–4, pp. 51, 54.

73. According to Gillian Clark, this emphasis on strict spiritual discipline "suggests the suicidal depression that afflicted Porphyry in the late 260s, which may have been intensified by Plotinus's death and the dispersal of his students." Gillian Clark, "Philosophic Lives and the Philosophic Life: Porphyry and Iamblichus," in *Greek Biography and Panegyric in Late Antiquity*, ed. Tomas Hägg and Philip Rousseau (Berkeley: University of California Press, 2000), 40.

74. *On Abstinence from Killing Animals* 2.1, 2.4.2, 2.4.3.

75. Nussbaum, *The Fragility of Goodness*, 37. See also Walter Burkert, "Greek Tragedy and Sacrificial Ritual," *Greek, Roman, and Byzantine Studies* 7 (1966): 87–121.

76. Plutarch, *Moralia*, 322n. On Porphyry's account, the supposed "consent" occurs when an animal bows its head to drink holy water that has been placed before it. *On Abstinence from Killing Animals* 2.9.3, p. 58.

77. *On Abstinence from Killing Animals* 2.5–2.6, pp. 56–57.

78. Ibid., 2.7.3, p. 57.

79. Ibid., 2.10.3, p. 58.

80. Ibid., 2.12.1–2.15.3, pp. 59–60. See also 2.25.7, p. 65: We tend to sacrifice animals that provide us, not the gods, with enjoyment.

81. At 2.61.2, p. 79, Porphyry says that honoring the gods should be like giving up one's seat to a good man, not like paying taxes.

82. Ibid., 2.22.1, p. 63. Theophrastus, too, believes in a "community of justice between human beings and animals." Dierauer, *Tier und Mensch im Denken der Antike*, 177.

83. *On Abstinence from Killing Animals* 2.28.2–3, p. 66. At 2.36.1, Porphyry says that the Pythagoreans sacrificed numbers and lines to the gods.

84. Ibid., 2.32.1, p. 68.

85. Ibid., 2.31.3, p. 68.

86. Ibid., 2.38.1–2.40.1, 2.42.3, pp. 70–73.

87. Ibid., 3.1.4, p. 80.

88. Ibid., 3.2.4, pp. 80–81.

89. Ibid., 3.3.3–4, p. 81.

90. Ibid., 3.3.6, 3.4.4, pp. 81–82.

91. Ibid., 3.9–10. Cf. 3.21.4, p. 92: "Every animate creature is *ipso facto* sentient."

92. Ibid., 3.10.4–5, p. 86 (sexual temperance), 3.11.1, p. 87 (marital chastity), 3.12.2, p. 87 (society with humans), 3.12.4, p. 87 (hostility toward humans).

93. Ibid., 3.21.6, p. 93.

94. Ibid., 3.19.2, p. 91.

95. Ibid., 3.20.3, p. 91.

96. Ibid., 3.20.4, p. 91. Lucretius attributes this argument to Epicurus; see *De rerum natura* (*On the Nature of Things*) 5.218–220. Lucretius, *On the Nature of Things*, Latin with English translation by W. H. D. Rouse, revised by Martin Ferguson Smith (Cambridge, Mass.: Harvard University Press, 1997), 395–97.

97. *On Abstinence from Killing Animals* 3.20.6, p. 92.

98. Ibid., 3.22–3.23, pp. 93–95.

99. Ibid., 3.23.8, p. 95.

100. Ibid., 3.18.3.

101. Ibid., 3.26.2, p. 97.

102. Ibid., 3.26.5–3.26.6.

103. Ibid., 4.1.1–4.1.2, 4.2.1, p. 100.

104. Ibid., 4.2.4–4.2.7.

105. Ibid., 4.5.2, p. 103. Cf. 4.3.3, p. 102: One measure employed by Lycurgus to discourage interest in wealth was to make money out of iron and to make it very large, "so that for the equivalent of ten minae you would need a large storeroom in the house and a team to carry it."

106. Ibid., 4.6.2–4.6.3, p. 104.

107. Ibid., 4.9.1–4.9.2, p. 106.

108. Ibid., 4.9.7, 4.9.9, 4.10.1, p. 107.

109. See ibid., 4.16.2, p. 112; cf. 1.6.3, p. 33, and 1.19.1–1.19.3, p. 38.

110. Ibid., 4.18.10, p. 115.

111. Ibid., 4.21.1, 4.20.7, pp. 116–17.

112. Ibid., 4.21.6, p. 118.

113. Ibid., 4.20.13, p. 117.

114. Ibid., 1.45.1, pp. 48–49.

115. Lawrence A. Babb, *Absent Lord: Ascetics and Kings in a Jain Ritual Culture* (Berkeley: University of California Press, 1996), 10.

Chapter 5: The Status of Animals in Medieval Christianity

1. Lynn White Jr., "The Historical Roots of Our Ecological Crisis," *Ecology and Religion in History*, ed. David Spring and Eileen Spring (New York: Harper Torchbooks, 1974), 24.

2. Ibid., 26.

3. Ibid., 28. On the ancient ideal of tree worship, see Sir James George Frazer, *The Golden Bough: A Study in Magic and Religion* (New York: Macmillan, 1922).

4. John Milton, *Paradise Lost*, ed. Roy Flannagan (New York: Macmillan, 1993), bk. 4, lines 331–40, p. 264; see also bk. 5, lines 303–7, p. 313 (vegetarian diet).

5. John Passmore, *Man's Responsibility for Nature: Ecological Problems and Western Traditions* (London: Duckworth, 1974), 6.

6. Ibid., 12–15.

7. Joseph Rickaby, S.J., *Moral Philosophy; or, Ethics and Natural Law* (London: Longmans, Green, and Co., 1912), 248–51.

8. James Gaffney, "Can Catholic Morality Make Room for Animals?" in *Animals on the Agenda: Questions about Animals for Theology and Ethics*, ed. Andrew Linzey and Dorothy Yamamoto (Urbana: University of Illinois Press, 1998), 104–5.

9. Contemporary scholarship has established that the early books of the Bible were composed of writings by three authors: the Yahwist, the Elohist, and the Priestly Writer(s). The orientations of these writers are very different; the Priestly Writer(s) emphasize human superiority over nature, while the Yahwist promotes a sense of community and continuity between human beings and nature. See Hiebert, *The Yahwist's Landscape*.

10. See in particular Romans 2:29, 8:5–8, 9:31–32, and 13:5; Mark 7:15–16; and Matthew 6:25, 6:33, 10:28.

11. Augustine, *The City of God against the Pagans*, ed. and trans. R. W. Dyson (Cambridge: Cambridge University Press, 1998), bk. 11, ch. 18, p. 471.

12. Augustine, *Eighty-Three Different Questions*, trans. David L. Mosher, Fathers of the Church, vol. 70 (Washington, D. C.: Catholic University of America Press, 1982), q. 9, p. 41.

13. Augustine, *The Teacher*, in *Against the Academicians and The Teacher*, trans. Peter King (Indianapolis: Hackett, 1995), sec. 12.40, p. 140.

14. Augustine, *On Free Choice of the Will*, trans. Thomas Williams (Indianapolis: Hackett, 1993), bk. 2, sec. 13, p. 56.

15. Augustine, *Tractates on the Gospel of John 28–54*, trans. John W. Rettig, Fathers of the Church, vol. 88 (Washington, D.C.: Catholic University of America Press, 1993), Tractate 29, sec. 6.2, p. 18.

16. Augustine, *Confessions*, trans. R. S. Pine-Coffin (London: Penguin, 1961), bk. 7, sec. 17, p. 151. Cf. bk. 10, sec. 17, p. 224: Animals have memory of sensory particulars but are incapable of the inward reflection that discloses God to human beings.

17. *On Free Choice of the Will*, bk. 1, sec. 8, p. 14; see also *City of God*, bk. 19, ch. 14, p. 940.

18. *On Free Choice of the Will*, bk. 1, sec. 9, p. 15; *Confessions*, bk. 10, sec. 31, p. 235.

19. *City of God*, bk.7, ch. 23, p. 294; Augustine, Letter 18, to Coelestinus, in *The Essential Augustine*, ed. Vernon J. Bourke (Indianapolis: Hackett, 1974), p. 46.

20. *City of God*, bk. 19, ch. 14, p. 941.

21. Augustine, *On Music*, in *The Immortality of the Soul, The Magnitude of the Soul, On Music, The Advantage of Believing, and On Faith in Things Unseen*, trans. Ludwig Schopp et al., Fathers of the Church, vol. 4 (Washington, D.C.: Catholic University of America Press, 1992), ch. 13, sec. 41, p. 365; see also ch. 15, sec. 50, p. 372.

22. *Confessions*, bk. 7, sec. 12–13, pp. 148–49.

23. Ibid., bk. 7, sec. 10, p. 147 and bk. 7, sec. 16, p. 151. See also *On Music*, 368: "The body also is a creature of God and is adorned with its own beauty, although of the lowest kind."

24. *Confessions*, bk. 10, sec. 35, p. 243. Moreover, Augustine believes that we can learn from the example of animals what we must do for the sake of our salvation; see Gillian Clark, "The Fathers and the Animals: The Rule of Reason?" in *Animals on the Agenda*, ed. Andrew Linzey and Dorothy Yamamoto, 67–79 (Urbana: University of Illinois Press, 1998), 73.

25. *Confessions*, bk. 10, sec. 28–29, pp. 232–33.

26. *On Free Choice of the Will*, bk. 2, sec. 18, p. 68.

27. *Confessions*, bk. 10, sec. 31, p. 235. Cf. bk. 10, sec. 35, p. 241: Even the curiosity of scientific theory counts as "gratification of the eye" [*concupiscentia oculorum*]. Thus the systematic scientific investigation of animals and other natural beings advocated by Bacon and Descartes would be anathema to Augustine.

28. Ibid, bk. 10, sec. 29, p. 233.

29. *City of God*, bk. 5, ch. 19, p. 224.

30. *Confessions*, bk. 2, sec. 3, p. 45; see also bk. 10, sec. 36, p. 244.

31. *Eighty-Three Different Questions*, q. 30, p. 57; q. 5, p. 39.

32. *City of God*, bk. 19, ch. 15, p. 942.

33. Ibid., bk. 1, ch. 20, p. 32. Here Augustine criticizes the Manichaeans for extending "this commandment [against killing] even to beasts and cattle."

34. Augustine, *The Catholic and Manichaean Ways of Life*, trans. Donald A. Gallagher and Idella J. Gallagher, Fathers of the Church, vol. 56 (Washington, D.C.: Catholic University of America Press, 1966), bk. 2, ch. 17, sec. 54, p. 102.

35. *Confessions*, bk. 10, sec. 31, p. 237.

36. *The Catholic and Manichaean Ways of Life*, bk. 2, ch. 17, sec. 59, p. 105. See also bk. 2, ch. 17, sec. 54, p. 102, where Augustine interprets the biblical story of the Gerasene swine (Matthew 8:28–34, Mark 5:1–20, Luke 8:26–39) as a confirmation that there is no "community of rights" between human beings and animals.

37. See Isaac's *Mystic Treatises*, cited in Vladimir Lossky, *The Mystical Theology of the Eastern Church* (Crestwood, N.Y.: St. Vladimir's Seminary Press, 1976), III. On the ideal of *caritas* (translated as "charity" in the King James Bible and as "love" in the New and Revised English Bibles) see I Corinthians 13:1–6.

38. Origen, *Contra Celsum*, trans. Henry Chadwick (Cambridge: Cambridge University Press, 1980), bk. I, sec. 74, pp. 242–43.

39. Ibid, bk. 4, sec. 85, p. 251.

40. Ibid, bk. 4, sec. 81, p. 249.

41. Ibid, bk. 4, sec. 78, p. 246. See also bk. 4, sec. 99, pp. 262–63.

42. Ibid, bk. 4, sec. 99, p. 263.

43. Ibid, bk. 4, sec. 78, p. 246.

44. Origen, *Homilies on Genesis*, in *Homilies on Genesis and Exodus*, trans. Ronald E. Heine, Fathers of the Church, vol. 71 (Washington, D.C.: Catholic University of America Press, 1982), homily I, sec. II, p. 60.

45. Ibid, homily I, sec. 13, p. 63.

46. Ibid, homily I, sec. 16, p. 69.

47. *Contra Celsum*, bk. 4, sec. 78, p. 246.

48. J. C. M. Van Winden, "Hexaemeron," in *Reallexikon für Antike und Christentum: Sachwörterbuch zur Auseinandersetzung des Christentums mit der antiken Welt*, vol. 14, pp. 1250–70 (Stuttgart: Hiersemann, 1988).

49. Giet, "Introduction," Basil of Caesarea, *Homélies sur l'Hexaéméron*, Greek with French translation, intro. and trans. Stanislas Giet, 2d ed. (Paris: Cerf, 1968), 18. Basil says that his "one aim" is "the edification of the Church" in *Homilies on the Hexaemeron*, in *Exegetic Homilies*, trans. Sister Agnes Clare Way, Fathers of the Church, vol. 46 (Washington, D.C.: Catholic University of America Press, 1963), homily 7, sec. 6, p. 114.

50. *Homilies on the Hexaemeron*, homily 7, sec. 3, p. 110 (Giet 406).

51. Ibid., homily 8, sec. I, p. 118.

52. Ibid., homily 8, sec. 2, p. 119 (making implicit reference to Leviticus 17:11).

53. Ibid.

54. Ibid., homily 9, sec. 3, p. 139.

55. Ibid., homily 9, sec. 5, p. 145.

56. Ibid., homily 7, sec. 6, p. 115; see also homily 8, sec. 8, p. 132.

57. Ibid., homily 9, sec. 3, p. 138; homily 7, sec. 3, p. 109.

58. Ibid., homily 7, sec. 3, p. 109.

59. Ibid., homily 7, sec. 4, p. 112.

60. Ibid., homily 9, sec. 3, p. 140.

61. Ibid., homily 9, sec. 6, p. 146.

62. Donald Attwater, *St. John Chrysostom: Pastor and Preacher* (London: Harvill, 1959), 59–60.

63. Saint John Chrysostom, *Homilies on Genesis 1–17*, trans. Robert C. Hill, Fathers of the Church, vol. 74 (Washington, D.C.: Catholic University of America Press, 1986), homily 8, sec. 4, p. 107.

64. Ibid., homily 7, sec. 15, p. 100.

65. Ibid., homily 7, sec. 12, p. 98.

66. Ibid., homily 8, sec. 18, p. 115. Here Chrysostom appeals to Galatians 2:20: "I am alive, though it is no longer me but Christ alive in me."

67. Saint John Chrysostom, *Homilies on Genesis 18–45*, trans. Robert C. Hill, Fathers of the Church, vol. 82 (Washington, D.C.: Catholic University of America Press, 1990), homily 26, sec. 10, p. 151.

68. Ibid., homily 28, sec. 5, p. 186.

69. Ibid., homily 28, sec. 7, p. 188.

70. Saint John Chrysostom, *Address on Vainglory and the Right Way for Parents to Bring Up Their Children*, in M. L. W. Laistner, *Christianity and Pagan Culture in the Later Roman Empire Together with An English Translation of John Chrysostom's Address on Vainglory and the Right Way for Parents to Bring Up Their Children* (Ithaca: Cornell University Press, 1967), sec. 90, p. 122. On the permissibility of meat eating, see sec. 43, p. 105 and *Homilies on Genesis 18–45*, homily 27, sec. 12, p. 172.

71. Andrew Linzey, *Christianity and the Rights of Animals* (New York: Crossroad, 1987), 17.

72. Passmore, *Man's Responsibility for Nature*, 112.

73. *Lives of St. Francis by Thomas of Celano*, "First Life," ch. 21, sec. 58, in *St. Francis of Assisi, Writings and Early Biographies: English Omnibus of the Sources for the Life of St. Francis*, ed. Marion A. Habig, 2 vols. (Quincy, Ill.: Franciscan Press, 1991), 1:278. See also *Little Flowers of St. Francis*, part 1, sec. 16, in *Writings and Early Biographies*, 2:1336–37.

74. *Little Flowers of St. Francis*, part 1, sec. 40, in *Writings and Early Biographies*, 2:1391, 2:1393.

75. *Lives of St. Francis by St. Bonaventure*, "Major Life," ch. 8, sec. 7, in *Writings and Early Biographies*, 1:693.

76. See Celano, "First Life," ch. 29, sec. 80, in *Writings and Early Biographies*, 1:296 (worms and bees); Bonaventure, "Major Life," ch. 8, sec. 6, in *Writings and Early Biographies*, 1:692 (lambs); Celano, "First Life," ch. 21, sec. 61, in *Writings and Early Biographies*, 1:280 (fish).

77. See *Legend of Perugia*, sec. 51, in *Writings and Early Biographies*, 2:1029 ("our sisters the flowers"); *Mirror of Perfection*, sec. 118–20, in *Writings and Early Biographies*, 2:1256–60 (moon, water, sun, fire).

78. *Mirror of Perfection*, sec. 115, in *Writings and Early Biographies*, 2:1255.

79. See *Admonition 18*, in *Writings and Early Biographies*, 1:84 (compassion for one's neighbor); *Admonition 25*, in *Writings and Early Biographies*, 1:86 (love of one's brother); "Letter to All the Faithful," in *Writings and Early Biographies*, 1:95 (love of one's enemies).

80. *Writings and Early Biographies*, 1:130.

81. *Writings and Early Biographies*, 1:134.

82. *The Rule of the Third Order*, "First Rule," ch. 2, in *Writings and Early Biographies*, 1:169. (Francis's own version of this rule has been lost, but Cardinal Ugolino's rewriting of the rule in 1221 is considered to contain the substance of Francis's version and thus is published among Francis's own writings.) See also *Mirror of Perfection*, sec. 42, in *Writings and Early Biographies*, 2:1167: "Blessed Francis was not ashamed to obtain meat for a sick friar."

83. *The Life of Brother Juniper*, ch. 1, in *The Little Flowers of St. Francis of Assisi* (Paterson, N.J.: St. Anthony Guild Press, 1958), 256.

84. Saint Thomas Aquinas, *Summa Theologica* 1, q. 65, art. 2, resp., in *Basic Writings of St. Thomas Aquinas*, ed. Anton C. Pegis, 2 vols. (Indianapolis: Hackett, 1997), 1:612.

85. Saint Thomas Aquinas, *Quaestiones disputatae de veritate*, q. 5, art. 8, resp., in *Truth*, trans. Robert W. Mulligan, James V. McGlynn, and Robert W. Schmidt, 3 vols. (Indianapolis: Hackett, 1995), 1:233. See also *Summa Contra Gentiles* 3, ch. 97, in *Basic Writings*, 2:189: "Things are arranged by divine providence according to a plan. . . . Now the closer a thing approaches the divine likeness, the more perfect it is."

86. Saint Thomas Aquinas, *Summa Contra Gentiles* 3, ch. 3, in *Basic Writings*, 2:8.

87. Aquinas, *Summa Theologica* 1, q. 115, art. 6, resp., in *Basic Writings*, 1:1066.

88. Aquinas, *Summa Contra Gentiles* 3, ch. 22, in *Basic Writings*, 2:36. Cf. *Summa Theologica* 1, q. 22, art. 2, repl. obj. 2, in *Basic Writings*, 1:233: "Man is not the author of nature, but he uses natural things for his own purposes in his works of art and virtue."

89. St. Thomas Aquinas, *Commentary on the Metaphysics of Aristotle*, trans. John P. Rowan, 2 vols. (Chicago: Regnery, 1961), 1:11.

90. Aquinas, *Summa Theologica* 2–2, q. 2, art. 3, resp., in *Basic Writings*, 2:1078 (emphasis in original).

91. Aquinas, *Summa Theologica* 1, q. 78, art. 4, resp., in *Basic Writings*, 1:742.

92. Ibid. See also *De veritate*, q. 25, art. 2, resp., in *Truth*, 3:220: "It is accordingly in virtue of the estimative power that animals are said to have a sort of prudence. . . . A sheep, for example, flees from a wolf whose hostility it has never sensed." Aquinas takes the sheep-wolf example from Avicenna, who believes that the sheep is capable of abstraction. Judith Barad argues that Aquinas follows Avicenna in this belief; but for reasons that will become clear presently, this is an implausible interpretation of Aquinas's position. See Judith Barad, *Aquinas on the Nature and Treatment of Animals* (San Francisco: International Scholars, 1995), 97.

93. Aquinas, *De veritate*, q. 22, art 4, resp., in *Truth*, 3:47.

94. Aquinas, *Summa Theologica* 1–2, q. 6, art. 2, resp., in *Basic Writings*, 2:229; q. 13, art. 2, repl. obj. 2, in *Basic Writings*, 2:280.

95. Aquinas, *Summa Theologica* 1–2, q. 13, art. 2, repl. obj. 3, in *Basic Writings*, 2:281.

96. Aquinas, *Summa Theologica* 1–2, q. 13, art. 2, resp., in *Basic Writings*, 2:280.

97. Aquinas, *Summa Theologica* 1–2, q. 40, art. 3, repl. obj. 1, in *The 'Summa Theologica' of St. Thomas Aquinas*, trans. Fathers of the English Dominican Province, 22 vols. (London: Burns Oats and Washbourne, 1920–1925), 6:460.

98. Aquinas, *Summa Theologica* 1, q. 78, art. 4, resp., in *Basic Writings* 2:742.

99. Aquinas, *Summa Theologica* 1–2, q. 6, art. 2, repl. obj. 3, in *Basic Writings* 2:229; *Summa Theologica* 1–2, q. 91, art. 2, repl. obj. 3, in *Basic Writings* 2:750.

100. Aquinas, *De veritate*, q. 24, art. 2, resp., in *Truth*, 3:146.

101. Ibid., ans. to diff. 3, in *Truth*, 3:147.

102. Ibid., ans. to diff. 6, in *Truth*, 3:147.

103. Aquinas, *De veritate*, q. 24, art. 1, resp., in *Truth*, 3:138.

104. Thomas Aquinas, *Commentary on the Posterior Analytics of Aristotle*, trans. F. R. Larcher (Albany: Magi, 1970), bk. 2, lecture 20, p. 237.

105. Thomas Aquinas, *Summa Contra Gentiles*, bk. 2, ch. 82 (Turin: Casa Editrice Marietti, 1946), 193: "Nulla igitur est operatio animae brutorum quae possit esse sine corpore."

106. Aquinas, *Summa Theologica* 1, q. 75, art. 6, resp., in *Basic Writings*, 1:692.

107. Aquinas, *Summa Theologica* 1–2, q. 96, art. 1, resp., in *Basic Writings*, 1:918.

108. Aquinas, *Summa Theologica* 1–2, q. 102, art. 6, repl. obj. 8, in *Basic Writings*, 2:905.

109. Aquinas, *Summa Contra Gentiles* 3, ch. 92, in *Basic Writings*, 2:222.

110. Aquinas, *Summa Theologica* 2–2, q. 64, art. 1, resp. and repl. obj. 1, 2, in *The 'Summa Theologica' of St. Thomas Aquinas*, 10:196.

111. Ibid., repl. obj. 3, p. 197.

112. Aquinas, *Summa Theologica* 1–2, q. 102, art. 6, in *Basic Writings*, 2:904.

113. Ibid.

114. Aquinas, *Summa Contra Gentiles* 3, ch. 92, in *Basic Writings*, 2:222.

115. Luther's *Lectures on Genesis* are particularly revealing in this connection. See Martin Luther, *Luther's Works*, vol. 2, *Lectures on Genesis Ch. 6–14*, ed. Jaroslav Pelikan and Daniel E. Poellot, trans. George V. Schick (St. Louis: Concordia, 1960), 133: In granting a carnivorous diet to Noah, "God sets himself up as a butcher; for with His Word He slaughters and kills the animals that are suited for food, in order to make up, as it were, for the great sorrow that pious Noah experienced during the flood. . . . It is a great liberty that with impunity man may kill and eat animals of every edible kind. . . . Animals are made subject to man for the purpose of serving him even to the extent of dying." And p. 142: Genesis "gives permission to slaughter animals for religious and private purposes but utterly forbids the killing of human beings, because man was created according to the image of God." See also *Luther's Works*, vol. 1, *Lectures on Genesis Ch. 1–5*, ed. Jaroslav Pelikan, trans. George V. Schick (St. Louis: Concordia, 1958), 81: "Man was created not for this physical life only, like the other animals, but for eternal life, just as God, who has ordered and ordained these practices, is eternal."

Chapter 6: Descartes on the Moral Status of Animals

1. "Caeterum a nulla tuarum opinionum animus meus, pro ea qua est mollitie ac teneritudine, aeque abhorret, ac ab internecina illa & iugulatrice sententia, quam in Methodo tulisti, brutis omnibus vitam sensumque eripiens." Henry More, letter to Descartes, December 11, 1648, *Oeuvres de Descartes* (cited hereafter as *Oeuvres* plus volume and page number), ed. Charles Adam and Paul Tannery, 12 vols. (Paris: Vrin, 1964–74), 5:243. For a translation of Descartes's correspondence with More concerning animal nature that includes the letter cited here, see Leonora D. Cohen, "Descartes and Henry More on the Beast-Machine—A Translation of Their Correspondence Pertaining to Animal Automatism," *Annals of Science: A Quarterly Review of the History of Science Since the Renaissance* 1 (1936): 48–61.

2. Descartes, *Discourse on Method*, *Oeuvres* 6:56–60, in *The Philosophical Writings of Descartes* (cited hereafter as *Philosophical Writings* plus volume and page number), ed. John Cottingham et al., 3 vols. (Cambridge: Cambridge University Press, 1984–91), 1:139–41.

3. See A. Boyce Gibson, *The Philosophy of Descartes* (New York: Garland, 1987), 214; and Norman Kemp Smith, *New Studies in the Philosophy of Descartes* (New York: Russell and Russell, 1963), 136.

4. Stephen Voss has suggested that Descartes touches upon as many as seven different criteria for distinguishing animals from human beings, namely life, soul, sensation, passions, thought, reason, and the use of language. Descartes, *The Passions of the Soul*, trans. Stephen H. Voss (Indianapolis: Hackett, 1989), 48n53. One implication of the following discussion is that these seven criteria actually resolve themselves into more basic ones; for example, it will become clear that for Descartes, thought and reason are not two different criteria but instead refer to the same criterion.

5. John Cottingham, "'A Brute to the Brutes?' Descartes's Treatment of Animals," *Philosophy* 53 (1978): 551–59.

6. Peter Harrison, "Descartes on Animals," *Philosophical Quarterly* 42 (1992): 219–27.

7. Stephen Gaukroger, *Descartes: An Intellectual Biography* (Oxford: Clarendon Press, 1995), 166, 278–90, 349.

8. Cottingham, "'A Brute to the Brutes?'" 559; Harrison, "Descartes on Animals," 227.

9. *Discourse on Method*, part 6, *Oeuvres* 6:62, *Philosophical Writings* 1:142 (translation altered).

10. See *Principles of Philosophy*, part 1, sections 19, 23–27, 54, 63; Third and Fourth Meditations; letter to More, February 5, 1649, *Oeuvres* 5:269–70, *Philosophical Writings* 3:361; and letter to More, April 15, 1649, *Oeuvres* 5:343, *Philosophical Writings* 3:373.

11. George Boas, *The Happy Beast in French Thought of the Seventeenth Century* (New York: Octagon Books, 1966), 1. Boas provides a detailed account of animal-friendly views in the seventeenth century, notably including the views of Montaigne's disciple Charron; see pp. 56–63.

12. Giovanni Battista Gelli, *Circe. Consisting of Ten Dialogues between Ulysses and several men transformed into beasts, satirically representing the various passions of mankind and the many infelicities of human life* (1549), trans. Thomas Brown, revised trans. and intro. Robert Adams (Ithaca: Cornell University Press, 1963). On Plutarch's *Gryllus* (*Bruta animalia ratione uti*), see chapter 4 above.

13. Gelli, *Circe*, 166. On Aquinas's treatment of the sheep-wolf example, see chapter 5 above. On Descartes's treatment of this example, see below.

14. Gelli, *Circe*, 168.

15. Ibid., 3. Cf. Giovanni Pico della Mirandola, *Oration on the Dignity of Man* (1486?), in *The Renaissance Philosophy of Man*, ed. Ernst Cassirer, Paul Oskar Kristeller, and John Herman Randall Jr. (Chicago: University of Chicago Press, 1948), 225: "Whatever seeds each man cultivates will grow to maturity and bear in him their own fruit. If they be vegetative, he will be like a plant. If sensitive, he will become

brutish. If rational, he will grow into a heavenly being. If intellectual, he will be an angel and the son of God. And if, happy in the lot of no created thing, he withdraws into the center of his own unity, his spirit, made one with God, in the solitary darkness of God, who is set above all things, shall surpass them all. Who would not admire this our chameleon?"

16. Adams, "Introduction" to Gelli, *Circe*, xxx.

17. See, e.g., Gelli, *Circe*, 167.

18. More unequivocal in its defense of animals is the work of Gelli's contemporary Rorarius. See the entry "Rorarius" in Pierre Bayle, *Historical and Critical Dictionary* (1702), trans. Richard Popkin with the assistance of Craig Bush (Indianapolis: Bobbs-Merrill, 1965), 213–54.

19. Michel de Montaigne, *Essays. Travel Journals. Letters*, trans. Donald M. Frame (Stanford: Stanford University Press, 1957), "Of Pedantry," 100; "Of Cannibals," 152.

20. Montaigne, *Essays*, "Of Cannibals," 153.

21. Montaigne, *Essays*, *Apology for Raymond Seybond*, "Man is no better than the Animals," 330–58; "Of Cruelty," 318.

22. Montaigne, *Essays*, "Of Cruelty," 317.

23. Montaigne, *Essays*, "Of Cruelty," 317–18.

24. Montaigne, *Essays*, *Apology for Raymond Seybond*, 358. At the same time, Montaigne asserts "that the elephants have some participation in religion" and that "we cannot . . . prove that [other animals] are without religion and cannot grasp any part of what is hidden from us." Ibid., 343.

25. *Oeuvres* 6:59, *Philosophical Writings* 1:141.

26. *Oeuvres* 6:57, *Philosophical Writings* 1:140.

27. *Oeuvres* 6:57–58, *Philosophical Writings* 1:140. On Descartes's conception of language and his reasons for denying language to mechanisms, see Margaret Wilson, "Cartesian Dualism," in *Descartes: Critical and Interpretive Essays*, ed. Michael Hooker (Baltimore: Johns Hopkins University Press, 1978), 203; and Jean-Pierre Séris, "Language and Machine in the Philosophy of Descartes," in *Essays on the Philosophy and Science of René Descartes*, ed. Stephen Voss, 177–92 (New York: Oxford University Press, 1993).

28. *Oeuvres* 6:59, *Philosophical Writings* 1:141.

29. Descartes to Reneri for Pollot, April or May 1638, *Oeuvres* 2:41, *Philosophical Writings* 3:99.

30. *Oeuvres* 2:41, *Philosophical Writings* 3:100.

31. Leibniz, for example, believed that animals cannot employ abstract reason, but can use memory only empirically to anticipate the immediate consequences of a familiar event; see *Monadology*, sections 24–29 (where Leibniz altogether denies that animals reason); and *New Essays on Human Understanding*, "Preface" and bk. 2, ch. 11, sec. 11 (where Leibniz says that animals can reason about particular ideas). G. W. Leibniz, *Monadology*, in *Philosophical Essays*, trans. Roger Ariew and Daniel Garber (Indianapolis: Hackett, 1989), 216–17; *New Essays on Human Understanding*, trans. and ed. Peter Remnant and Jonathan Bennet (Cambridge: Cambridge University Press, 1996), 50, 143. On Hobbes, Locke, and Hume, see chapter 7 below. On Descartes

and his critics regarding animal capacities, see also Margaret Wilson, "Animal Ideas," *Proceedings and Addresses of the American Philosophical Association* 69 (November 1995): 7–25.

32. "Fifth Set of Objections," *Oeuvres* 7:262, *Philosophical Writings* 2:183.

33. "Fifth Set of Objections," *Oeuvres* 7:270–71, *Philosophical Writings* 2:189.

34. "Fifth Set of Objections," *Oeuvres* 7:272, *Philosophical Writings* 2:190; cf. Second Meditation, *Oeuvres* 7:32, *Philosophical Writings* 2:21.

35. "Author's Replies to the Fifth Set of Objections," *Oeuvres* 7:358, *Philosophical Writings* 2:247–48.

36. "Author's Replies to the Fifth Set of Objections," *Oeuvres* 7:359, *Philosophical Writings* 2:248.

37. Rule Twelve, *Oeuvres* 10:415, *Philosophical Writings* 1:42.

38. Gaukroger, *Descartes: An Intellectual Biography*, 166.

39. Letter to the Marquess of Newcastle, November 23, 1646, *Oeuvres* 4:576, *Philosophical Writings* 3:304: "Si elles pensoient ainsi que nous, elles aurioent une ame immortelle aussi bien que nous."

40. Gaukroger, *Descartes: An Intellectual Biography*, 454n165.

41. *Oeuvres* 4:574–75, *Philosophical Writings* 3:303. See also "Author's Replies to the Sixth Set of Objections," *Oeuvres* 7:426, *Philosophical Writings* 2:287–88: "In fact the brutes possess no thought [*cogitationem*] whatsoever; I not only stated this, as my critics here imply, but proved it by very strong arguments which no one has refuted up to now."

42. Letter to More, February 5, 1649, *Oeuvres* 5:277, *Philosophical Writings* 3:366. See also letter to the Marquess of Newcastle, November 23, 1646, *Oeuvres* 4:576, *Philosophical Writings* 3:304.

43. *Oeuvres* 5:276, *Philosophical Writings* 3:365.

44. Harrison, "Descartes on Animals," 227.

45. This concession on Descartes's part is based not only on his "a posteriori" approach to understanding animals, but also on his acknowledgement that God may have made things differently than they appear to our reason: "And so I boldly assert that God can do everything which I perceive to be possible, but I am not so bold as to assert the converse, namely that he cannot do what conflicts with my conception of things—I merely say that it involves a contradiction." Letter to More, February 5, 1649, *Oeuvres* 5:272, *Philosophical Writings* 3:363.

46. *Oeuvres* 5:277, *Philosophical Writings* 3:365–66.

47. *Oeuvres* 5:276, *Philosophical Writings* 3:365.

48. Letter to Plempius for Fromondus, October 3, 1637, *Oeuvres* 1:414–15, *Philosophical Writings* 3:62. Here Descartes appeals to the scriptural authority of Leviticus and Deuteronomy in support of his view. See also Descartes's letter to Buitendijck, 1643, *Oeuvres* 4:65, *Philosophical Writings* 3:230: "I would prefer to say with Holy Scripture (Deuteronomy 12:23) that blood is their soul [viz. the soul of animals], for blood is a fluid body in very rapid motion, and its more rarefied parts are called spirits. It is these which move the whole mechanism of the body."

49. *Oeuvres* 7:426, *Philosophical Writings* 2:288.

50. *Oeuvres* 7:425–26, *Philosophical Writings* 2:287.

51. "Author's Replies to the Fourth Set of Objections," *Oeuvres* 7:230, *Philosophical Writings* 2:161–62. See also Descartes's letter to Regius, May 1641, *Oeuvres* 3:370, *Philosophical Writings* 3:181: "I do not admit that the powers of growth and sensation in animals deserve the name 'soul', as does the mind in human beings. This common view is based on ignorance of the fact that animals lack a mind. So the term 'soul' is ambiguous as used of animals and of human beings."

52. Marleen Rozemond, "The Role of the Intellect in Descartes's Case for the Incorporeity of the Mind," in *Essays on the Philosophy and Science of Descartes*, ed. Stephen Voss (New York: Oxford University Press, 1993), 101. On Descartes's denial that animals have immortal souls, see Gilson's remarks in Descartes, *Discours de la Méthode*, 420–38.

53. "Fifth Set of Objections," *Oeuvres* 7:269, *Philosophical Writings* 2:187–88.

54. "Fifth Set of Objections," *Oeuvres* 7:270, *Philosophical Writings* 2:188.

55. Cottingham, "'A Brute to the Brutes?'" 553; see also Smith, *New Studies in the Philosophy of Descartes*, 135.

56. Cottingham, "'A Brute to the Brutes?'" 558; see also p. 556.

57. Gaukroger, *Descartes: An Intellectual Biography*, 288; see also pp. 166–67, 278–90, and 349–50.

58. Letter to Plempius for Fromondus, October 3, 1637, *Oeuvres* 1:413–14, *Philosophical Writings* 3.61–62.

59. "Author's Replies to the Fourth Set of Objections," *Oeuvres* 7:230, *Philosophical Writings* 2:161 (italics mine). (Here Descartes provides a mechanistic account of the sheep-and-wolf example earlier employed by Avicenna and Aquinas; see chapter 5 above.) See also *The Passions of the Soul*, art. 16, *Oeuvres* 11:341–42, *Philosophical Writings* 1:335: "Thus every movement we make without any contribution from our will—as often happens when we breathe, walk, eat and, indeed, when we perform any action which is common to us and the beasts—depends solely on the arrangement of our limbs and on the route which the spirits, produced by the heat of the heart, follow naturally in the brain, nerves, and muscles. This occurs in the same way as the movement of a watch is produced merely by the strength of its spring and the configuration of its wheels." Cf. *The Passions of the Soul*, art. 38, *Oeuvres* 11:358, *Philosophical Writings* 1:342–43.

60. *The Passions of the Soul*, art. 50, *Oeuvres* 11:370, *Philosophical Writings* 1:348. See also letter to the Marquess of Newcastle, November 23, 1646, *Oeuvres* 4:575–76, *Philosophical Writings* 3:304: "Doubtless when the swallows come in spring, they operate like clocks. The actions of honeybees are of the same nature; so also is the discipline of cranes in flight, and of apes in fighting, if it is true that they keep discipline. . . . they act only by instinct and without thinking."

61. *Oeuvres* 11:369, *Philosophical Writings* 1:348.

62. Bernard Williams, *Descartes: The Project of Pure Enquiry* (Harmondsworth: Penguin, 1978), 284. See also L. J. Beck, *The Method of Descartes: A Study of the 'Regulae'* (New York: Garland, 1987), 24: for Descartes, animals are "highly complex machines" with "no consciousness at all." See also Daisie Radner and Michael Radner, *Animal Consciousness* (Buffalo: Prometheus Books, 1989), 64: "Descartes's assertion that animals do not think . . . commits him to the thesis that animals are

devoid of feelings and sensations" except in the "purely mechanical" sense; animals fundamentally lack "sensation as a form of awareness." Gaukroger claims that in calling animals "automata," Descartes is not saying that animals are mere machines, inasmuch as "in seventeenth-century usage [the term 'automaton'] meant little more than 'a self-moving thing.'" Gaukroger, *Descartes: An Intellectual Biography*, 287. See also Cottingham, "A Brute to the Brutes?" 553 (where Cottingham invokes Leibniz's discussion of "spiritual automata"). But a careful examination of each of Descartes's references to animals as automata shows that he is indeed employing the mechanistic sense of automatism. See Descartes's letter to Mersenne, July 30, 1640, *Oeuvres* 3:121, *Philosophical Writings* 3:149; Letter to Reneri for Pollot, April or May 1638, *Oeuvres* 2:41, *Philosophical Writings* 3:100; and letter to Plempius for Fromondus, October 3, 1637, *Oeuvres* 1:413—14, *Philosophical Writings* 3:61—62. On the terms and influence of Descartes's doctrine of animal automatism, see Leonora Cohen Rosenfeld, *From Beast-Machine to Man-Machine: Animal Soul in French Letters from Descartes to La Mettrie*, new and enlarged edition (New York: Octagon Books, 1968).

63. Letter to Gibieuf, January 19, 1642, *Oeuvres* 3:479, *Philosophical Writings* 3:203—4: "We observe in animals movements similar to those which result from our imaginations and sensations; but that does not mean that we observe imaginations and sensations in them. On the contrary, these same movements can take place without imagination, and we have arguments to prove that they do so take place in animals, as I hope to show clearly by describing in detail the structure of their limbs and the causes of their movements."

64. Letter to Mersenne, end of May, 1637, *Oeuvres* 1:366, *Philosophical Writings* 3:56. See also letter to Reneri for Pollot, April or May 1638, *Oeuvres* 2:36, *Philosophical Writings* 3:97: "Not only meditations and acts of the will, but the activities of seeing and hearing and deciding on one movement rather than another, so far as they depend on the soul, are all thoughts." See also "Author's Replies to the Sixth Set of Objections," *Oeuvres* 7:436—37, *Philosophical Writings* 2:294—95.

65. Marjorie Grene, *Descartes* (Minneapolis: University of Minnesota Press, 1985), 47.

66. Letter to Mersenne, June 11, 1640, *Oeuvres* 3:85, *Philosophical Writings* 3:148.

67. Letter to More, February 5, 1649, *Oeuvres* 5:277, *Philosophical Writings* 3:365.

68. Letter to Reneri for Pollot, April or May, 1638, *Oeuvres* 2:41, *Philosophical Writings* 3:100.

69. Grene, *Descartes*, 50. See also Gaukroger, *Descartes: An Intellectual Biography*, 393.

70. Letter to the Marquess of Newcastle, November 23, 1646, *Oeuvres* 4:574, *Philosophical Writings* 3:303.

71. Grene, *Descartes*, 50—51.

72. *Oeuvres* 4:574—75, *Philosophical Writings* 3:303.

73. *Oeuvres* 4:574, *Philosophical Writings* 3:303.

74. Margaret Wilson argues for a conclusion that is complementary to Grene's, namely that the later Descartes comes to acknowledge the possibility that animals can think. Wilson does so by appealing to several statements made by Descartes in his later writings that equivocate on the question whether animals are capable of thought. See Wilson, "Animal Ideas," 12. The remarks to which Wilson appeals are

Descartes's statement in *The Passions of the Soul* that animals "lack reason, and perhaps even thought" (article 50, *Oeuvres* 11:369, *Philosophical Writings* 1:348) and his statement in the November 23, 1646, letter to the Marquess of Newcastle that "it may be conjectured that there is attached to [the] organs [of animals] some thought such as we experience in ourselves, but of a very much less perfect kind" (*Oeuvres* 4:576, *Philosophical Writings* 3:304). But the context of each of these passages makes it clear that Descartes withholds from a definitive claim about thought in animals not because he considers such thought likely but rather because, as he notes in his February 5, 1649, letter to More, the fact that "the human mind does not reach in to [the] hearts [of animals]" makes a definitive resolution of the question impossible. In both of the passages in question Descartes's position is obviously, if only implicitly, that animals in all likelihood lack any capacity for thought; in article 50 of the *Passions* he asserts that animals lack passions of the soul (on the grounds, examined below, that passions of the soul depend on thought), and in the letter to the Marquess of Newcastle he deems it "unlikely" that animals think inasmuch as the natures of many animals "are too imperfect for [thinking in animals] to be credible."

75. Letter to Plempius, February 15, 1638, *Oeuvres* 1:523–27, *Philosophical Writings* 3:80–82.

76. *Oeuvres* 11:241, *Philosophical Writings* 1:317.

77. *Oeuvres* 11:242–43, *Philosophical Writings* 1:317–18.

78. Harrison, "Descartes on Animals," 220. Curiously, Harrison seems to find no tension between this claim and his observation that the poet Racine "was both an enthusiastic advocate of the beast-machine hypothesis and a devoted dog owner." See "Descartes on Animals," 220n10.

79. *Discourse on Method*, part 3, *Oeuvres* 6:22, *Philosophical Writings* 1:122; see also Gilson's remarks on the definitive morality in *Discours de la Méthode: Texte et commentaire*, 231. I have examined Descartes's views on morality at length in *Descartes as a Moral Thinker: Christianity, Technology, Nihilism* (Amherst, N.Y.: Prometheus/Humanity Books, 2004).

80. *Oeuvres* 9B:14, *Philosophical Writings* 1:186.

81. For an excellent historically contextualized analysis of Descartes's theory of the passions and its relationship to morality, see Anthony Levi, S.J., *French Moralists: The Theory of the Passions, 1585–1649* (Oxford: Clarendon, 1964).

82. *Descartes: His Moral Philosophy and Psychology*, trans. and intro. John J. Blom (New York: NYU Press, 1978), 12.

83. *The Passions of the Soul*, art. 153, *Oeuvres* 11:446, *Philosophical Writings* 1:384. See also article 48, *Oeuvres* 11:367, *Philosophical Writings* 1:347: The will's "proper weapons" in conquering the passions are "firm and determinate judgments bearing upon the knowledge of good and evil, which the soul has resolved to follow in guiding its conduct." See also art. 144, *Oeuvres* 11:436, *Philosophical Writings* 1:379: The "chief utility of morality" consists in controlling or regulating our desires.

84. *The Passions of the Soul*, art. 152, *Oeuvres* 11:445, *Philosophical Writings* 1:384.

85. *The Passions of the Soul*, article 50, *Oeuvres* 11:369, *Philosophical Writings* 1:348. On Descartes's views concerning the mastery of the passions, see also Descartes's letter

to Elizabeth, September 15, 1645, *Oeuvres* 4:281–87, *Philosophical Writings* 3:262–65; letter to Chanut, February 1, 1647, *Oeuvres* 4:600–617, *Philosophical Writings* 3:305–14; and letter to Christine, November 20, 1647, *Oeuvres* 5:81–86, *Philosophical Writings* 3:324–26.

86. *The Passions of the Soul*, art. 17, *Oeuvres* 11:342, *Philosophical Writings* 1:335; art. 18 and 19, *Oeuvres* 11:343, *Philosophical Writings* 1:335–36.

87. Harrison attributes to Cottingham the mistaken view that "Descartes wedges animal feelings into the gap between self-consciousness . . . and consciousness." Harrison, "Descartes on Animals," 222. For Descartes to do so he would have had to grant that animals possess some kind or degree of consciousness; and yet this is precisely what Descartes denies. Furthermore, it is not clear why we should have to bring *self*-consciousness into the discussion at all in attempting to attribute a morally relevant sense of feeling to animals; all that would be required is the appeal to an inner level of experience that transcends mere mechanism and that is analogous to consciousness in human beings.

88. The complexities involved in reflecting on animal experience are detailed in Thomas Nagel's classic essay "What is it like to be a bat?"

Chapter 7: The Empiricists, the Utilitarians, and Kant

1. Hobbes, "Third Set of Objections with the Author's Replies," in Descartes, *Oeuvres* 7:173, and Descartes, *Philosophical Writings* 2:122. Cf. Descartes's reply, *Oeuvres* 7:174, *Philosophical Writings* 2:123: Hobbes "wants to prevent [thought from] being separated from the body"; but "his method lumps together a large number of different items, whereas I aim to distinguish each individual item as far as I can."

2. Thomas Hobbes, *Leviathan* (Harmondsworth: Penguin, 1985), "Introduction," 81.

3. Ibid.; see also Carl Schmitt, "Der Staat als Mechanismus bei Hobbes und Descartes," in *Dem Gedächtnis an René Descartes (300 Jahre Discours de la Méthode): Erinnerungsausgabe der Internationalen Vereinigung für Rechts- und Sozialphilosophie*, ed. C. A. Emge (Berlin: Verlag für Staatswissenschaften und Geschichte, 1937), 158–68.

4. *Leviathan*, pt. I, ch. I, p. 86.

5. Ibid, pt. I, ch. 2, p. 88.

6. Ibid., pt. I, ch. 2, p. 93.

7. Ibid., pt. I, ch. 6, p. 119.

8. Ibid., pt. I, ch. 2, pp. 93–94.

9. Ibid., pt. I, ch. 4, pp. 101–2.

10. Ibid., pt. I, ch. 3, pp. 96–97; ch. 5, p. 112.

11. Ibid., pt. I, ch. 6, p. 127.

12. Ibid., pt. 2, ch. 26, p. 317.

13. Thomas Hobbes, *On the Citizen*, ed. and trans. Richard Tuck and Michael Silverthorne (Cambridge: Cambridge University Press, 2000), ch. 8, sec. 10, p. 105.

14. See *Leviathan*, pt. I, ch. 14 and 15, pp. 190, 201.

15. John Locke, *An Essay Concerning Human Understanding*, ed. Peter H. Nidditch (Oxford: Clarendon, 1990), bk. 2, ch. 27, sec. 8, pp.333–35.

16. Ibid., bk. 2, ch. 1, sec. 19, p. 116.

17. Ibid., bk. 2, ch. 11, sec. 9, p. 159; cf. bk. 4, ch. 7, sec. 9, p. 595.

18. Ibid, bk. 2, ch. 11, sec. 10, pp. 159–60.

19. Ibid., sec. 11, p. 160.

20. Ibid., sec. 11, p. 160; sec. 5, p. 157.

21. Ibid., bk. 4, ch. 4, sec. 18, p. 573.

22. Ibid., bk. 1, ch. 1, sec. 1, p. 43.

23. John Locke, *Second Treatise of Government*, in *Two Treatises of Government*, ed. Peter Laslett (Cambridge: Cambridge University Press, 1988), ch. 2, sec. 6, p. 271.

24. John Locke, *First Treatise of Government*, in *Two Treatises of Government*, ch. 4, sec. 30, p. 162.

25. Ibid., sec. 39–41, pp. 167–69; see also sec. 28–30, pp. 160–62.

26. Locke, *Second Treatise of Government*, ch. 2, sec. 6, p. 271.

27. Locke, *First Treatise of Government*, ch. 9, sec. 92, p. 209.

28. David Hume, "Of Suicide," in *Essays Moral, Political, and Literary*, 2 vols., ed. T. H. Green and T. H. Grose (London: Longmans, Green, and Co., 1882), 2:410.

29. David Hume, *An Enquiry Concerning Human Understanding*, in *Enquiries Concerning Human Understanding and Concerning the Principles of Morals*, 3d ed., ed. P. H. Nidditch (Oxford: Clarendon, 1979), sec. 9, p. 104; see also David Hume, *A Treatise of Human Nature*, 2d ed., ed. P. H. Nidditch (Oxford: Clarendon, 1981), bk. 1, pt. 3, sec. 16, p. 176 and bk. 2, pt. 1, sec. 12, p. 325.

30. *An Enquiry Concerning Human Understanding*, sec. 9, p. 105.

31. *A Treatise of Human Nature*, bk. 1, pt. 4, sec. 1, p. 183.

32. See ibid., bk. 1, pt. 3, sec. 6, pp. 86–94.

33. *An Enquiry Concerning Human Understanding*, sec. 9, p. 108; *A Treatise of Human Nature*, bk. 1, pt. 3, sec. 16, p. 179.

34. *A Treatise of Human Nature*, bk. 1, pt. 3, sec. 1–2, pp. 69–73; bk. 2, pt. 3, sec. 9, p. 448.

35. Ibid., bk. 2, pt. 2, sec. 12, pp. 397–98.

36. Ibid., bk. 3, pt. 1, sec. 1, p. 468.

37. Ibid., bk. 2, pt. 3, sec. 12, p. 326.

38. Ibid., bk. 3, pt. 3, sec. 4, p. 610.

39. Ibid., bk. 3, pt. 2, sec. 2, p. 490; sec. 3, p. 506.

40. Ibid., bk. 3, pt. 2, sec. 2, pp. 489, 498.

41. Ibid., bk. 3, pt. 2, sec. 3, p. 509.

42. David Hume, *An Enquiry Concerning the Principles of Morals*, in *Enquiries Concerning Human Understanding and Concerning the Principles of Morals*, sec. 2, pt. 2, p. 179.

43. Ibid., bk. 3, pt. 1, sec. 2, p. 470.

44. Bentham printed the first part of the *Principles* in 1780, published the entire work in 1789, and issued an edition with final corrections in 1823.

45. Jeremy Bentham, *An Introduction to the Principles of Morals and Legislation* (New York: Hafner/Macmillan, 1948), ch. 1, sec. 2, par. 8, p. 101.

46. Ibid., ch. 14, par. 28, p. 188.

47. Ibid., ch. 1, par. 2, p. 2n1.

48. Ibid., ch. 1, par. 1, pp. 1, 1n1.

49. Ibid., ch. 17, par. 4, pp. 310—11n1.

50. Ibid., p. 310. Presumably Bentham has the Stoics in mind here.

51. Ibid., pp. 310—11n.

52. John Stuart Mill, "Whewell on Moral Philosophy," in *Utilitarianism and Other Essays: J. S. Mill and Jeremy Bentham*, ed. Alan Ryan, 228—70 (Harmondsworth: Penguin, 1987), 253.

53. Ibid., 252—53.

54. John Stuart Mill, *Principles of Political Economy* (Oxford: Oxford University, 1994), bk. 5, ch. 11, sec. 9, p. 344. Here Mill argues that the same reasoning justifies legal intervention on behalf of slaves.

55. Mill, "Nature," in *Three Essays on Religion*, 3—65 (New York: Henry Holt and Co., 1878), 65.

56. Ibid., 20—21.

57. Mill, *Utilitarianism*, in *On Liberty and Other Essays*, pt. 2, p. 138.

58. Ibid., 138—39.

59. Ibid., 140.

60. Ibid., pt. 5, p. 187.

61. Ibid., pt. 2, p. 140.

62. See Hume, *A Treatise of Human Nature*, bk. 3, pt. 2, sec. 2, p. 491.

63. Immanuel Kant, *Grounding for the Metaphysics of Morals*, trans. James W. Ellington (Indianapolis: Hackett, 1981), 46 (Ak. 442).

64. Ibid., 12 (Ak. 399).

65. Ibid., 13—14 (Ak. 401).

66. Ibid., 35 (Ak. 428).

67. Ibid., 36 (Ak. 428).

68. Ibid., 35—36 (Ak. 428).

69. Ibid., 36 (Ak. 429).

70. Kant, "Idea for a Universal History with a Cosmopolitan Purpose," in *Political Writings*, ed. H. S. Reiss (Cambridge: Cambridge University Press, 1991), 43.

71. Kant, *Critique of Judgment*, sec. 90, pp. 356—57nn64, 66 (translation altered; emphasis in original).

72. Immanuel Kant, *Lectures on Ethics*, ed. Peter Heath and J. B. Schneewind, trans. Peter Heath (Cambridge: Cambridge University Press, 1997), 125.

73. Ibid., 60.

74. Ibid., 218.

75. "Idea for a Universal History with a Cosmopolitan Purpose," in *Political Writings*, 43. See also *Lectures on Ethics*, 234: "*Necessitatio* of my *arbitrium* is either *pathologica* or *practica*. The former is *obligatio arbitrii bruti* [obligation of animal choice], but the latter, *liberi* [obligation of free choice]. The former is necessitation through sensory impulses, but the latter, from motivating grounds. These grounds always have to do with free actions; but those impulses, with involuntary ones. For animals have no free choice, their actions being necessarily determined by sensory impulses."

76. Kant, "The Contest of Faculties," in *Political Writings*, 180; *Critique of Judgment*, sec. 86, p. 334 (Ak. 445).

77. See Kant, *Grounding for the Metaphysics of Morals*, 39 (Ak. 433).

78. Kant, "The Doctrine of Virtue," in *The Metaphysics of Morals*, ed. Mary Gregor (Cambridge: Cambridge University Press, 1996), pt. 1, bk. 1, ch. 2, sec. 11, p. 186 (Ak. 434–35).

79. Kant, *Critique of Judgment*, sec. 60, p. 232 (Ak. 356); *Religion within the Limits of Reason Alone*, trans. Theodore M. Greene and Hoyt H. Hudson (New York: Harper Torchbooks, 1960), 21.

80. Kant, *Lectures on Ethics*, 147 (translation altered).

81. Kant, *Critique of Judgment*, sec. 83, p. 318 (Ak. 431).

82. Ibid., sec. 83, pp. 318 (Ak. 431), 320 (Ak. 432); see also sec. 86.

83. Ibid., 320 (Ak. 432). Kant articulates his cosmopolitan ideal in "Idea for a Universal History with a Cosmopolitan Purpose," in *Political Writings*, 41, 51; and "The Contest of Faculties," in *Political Writings*, 188.

84. Kant, *Lectures on Ethics*, 156.

85. Ibid., 381 (translation altered); relations between animals are confined to procreation ("Vermischung verschiedenen Geschlechts"). On the Stoics' view that animals can have community among themselves, see chapter 3 above.

86. Immanuel Kant, *Critique of Practical Reason*, 3d ed., trans. Lewis White Beck (Upper Saddle River, N.J.: Library of Liberal Arts, 1993), pt. 1, bk. 1, ch. 3, p. 80.

87. Kant, "The Doctrine of Virtue," in *The Metaphysics of Morals*, sec. 17, p. 193 (Ak. 443), emphasis in original.

88. Ibid., 192–93 (Ak. 443). See also Kant, *Lectures on Ethics*, 212.

89. Ibid.

90. Kant, *Lectures on Ethics*, 213.

91. Kant, "The Doctrine of Virtue," in *The Metaphysics of Morals*, sec. 17, p. 193 (Ak. 443).

Chapter 8: Conceptions of Continuity

1. Kant, *Grounding for the Metaphysics of Morals*, 58–59 (Ak. 459).

2. Friedrich Nietzsche, *The Will to Power*, trans. Walter Kaufmann and R. J. Hollingdale (New York: Vintage/Random House, 1968), bk. 1, sec. 30, p. 20 (Nachlaß, November 1887–March 1888).

3. Isaiah Berlin, *The Roots of Romanticism*, the A. W. Mellon Lectures in the Fine Arts, 1965 (Princeton: Princeton University Press, 2001), 1.

4. Frederick C. Beiser, *The Fate of Reason: German Philosophy from Kant to Fichte* (Cambridge, Mass.: Harvard University Press, 1987), 128–29.

5. Novalis (Friedrich von Hardenberg), "The Universal Brouillon: Materials for an Encyclopaedia," sec. 857, in *The Early Political Writings of the German Romantics*, ed. Frederick C. Beiser (Cambridge: Cambridge University, 1996), 90.

6. Friedrich Daniel Ernst Schleiermacher, "Monologue III: Worldview," in *The Early Political Writings of the German Romantics*, 194. Here Schleiermacher gives equal primacy to imagination and faith ("lebendige Fantasie und starken Glauben").

Friedrich Daniel Ernst Schleiermacher, *Schriften aus der Berliner Zeit 1800–1802*, ed. Günter Meckenstock (Berlin: Walter de Gruyter, 1988), 35.

7. Robert J. Richards, *The Romantic Conception of Life: Science and Philosophy in the Age of Goethe* (Chicago: University of Chicago Press, 2002), 19.

8. William Wordsworth, "Lines Composed a Few Miles above Tintern Abbey, On Revisiting the Banks of the Wye during a Tour. July 13, 1798," lines 102–11, in *Poems*, selected by Seamus Heaney (New York: Faber and Faber, 2001), 37.

9. Étienne Bonnot de Condillac, *Essay on the Origin of Human Knowledge*, ed. Hans Aarsleff (Cambridge: Cambridge University Press, 2001), pt. 1, sec. 2, art 39, p. 37. On the types of signs, see pt. 1, sec. 2, art. 35.

10. Ibid., pt. 1, sec. 2, art. 47, p. 41.

11. Ibid., pt. 2, sec. 1, art. 3, 5, 6, pp. 115–16.

12. Ibid., pt. 2, sec. 2, art. 34, p. 211.

13. Étienne Bonnot de Condillac, *Traité des Animaux*, in *Oeuvres philosophiques de Condillac*, vol. 1, ed. Georges Le Roy (Paris: Presses Universitaires de France, 1947), 338–79.

14. Ibid., pt. 2, ch. 4, pp. 361–62.

15. Ibid., pt. 2, ch. 5, pp. 362–63. Nonetheless, Condillac argues at length in part 1, animals are sentient beings, not the mechanisms that Descartes and Buffon considered them to be.

16. Ibid., pt. 2, ch. 5, p. 363; pt. 2, ch. 10, p. 378.

17. Ibid., pt. 2, ch. 10, p. 379; see also pt. 2, ch. 6 (knowledge of God) and ch. 7 (knowledge of the principles of morality).

18. Condillac, *Essay on the Origin of Human Knowledge*, pt. 1, sec. 2, art. 40, p. 37.

19. Ibid., pt. 1, sec. 2, art. 41, p. 38.

20. Ibid., pt. 1, sec. 2, art. 43, p. 39.

21. Ibid., pt. 1, sec. 2, art. 40, p. 38. For Condillac, this ability to form precise ideas depends on the ability to employ conventional signs; as Aarsleff notes, Condillac makes "speech and words the condition for discursivity and thus the agency of knowledge and the exercise of reason." Ibid., xv.

22. Ibid., pt. 1, sec. 2, art. 43, p. 39.

23. Ibid., pt. 1, sec. 2, art. 46, p. 40; art. 43, p. 39.

24. Jean-Jacques Rousseau, *Discourse on the Origin and Foundations of Inequality Among Men*, in *Rousseau's Political Writings*, ed. Alan Ritter and Julia Conaway Bondanella (New York: Norton, 1988), 27n8, 27, 32.

25. Ibid., 20.

26. Ibid., 11, 28–29, 31.

27. Ibid., 27n9. Cf. 27: Therefore Hobbes is wrong to characterize the state of nature as one of violent enmity among human beings.

28. Ibid., 15–16.

29. Ibid., 23–24.

30. Ibid., 16.

31. See ibid., 10.

32. Jean-Jacques Rousseau, *Émile, Or Treatise on Education*, trans. William H. Payne (Amherst, N.Y.: Prometheus, 2003), 18–19, 226.

33. *Discourse on the Origin of Inequality*, in *Rousseau's Political Writings*, 28.

34. Ibid., 17n3.

35. Ibid., 35, 33.

36. Ibid., 14.

37. Ibid., 40.

38. Ibid., 12.

39. *Émile*, 256.

40. *Discourse on the Origin of Inequality*, in *Rousseau's Political Writings*, 7.

41. *Émile*, 237–38.

42. See ibid., 22; and *Discourse on the Origin of Inequality*, in *Rousseau's Political Writings*, 13, 20.

43. *Émile*, 291.

44. Mary Wollstonecraft, *A Vindication of the Rights of Woman* (1791–92), in *A Vindication of the Rights of Men and A Vindication of the Rights of Woman*, ed. Sylvia Tomaselli (Cambridge: Cambridge University Press, 1995), ch. 1, p. 82n2. One must be on guard against the conventional wisdom that Rousseau categorically idealizes a vegetarian diet. This view is maintained by Carol J. Adams, who states that Rousseau's "Emile, Sophie, and Julie were all vegetarians." *The Sexual Politics of Meat*, 115. Adams bases this claim on the work of Madelaine A. Simons, who suggests that "the models [Rousseau] proposed for mankind, Emile and Julie, were vegetarians." "Rousseau's Natural Diet," *Romantic Review* 45 (1954): 18.

45. Condillac, *Traité des Animaux*, pt. 2, ch. 3, pp. 358–59.

46. Ibid., conclusion to pt. 2, p. 379.

47. Wollstonecraft, *A Vindication of the Rights of Woman*, 81.

48. Johann Gottfried von Herder, *Outlines of a Philosophy of the History of Man* (1784–90), trans. T. Churchill (New York: Bergman, 1800), pt. 1, bk. 5, ch. 1, p. 107.

49. Ibid., pt. 1, bk. 2, ch. 3, p. 35.

50. Ibid., pt. 1, bk. 2, ch. 4, p. 39.

51. Johann Gottfried von Herder, *Treatise on the Origin of Language*, in *Philosophical Writings*, trans. and ed. Michael N. Forster (Cambridge: Cambridge University Press, 2002), 99, 127, 55.

52. Ibid., 75–76, 104, 164.

53. Ibid., 136.

54. Ibid., 121; see also Herder, *Fragments on Recent German Literature* (1767–68), in *Philosophical Writings*, 49.

55. Herder, *Treatise on the Origin of Language*, 83.

56. Ibid., 87–88.

57. See ibid., 87–92.

58. Ibid., 128–30, 133.

59. Ibid., 155 (translation altered).

60. See ibid., 128–30 (where Forster translates *sammeln* and *Sammlung* variously as "achieve" and "conscious control").

61. Ibid., 193.

62. Herder, *On the Cognition and Sensation of the Human Soul*, in *Philosophical Writings*, 214.

63. Ibid., 216.

64. Herder, *Treatise on the Origin of Language*, in *Philosophical Writings*, 145.

65. Herder, *Outlines of a Philosophy of the History of Man*, pt. 1, bk. 2, ch. 4, p. 40.

66. Ibid., pt. 1, bk. 4, ch. 1, pp. 79, 81.

67. Ibid., pt. 1, bk. 4, ch. 2, pp. 87, 89; bk. 4, ch. 6, pp. 102–4.

68. Ibid., pt. 1, bk. 4, ch. 4, p. 91.

69. Ibid., pt. 1, bk. 7, ch. 1, p. 166.

70. Ibid., pt. 1, bk. 8, ch. 3, p. 206.

71. Ibid., pt. 1, bk. 5, ch. 1, p. 107.

72. See Friedrich Nietzsche, "On Truth and Lies in a Nonmoral Sense" (1873), in *Philosophy and Truth: Selections from Nietzsche's Notebooks of the Early 1870's*, ed. and trans. Daniel Breazeale (New Jersey: Humanities Press International, 1992), 79.

73. Arthur Schopenhauer, *The World as Will and Representation*, vol. 1, trans. E. F. J. Payne (Indian Hills, Colo.: Falcon's Wing, 1958), bk. 2, sec. 27, p. 149; bk. 2, sec. 29, p. 164.

74. Ibid., bk. 1, sec. 6, p. 19.

75. Ibid., bk. 1, sec. 6, pp. 20–21. To say that a being understands is to say that it "perceives as object in space the cause affecting its body."

76. Ibid., bk. 1, sec. 7, p. 30; bk. 1, sec. 6, p. 23.

77. Arthur Schopenhauer, "On Religion," sec. 177, in *Parerga and Paralipomena*, trans. E. F. J. Payne, 2 vols. (Oxford: Clarendon, 2000), 2:375. In arguing for the conclusion that animals share in understanding, Schopenhauer invokes the authority of Plutarch and Porphyry. See Arthur Schopenhauer, *The Fourfold Root of the Principle of Sufficient Reason*, trans. E. F. J. Payne (La Salle, Ill.: Open Court, 1974), ch. 4, sec. 21, pp. 109–10.

78. Schopenhauer, *The Fourfold Root of the Principle of Sufficient Reason*, ch. 5, sec. 27, p. 151 (emphasis in original).

79. Schopenhauer, *The World as Will and Representation*, vol. 1, bk. 1, sec. 16, p. 84.

80. Ibid., bk. 1, sec. 8, p. 35; bk. 1, sec. 6, pp. 22–23; bk. 1, sec. 12, p. 55; Schopenhauer, *The World as Will and Representation*, vol. 2, trans. E. F. J. Payne (New York: Dover, 1958), ch. 31, p. 382. See also *The Fourfold Root of the Principle of Sufficient Reason*, 238.

81. Schopenhauer, *The World as Will and Representation*, vol. 1, bk. 2, sec. 26, p. 132.

82. Schopenhauer, *The World as Will and Representation*, vol. 2, ch. 5, p. 60; see also *The World as Will and Representation*, vol. 1, bk. 1, sec. 8, p. 36

83. Schopenhauer, *The World as Will and Representation*, vol. 1, bk. 1, sec. 8, p. 37; see also "Additional Remarks on the Doctrine of the Suffering of the World," in *Parerga and Paralipomena*, vol. 2, ch. 12, sec. 153, p. 295.

84. Schopenhauer, *The World as Will and Representation*, vol. 1, bk. 1, sec. 8, p. 37.

85. Ibid., bk. 1, sec. 7, p. 30.

86. Schopenhauer, "Additional Remarks on the Doctrine of the Suffering of the World," in *Parerga and Paralipomena*, vol. 2, ch. 12, sec. 153, p. 294.

87. Arthur Schopenhauer, *On the Basis of Morality*, trans. E. F. J. Payne (Providence: Berghahn Books, 1995), pt. 3, sec. 16, p. 144.

88. Schopenhauer, *The World as Will and Representation*, vol. 1, bk. 4, sec. 67, pp. 375–76.

89. Schopenhauer, "Fragments for the History of Philosophy," in *Parerga and Paralipomena*, vol. I, sec. 12, p. 73.

90. Schopenhauer, *On the Basis of Morality*, pt. 2, sec. 8, pp. 95–96.

91. Ibid., pt. 3, sec. 19, pp. 175, 179.

92. Ibid., pt. 3, sec. 16, p. 151.

93. Schopenhauer, "On Religion," in *Parerga and Paralipomena*, vol. 2, ch. 15, sec. 177, pp. 372, 376.

94. Ibid., p. 370.

95. Ibid., pp. 375, 370–71.

96. Schopenhauer, *On the Basis of Morality*, pt. 2, sec. 8, p. 96.

97. Schopenhauer, "On Religion," in *Parerga and Paralipomena*, vol. 2, ch. 15, sec. 177, pp. 373–74.

98. Ibid. On Blumenbach's notion of the *Bildungstrieb* (developmental drive) and its contribution to a Romantic sense of continuity between human beings and other living things, see Richards, *The Romantic Conception of Life*, 216ff.

99. Schopenhauer, "On Religion," in *Parerga and Paralipomena*, vol. 2, ch. 15, sec. 177, pp. 373–74.

100. Schopenhauer, *On the Basis of Morality*, pt. 3, sec. 19, p. 182. See also "On Religion," in *Parerga and Paralipomena*, vol. I, ch. 15, sec. 177, p. 375.

101. Schopenhauer, *On the Basis of Morality*, pt. 3, sec. 20, p. 192.

102. On the influence of these thinkers on Darwin, see Richards, *The Romantic Conception of Life*. Richards also discusses the role of Darwin's father Erasmus in this lineage of thinking.

103. Charles Darwin, *The Origin of Species*, in *The Origin of Species by Means of Natural Selection or the Preservation of Favored Races in the Struggle for Life and The Descent of Man and Selection in Relation to Sex* (New York: Modern Library, no date), 353; Charles Darwin, *The Descent of Man*, in *The Origin of Species by Means of Natural Selection or the Preservation of Favored Races in the Struggle for Life and The Descent of Man and Selection in Relation to Sex*, 909–10.

104. Darwin, *The Origin of Species*, 361.

105. Darwin, *The Descent of Man*, 446.

106. Ibid., 448.

107. See Darwin, *The Descent of Man*, 448–50; 475–76.

108. Charles Darwin, *The Expression of the Emotions in Man and Animals*, 3d ed., ed. Paul Ekman (New York: Oxford University Press, 1998), 360.

109. Darwin, "Introduction to the First Edition," in *The Expression of the Emotions in Man and Animals*, 19; see also 355.

110. Darwin, *The Descent of Man*, ch. 3, p. 448; *The Expression of the Emotions in Man and Animals*, 347.

111. Darwin, *The Descent of Man*, 463. See also Darwin, *The Expression of the Emotions in Man and Animals*, 92.

112. Charles Darwin, *The Autobiography of Charles Darwin*, ed. Francis Darwin (Amherst, N.Y.: Prometheus Books, 2000), 66.

113. As Richards notes, however, Darwin fails to see the usefulness of the ability to communicate emotions, even though he recognizes that mental abilities as a whole contribute to survival. See Robert J. Richards, *Darwin and the Emergence of*

Evolutionary Theories of Mind and Behavior (Chicago: University of Chicago Press, 1987), 230–31.

114. Darwin, *The Expression of the Emotions in Man and Animals*, 353.

115. Darwin, *The Descent of Man*, 453.

116. Ibid., 454.

117. Ibid., 446.

118. Ibid., 454–55.

119. Ibid., 455.

120. Ibid., 460.

121. Ibid., 462–63.

122. Ibid., 461–62.

123. Ibid., 495.

124. Ibid.

125. Ibid., 460.

126. Ibid., 467–68. One might even say of "most savages . . . that their aesthetic faculty was not so highly developed as in certain animals."

127. Ibid., 462.

128. Ibid., 472n.

129. Ibid., 471.

130. Ibid., 472–73.

131. Ibid., 476–77.

132. Ibid., 478; on *oikeiosis*, see chapter 3 above.

133. Ibid., 476–77.

134. Ibid., 478. Cf. 480: This holds for human beings as well as for animals.

135. Ibid., 478.

136. Richards, *Darwin and the Emergence of Evolutionary Theories of Mind and Behavior*, 219, 237.

137. Ibid., 115.

138. Darwin, *The Descent of Man*, 490.

139. Ibid., 473.

140. See in particular ibid., 481.

141. Ibid., 482–83, 485.

142. Ibid., 493.

143. Ibid., 494.

144. Ibid., 473.

145. See Darwin, *The Autobiography of Charles Darwin*, 60 (citing letter to Abbott, November 16, 1871); 249 (citing letter to Gray, May 22, 1860). See also Darwin, *On the Origin of Species*, 367–68. But cf. Charles Darwin, *The Variation of Plants and Animals under Domestication*, 2 vols. (New York: Orange Judd and Co., 1868), 2:516: The principle of variation seems incompatible with the idea of "an omnipotent and omniscient creator [who] preordains everything. Thus we are brought face to face with a difficulty as insoluble as that of free will and predestination."

146. Darwin, *The Descent of Man*, 492.

147. Darwin, *The Autobiography of Charles Darwin*, 305–6.

148. Ibid., 306.

149. Darwin, *The Variation of Plants and Animals Under Domestication*, 2:484.

150. Darwin, *The Descent of Man*, 920. Richards advances an intriguing thesis that would account for Darwin's claim of human superiority: that "Darwin never referred to or conceived of natural selection as operating in a mechanical fashion, [but instead] the nature to which selection gave rise was perceived in its parts and in the whole as a teleologically self-organizing structure." Richards, *The Romantic Conception of Life*, 536. Cf. Richards, *Darwin and the Emergence of Evolutionary Theories*, 240: In ethics, "Darwin replaced God with nature." For a full exposition of the argument that Darwin's theory of natural selection involves a notion of teleology or progress, see Robert J. Richards, *The Meaning of Evolution: The Morphological Construction and Ideological Reconstruction of Darwin's Theory* (Chicago: University of Chicago Press, 1992).

151. Albert Schweitzer, *Civilization and Ethics: The Philosophy of Civilization Part II*, trans. John Naish (London: A&C Block, 1923), viii.

152. Ibid., xi.

153. Ibid., 6f.

154. Ibid., 68 (mastery of nature); 108 (Enlightenment philosophies of history).

155. Ibid., xii–xiii.

156. Ibid., 8.

157. Ibid., 30.

158. Ibid., 17.

159. Ibid., 41–42.

160. Ibid., 62; 94.

161. Ibid., 65.

162. Ibid., 175–76.

163. Ibid., 197.

164. Ibid., 207–8.

165. Ibid., 210.

166. Ibid., 223.

167. Ibid., 211.

168. Ibid., xvii–xviii; see also 290.

169. Ibid., 218–19.

170. Ibid., 238, 241–42; 264–65.

171. Ibid., 249.

172. Ibid., 254.

173. Ibid., 263, 266, 269.

174. Ibid., 278.

175. Ibid., 282.

176. Ibid., 286.

177. Ibid., 237.

178. Ibid., 258.

179. Ibid., 262.

Chapter 9: Postmodern Conceptions
of the Human-Animal Boundary

1. Sigmund Freud, *Civilization and Its Discontents*, trans. James Strachey (New York: Norton, 1989), 42 (translation altered).

2. The definitive study of the dangers of central planning and the need for liberal individualism, particularly as these bear on Nazi Germany and the Soviet Union, is F. A. Hayek's *The Road to Serfdom* (Chicago: University of Chicago Press, 1994).

3. Freud, *Civilization and Its Discontents*, 42.

4. Immanuel Kant, "The Canon of Pure Reason," in *Critique of Pure Reason*, trans. Norman Kemp Smith (New York: Humanities, 1950), 635 (A805/B833, translation altered).

5. Karl Löwith, "Der Weltbegriff der neuzeitlichen Philosophie," *Sitzungsberichte der Heidelberger Akademie der Wissenschaften, Philosophisch-historischer Klasse* 44 (1960): 7, 19.

6. Martin Heidegger, "Introduction to 'What Is Metaphysics?'," in *Pathmarks*, trans. William McNeill (Cambridge: Cambridge University Press, 1998), 284.

7. Ibid.

8. Martin Heidegger, "Letter on 'Humanism'," in *Pathmarks*, 247.

9. Martin Heidegger, "What Is Metaphysics?" in *Pathmarks*, 88.

10. Martin Heidegger, "Postscript to 'What Is Metaphysics?'," in *Pathmarks*, 234.

11. Heidegger, "What Is Metaphysics?" in *Pathmarks*, 91.

12. Martin Heidegger, *Being and Time*, trans. John Macquarrie and Edward Robinson (New York: Harper and Row, 1962), 232. Italics in original.

13. Heidegger, *Being and Time*, 288–89.

14. Heidegger, *Being and Time*, 32. This is Dasein's "special distinctiveness as compared with other entities."

15. Heidegger, *Being and Time*, 310.

16. Heidegger, "What Is Metaphysics?" in *Pathmarks*, 96 (translation altered).

17. Martin Heidegger, "The Question Concerning Technology," in *The Question Concerning Technology and Other Essays*, trans. William Lovitt (New York: Harper and Row, 1977), 35 (translation altered).

18. Heidegger, *Being and Time*, 291. Alternately, we may speak of the "demise" [*Ableben*] of living beings.

19. Martin Heidegger, "The Origin of the Work of Art," in *Poetry, Language, Thought*, trans. Albert Hofstadter (New York: Perennial Classics/HarperCollins, 2001), 71 (translation altered).

20. Martin Heidegger, "Language," in *Poetry, Language, Thought*, 196.

21. Martin Heidegger, "The Nature of Language," in *On the Way to Language*, trans. Peter D. Hertz (San Francisco: Harper and Row, 1982), 107 (translation altered).

22. Heidegger, "Letter on 'Humanism'," in *Pathmarks*, 248. "Ek-sistent" refers to the way in which human Dasein is held out into the Nothing.

23. Ibid.

24. Heidegger, "What is Metaphysics?" in *Pathmarks*, 91: "Without the original manifestness of the nothing, no selfhood and no freedom."

25. Martin Heidegger, *Die Grundbegriffe der Metaphysik: Welt—Endlichkeit—Einsamkeit*, Gesamtausgabe, vol. 29/30 (Frankfurt: Klostermann, 1983), 261, 263. (All translations of passages from this text are my own. The English translation is Martin Heidegger, *The Fundamental Concepts of Metaphysics: World, Finitude, Solitude*, trans. William McNeill and Nicholas Walker [Bloomington: Indiana University Press, 1995]. The English translation includes page-by-page cross-references to the German pagination.)

26. Heidegger, *Die Grundbegriffe der Metaphysik*, 284, 287, 285.

27. Ibid., 285, 294.

28. Ibid., 384–85. On *Benommenheit*, see also Martin Heidegger, "What Are Poets For?" in *Poetry, Language, Thought*, 106 (where Hofstadter translates *benommen* as 'benumbed').

29. Heidegger, *Die Grundbegriffe der Metaphysik*, 390–91. "The animal is . . . *open in a nondisconcealment*." Giorgio Agamben, *The Open: Man and Animal*, trans. Kevin Attell (Stanford: Stanford University Press, 2004), 59.

30. Ibid., 402.

31. See Heidegger's discussion of the as-structure in *Being and Time*, par. 31 and 32; Martin Heidegger, *Logik: Die Frage nach der Wahrheit*, Gesamtausgabe, vol. 21 (Frankfurt: Klostermann, 1976), 135–61; and *Die Grundbegriffe der Metaphysik*, 414–507. See also Martin Heidegger, *Parmenides*, Gesamtausgabe, vol. 54 (Frankfurt: Klostermann, 1982), 225–40.

32. Heidegger, *Die Grundbegriffe der Metaphysik*, 391.

33. William McNeill has suggested, against Heidegger, that even if animals lack freedom, they must in some sense be capable of the "as," e.g., the cat must be able to relate to the mouse *as* its potential dinner. See William McNeill, "Life Beyond the Organism: Animal Being in Heidegger's Freiburg Lectures, 1929–30," in *Animal Others: On Ethics, Ontology, and Animal Life*, ed. Peter Steeves (Albany: SUNY Press, 1999), 240–41. This criticism is best assessed against the background of Allen and Hauser's distinction between perceiving an *X* and perceiving something as an *X* (see chapter 1 above): it is not clear why the "as" must be assumed to be at work here.

34. Heidegger, *Die Grundbegriffe der Metaphysik*, 393.

35. Ibid., 396.

36. Ibid., 285.

37. Ibid., 398.

38. Martin Heidegger, "On the Essence of Truth," in *Pathmarks*, 144–48. See also *Die Grundbegriffe der Metaphysik*, 492: The capacity for apophantic (i.e., thematic, predicative) *logos* "is grounded in a *being-free for beings as such*."

39. Martin Heidegger, *Schellings Abhandlung über das Wesen der menschlichen Freiheit* (1809), ed. Hildegard Feick (Tübingen: Niemeyer, 1971), 173–74.

40. Heidegger, *Die Grundbegriffe der Metaphysik*, 286–87.

41. *Mut* is derived from Middle High German/Old High German *muot*, which signifies "power of thinking, sensing, willing; sense, soul, spirit; disposition, mood, mindedness; arrogance; the thought of a deed, decision, intention." Friedrich Kluge, *Etymologisches Wörterbuch der deutschen Sprache*, ed. Walther Mitzka, 20th ed. (Berlin: de Gruyter, 1967), 496.

42. Nagel, "What is it like to be a bat?"

43. Hub Zwart, "What Is an Animal? A Philosophical Reflection on the Possibility of a Moral Relationship with Animals," *Environmental Values* 6 (1997): 386.

44. See "Postscript to 'What is Metaphysics?" in *Pathmarks*, 232. See also "Letter on 'Humanism'," in *Pathmarks*, 261; "The Thing," in *Poetry, Language, Thought*, 179, 182.

45. One might also ask whether animals are incapable of history, as Heidegger and the tradition have assumed. David Krell suggests that Heidegger's "reluctance to think life in terms of occurrence, essential unfolding, and the fateful-fatal sending weakens his achievement [in thinking about animals] considerably. It ruins his chance to integrate history and nature in a way Dilthey dreamed of but could not fulfill." David Farrell Krell, *Daimon Life: Heidegger and Life-Philosophy* (Bloomington: Indiana University Press, 1992), 333n22. In chapter 10, I return to the problem of integrating history and nature.

46. Emmanuel Levinas, "The Name of a Dog, or Natural Rights," *Difficult Freedom: Essays on Judaism*, trans. Seán Hand (Baltimore: Johns Hopkins University Press, 1990), 153.

47. Ibid.

48. Ibid, 151, 152.

49. David Clark, "On Being 'The Last Kantian in Nazi Germany': Dwelling with Animals after Levinas," in *Animal Acts: Configuring the Human in Western History*, ed. Jennifer Ham and Matthew Senior (New York: Routledge, 1997), 178.

50. See Emmanuel Levinas, "As If Consenting to Horror," *Critical Inquiry* 15 (1989): 485–88. Cf. Martin Heidegger, "Das Ge-Stell" (unpublished essay, 1949), cited in Wolfgang Schirmacher, *Technik und Gelassenheit: Zeitkritik nach Heidegger* (Freiburg: Alber, 1983), 25: "Agriculture is now motorized food industry, essentially [im Wesen] the same as the manufacture of corpses in gas chambers and death camps, the same as the blockade and starvation of countries, the same as the manufacture of hydrogen bombs."

51. Clark, "On Being 'The Last Kantian,'" 192.

52. Emmanuel Levinas and Richard Kearney, "Dialogue with Emmanuel Levinas," in *Face to Face with Levinas*, ed. Richard A. Cohen (Albany: SUNY Press, 1986), 29.

53. Ibid, 26, 23.

54. Tamra Wright, Peter Hughes, and Alison Ainley, "The Paradox of Morality: An Interview with Emmanuel Levinas," in *The Provocation of Levinas: Rethinking the Other*, ed. Robert Bernasconi and David Wood (London: Routledge, 1988), 172.

55. Ibid, 170.

56. Ibid, 172.

57. Ibid, 169.

58. Levinas and Kearney, "Dialogue with Emmanuel Levinas," 25.

59. Jacques Derrida, "'Eating Well', or the Calculation of the Subject: An Interview with Jacques Derrida," in *Who Comes after the Subject?* ed. Eduardo Cadava, Peter Connor, and Jean-Luc Nancy (New York: Routledge, 1991), 100.

60. Ibid, 102.

61. Ibid, 105.

62. Ibid, 102. Cf. p. 107, where Derrida stresses "the irreducibility of the relation to the other."

63. Ibid, 107, 112.

64. Ibid, 112. See also Jacques Derrida, *Of Spirit: Heidegger and the Question*, trans. Geoffrey Bennington and Rachel Bowlby (Chicago: University of Chicago Press, 1991), 55–56: In his discussion of human Dasein, Heidegger "cannot avoid a certain anthropocentric or even humanist teleology" that places human beings above animals.

65. Derrida, "Eating Well," 113. "Citizens who are also women and/or vegetarians" can be included in the ethical sphere only when the notion of responsibility has been deconstructed. The same would presumably apply to animals, though Derrida conspicuously refrains from saying this; I return to this omission below.

66. Ibid, 113.

67. Jacques Derrida, "Force of Law: The 'Mystical Foundation of Authority'," trans. Mary Quaintance, *Cardozo Law Review* 11 (1989–90): 953.

68. Derrida, *Of Spirit*, 54.

69. Jacques Derrida, *Aporias*, trans. Thomas Dutoit (Stanford: Stanford University Press, 1993), 14.

70. Ibid, 31, 35.

71. Ibid, 22.

72. Ibid, 37.

73. Ibid, 42.

74. David Wood, "*Comment ne pas manger*—Deconstruction and Humanism," in *Animal Others: On Ethics, Ontology, and Animal Life*, ed. H. Peter Steeves (Albany: SUNY Press, 1999), 30.

75. Derrida, "Eating Well," 110. Derrida never gets beyond vague suggestions such as "against, or without, Heidegger, one could point to a thousand signs that show that animals also *die*." *Aporias*, 75.

76. "Eating Well," 112.

77. "Eating Well," 118.

78. Jacques Derrida, "On Reading Heidegger: An Outline of the Essex Colloquium," *Research in Phenomenology* 17 (1987): 173.

79. *Of Spirit*, 84. Cf. p. 1: "I shall speak of ghost [*revenant*], of flame, and of ashes. And of what, for Heidegger, *avoiding* means."

80. Derrida, "Eating Well," 113; Wood, "*Comment ne pas manger*," 15.

81. Derrida, *Of Spirit*, 109.

82. Heidegger, "What Are Poets For?" in *Poetry, Language, Thought*, 108.

83. Ibid, 130.

84. Derrida, *Of Spirit*, 130.

85. Ibid, 132.

86. Derrida, "Eating Well," 116.

Chapter 10: Rethinking the Moral Status of Animals

1. Sorabji, *Animal Minds and Human Morals*, 216–17.

2. Regan, *The Case for Animal Rights*, 25–34. But Regan also recognizes this danger of bias. See Regan, "The Nature and Possibility of an Environmental Ethic," 30.

3. Sorabji, *Animal Minds and Human Morals*, 217.

4. See ibid., ch. 11.

5. Regan, "The Nature and Possibility of an Environmental Ethic," 21.

6. Ibid., 30.

7. See chapter 1 above for discussion of the lifeboat dilemma.

8. Nussbaum, "Animal Rights," 1521.

9. Ibid., 1543. Cf. p. 1535: Nussbaum calls her own approach the "capabilities" view, by which she means that we must recognize "the presence of certain powers, deemed valuable in themselves" and worthy of growth and flourishing in living beings.

10. Edmund Husserl, *The Crisis of the European Sciences and Transcendental Phenomenology*, trans. David Carr (Evanston: Northwestern University Press, 1970), 16 (translation altered). Cf. Husserl, "The Vienna Lecture," in ibid., 299: The purported failure of rationalism is merely an *apparent* failure.

11. Sigmund Freud, *The Future of an Illusion*, trans. James Strachey (New York: Norton, 1989), sec. 10, p. 65 (translation altered).

12. Luc Ferry, *The New Ecological Order*, trans. Carol Volk (Chicago: University of Chicago Press, 1995), xx–xxi.

13. Ibid., xxi. "Khaki" is an oblique reference to the SA (Sturmabteilung), also known as storm troopers or Brownshirts, a violent security force for Nazi rallies organized in 1921 by Ernst Röhm. Starting in 1924, all party members wore the brown shirts worn by the SA.

14. Ferry, *The New Ecological Order*, xviii, xxiv.

15. As some of the Stoics argue, compare creatures such as spiders, which weave a perfect web on the very first attempt: this fact signifies that such creatures act purely from instinct or nature, that they lack reason, and hence that they are inferior to human beings.

16. Ferry, *The New Ecological Order*, 18.

17. Ibid., 10. Cf. p. 41: "Men and animals seem to be separated by an abyss which bears [the] name . . . history."

18. Ibid., xxix, 18, 52–56.

19. Ibid., 67, 69.

20. Ibid., 89

21. Ibid., 93.

22. On the terms of this conservative revolutionary critique of modernity, see Richard Wolin, *Heidegger's Children: Hannah Arendt, Karl Löwith, Hans Jonas, and Herbert Marcuse* (Princeton: Princeton University Press, 2001), 179; Gary Steiner, "The Perils of a Total Critique of Reason: Rethinking Heidegger's Influence," *Philosophy Today* 47 (2003): 94.

23. Ferry, *The New Ecological Order*, 90.

24. Ibid., 98, 106.

25. See Giese and Kahler, *Das deutsche Tierschutzrecht: Bestimmungen zum Schutze der Tiere (Tierschutzgesetz, Schlachtgesetz, Eisenbahnsverkehrsordnung, Reichsjagdgesetz, Reichsnaturschutzgesetz, Straßenverkehrsordnung mit den dazu ergangenen Verordnungen)*, 3d ed. (Berlin: Duncker and Humboldt, 1944). A translation of the expanded 1938 version of the Animal Protection Law, together with a chronology of the relevant laws, orders, and decrees is provided in Boria Sax, *Animals in the Third Reich: Pets, Scapegoats, and the Holocaust* (New York: Continuum, 2000), 175–82. Background on the Green Nazi movement is provided in Anna Bramwell, *Blood and Soil: Richard Walther Darré and Hitler's 'Green Party'* (Abbotsbrook: Kensal House, 1985). Darré was minister of agriculture under the Nazis from 1933 to 1942.

26. Sax, *Animals in the Third Reich*, 41–42.

27. Ibid., 43. Cf. p. 115: Sax notes that this was a logic according to which, for example, animals were to be treated better than concentration camp inmates.

28. Ferry, *The New Ecological Order*, 112; Hayek, *The Road to Serfdom*.

29. Ferry, *The New Ecological Order*, 129.

30. Ibid., 131. Italics in original.

31. Ferry, ibid., p. 151.

32. See John Rawls, *A Theory of Justice*, revised ed. (Cambridge, Mass.: Belknap Press of Harvard University Press, 1999), 441, 448: Animals are owed no justice because they lack "the capacity for a sense of justice." Nonetheless, like Kant, Rawls acknowledges that it is possible to argue for duties such as compassion toward animals; but all such duties are "outside the scope of the theory of justice, and it does not seem possible to extend the contract doctrine so as to include them in a natural way."

33. Karl Löwith, *Meaning in History: The Theological Implications of the Philosophy of History* (Chicago: University of Chicago Press, 1962), 68.

34. Richard Wolin makes this charge, and succinctly explains the dangers of such a "total critique of reason," in *Heidegger's Children*; see in particular pp. 78–79, 95–100.

35. Karl Löwith, "Heidegger: Thinker in a Destitute Time," in *Martin Heidegger and European Nihilism*, ed. Richard Wolin, trans. Gary Steiner (New York: Columbia University Press, 1995), 43 (citing Heidegger's "What is Metaphysics?").

36. Heidegger uses the Greek term *physis* (φύσις) to characterize nature as a mysterious presence that emerges from an origin that is forever hidden from human beings; Heidegger appeals to *physis* to counter the modern scientific conception of nature as a set of objects that are fully knowable and controllable by human beings.

37. Löwith, "Heidegger: Thinker in a Destitute Time," 86, 91.

38. Löwith, *Meaning in History*, 21.

39. Löwith, *Martin Heidegger and European Nihilism*, 95.

40. Löwith, *Meaning in History*, 25, 21.

41. Heidegger follows Friedrich Hölderlin in seeing the problem of homelessness as a problem of the flight of the gods: Modernity is "the age of the gods who have fled and of the one to come. It is the *destitute* time, because it stands

under a double lack and a double not: the no-longer of gods who have fled, and the not-yet of the one to come." Martin Heidegger, "Hölderlin and the Essence of Poetry," in *Existence and Being*, ed. Werner Brock (Washington, D.C.: Regnery/ Gateway, 1988), 289 (translation altered).

42. Karl Löwith, "Natur und Humanität des Menschen," in *Welt und Menschenwelt: Beiträge zur Anthropologie*, Sämtliche Schriften, vol. 1 (Stuttgart: Metzler, 1981), 294.

43. Karl Löwith, "Welt und Menschenwelt," in *Welt und Menschenwelt*, 295.

44. Ibid., 303.

45. See Steiner, *Descartes as a Moral Thinker*, ch. 4.

46. Hans Jonas, *The Imperative of Responsibility: In Search of an Ethics for the Technological Age* (Chicago: University of Chicago Press, 1984), 141.

47. Hans Jonas, "The Practical Uses of Theory," in *The Phenomenon of Life: Toward a Philosophical Biology* (Chicago: University of Chicago Press, 1982), 195.

48. Hans Jonas, "Seventeenth Century and After: The Meaning of the Scientific and Technological Revolutions," in *Philosophical Essays: From Ancient Creed to Technological Man* (Chicago: University of Chicago Press, 1980), 70.

49. Wolin, *Heidegger's Children*, 103.

50. See Hans Jonas, *Morality and Mortality: A Search for the Good after Auschwitz*, ed. Lawrence Vogel (Evanston, Ill.: Northwestern University Press, 1996).

51. Hans Jonas, *The Gnostic Religion: The Message of the Alien God and the Beginnings of Christianity*, 2d ed. (Boston: Beacon, 1991), 340.

52. Ferry, *The New Ecological Order*, p. 77.

53. Ibid., 82–83.

54. Jonas, *The Imperative of Responsibility*, 202; see also pp. 26–27.

55. Ferry, *The New Ecological Order*, 112.

56. Wolin, *Heidegger's Children*, 123–26.

57. Jonas, *The Imperative of Responsibility*, 147.

58. Ibid., 149.

59. Sorabji, *Animal Minds and Human Morals*, 216.

60. Sue Savage-Rumbaugh, Stuart G. Shanker, and Talbot J. Taylor, *Apes, Language, and the Human Mind* (New York: Oxford University, 1998), 4.

61. E. Sue Savage-Rumbaugh, *Ape Language: From Conditioned Response to Symbol* (New York: Columbia University Press, 1986), 379.

62. Ibid., chaps. 9, 10, 14.

63. Ibid., 329.

64. Ibid., 334.

65. Douglas Keith Candland, *Feral Children and Clever Animals: Reflections on Human Nature* (New York: Oxford University Press, 1993), 343. For the details of these experiments, see Savage-Rumbaugh, *Ape Language*, ch. 7, and Candland, *Feral Children and Clever Animals*, 336.

66. Savage-Rumbaugh et al., *Apes, Language, and the Human Mind*, 139–40.

67. Ibid., 165.

68. Dorothy L. Cheney and Robert M. Seyfarth, *How Monkeys See the World: Inside the Mind of Another Species* (Chicago: University of Chicago Press, 1990), 9–10; see also H. Markl, "Manipulation, Modulation, Information, Cognition: Some of the Riddles

of Communication," in *Experimental Behavioral Ecology and Sociobiology*, ed. B. Holldobler and M. Lindauer (Sunderland, Mass.: Sinauer Associates, 1985), 163–94.

69. Savage-Rumbaugh et al., *Apes, Language, and the Human Mind*, 167. Italics in original. Cf. p. 141: The complex "metalinguistic claim" for which the authors argue is that laboratory-reared apes such as Kanzi "really understand what a spoken English sentence means"; that "the signs and lexigrams that some apes have learned to produce really mean or refer" to specific objects and states of affairs; that "these apes, when producing or responding to communicational behavior, [are] really following ([at least] simple) linguistic rules"; and that "any such ape knows what it is doing when it produces or responds to language . . . it really [understands], as we do, that language is for communicating thoughts and intentions to others, for speaking truly (and sometimes falsely) of the world, and for attaining particular communicational goals."

70. T. T. Struhsaker, *The Red Colobus Monkey* (Chicago: University of Chicago Press, 1967).

71. See D. L. Cheney and R. M. Seyfarth, "How Vervet Monkeys Perceive their Grunts: Field Playback Experiments," *Animal Behavior* 30 (1982): 739–51.

72. Cheney and Seyfarth, *How Monkeys See the World*, 137–38. Cheney and Seyfarth have elaborated Struhsaker's work on vervet alarm calls and have determined that the responses of vervets are not uniform in response to a given alarm call; for example, "vervet eagle alarm calls elicit at least four different responses. Animals on the ground may look up or run into a bush, whereas animals in a tree may run down out of the tree. In either case, a listener can also do nothing. . . . The simplest explanation is that eagle alarm calls refer not to particular escape responses but to certain broad classes of danger." *How Monkeys See the World*, 167–68. Cf. p. 169 for a discussion of the ways in which vervet monkeys in Cameroon respond to threats specific to the area, such as feral dogs.

73. Ibid., 173.

74. S. Gouzoules, H. Gouzoules, and P. Marler, "Rhesus Monkey (*Macaca mulatta*) Screams: Representational Signalling in the Recruitment of Agonistic Aid," *Animal Behavior* 32 (1984): 182–93.

75. S. Gouzoules, H. Gouzoules, and P. Marler, "Vocal Communication: A Vehicle for the Study of Relationships," in *The Cayo Santiago Macaques: History, Behavior, and Biology*, ed. Richard G. Rawlins (Albany: SUNY Press, 1986), 111–29.

76. For a summary of the research on cockerels, see Griffin, *Animal Minds*, 162–63.

77. William A. Hillix and Duane M. Rumbaugh, *Animal Bodies, Human Minds: Ape, Dolphin, and Human Language Skills* (New York: Kluwer Academic/Plenum, 2004), 252. Hillix and Rumbaugh provide a detailed discussion and evaluation of Alex's linguistic abilities.

78. Griffin, *Animal Minds*, 174.

79. See Marc Bekoff, "Play Signals as Punctuation: The Structure of Social Play in Canids," *Behavior* 132 (1995): 419–29; "Animal Play, Problems and Perspectives," *Perspectives in Ethology* 2 (1976): 165–88; "Social Play and Play-Soliciting by Infant Canids," *American Zoologist* 14 (1974): 323–40.

80. Marc Bekoff, *Minding Animals: Awareness, Emotions, and Heart* (Oxford: Oxford University Press, 2002), 120; see also Marc Bekoff and John A. Byers, eds., *Animal Play: Evolutionary, Comparative, and Ecological Perspectives* (Cambridge: Cambridge University Press, 1998).

81. Martin E. P. Seligman, *Helplessness: On Depression, Development, and Death* (San Francisco: W. H. Freeman, 1975), 22.

82. Ibid., 47.

83. Ibid., 31. Cf. p. 51: The representation consists in "learning that [the] outcome is independent of [the] response."

84. Ibid., 51.

85. Ibid., 59 (referring to Richter's experiments with rats).

86. Stephen R. L. Clark, "The Reality of Shared Emotions," 468.

87. Ibid., 459.

88. Ibid., 465.

89. James L. Gould and William F. Towne, "Evolution of the Dance Language," *American Naturalist* 130 (1987): 318–19, 336.

90. Griffin, *Animal Minds*, 191, 241.

91. James L. Gould and Carol Grant Gould, "Invertebrate Intelligence," in *Animal Intelligence: Insights into the Animal Mind*, ed. R. J. Hoage and Larry Goldman, 21–36 (Washington, D.C.: Smithsonian Institution, 1986), 24.

92. See ibid., 28: "There is no reason to suppose that the learning requires any active intelligence on the part of the 'student'. Relatively rigid mental rules underlie trial-and-error learning, which animals appear to be unable to overcome even when it seems obvious that they are poorly matched to the situation."

93. Nagel, "What is it like to be a bat?" 166.

94. See Candland, *Feral Children and Clever Animals*, 369: "We do not know whether chickens, and fish [subjectively relate to other minds, as humans do], but do we not, in our own minds, believe that these beasts also have rich and complex beliefs about their own minds—and perhaps about ours? When my dog barks at me, do I not attribute to the dog some purpose, a purpose reflected in my reflecting about the contents of the dog-mind? In this way, the mind of my dog is inextricably bound to my mind, *for I have no way to create its mind than by applying the categories and concepts of my own*" (italics added).

95. Griffin, *Animal Minds*, 237–38. Griffin gives the example of understanding echolocation in bats by analogy to the audible cues that blind humans use (so-called facial vision). Nagel gives the same example but makes little of it; see "What is it like to be a bat?" 172n8.

96. Daisie Radner, "Heterophenomenology: Learning about the Birds and the Bees," *Journal of Philosophy* 91 (1994): 398.

97. Ibid., 393.

98. Gould and Gould, *The Honey Bee*, 41–43.

99. Karl von Frisch, *The Dance Language and Orientation of Bees*, trans. Leigh E. Chadwick (Cambridge, Mass.: Harvard University Press, 1993), 482–83.

100. Radner, "Heterophenomenology," 396.

101. Charles R. Gallistel, *The Organization of Learning* (Cambridge, Mass.: M.I.T. Press, 1990), 103.

102. Ibid., 133.

103. F. C. Dyer and J. L. Gould, "Honey Bee Orientation: A Backup System for Cloudy Days," *Science* 214 (1981): 1041–42. See also Gallistel, *The Organization of Learning*, 131–40.

104. For the specific details of these dances, see von Frisch, *The Dance Language and Orientation of Bees*, chs. 3 and 4.

105. Griffin, *Animal Minds*, 182, 185, 241.

106. Ibid., 10, 249.

107. Gould and Gould, *The Honey Bee*, 219.

108. Ibid., 225.

109. Paul W. Taylor, *Respect for Nature: A Theory of Environmental Ethics* (Princeton: Princeton University Press, 1986), 99–100.

110. Ibid., 308.

111. Ibid., 312.

112. Ibid., 260, 198–218.

113. Ibid., 276, 282–87.

114. See ibid., 11–12. Much has been written on the problem of developing a nonanthropocentric ethic of reverence for nature. In addition to Taylor's work, texts that are particularly worth mention are Robin Attfield, *The Ethics of Environmental Concern*, 2d ed. (Athens: University of Georgia Press, 1991); J. Baird Callicott, "Animal Liberation: A Triangular Affair," in *The Animal Rights/Environmental Ethics Debate: The Environmental Perspective*, ed. Eugene C. Hargrove, 37-69 (Albany: SUNY Press, 1992); Aldo Leopold, *A Sand County Almanac and Sketches Here and There* (New York: Oxford University, 1949).

115. Taylor, *Respect for Nature*, 99, 308.

BIBLIOGRAPHY

Adams, Carol J. *The Sexual Politics of Meat: A Feminist-Vegetarian Critical Theory*. New York: Continuum, 1990.

Agamben, Giorgio. *The Open: Man and Animal*. Translated by Kevin Attell. Stanford: Stanford University Press, 2004.

Allen, Colin. "Mental Content." *British Journal for the Philosophy of Science* 43 (1992): 537–53.

———. "Mental Content and Evolutionary Explanation." *Biology and Philosophy* 7 (1992): 1–12.

Allen, Colin, and Marc D. Hauser. "Concept Attribution in Nonhuman Animals: Theoretical and Methodological Problems in Ascribing Complex Mental Processes." *Philosophy of Science* 58 (1991): 221–40.

Aquinas, Saint Thomas. *Basic Writings of St. Thomas Aquinas*. Edited by Anton C. Pegis. 2 vols. Indianapolis: Hackett, 1997.

———. *Commentary on the Metaphysics of Aristotle*. Translated by John P. Rowan. 2 vols. Chicago: Regnery, 1961.

———. *Commentary on the Posterior Analytics of Aristotle*. Translated by F. R. Larcher. Albany: Magi, 1970.

———. *Summa Contra Gentiles*. Turin: Casa Editrice Marietti, 1946.

———. *The 'Summa Theologica' of St. Thomas Aquinas*. Translated by Fathers of the English Dominican Province. 22 vols. London: Burns Oats and Washbourne, 1920–1925.

———. *Truth*. Translated by Robert W. Mulligan, James V. McGlynn, and Robert W. Schmidt. 3 vols. Indianapolis: Hackett, 1995.

Aristotle. *Aristotle's "De Partibus Animalium I" and "De Generatione Animalium I" (with Passages from II.1–3)*. Greek with English translation by D. M. Balme. Oxford: Clarendon, 1972.

———. *The Complete Works of Aristotle*. Edited by Jonathan Barnes. 2 vols. Revised Oxford Translation. Princeton: Princeton University Press, Bollingen, 1995.

———. *History of Animals, Books IV–VI*. Greek with English translation by A. L. Peck. Cambridge, Mass.: Harvard University Press, 2002.

———. *History of Animals, Books VII–X*. Greek with English translation and edited by D. M. Balme. Cambridge, Mass.: Harvard University Press, 1991.

———. *Parts of Animals, Movement of Animals, Progression of Animals*. Greek with English translation by A. L. Peck and E. S. Forster. Cambridge, Mass.: Harvard University Press, 1998.

Attfield, Robin. *The Ethics of Environmental Concern*. 2d ed. Athens: University of Georgia, 1991.

Attwater, Donald. *St. John Chrysostom: Pastor and Preacher*. London: Harvill, 1959.

Augustine, Saint. *Against the Academicians, and The Teacher*. Translated by Peter King. Indianapolis: Hackett, 1995.

———. *The Catholic and Manichaean Ways of Life*. Translated by Donald A. Gallagher and Idella J. Gallagher. Fathers of the Church, vol. 56. Washington, D.C.: Catholic University of America Press, 1966.

———. *The City of God against the Pagans*. Edited and translated by R. W. Dyson. Cambridge: Cambridge University Press, 1998.

———. *Confessions*. Translated by R. S. Pine-Coffin. London: Penguin, 1961.

———. *Eighty-Three Different Questions*. Translated by David L. Mosher. Fathers of the Church, vol. 70. Washington, D.C.: Catholic University of America Press, 1982.

———. *The Essential Augustine*. Edited by Vernon J. Bourke. Indianapolis: Hackett, 1974.

———. *On Free Choice of the Will*. Translated by Thomas Williams. Indianapolis: Hackett, 1993.

———. *On Music*, in *The Immortality of the Soul, The Magnitude of the Soul, On Music, The Advantage of Believing, and On Faith in Things Unseen*. Translated by Ludwig Schopp et al. Fathers of the Church, vol. 4. Washington, D.C.: Catholic University of America Press, 1992.

———. *Tractates on the Gospel of John 28–54*. Translated by John W. Rettig. Fathers of the Church, vol. 88. Washington, D.C.: Catholic University of America Press, 1993.

Babb, Lawrence A. *Absent Lord: Ascetics and Kings in a Jain Ritual Culture*. Berkeley: University of California Press, 1996.

Barad, Judith. *Aquinas on the Nature and Treatment of Animals*. San Francisco: International Scholars, 1995.

Basil of Caesarea. *Exegetic Homilies*. Translated by Sister Agnes Clare Way. Fathers of the Church, vol. 46. Washington, D.C.: Catholic University of America Press, 1963.

———. *Homélies sur l'Hexaéméron*. Greek with French translation. Translated with an introduction by Stanislas Giet. 2d ed. Paris: Cerf, 1968.

Bayle, Pierre. *Historical and Critical Dictionary*. Translated by Richard Popkin with the assistance of Craig Bush. Indianapolis: Bobbs-Merrill, 1965.

Beck, L. J. *The Method of Descartes: A Study of the 'Regulae'*. New York: Garland, 1987.

Beiser, Frederick C., ed. *The Early Political Writings of the German Romantics*. Cambridge: Cambridge University Press, 1996.

———. *The Fate of Reason: German Philosophy from Kant to Fichte*. Cambridge, Mass.: Harvard University, 1987.

Bekoff, Marc. "Animal Play, Problems and Perspectives." *Perspectives in Ethology* 2 (1976): 165–88.

———. *Minding Animals: Awareness, Emotions, and Heart.* Oxford: Oxford University, 2002.

———. "Play Signals as Punctuation: The Structure of Social Play in Canids." *Behavior* 132 (1995): 419–29.

———. "Social Play and Play-Soliciting by Infant Canids." *American Zoologist* 14 (1974): 323–40.

Bekoff, Marc, and John A. Byers, eds. *Animal Play: Evolutionary, Comparative, and Ecological Perspectives.* Cambridge: Cambridge University Press, 1998.

Bentham, Jeremy. *An Introduction to the Principles of Morals and Legislation.* New York: Hafner/Macmillan, 1948.

Berlin, Isaiah. *The Roots of Romanticism.* The A. W. Mellon Lectures in the Fine Arts, 1965. Princeton: Princeton University Press, 2001.

Boas, George. *The Happy Beast in French Thought of the Seventeenth Century.* New York: Octagon Books, 1966.

Bramwell, Anna. *Blood and Soil: Richard Walther Darré and Hitler's 'Green Party'.* Abbotsbrook: Kensal House, 1985.

Burkert, Walter. "Greek Tragedy and Sacrificial Ritual." *Greek, Roman, and Byzantine Studies* 7 (1966): 87–121.

Callicott, J. Baird. "Animal Liberation: A Triangular Affair." In *The Animal Rights/ Environmental Ethics Debate: The Environmental Perspective,* edited by Eugene C. Hargrove, 37–69. Albany: SUNY Press, 1992.

Candland, Douglas Keith. *Feral Children and Clever Animals: Reflections on Human Nature.* New York: Oxford University, 1993.

Cassirer, Ernst, Paul Oskar Kristeller, and John Herman Randall Jr. *The Renaissance Philosophy of Man.* Chicago: University of Chicago Press, 1948.

Cheney, Dorothy L., and Robert M. Seyfarth. *How Monkeys See the World: Inside the Mind of Another Species.* Chicago: University of Chicago Press, 1990.

———. "How Vervet Monkeys Perceive their Grunts: Field Playback Experiments." *Animal Behavior* 30 (1982): 739–51.

Chomsky, Noam. "Linguistics and Philosophy." In *Language and Philosophy: A Symposium,* edited by Sidney Hook, 51–94. New York: New York University Press; London: University of London Press, 1969.

———. *New Horizons in the Study of Language and Mind.* Cambridge: Cambridge University Press, 2000.

———. *On Nature and Language.* Edited by Adriana Belletti and Luigi Rizzi. Cambridge: Cambridge University Press, 2002.

———. *Reflections on Language.* New York: Pantheon, 1975.

———. *Rules and Representations.* Oxford: Blackwell, 1980.

Chrysostom, Saint John. *Homilies on Genesis 1–17.* Translated by Robert C. Hill. Fathers of the Church, vol. 74. Washington, D.C.: Catholic University of America Press, 1986.

———. *Homilies on Genesis 18–45.* Translated by Robert C. Hill. Fathers of the Church, vol. 82. Washington, D.C.: Catholic University of America Press, 1990.

Cicero. *De Finibus Bonorum et Malorum.* Latin with English trans. by H. Rackham. Cambridge, Mass.: Harvard University Press, 1999.

Clark, David. "On Being 'The Last Kantian in Nazi Germany': Dwelling with Animals after Levinas." In *Animal Acts: Configuring the Human in Western History*, edited by Jennifer Ham and Matthew Senior, 165–98. New York: Routledge, 1997.

Clark, Gillian. "The Fathers and the Animals: The Rule of Reason?" In *Animals on the Agenda*, edited by Andrew Linzey and Dorothy Yamamoto, 67–79. Urbana: University of Illinois Press, 1998.

——. "Philosophic Lives and the Philosophic Life: Porphyry and Iamblichus." In *Greek Biography and Panegyric in Late Antiquity*, edited by Tomas Hägg and Philip Rousseau, 29–51. Berkeley: University of California Press, 2000.

Clark, Stephen R. L. "The Reality of Shared Emotions." In *Interpretation and Explanation in the Study of Animal Behavior*, Vol. 1: *Interpretation, Intentionality, and Communication*, edited by Marc Bekoff and Dale Jamieson, 449–72. Boulder: Westview, 1990.

Cohen, Leonore D. "Descartes and Henry More on the Beast-Machine—A Translation of Their Correspondence Pertaining to Animal Automatism." *Annals of Science: A Quarterly Review of the History of Science since the Renaissance* 1 (1936): 48–61.

Condillac, Étienne Bonnot de. *Essay on the Origin of Human Knowledge*. Edited by Hans Aarsleff. Cambridge: Cambridge University Press, 2001.

——. *Traité des Animaux*. In *Oeuvres philosophiques de Condillac*, vol. 1, edited by Georges Le Roy, 338–79. Paris: Presses Universitaires de France, 1947.

Cooper, John M. "Reason, Moral Virtue, and Moral Value." In *Rationality in Greek Thought*, edited by Michael Frede and Gisela Striker, 81–114. Oxford: Clarendon, 1996.

Cottingham, John. "'A Brute to the Brutes?': Descartes' Treatment of Animals." *Philosophy* 53 (1978): 551–59.

Darwin, Charles. *The Autobiography of Charles Darwin*. Edited by Francis Darwin. Amherst, N.Y.: Prometheus Books, 2000.

——. *The Expression of the Emotions in Man and Animals*. Edited by Paul Ekman. 3d ed. New York: Oxford University Press, 1998.

——. *The Origin of Species by Means of Natural Selection or the Preservation of Favored Races in the Struggle for Life and The Descent of Man and Selection in Relation to Sex*. New York: Modern Library, n.d.

——. *The Variation of Plants and Animals under Domestication*. 2 vols. New York: Orange Judd and Co., 1868.

Davidson, Donald. "Rational Animals." In *Actions and Events: Perspectives on the Philosophy of Donald Davidson*, edited by Ernest LePore and Brian McLaughlin, 473–80. Oxford: Basil Blackwell, 1985.

DeGrazia, David. *Taking Animals Seriously: Mental Life and Moral Status*. Cambridge: Cambridge University Press, 1996.

Dennett, Daniel C. *Content and Consciousness*. London: Routledge and Kegan Paul, 1969.

Derrida, Jacques. *Aporias*. Translated by Thomas Dutoit. Stanford: Stanford University Press, 1993.

——. "'Eating Well', or the Calculation of the Subject: An Interview with Jacques Derrida." In *Who Comes After the Subject?* edited by Eduardo Cadava, Peter Connor, and Jean-Luc Nancy, 96–119. New York: Routledge, 1991.

——. "Force of Law: The 'Mystical Foundation of Authority.'" Translated by Mary Quaintance. *Cardozo Law Review* 11 (1989–90): 919–1045.

——. *Of Spirit: Heidegger and the Question.* Translated by Geoffrey Bennington and Rachel Bowlby. Chicago: University of Chicago Press, 1991.

——. "On Reading Heidegger: An Outline of the Essex Colloquium." *Research in Phenomenology* 17 (1987): 171–87.

Descartes, René. *Descartes: His Moral Philosophy and Psychology.* Translated with an introduction by John J. Blom. New York: NYU Press, 1978.

——. *Discours de la Méthode: Texte et commentaire.* 5th ed. Edited by Étienne Gilson. Paris: Vrin, 1976.

——. *Oeuvres de Descartes.* Edited by Charles Adam and Paul Tannery. 12 vols. Paris: Vrin, 1964–74.

——. *The Passions of the Soul.* Translated by Stephen H. Voss. Indianapolis: Hackett, 1989.

——. *The Philosophical Writings of Descartes.* Edited by John Cottingham et al. 3 vols. Cambridge: Cambridge University Press, 1984–1991.

Diamond, Cora. "Eating Meat and Eating People." *Philosophy* 53 (1978): 465–79.

Diels, Hermann, trans., and Walther Kranz, ed. *Die Fragmente der Vorsokratiker.* 3 vols. Zurich: Weidmann, 1964.

Dierauer, Urs. *Tier und Mensch im Denken der Antike: Studien zur Tierpsychologie, Anthropologie und Ethik.* Amsterdam: Grüner, 1977.

Diogenes Laertius. *Lives of Eminent Philosophers.* Vol. 2. Greek with English translation by R. D. Hicks. Cambridge, Mass.: Harvard University Press, 2000.

Dombrowski, Daniel. *Babies and Beasts: The Argument from Marginal Cases.* Urbana: University of Illinois, 1997.

——. *The Philosophy of Vegetarianism.* Amherst: University of Massachusetts Press, 1984.

Dyer, F. C., and J. L. Gould. "Honey Bee Orientation: A Backup System for Cloudy Days." *Science* 214 (1981): 1041–42.

Epictetus. *The Discourses as Reported by Arrian, Books I–II.* Greek with English trans. by W. A. Oldfather. Cambridge, Mass.: Harvard University Press, 2000.

——. *The Discourses Books III–IV. Fragments. Encheiridion.* Greek with English trans. by W. A. Oldfather. Cambridge, Mass.: Harvard University Press, 2000.

Ferry, Luc. *The New Ecological Order.* Translated by Carol Volk. Chicago: University of Chicago Press, 1995.

Fortenbaugh, William W. "Aristotle: Animals, Emotion, and Moral Virtue." *Arethusa* 4 (1971): 137–65.

Francione, Gary L. *Introduction to Animal Rights: Your Child or the Dog?* Philadelphia: Temple University Press, 2000.

Francis of Assisi, Saint. *The Little Flowers of St. Francis of Assisi.* Paterson, N.J.: St. Anthony Guild Press, 1958.

——. *Writings and Early Biographies: English Omnibus of the Sources for the Life of St. Francis.* Edited by Marion A. Habig. 2 vols. Quincy, Ill.: Franciscan Press, 1991.

Frazer, Sir James George. *The Golden Bough: A Study in Magic and Religion,* New York: Macmillan, 1922.

Freud, Sigmund. *Civilization and Its Discontents*. Translated by James Strachey. New York: Norton, 1989.

——. *The Future of an Illusion*. Translated by James Strachey. New York: Norton, 1989.

Frey, R. G. *Interests and Rights: The Case against Animals*. Oxford: Clarendon, 1980.

Friedman, Richard Elliott. *Who Wrote the Bible?* 2d ed. San Francisco: HarperCollins, 1997.

Frisch, Karl von. *The Dance Language and Orientation of Bees*. Translated by Leigh E. Chadwick. Cambridge, Mass.: Harvard University Press, 1993.

Gaffney, James. "Can Catholic Morality Make Room for Animals?" In *Animals on the Agenda: Questions about Animals for Theology and Ethics*, edited by Andrew Linzey and Dorothy Yamamoto, 100–112. Urbana: University of Illinois Press, 1998.

Gallistel, Charles R. *The Organization of Learning*. Cambridge, Mass.: M.I.T. Press, 1990.

Gaukroger, Stephen. *Descartes: An Intellectual Biography*. Oxford: Clarendon Press, 1995.

Gelli, Giovanni Battista. *Circe. Consisting of Ten Dialogues between Ulysses and several men transformed into beasts, satirically representing the various passions of mankind and the many infelicities of human life*. Translated by Thomas Brown, revised translation and introduction by Robert Adams. Ithaca: Cornell University Press, 1963.

Gibson, A. Boyce. *The Philosophy of Descartes*. New York: Garland, 1987.

Giese and Kahler. *Das deutsche Tierschutzrecht: Bestimmungen zum Schutze der Tiere (Tierschutzgesetz, Schlachtgesetz, Eisenbahnsverkehrsordnung, Reichsjagdgesetz, Reichsnaturschutzgesetz, Straßenverkehrsordnung mit den dazu ergangenen Verordnungen)*. 3d ed. Berlin: Duncker and Humboldt, 1944.

Gould, James L., and Carol Grant Gould. *The Honey Bee*. New York: Scientific American Books, 1988.

——. "Invertebrate Intelligence." In *Animal Intelligence: Insights into the Animal Mind*, edited by R. J. Hoage and Larry Goldman, 21–36. Washington, D.C.: Smithsonian Institution, 1986.

Gould, James L., and William F. Towne. "Evolution of the Dance Language." *American Naturalist* 130 (1987): 318–38.

Gouzoules, S., H. Gouzoules, and P. Marler. "Rhesus Monkey (*Macaca mulatta*) Screams: Representational Signalling in the Recruitment of Agonistic Aid." *Animal Behavior* 32 (1984): 182–93.

——. "Vocal Communication: A Vehicle for the Study of Relationships" In *The Cayo Santiago Macaques: History, Behavior, and Biology*, edited by Richard G. Rawlins, 111–29. Albany: SUNY Press, 1986.

Grene, Marjorie. *Descartes*. Minneapolis: University of Minnesota Press, 1985.

Griffin, Donald R. *Animal Minds*. Chicago: University of Chicago Press, 1994.

Hampshire, Stuart. "Morality and Pessimism." In *Public and Private Morality*, edited by S. Hampshire et al., 1–22. Cambridge: Cambridge University Press, 1978.

Harrison, Peter. "Descartes on Animals." *Philosophical Quarterly* 42 (1992): 219–27.

Haussleiter, Johannes. *Der Vegetarismus in der Antike*. Religionsgeschichtliche Versuche und Vorarbeiten, vol. 24. Berlin: Alfred Töpelmann, 1935.

Hayek, F. A. *The Road to Serfdom*. Chicago: University of Chicago, 1994.

Heidegger, Martin. *Being and Time*. Translated by John Macquarrie and Edward
Robinson. New York: Harper and Row, 1962.
——. *Existence and Being*. Edited by Werner Brock. Washington, D.C.: Regnery/
Gateway, 1988.
——. *The Fundamental Concepts of Metaphysics: World, Finitude, Solitude*. Translated by William
McNeill and Nicholas Walker. Bloomington: Indiana University Press, 1995.
——. *Die Grundbegriffe der Metaphysik: Welt—Endlichkeit—Einsamkeit*. Gesamtausgabe, vol. 29/
30, Frankfurt: Klostermann, 1983.
——. *Logik: Die Frage nach der Wahrheit*. Gesamtausgabe, vol. 21. Frankfurt:
Klostermann, 1976.
——. *On the Way to Language*. Translated by Peter D. Hertz. San Francisco: Harper and
Row, 1982.
——. *Parmenides*. Gesamtausgabe, vol. 54. Frankfurt: Klostermann, 1982.
——. *Pathmarks*. Translated by William McNeill. Cambridge: Cambridge University
Press, 1998.
——. *Poetry, Language, Thought*. Translated by Albert Hofstadter. New York: Perennial
Classics/HarperCollins, 2001.
——. *The Question Concerning Technology and Other Essays*. Translated by William Lovitt. New
York: Harper and Row, 1977.
——. *Schellings Abhandlung über das Wesen der menschlichen Freiheit*. Edited by Hildegard Feick.
Tübingen: Niemeyer, 1971.
Herder, Johann Gottfried von. *Outlines of a Philosophy of the History of Man*. Translated by
T. Churchill. New York: Bergman, 1800.
——. *Philosophical Writings*. Translated and edited by Michael N. Forster. Cambridge:
Cambridge University Press, 2002.
Herrnstein, R. J. "Objects, Categories, and Discriminative Stimuli." In *Animal
Cognition: Proceedings of the Harry Frank Guggenheim Conference, June 2–4, 1982*, edited by H.
L. Roitblat, T. G. Bever, and H. S. Terrace, 233–61. Hillsdale, N.J.: Lawrence
Erlbaum Associates, 1984.
Herrnstein, R. J., D. H. Loveland, and C. Cable. "Natural Concepts in Pigeons."
Journal of Experimental Psychology: Animal Behavior Processes 2 (1976): 285–302.
Hesiod. *Hesiod*. Translated by Richard Lattimore. Ann Arbor: University of
Michigan Press, 1959.
Hiebert, Theodore. *The Yahwist's Landscape: Nature and Religion in Early Israel*. New York:
Oxford University Press, 1996.
Hillix, William A., and Duane Rumbaugh. *Animal Bodies, Human Minds: Ape, Dolphin, and
Parrot Language Skills*. New York: Kluwer Academic/Plenum, 2004.
Hobbes, Thomas. *On the Citizen*. Edited and translated by Richard Tuck and Michael
Silverthorne. Cambridge: Cambridge University Press, 2000.
——. *Leviathan*. Harmondsworth: Penguin, 1985.
Homer. *The Iliad*. Translated by Robert Fagles. New York: Penguin, 1990.
——. *The Odyssey*. Translated by Robert Fitzgerald. Garden City, N.Y.: Doubleday,
1961.
Hume, David. *Enquiries Concerning Human Understanding and Concerning the Principles of Morals*.
3d ed. Edited by P. H. Nidditch. Oxford: Clarendon, 1979.

——. "Of Suicide." In *Essays Moral, Political, and Literary*, 2 vols., new edition, edited by T. H. Green and T. H. Grose, 2:406–14. London: Longmans, Green, and Co., 1882.

——. *A Treatise of Human Nature*. 2d ed. Edited by P. H. Nidditch. Oxford: Clarendon, 1981.

Hursthouse, Rosalind. *On Virtue Ethics*. Oxford: Oxford University Press, 1999.

Husserl, Edmund. *The Crisis of the European Sciences and Transcendental Phenomenology*. Translated by David Carr. Evanston: Northwestern University Press, 1970.

Iamblichus. *On the Pythagorean Life*. Translated by Gillian Clark. Liverpool: Liverpool University, 1989.

Inwood, Brad. *Ethics and Human Action in Early Stoicism*. Oxford: Clarendon, 1985.

Jamieson, Dale. "Rights, Justice, and Duties to Provide Assistance: A Critique of Regan's Theory of Rights." *Ethics* 100 (1990): 349–62.

Jonas, Hans. *The Gnostic Religion: The Message of the Alien God and the Beginnings of Christianity*. 2d ed. Boston: Beacon Press, 1991.

——. *The Imperative of Responsibility: In Search of an Ethics for the Technological Age*. Chicago: University of Chicago Press, 1984.

——. *Morality and Mortality: A Search for the Good after Auschwitz*. Edited by Lawrence Vogel. Evanston: Northwestern University Press, 1996.

——. *The Phenomenon of Life: Toward a Philosophical Biology*. Chicago: University of Chicago Press, 1982.

——. *Philosophical Essays: From Ancient Creed to Technological Man*. Chicago: University of Chicago Press, 1980.

Kahn, Charles H. *Pythagoras and the Pythagoreans: A Brief History*. Indianapolis: Hackett, 2001.

Kant, Immanuel. *Critique of Judgment*. Translated by Werner S. Pluhar. Indianapolis: Hackett, 1987.

——. *Critique of Practical Reason*. 3d ed. Translated by Lewis White Beck. Upper Saddle River, N.J.: Library of Liberal Arts, 1993.

——. *Critique of Pure Reason*. Translated by Norman Kemp Smith. New York: Humanities, 1950.

——. *Grounding for the Metaphysics of Morals*. Translated by James W. Ellington. Indianapolis: Hackett, 1981.

——. *Lectures on Ethics*. Edited by Peter Heath and J. B. Schneewind, translated by Peter Heath. Cambridge: Cambridge University Press, 1997.

——. *The Metaphysics of Morals*. Edited by Mary Gregor. Cambridge: Cambridge University Press, 1996.

——. *Political Writings*. Edited by H. S. Reiss. Cambridge: Cambridge University Press, 1991.

——. *Religion within the Limits of Reason Alone*. Translated by Theodore M. Greene and Hoyt H. Hudson. New York: Harper Torchbooks, 1960.

Kirk, G. S., and J. E. Raven. *The Presocratic Philosophers: A Critical History with a Selection of Texts*. Cambridge: Cambridge University Press, 1979.

Kluge, Friedrich. *Etymologisches Wörterbuch der deutschen Sprache*. Edited by Walther Mitzka. 20th ed. Berlin: de Gruyter, 1967.

Krell, David Farrell. *Daimon Life: Heidegger and Life-Philosophy*. Bloomington: Indiana University Press, 1992.

Labarrière, Jean-Louis. "De la *phronesis* animale." In *Biologie, logique et métaphysique chez Aristotle*, edited by Daniel Devereux and Pierre Pellegrin, 405–28. Paris: Éditions du Centre National de la Recherche Scientifique, 1990.

Laistner, M. L. W. *Christianity and Pagan Culture in the Later Roman Empire Together with An English Translation of John Chrysostom's Address on Vainglory and the Right Way for Parents to Bring Up Their Children*. Ithaca: Cornell University Press, 1967.

Leibniz, G. W. *New Essays on Human Understanding*. Translated and edited by Peter Remnant and Jonathan Bennett. Cambridge: Cambridge University Press, 1996.

——. *Philosophical Essays*. Translated by Roger Ariew and Daniel Garber. Indianapolis: Hackett, 1989.

Leopold, Aldo. *A Sand County Almanac and Sketches Here and There*. New York: Oxford University Press, 1949.

Levi, Anthony, S.J. *French Moralists: The Theory of the Passions, 1585–1649*. Oxford: Clarendon, 1964.

Levinas, Emmanuel. "As if Consenting to Horror." *Critical Inquiry* 15 (1989): 485–88.

——. "The Name of a Dog, or Natural Rights." In *Difficult Freedom: Essays on Judaism*, translated by Seán Hand, 151–53. Baltimore: Johns Hopkins University Press, 1990.

Levinas, Emmanuel, and Richard Kearney. "Dialogue with Emmanuel Levinas." In *Face to Face with Levinas*, edited by Richard A. Cohen, 13–33. Albany: SUNY, 1986.

Linzey, Andrew. *Christianity and the Rights of Animals*. New York: Crossroad, 1987.

Locke, John. *An Essay Concerning Human Understanding*. Edited by Peter H. Nidditch. Oxford: Clarendon, 1990.

——. *Two Treatises of Government*. Edited by Peter Laslett. Cambridge: Cambridge University Press, 1988.

Long, A. A. *Epictetus: A Stoic and Socratic Guide to Life*. Oxford: Clarendon, 2002.

Long, A. A., and D. N. Sedley, eds. and trans. *The Hellenistic Philosophers*. 2 vols. Cambridge: Cambridge University Press, 1990.

Long, Herbert Strainge. *A Study of the Doctrine of Metempsychosis in Greece from Pythagoras to Plato*. Princeton: n.p., 1948.

Lorenz, Konrad. *Studies in Animal and Human Behavior*. 2 vols. Translated by R. Martin. Cambridge, Mass.: Harvard University Press, 1970–1971.

Lossky, Vladimir. *The Mystical Theology of the Eastern Church*. Crestwood, N.Y.: St. Vladimir's Seminary Press, 1976.

Löwith, Karl. *Martin Heidegger and European Nihilism*. Edited by Richard Wolin, translated by Gary Steiner. New York: Columbia University Press, 1995.

——. *Meaning in History: The Theological Implications of the Philosophy of History*. Chicago: University of Chicago Press, 1962.

——. *Welt und Menschenwelt: Beiträge zur Anthropologie*. Sämtliche Schriften, vol. 1. Stuttgart: Metzler, 1981.

——. "Der Weltbegriff der neuzeitlichen Philosophie." *Sitzungsberichte der Heidelberger Akademie der Wissenschaften, Philosophisch-historischer Klasse* 44 (1960): 7–23.

Lucretius. *On the Nature of Things*. Translated by W. H. D. Rouse. Revised by Martin F. Smith. Cambridge, Mass.: Harvard University Press, 1997.

Luther, Martin. *Luther's Works*. Vol. 1, *Lectures on Genesis Ch. 1–5*. Edited by Jaroslav Pelikan, translated by George V. Schick. St. Louis: Concordia, 1958.

——. *Luther's Works*. Vol. 2, *Lectures on Genesis Ch. 6–14*. Edited by Jaroslav Pelikan and Daniel E. Poellot, translated by George V. Schick. St. Louis: Concordia, 1960.

Malcolm, Norman. "Thoughtless Brutes." *Proceedings and Addresses of the American Philosophical Association* 46 (1972–3): 5–20.

Markl, H. "Manipulation, Modulation, Information, Cognition: Some of the Riddles of Communication." In *Experimental Behavioral Ecology and Sociobiology*, edited by B. Holldobler and M. Lindauer, 163–94. Sunderland, Mass.: Sinauer Associates, 1985.

McNeill, William. "Life Beyond the Organism: Animal Being in Heidegger's Freiburg Lectures, 1929–30." In *Animal Others: On Ethics, Ontology, and Animal Life*, edited by Peter Steeves, 197–248. Albany: SUNY, 1999.

Mill, John Stuart. *On Liberty and Other Essays*. Edited by John Gray. Oxford: Oxford University Press, 1998.

——. *Principles of Political Economy*. Oxford: Oxford University Press, 1994.

——. *Three Essays on Religion*. New York: Henry Holt and Co., 1878.

——. "Whewell on Moral Philosophy." In *Utilitarianism and Other Essays: J. S. Mill and Jeremy Bentham*, edited by Alan Ryan, 228–70. Harmondsworth: Penguin, 1987.

Milton, John. *Paradise Lost*. Edited by Roy Flannagan. New York: Macmillan, 1993.

Montaigne, Michel de. *Essays. Travel Journals. Letters*. Translated by Donald M. Frame. Stanford: Stanford University Press, 1957.

Nagel, Thomas. "What is it like to be a bat?" In *Mortal Questions*, 165–80. Cambridge: Cambridge University, 1979.

Nietzsche, Friedrich. "On Truth and Lies in a Nonmoral Sense." In *Philosophy and Truth: Selections from Nietzsche's Notebooks of the Early 1870's*, edited and translated by Daniel Breazeale, 79–97. Atlantic Highlands, N.J.: Humanities Press International, 1992.

——. *The Will to Power*. Translated by Walter Kaufmann and R. J. Hollingdale. New York: Vintage/Random House, 1968.

Nussbaum, Martha C. "Animal Rights: The Need for a Theoretical Basis." Review discussion of *Rattling the Cage: Toward Legal Rights for Animals*, by Steven M. Wise. *Harvard Law Review* 114 (2001): 1506–49.

——. *Aristotle's De Motu Animalium*. Princeton: Princeton University Press, 1978.

——. *The Fragility of Goodness: Luck and Ethics in Greek Tragedy and Philosophy*. Cambridge: Cambridge University Press, 1987.

——. *The Therapy of Desire: Theory and Practice in Hellenistic Ethics*. Princeton: Princeton University Press, 1994.

——. *Upheavals of Thought: The Intelligence of Emotions*. Cambridge: Cambridge University Press, 2001.

Origen. *Contra Celsum*. Translated by Henry Chadwick. Cambridge: Cambridge University Press, 1980.

——. *Homilies on Genesis and Exodus*. Translated by Ronald E. Heine. Fathers of the Church, vol. 71. Washington, D.C.: Catholic University of America Press, 1982.

Orlans, F. Barbara, et al. *The Human Use of Animals: Case Studies in Ethical Choice*. New York: Oxford University Press, 1998.

Ovid. *Metamorphoses*. 2 vols. Latin with English translation by Frank Justus Miller. Cambridge, Mass.: Harvard University, 1977.

Passmore, John. *Man's Responsibility for Nature: Ecological Problems and Western Traditions*. London: Duckworth, 1974.

Pembroke, S. G. "Oikeiosis." In *Problems in Stoicism*, edited by A. A. Long, 114–49. London: University of London/Athlone Press, 1971.

Petitto, Laura Ann, and Paula F. Marentette. "Babbling in the Manual Mode: Evidence for the Ontogeny of Language." *Science* 251 (1991): 1493–96.

Philip, J. A. *Pythagoras and Early Pythagoreanism*. Phoenix: *Journal of the Classical Association of Canada*, supp. vol. 7. Toronto: University of Toronto Press, 1966.

Plato. *The Collected Dialogues of Plato Including the Letters*. Edited by Edith Hamilton and Huntington Cairns. Princeton: Bollingen, 1961.

Plutarch. *Moralia*. Vol. 12. Greek with English translated by Harold Cherniss and William C. Helmbold. Cambridge, Mass.: Harvard University Press, 1995.

——. *Plutarch's Lives*. Vol. 2. Greek with English translated by by Bernadotte Perrin. Cambridge, Mass.: Harvard University; London: William Heinemann, 1985.

Porphyry. *On Abstinence from Killing Animals*. Translated by Gillian Clark. Ithaca: Cornell University Press, 2000.

——. *Vie de Pythagore. Lettre à Marcella*. Greek with French translated by Édouard des Places, S.J. Paris: Société d'Édition 'Les belles lettres', 1982.

Povinelli, Daniel J., in collaboration with James E. Reaux, Laura A. Theall, and Steve Giambrone. *Folk Physics for Apes: The Chimpanzee's Theory of How the World Works*. New York: Oxford University Press, 2000.

Radner, Daisie. "Heterophenomenology: Learning about the Birds and the Bees." *Journal of Philosophy* 91 (1994): 389–403.

Radner, Daisie, and Michael Radner. *Animal Consciousness*. Buffalo: Prometheus Books, 1989.

Rawls, John. *A Theory of Justice*. Revised ed. Cambridge, Mass.: Belknap Press of Harvard University Press, 1999.

Regan, Tom. *The Case for Animal Rights*. Berkeley: University of California Press, 1983.

——. "The Nature and Possibility of an Environmental Ethic." *Environmental Ethics* 3 (1981): 19–34.

Richards, Robert J. *Darwin and the Emergence of Evolutionary Theories of Mind and Behavior*. Chicago: University of Chicago Press, 1987.

——. *The Meaning of Evolution: The Morphological Construction and Ideological Reconstruction of Darwin's Theory*. Chicago: University of Chicago Press, 1992.

——. *The Romantic Conception of Life: Science and Philosophy in the Age of Goethe*. Chicago: University of Chicago Press, 2002.

Rickaby, Joseph, S.J. *Moral Philosophy, or Ethics and Natural Law*. London: Longmans, Green, and Co., 1912.

Rifkin, Jeremy. *Beyond Beef: The Rise and Fall of the Cattle Culture*. New York: Dutton, 1992.

Roethke, Theodore. *The Collected Poems of Theodore Roethke*. Garden City, N.Y.: Doubleday, 1966.

Rosenfeld, Leonora Cohen. *From Beast-Machine to Man-Machine: Animal Soul in French Letters from Descartes to La Mettrie*. New and enlarged ed. New York: Octagon Books, 1968.

Rousseau, Jean-Jacques. *Émile, or Treatise on Education*. Translated by William H. Payne. Amherst, N.Y.: Prometheus, 2003.

———. *Rousseau's Political Writings*. Edited by Alan Ritter and Julia Conaway Bondanella. New York: Norton, 1988.

Rozemond, Marleen. "The Role of the Intellect in Descartes's Case for the Incorporeity of the Mind." In *Essays on the Philosophy and Science of Descartes*, edited by Stephen Voss, 97–114. New York: Oxford University, 1993.

Sälzle, Karl. *Tier und Mensch. Gottheit und Dämon. Das Tier in der Geistesgeschichte der Menschheit*. Munich: Bayerischer Landschaftsverlag, 1965.

Sapontzis, S. F. *Morals, Reason, and Animals*. Philadelphia: Temple University Press, 1987.

Savage-Rumbaugh, E. Sue. *Ape Language: From Conditioned Response to Symbol*. New York: Columbia University Press, 1986.

Savage-Rumbaugh, Sue, Stuart G. Shanker, and Talbot J. Taylor. *Apes, Language, and the Human Mind*. New York: Oxford University Press, 1998.

Sax, Boria. *Animals in the Third Reich: Pets, Scapegoats, and the Holocaust*. New York: Continuum, 2000.

Schama, Simon. *The Embarrassment of Riches: An Interpretation of Dutch Culture in the Golden Age*. New York: Knopf, 1987.

Schirmacher, Wolfgang. *Technik und Gelassenheit: Zeitkritik nach Heidegger*. Freiburg: Alber, 1983.

Schleiermacher, Friedrich Daniel Ernst. *Schriften aus der Berliner Zeit 1800–1802*. Edited by Günter Meckenstock. Berlin: Walter de Gruyter, 1988.

Schmitt, Carl. "Der Staat als Mechanismus bei Hobbes und Descartes." In *Dem Gedächtnis an René Descartes (300 Jahre Discours de la Méthode): Erinnerungsausgabe der Internationalen Vereinigung für Rechts- und Sozialphilosophie*, edited by C. A. Emge, 158–68. Berlin: Verlag für Staatswissenschaften und Geschichte, 1937.

Schopenhauer, Arthur. *The Fourfold Root of the Principle of Sufficient Reason*. Translated by E. F. J. Payne. La Salle, Ill.: Open Court, 1974.

———. *On the Basis of Morality*. Translated by E. F. J. Payne. Providence: Berghahn Books, 1995.

———. *Parerga and Paralipomena*. 2 vols. Translated by E. F. J. Payne. Oxford: Clarendon, 2000.

———. *The World as Will and Representation*. Vol. 1. Translated by E. F. J. Payne. Indian Hills, Colo.: Falcon's Wing, 1958.

———. *The World as Will and Representation*. Vol. 2. Translated by E. F. J. Payne. New York: Dover, 1958.

Schuster, Max. *Untersuchungen zu Plutarchs Dialog "De sollertia animalium" mit besonderer Berücksichtigung der Lehrtätigkeit Plutarchs*. Augsburg: J. P. Himmer, 1917.

Schweitzer, Albert. *Civilization and Ethics: The Philosophy of Civilization Part II.* Translated by John Naish. London: A&C Block, 1923.

Searle, John. "Animal Minds." Unpublished manuscript, cited in David DeGrazia, *Taking Animals Seriously: Mental Life and Moral Status.* Cambridge: Cambridge University, 1996.

———. "Intentionality and Its Place in Nature." *Synthese* 61 (1984): 3–16.

Seligman, Martin E. P. *Helplessness: On Depression, Development, and Death.* San Francisco: W. H. Freeman, 1975.

Seneca. *Ad Lucilium Epistulae Morales.* Vol. 2. Latin with English translation by Richard M. Gummere. London: Heinemann; New York: G. P. Putnam's Sons, 1930.

———. *Ad Lucilium Epistulae Morales.* Vol. 3. Latin with English translation by Richard M. Gummere. London: Heinemann; New York: G. P. Putnam's Sons, 1925.

———. *Moral Essays.* Vol. 1. Latin with English translation by John W. Basore. London: Heinemann; New York: G. P. Putnam's Sons, 1928.

———. *Naturales Quaestiones I.* Seneca in Ten Volumes, vol. 7. Latin with English translation by Thomas H. Corcoran. Cambridge, Mass.: Harvard University Press; London: William Heinemann, 1971.

Séris, Jean-Pierre. "Language and Machine in the Philosophy of Descartes." In *Essays on the Philosophy and Science of René Descartes,* edited by Stephen Voss, 177–92. New York: Oxford University Press, 1993.

Sextus Empiricus. *Sextus Empiricus.* Vol. 3. Greek with English translation by R. G. Bury. Cambridge, Mass.: Harvard University Press, 1936.

———. *The Skeptic Way: Sextus Empiricus's "Outlines of Pyrrhonism."* Translated by Benson Mates. New York: Oxford University Press, 1996.

Sihvola, Juha. "Emotional Animals: Do Aristotelian Emotions Require Beliefs?" *Apeiron* 29 (1996): 105–44.

Simons, Madelaine A. "Rousseau's Natural Diet." *Romantic Review* 45 (1954): 18–28.

Singer, Peter. *Animal Liberation.* 2d ed. London: Jonathan Cape, 1990.

———. *Practical Ethics.* 2d ed. Cambridge: Cambridge University Press, 1993.

———. "Utilitarianism and Vegetarianism." *Philosophy and Public Affairs* 9 (1980): 325–37.

Smith, Norman Kemp. *New Studies in the Philosophy of Descartes.* New York: Russell and Russell, 1963.

Snell, Bruno. *The Discovery of the Mind in Greek Philosophy and Literature.* New York: Dover, 1982.

Sorabji, Richard. *Animal Minds and Human Morals: The Origins of the Western Debate.* Ithaca: Cornell University Press, 1993.

———. "Rationality." In *Rationality in Greek Thought,* edited by Michael Frede and Gisela Striker, 311–34. Oxford: Clarendon, 1996.

Steiner, Gary. *Descartes as a Moral Thinker: Christianity, Technology, Nihilism.* Amherst, N.Y.: Prometheus/Humanity Books, 2004.

———. "The Perils of a Total Critique of Reason: Rethinking Heidegger's Influence." *Philosophy Today* 47 (2003): 93–111.

Stich, Steven. "Do Animals Have Beliefs?" *Australasian Journal of Philosophy* 57 (1979): 15–28.

———. *From Folk Psychology to Cognitive Science: The Case against Belief.* Cambridge, Mass.: M.I.T. Press, 1983.

Striker, Gisela. "The Role of *Oikeiosis* in Stoic Ethics." In *Oxford Studies in Ancient Philosophy* 1, edited by Julia Annas, 145–67. Oxford: Clarendon, 1983.

Struhsaker, T. T. *The Red Colobus Monkey.* Chicago: University of Chicago Press, 1967.

Taylor, Paul W. *Respect for Nature: A Theory of Environmental Ethics.* Princeton: Princeton University Press, 1986.

Tsekourakis, Damianos. "Pythagoreanism or Platonism and Ancient Medicine? The Reasons for Vegetarianism in Plutarch's 'Moralia'." In *Aufstieg und Niedergang der Römischen Welt: Geschichte und Kultur Roms im Spiegel der neueren Forschung* II.36.1, edited by Wolfgang Haase, 366–93. Berlin: de Gruyter, 1987.

Vygotsky, Lev. *Thought and Language.* Translated and edited by Alex Kozulin. Cambridge, Mass.: M.I.T. Press, 1986.

Waal, Franz de. *Chimpanzee Politics.* London: Jonathan Cape, 1982.

White, Lynn, Jr. "The Historical Roots of Our Ecological Crisis." In *Ecology and Religion in History*, edited by David Spring and Eileen Spring, 15–31. New York: Harper Torchbooks, 1974.

White, Nicholas P. "The Basis of Stoic Ethics." *Harvard Studies in Classical Philology* 83 (1979): 143–78.

Williams, Bernard. *Descartes: The Project of Pure Enquiry.* Harmondsworth: Penguin, 1978.

Wilson, Margaret. "Animal Ideas." *Proceedings and Addresses of the American Philosophical Association* 69 (November 1995): 7–25.

———. "Cartesian Dualism." In *Descartes: Critical and Interpretive Essays*, edited by Michael Hooker, 197–211. Baltimore: Johns Hopkins University Press, 1978.

Winden, J. C. M. Van. "Hexaemeron." In *Reallexikon für Antike und Christentum: Sachwörterbuch zur Auseinandersetzung des Christentums mit der antiken Welt*, vol. 14, pp. 1250–70. Stuttgart: Hiersemann, 1988.

Wittgenstein, Ludwig. *Philosophical Investigations.* 3d ed. Translated by G. E. M. Anscombe. New York: Macmillan, 1968.

Wolin, Richard. *Heidegger's Children: Hannah Arendt, Karl Löwith, Hans Jonas, and Herbert Marcuse.* Princeton: Princeton University Press, 2001.

Wollstonecraft, Mary. *A Vindication of the Rights of Men and A Vindication of the Rights of Woman.* Edited by Sylvia Tomaselli. Cambridge: Cambridge University Press, 1995.

Wood, David. "*Comment ne pas manger*—Deconstruction and Humanism." In *Animal Others: On Ethics, Ontology, and Animal Life*, edited by H. Peter Steeves, 15–35. Albany: SUNY Press, 1999.

Wordsworth, William. *Poems.* Selected by Seamus Heaney. New York: Faber and Faber, 2001.

Wright, Tamra, Peter Hughes, and Alison Ainley. "The Paradox of Morality: An Interview with Emmanuel Levinas." In *The Provocation of Levinas: Rethinking the Other*, edited by Robert Bernasconi and David Wood, 168–81. London: Routledge, 1988.

Zwart, Hub. "What Is an Animal? A Philosophical Reflection on the Possibility of a Moral Relationship with Animals." *Environmental Values* 6 (1997): 377–92.

INDEX

Allen, Colin, 21–23, 25–26, 301n33
analogy, 58, 240; Aristotle, 72–76,
264n35; Descartes, 148; Griffin, 20,
308n95; heterophenomenology, 246;
Hume, 160; Kant, 167; Nagel, 246
ants: Aristotle, 61, 266n74; Cleanthes'
story, 98; Darwin, 193; Origen, 120;
Plato, 56; Plutarch, 98; Stoics, 90
apes, 20–22, 214, 250; bonobos, 8, 239–
41; chimpanzees, 8, 20, 32, 239–40,
253; Chomsky on, 35; Herder on, 183;
language capacity in, 7, 22, 32–35,
238–41, 243; Savage-Rumbaugh on,
238–42; Singer on, 7; Vygotsky on,
32–34
Aquinas, Saint Thomas, 2, 27, 38, 126–
31, 186, 189, 195; animals are governed
by instinct, 128–30, 154, 168; human
beings superior to animals because not
governed by instinct, 130, 170–71
Aristotle, 2, 6, 14, 38–39, 50, 105, 113,
172, 182, 202, 209, 224, 233–34,
249; on belief, 57, 62, 67; characterization of Empedocles, 50; characterization of Pythagoras, 48; contrast with
Stoic thought, 78–81, 83–84, 87–88,
91, 100; on emotion in animals, 75,
267n106; ethical and psychological
texts, 59–72; happiness (eudaimonia),
60; imagination (phantasia), 63, 66–67;
influence on Aquinas, 127–29;
influence on Descartes, 134–35, 141–
43; influence on Locke, 158; influence

on the Romantics, 180; intellectual
pleasures superior to brute pleasures,
9; on memory, 68, 70; on primitive
universals, 68–69; on practical wisdom
(phronesis), 70–71; on rationality and
language, 57, 63, 67, 70, 73–75, 100;
on sensation, 64–65, 67; Sorabji on
crisis caused by Aristotle, 53–55, 57,
71, 92; on soul, 76; on teleology, 59,
91; theory, conception of, 234; virtue,
animals incapable of, 61, 62; zoological
texts, 72–76
asceticism, 48, 103, 105, 107–08, 111
associations, capacities of animals to make,
33, 35, 64, 127–28, 158, 160–61, 175–
76, 191–93
Augustine, Saint, 2, 38, 122, 149; animals
exist for the sake of human beings, 116–
19; contempt for the world (contemptus
mundi), 118; influence on Aquinas, 126,
130; influence on Descartes, 142; on
memory, 208; no moral obligations to
animals, 114, 144; theoretical curiosity
as gratification of the eye (concupiscentia
oculorum), 149
automata, animals conceived as, 130;
Aquinas on, 129; Condillac on, 177;
Descartes on, 139, 146–48; Kant on,
167–68. See also mechanisms, animals
conceived as
autonomy, 224, 237; Ferry on, 227–30;
Kant on, 10, 168, 172, 212, 230;
Regan on, 10